Best wis...
and happy reading!

[signature]

The King and His Man

ALSO BY JEAN ZEB DE LA GRAVES

Fiction

Zazi, Un Chat de Paris (2020)

The Boy Who Healed Death (2020)

Pictures from an Exhibition (2021)

Non-Fiction

The Big Book of Flax (2011, co-author)

Everyday Furniture of the Mahantongo - Not Chust For Nice
(2028, co-author)

Plays

Bravo, Da Ponte!

Shostakovich, or The End of Time

The King and His Man

a novel

by Jean Zeb de la Graves

THE KING AND HIS MAN

Set in 12 point Palatino Linotype.
Book design and layout by Jean Zeb de la Graves.
Cover illustration by Zephram de Colebi.

Published by The Hermitage Press
Pitman, Pennsylvania 17964

"L'oeuvre d'art a besoin de temps et de silence."

Rainer Maria Rilke

CONTENTS

FORWARD

This work of fiction takes place in an alternate Britain and there are some significant differences. The author has made changes to certain locations, such as the city of Durham and the layout of its cathedral, for heightened dramatic effect.

Also, the Royal Family of the novel diverges from ours at Edward VII, who now lives into the 1920s. In this novel, he sends a ship to rescue the family of the Russian Tsar. Edward then proceeds to outlive most of his children, and a different child ascends the throne, thereby creating an entirely new line of descendants, as shown on an accompanying genealogy chart. This Royal Family is called The House of Britain.

The monarchs of the book have rather more actual power than the British monarchs of our world. There are also differences in protocol and ritual, among others, and even differences in locations as well. And in this world the Church of England recognizes same-sex marriage.

The Britain of the novel is somewhat less secure and therefore more threatened than our own Britain, and so security is appropriately tighter, but still discrete and reserved in the British tradition.

I have used British slang only when I've actually heard the word or phrase used in conversation. Hopefully I've used them correctly.

I have relegated British spellings that reflect class and education to dialogue, while using American spellings

Certain phrases are translated at the end of the book.

Selected Genealogy of the House of Britain

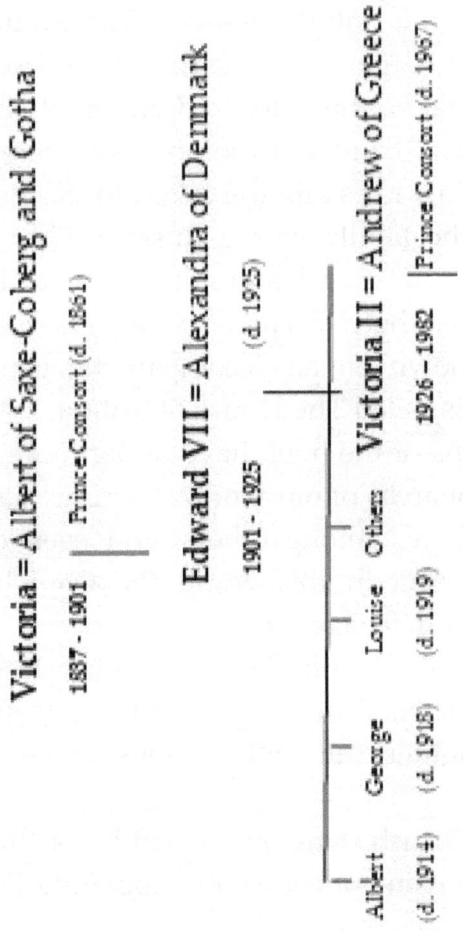

Victoria = Albert of Saxe-Coberg and Gotha
1837 - 1901 | Prince Consort (d. 1861)

Edward VII = Alexandra of Denmark
1901 - 1925 (d. 1925)

Albert   George   Louise Others Victoria II = Andrew of Greece
(d. 1914) (d. 1915) (d. 1919)   1926 – 1982 | Prince Consort (d. 1967)

Selected Genealogy of the House of Britain

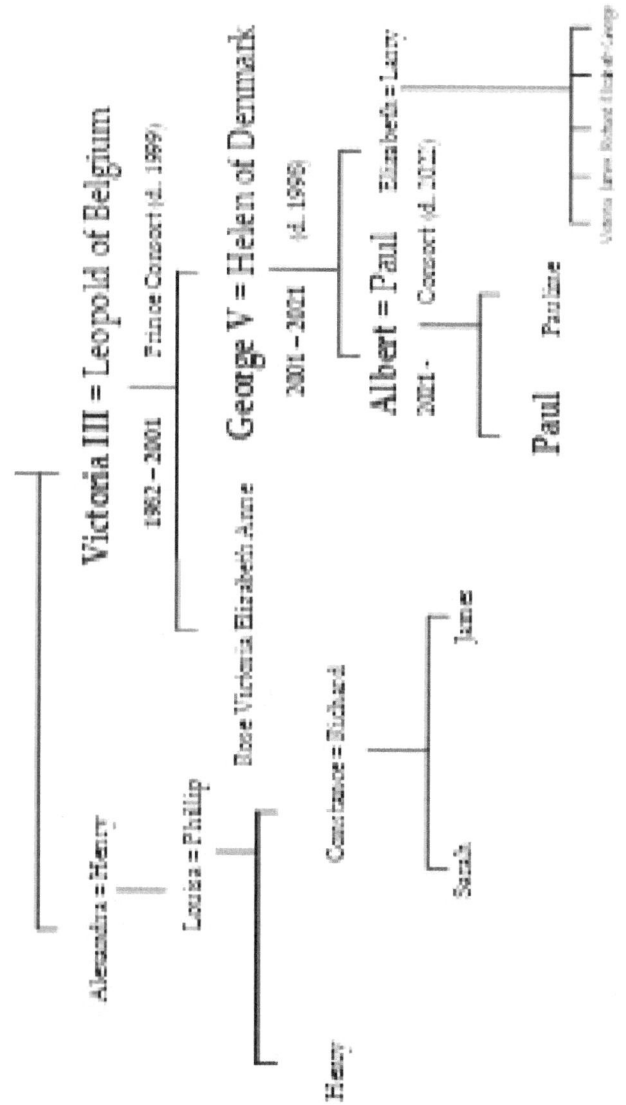

PART 1

CHAPTER 1

The Prince's valet quietly opened the door to the bedchamber. The Prince was asleep, with nothing over him, naked, on the vast bed, on his back, a forearm covering his eyes. His clothes were strewn on the floor where he'd dropped them as he took them off. This was Cunningham's favorite part of his day, when it was just the two of them, before the Prince was taken away by duty, when Cunningham had the Prince to himself.,

He looked at Albert's body, its solid musculature, its definition, and felt, once again, the daily regret that he could look at the Prince but never, in the way he really wanted, to touch him. For a man in Cunningham's position, being in the presence of the Prince was all he would ever have, and yet it was a gift he didn't have to share with anyone else on the planet. He stared at the Prince for a long time, then went to the curtains and quickly pulled them back. The glorious sunshine of a spring day in London filled the bed chamber, and a shaft of early morning light struck the bed and illuminated the sleeping body in gold. Cunningham gasped at the beauty of the image, when Albert rolled over, pulled a pillow over his head and bellowed in a surprisingly theatrical voice, "No! No! No! No!"

"A long night, sir?"

"Fortunately, I've forgotten," the Prince replied testily. Actually, he remembered everything: the dimly-lit back corridor of the club, standing naked against a wall while other naked men pressed themselves against him, kissing him, rubbing their hands over his sweating body, some were at his groin, alternating taking his manhood into their mouths, while one ran a finger up the royal backside and massaged Albert's sphincter until he carefully pushed it inside, which always made Albert gasp in delight. He smiled at the memory when Cunningham reminded him, "Durham today, sir."

"Damn Durham!" shouted Albert as he sat up furiously. Cunningham smiled because he was used to Albert this way and proceeded with the methodical care of a professional.

"Shall I put out a selection of clothes, or do you want to choose?"

"You choose," replied Albert, reconciling to the requirements of the day. "A boys' school, isn't it?"

"Yes, sir, a trades and arts school funded by one of your charities."

"Very well. Nothing formal. Nothing to put the lads off. I want to talk with them, not intimidate them. A blazer, I'm sure a tie is expected, but a striped shirt, slacks, Oxfords."

"Very well, sir."

Albert got out of bed and went to the loo while Cunningham picked out his ensemble. Albert closed the door and then stood at the urinal to pee. He was glad he'd had it installed, though he realized the thing probably made it look like the men's room at Paddington Station, not that he'd ever been there, of course. But there were many mornings when he couldn't even pee straight into a toilet and so made a mess of things. At least he could usually stand at a urinal and get it all in.

Before taking a shower, he went to the sink and looked at himself in the mirror. He was vain about his good looks and about his body. The looks came, fortunately, from his mother's side, as the picture of her on his bedside table attested. Having died when he and his twin sister were five, he had fleeting, if treasured, memories of her. But his father, still a widower after all these years, spoke about her often enough, as did others at court who remembered her. She was well-liked in life and fondly remembered in death.

He had inherited his father's shapeless English body, but years of swimming and water polo had given shape and definition, and he conscientiously worked out daily with his trainer, so what he saw in the mirror always pleased him, with its thick chest, chiseled abs, and, as he turned to see himself from the side, an admirably flat stomach.

He felt his people wanted to see an idealized version of themselves, and he knew that the confidence and pride he felt in his body communicated itself to others. He wanted to be worthy of his people's admiration, both as Prince of Wales and their future King. Yet he realized, as an openly gay man leading an openly sexually promiscuous life, that he was also an item of ridicule and scorn, as his father never ceased to remind him.

"As Prince of Wales you are expected to sow a few wild oats, but what was overlooked at university is now an embarrassment in your late twenties. You need to find a partner of good breeding and settle down. We know the succession will pass to Lizzie and that brood of hers, but you need to set an example of stability and maturity before you become King."

The son admired the distance his father had traveled since Albert came out to him at the age of twelve. His father's first idea was the traditional one for monarchs in such a position, namely a marriage of convenience to a woman for the public image and to continue the line of succession, while having men on the side.

But Albert knew what he wanted even then, and insisted he would only marry another man, much to his father's dismay and surprise. Gradually his father came to accept that but was still waiting for it to happen. So was Albert, frankly. He looked at himself in the mirror. His personal life was sexually satisfying but loveless. He had no companion to share his isolated and, admittedly, artificial life. He woke up every morning in a vast, lonely bed. A man with whom he could share his life would not be found in dimly lit back corridors of clubs because he didn't see how he could trust anyone he met there or, frankly, any place else. He was the most famous, and most desired, shirt-lifter in the kingdom. When men looked at him, they saw wealth, power, prestige, and position, but they didn't see him as anything other than someone to be used.

"And you're certainly not going to find anyone at a boys' school," he said to himself in the mirror.

The warm water of the shower massaged his skin as he lathered soap and rubbed it over his body. He loved the oily feel of it on his legs, his chest, on each arm, his groin, his backside. He loved the pure sensuality of it, then let the water flush the soap away. But he did have to get going, so he turned off the taps, opened the glass door, got a towel from the nearby stand, and dried himself off. He shaved, brushed his teeth, gargled, brushed his hair, and then returned to see what Cunningham had laid out for him.

The choices were on the bed, and the clothes that had littered the floor were gone. Cunningham had withdrawn, knowing the Prince preferred to dress himself, at least with an outfit this simple. Quickly ready, he looked at himself in the full-length dressing mirror.

"Good enough for Durham," he thought, and then left to start his day. He didn't want to keep the boys waiting.

CHAPTER 2

The royal helicopter was flying over the Midlands behind its escort. The sound of the rotors and engines gave a muffled roar that made hearing difficult. In the main compartment was the Prince; Sir Humphrey, his principal private secretary; and Graham, his long-time protection officer. Sir Humphrey was explaining the day's itinerary.

"We will land on the playing field in front of St. Giles, where we will be met by the headmaster and selected staff and pupils. This is one of your Endeavour Schools. In addition to vocational and computer work, it has an extensive arts component, so the boys are not chosen strictly on income, but also on ability and potential, while, of course, tuition, along with room and board, are free. Most go on to some form of advanced training and education.

"You'll recall that a similar Endeavour School for girls is located in New Castle under your sister's patronage, but its funding is actually paid by you as well."

Albert understood perfectly, thinking ruefully about Lizzie's penchant for appearing concerned about the country's welfare, but not actually willing to commit any of her vast resources to doing anything about it.

Sir Humphrey continued: "You will visit a few classrooms and there will be time to speak with students and teachers, then everyone will gather in the dining hall where the boys will provide some entertainment; then there will be lunch."

Albert looked at him questioningly.

"Yes, sir," said Sir Humphrey, anticipating the Prince's concern: "St. Giles is aware that you only eat fish as a meat, but with the river right there and the North Sea not far away, having locally sourced fish is not a problem. After that, you'll proceed by car to the cathedral, where the Lord Bishop will show you the newly restored organ, paid for by another of Your Highness's charities, then the choristers will present a short program with organ accompaniment."

Unexpectedly mimicking the dry, professional tone of a tour guide, Sir Humphrey said, "Please note the various styles of Norman columns in the nave which are almost unique in the Kingdom."

Albert smiled, "I'm sure the Lord Bishop will point them out."

"Count on it, sir," explained Sir Humphrey. "He's quite proud of his cathedral. And then that's it for Durham. You'll fly back to the palace in time for a private dinner with your father, your sister, and her husband."

"Oh joy," said Albert sarcastically as he looked over at Graham, who was well aware of the tensions and competition between the twins. Albert sullenly shook his head again and then sat back in the seat and shut his eyes to block out all but the roar of the engines.

He dreaded another tedious family dinner, probably with pale, poached salmon from Balmoral. Though Scotland was independent, the transfer agreement stipulated that the estate remained English soil upon which the Crown paid no taxes, to the Scottish government's constant irritation. The King had weekly shipments of trout and salmon flown to Buckingham Palace where they formed an essential part of his diet. Albert thought the whole thing a boring and unnecessary expense.

He opened his eyes and looked out the window. They were still over the Midlands. He glanced again at Graham, who had taken the opportunity to nap. Albert smiled gently, which Sir Humphrey caught. He knew something had occurred years before between the two but wasn't sure what it was. Still, he knew the personal attachment that Graham felt towards the Prince made him more protective than mere professionalism and loyalty to the post could provide. There was a bond between them that could not be purchased.

Albert still thought Graham was one of the handsomest men he had ever seen and, when Albert was a precocious twelve, Graham was the first man to whom he was sexually attracted. In fact, he had literally thrown himself upon Graham one day when they found themselves alone in an isolated hallway. Instinctively, Graham grabbed the Prince to hold him safe, and their close proximity made it easy for Albert to cover Graham's face with kisses. Graham looked at the Prince in surprise, then closed his eyes and passionately pressed Albert full on the lips with a long, drawn-out kiss, then opened his eyes, looked at the lad in shock, and gently set him down on his feet. His professionalism returned to help cover his momentary lapse.

"Your Highness, I appreciate the honor you do me and will forever treasure it. But we cannot let this happen again. You are the future King, and I am a member of your staff. And anyway [and he said this with a gentle smile], you need boys of your own age."

Angry at being frustrated this way, and angry at Graham for not fully returning his own passion, Albert ran to his room, slammed the door, and flung himself on his bed, weeping. It was only years later when he realized the jeopardy in which he'd placed Graham and, by that time, he was grateful at how things had turned out.

Graham must have said something to the King because, while he kept his job, soon after Albert was sent to boarding school where he indeed found eager lads his own age. Even now, a decade and a half later, Graham remained a significant and trusted part of his life. Yet, as Albert looked at the dozing Graham, he realized part of the old feeling remained.

He looked again out the window. The farmland and forests of the Midlands were now behind them and they were flying over the northern moors; Durham was ahead.

CHAPTER 3

The escort helicopter landed first, and the security detail exited and took their positions to protect the Prince from, well, from anything. Albert appreciated their presence because he knew in this day and age that one could not be too careful. When they were in position, word was given to lower the ramp so Albert, accompanied by Sir Humphrey and Graham, who descended first and carefully scrutinized the location before giving a curt nod of his head for the others to exit. They made their way to the broad steps that led up to a landing before the main doors where the welcoming party waited, with everyone smiling. As Albert approached, he noticed students and staff crowding the windows of the two-story building to see him. They pointed to him, smiled, waved, and Albert acknowledged them and smiled and waved back. He did notice one unsmiling lad who defiantly gave him a very-American middle finger, though Albert knew what it meant.

"Must be a republican," Albert thought to himself. "Well, we are close to Scotland."

Albert still smiled and waved to the lad, who refused to smile back. "Can't win all hearts and minds," Albert realized from long experience.

The headmaster and the others bowed as Albert approached. The students were in their uniforms that included white shirts, dark ties, and black jackets with red edging. Albert acknowledged them with a slight nod of his own. The headmaster greeted him in the name of St. Giles, its students and staff, and said that, with the Prince's approval, they would start with a tour of several classrooms.

"Lead on, Headmaster; I'm looking forward to it," Albert replied, as he motioned for the headmaster to begin the tour. They passed several classrooms and Albert looked inside to see the boys looking curiously back at him. Obviously, he was the lesson for the day.

He followed the headmaster into a classroom where the teacher had been writing an advanced math problem on the board. Math was not one of Albert's strong suits. The boys stood in honor. "Thank you," he said, "Please continue. I'll be as quiet as a mouse." A weak joke, but he was pleased to see the boys, most of them at least, smile.

The teacher continued the lesson by calling on Albert to finish the equation. He didn't like being put on the spot but hid his anger and embarrassment by saying with a smile, "That is far above my pay scale." Now all the boys laughed, and Albert responded with a broad smile.

"But it's so simple," said one of the students eagerly, who then went up and quickly finished the formula. Albert was impressed and looked at the teacher.

"Is it correct?"

"It is, Your Highness."

"Then well done, lad," who beamed under the royal compliment. "And well done to you all. I can see the future of the kingdom is in good hands."

He left the room leaving good cheer behind him, while admitting to the headmaster that he had no idea what the students were doing.

"Frankly, sir, neither did I," replied the headmaster with a smiling shake of his head.

The next classroom they entered was studying British history and once again the students stood and, again, Albert thanked them and motioned to their seats. Albert then noticed on the wall one of his father's official portraits, the kind he hated doing because everything took so long to prepare, including himself in his regalia. He drew a line at makeup, however, saying "Let them see me wrinkles and all." Even so, his was a regal presence; his salt and pepper beard made him look remarkably like his great-great-grandfather Edward. He always complained at how heavy the robes of state were ("Like being encased in an elephant hide" he said disdainfully.) Still, wearing the Crown of St. Edward (which he rarely did any more; mainly for the opening of Parliament), while holding the orb and Sceptre made him the monarch he was to the kingdom and Commonwealth, and much more than the father Albert knew.

While understanding the role he played, and never did he feel closer to the acting profession than when attired like this, George retained both his sense of humor (which endeared him to Albert while also being a role model for taking the role of monarch seriously, but not himself as a man).

"Just wait until it's your turn," George promised his son.

"I swear I look like a bearded Victoria," he always said when reviewing the proofs. And so, he did, thought Albert to himself, which he would never tell his father.

Returning from his momentary reverie, Albert pointed to the photograph and said with a grin, "I know that man!" The students laughed, and Albert felt more at ease now. He saw a wall chart of the monarchs of British history going back to William the Conqueror.

Pointing to the Norman king, Albert asked, "I wonder why it took a Frenchman to unite the English?"

While meaning it as a rhetorical question, one of the students raised his hand. "I know, sir," he said enthusiastically.

"Yes?" asked a bemused Albert.

The lad stood up beside his desk to reply. "He took it by

force, didn't he, Sir? He brought over an army, and made himself King, and your lot have stayed on the throne by force ever since, haven't you?"

"Sit down, young man!" shouted the headmaster, livid with rage. "The impertinence!"

"No, no," said Albert, who approached the lad now seated in his chair, but who stared at Albert defiantly.

"Let him speak."

And he knelt beside the student and said gently, "Tell me your name, lad."

Now embarrassed, he said softly to the titters of his classmates, "William, Sir."

"Ah," said Albert with a smile, "Named for the Conqueror, evidently."

The lad begrudgingly admitted, "Yes, Your Majesty."

Albert gently corrected him, "That's for the King, and my father lives. But you're right. William, your namesake, did take England by force when the British King Harold II was killed at the Battle of Hastings, which all of you know."

The students enthusiastically nodded.

"Nonetheless, he forged a united country where, previously, there were just tribes of Angles, Saxons, and Britons of all kinds. And it was William who set up an administrative system and laws to govern the country that still forms the basis of who we are today.

"But keep in mind that things have also changed greatly since your namesake's time and so has the monarchy."

By now, the lad and his classmates were listening intently.

"He, indeed, had absolute power. At just a word from him, entire villages could be destroyed and were. He fought wars and levied taxes to pay for them, whereas I can't do any of that."

"Then what good are you?" asked the lad, still defiant.

"William!" said the headmaster threateningly.

"No," protested Albert again, looking at the headmaster. "It's a very good question, and if I can't answer it, then I don't deserve to be in line for the throne. It's also a question that each new generation, and each new monarch, must ask as well."

Then he turned back to the student.

"William, I stand on a thousand years of English history, the very DNA of my body goes back beyond the Conqueror to Alfred the Great and the tribal kings before him. And while that's true for many of you, it's the Royal Family that encapsulates British history as no other family in the country does. We provide continuity and tradition in a rapidly changing world, when what it means to be a British man or woman is constantly called into question. My father has remarkably little real power, almost none. It's Parliament, and the prime minister, who carry out the will of the people. That's you, William, and all you lads in this room, and your families, your neighbors, Durham itself, and all of the North, and all of the United Kingdom, such as it is these days," he said with a rueful smile, then continued.

"Ruling the country as William the Conqueror did, and all those Henrys and Charleses and Jameses, and the Marys and Georges, is not what we, as a Royal Family, do any more. But we do stand for something. We represent the country as a whole. Our job is to be the very best we can be, so that when you see us, even a picture of us, like that one [and he pointed to his father's photograph], you can take pride in being part of a country that has lasted a thousand years, through good times and some very hard times, but we, as a people, are still here, and may we be here another thousand years, on this blessed isle!"

There was stunned silence, then wildly enthusiastic applause from students and staff alike.

Albert waited for a moment, then raised his hand for quiet, and again spoke to the lad before him. "And so, you, my dear young William, are part of that line as well, and I wish you, and your descendants, a glorious future. And be the best Brit you can be!"

William glowed with the attention of the Prince and of his classmates. sir Humphrey, standing in the classroom doorway, leaned over to Graham beside him and said quietly, "And that is why the monarchy will continue." Graham simply nodded.

The tour continued through the school's corridors, with the headmaster pointing out various classrooms. Students in these classrooms eagerly looked at the Prince as he passed by, and many waved, and he waved back. One called out, "How do you like Durham, sir?"

"Smashing!" replied Albert, to applause and gleeful hoots.

The last classroom before the entertainment and lunch was a woodworking class at the far end of the school. After seeing computer classrooms and media centers with the latest high-end technology, Albert was surprised to see students doing something so apparently old-fashioned like turning wood on lathes and making tables and chairs. The headmaster explained the object was not just to produce furniture, but to train students in eye-hand coordination, while providing useful, life-long skills and, most importantly, the value of teamwork and collaboration.

The young men were already standing at their workstations, but they stopped whatever they were doing, turned off the machinery, and the once-noisy classroom because eerily silent.

Albert glanced around the room – all of the students were staring back at him – when he saw one young man whose beauty made him gasp. High cheek bones; deep-set, piercing eyes; dramatic, chocolate-colored skin; Albert caught himself before doing something obvious and foolish, like staring too long. He quickly turned away to survey the rest of the room. "Please continue," he managed to say, and then made his way around the room, from station to station, talking briefly with each group, and finally found himself standing in front of the young man and his team.

Trying to seem relaxed and sociable, Albert asked the four of them what their particular project was. One of the lads started to explain the machine at their station, while the student with the chocolate skin stared at him intensely, with his clear, chocolate eyes, but then unexpectedly turned bashfully away, which Albert found even more endearing.

Fighting to remain outwardly calm, Albert knew not to embarrass himself or the lad, so when the brief explanation was over and Albert had finished the circuit of the room, he returned to the door but turned back to speak to the class.

"Well done, lads!" he said. "I'm impressed with you and your work."

He glanced briefly at the beautiful young man who once again stared calmly back at him, but with an erotic undercurrent that made Albert's groin stir. Before making a fool of himself, Albert broadened his stare to include the entire class.

"Now, enough diligence and application. I understand you have an entertainment for me, and then we eat!"

The students broke into applause as Albert turned backed to the door where the headmaster waited, but not before he looked back one last time to the young man who captured his attention, and who was still staring calmly at him with an erotic frisson that continued throbbing between Albert's legs. He abruptly turned and followed the headmaster down the hallway. The brief encounter was not missed by Sir Humphrey or Graham, who looked at each other with a knowing look, recalling past situations, before following the Prince.

The school's large dining room was set up for the luncheon, with rows of tables set at right angles to the stage. In the center of the stage was a single table where the Prince, the headmaster, a representative teacher, and Sir Humphrey sat. A small grand piano was to the right, near risers for the school's choir. The Prince and the others took their places at the head table and chatted among themselves as students filed in and took their places at the tables which were set for the meal. As they sat down, the students kept looking at the Prince and pointing to him as they spoke among themselves. Teachers sat with their classes, with the support staff at the back. Graham was in the wings, keeping track of the security detail, several of whom were stationed in the hall where they could see the doors while keeping an eye on the students. Others were in the kitchen, inspecting the food preparation, and still others were stationed in and around the building, so all access routes were covered. Such preparations were unheard of even earlier in George's reign, when security was present but not obvious; a time when the royal helicopter could fly anywhere in the country unescorted, but with drones and terrorist cells and increasing fragility in international affairs, Britain gradually, if reluctantly, realized it was better to be safe than sorry, and so adopted the American model of an obvious security presence that still did not mix comfortably with traditional British sangfroid.

When the school was assembled and seated, the headmaster rose and tapped his glass with a knife. A bright, crystal pinging was heard throughout the room, and the low roar of conversation quickly stopped, and the students and staff rose as one. The headmaster spoke a few words of greeting to the Prince, who acknowledged them with a smile and a slight nod of his head and motioned to the assembly to take their seats.

In few words, Albert said how glad he was to be at St. Giles; that he was impressed with what he saw, and he was looking forward to the entertainment "as I know all of you are."

The students enthusiastically applauded as Albert took his seat, followed by the headmaster, and the eight members of the school's chamber choir entered and took their places. Albert was surprised to see the handsome young man from the shop class among them. He smiled brightly at Albert, bemused by Albert's disconcerted look. All the young men smiled at the Prince, then turned to their conductor, who motioned to the pianist to begin the introduction to the first song. They sang a selection of North Country folk songs, and at the end there was enthusiastic applause from the students and the Prince. Many students were holding up their cell phones to record the event.

Then the conductor turned to the Prince and explained that graduating senior Paul McGregor [At this, the headmaster leaned over to Albert and said quietly, "One of our most promising students in years."] had prepared a special song to honor the Prince, who smiled and nodded. To his surprise, it was the young man himself who stepped down off the risers to stand by the piano.

McGregor explained in a clear voice that reached the back of the hall even without amplification, that he'd only just replaced the song he'd originally planned to sing with another that he and his accompanist had not had time to rehearse together, so he apologized in advance for any mistakes the two of them might make. Again, the Prince nodded graciously, then the pianist began to play, and Paul quickly entered, singing in a pleasant, light baritone voice, "I sat down under his shadow with great delight, with great delight, and his fruit was sweet to my taste."

That was when the tittering and giggles started and

quickly spread throughout the room as some boys laughed openly. The headmaster stood up abruptly and repeatedly hit the glass with his knife until the laughter died down but didn't stop completely, while Paul continued his song.

"He brought me to the banqueting house, and his banner over me, his banner over me was love." By now the boys could barely contain themselves, even though the headmaster was glaring angrily across the room, while Albert was enchanted and thought it was the most beautiful thing he'd ever heard, sung by the most beautiful young man he'd ever seen.

The song concluded as it began, and as quietly, "I sat down under his shadow." Pianist and singer stopped together, and there was, surprisingly, an unexpected moment of complete silence before the room exploded with applause, which covered up scattered laughter.

Paul smiled and motioned to his accompanist, who stood, and they accepted the applause together, smiling and bowing. Paul looked directly at the Prince and smiled. Albert was transfixed, as though he'd heard the voice of an angel, and then broke into applause himself. Paul continued smiling at him, then turned back to the students to bow once more, then returned to his place on the risers with the other singers.

The headmaster raised his hand, and the room quickly fell silent. Even though he was unnerved by what had happened and simply wanted to move quickly on. "To conclude the entertainment," he said, "The boys have prepared a song specifically for the Prince."

The pianist started the song that needed no further introduction, and the members of the choir, Paul included, started swaying and snapping their fingers rhythmically and then sang out, "Y . . . M. C. A.! Y . . . M. C. A.!" And then the dining hall erupted into cheers as some boys immediately got up and started dancing in the aisles, then all the students were up and singing and dancing, and the dining hall instantly became a dance floor.

The headmaster looked triumphantly at Albert, who laughed, then stood and danced his way across the stage and down the steps to the main floor where he joined the lads in dancing, and they cheered him on. Paul and the chamber choir also came down to the main floor to dance and sing as well. Albert threw himself into the moves with gusto, as he was surrounded by dancing and singing lads, many of whom were whooping with joy. Sir Humphrey looked into the wings to catch Graham's attention, and they both just shook their heads and smiled.

Paul made his way towards the Prince, who beamed with joy at seeing him approach. They danced suggestively with each other, body close to body, and it was obviously more than just a disco dance; it quickly turned into a mating ritual. And this was when Sir Humphrey and Graham lost their smiles, because they saw how many phones were recording at this moment, and they knew, with sinking hearts, just how quickly what had been a positive photo op was becoming a scandal they couldn't stop.

Finally, to their relief, the song ended, and Albert and Paul stood looking at each other, sweating, aroused, wanting to touch the other, but knowing they couldn't, and shouldn't, so Albert broke away, raised both hands in fists of triumph as the room exploded in cheers, and made his way back up the steps and the stage where, to the great relief of the adults in the room, he sat down. But the cheering kept on and on, so Albert stood again, raised a hand for silence, got it, then said, "Durham, you're fabulous!" And cheering continued as the Prince stood looking proudly at his subjects. Then he sat again, the room quieted down, and the headmaster, who, wisely, had let things take their course, nodded to the conductor, who motioned for all the students to rise, which they did, then he started to lead the national anthem, which also needed no introduction.

"God save our gracious King,
Long live our noble King,
God save the King.
Send him victorious,
Happy and glorious,
Long to reign over us,
God save the King."

Actually, Albert loved the national anthem and never tired of hearing it and singing it with his people as they joined in mutual respect for monarch and kingdom. Albert had great respect for the office he would one day hold himself; he just didn't want to hold it any time soon.

Then it was time for lunch. The headmaster explained that, in honor of the Prince's visit, the menu featured poached North Sea salmon. "My favorite," replied a gracefully smiling Albert, without a hint of sarcasm.

At the end of the meal, the students rose to return to their classrooms; many waved to the Prince as they left, and he acknowledged them with a nod. He chatted briefly with the headmaster, then the morning's events were over, and it was time to head to the cathedral for the afternoon.

As the group entered the hallway leading to the front entrance, they passed a sign for the students' toilet, and Albert stopped to enter. The headmaster said the faculty toilet at the other end had been set aside for the Prince's use.

"I'll just be a minute, if you don't mind," said Albert rather imperiously.

Abashed, the headmaster stepped back. "Of course, Your

Highness ,"
he said with a slight bow of the head.

Feeling pressured, Albert entered quickly, without waiting for Graham to
make his usual check for occupants before its use by the Prince. Albert stood at the loo, unzipped his pants and peed into the porcelain urinal. "About fucking time," he thought, relieved, then zipped up his pants. He went to the wash basin to clean his hands and then looked at himself in the mirror. He was pleased that the day was going well and gave himself a brief smile. Behind him in the mirror he noticed a row of closed stalls when, to his great surprise, one of the doors opened and out stepped Paul McGregor, as though he'd been waiting for him, though he was also putting on his jacket, so perhaps he'd actually been using the stall. He stood beside the Prince at another basin and turned on the spigot to wash his hands.

Albert was shocked.

"You're not supposed to be here, when I'm here."

Paul looked at him bemusedly in the mirror.

"The sign on the door says 'Students.' I'm a student; you're not."

"But I'm the Prince of Wales."

"I didn't know when I came in how could I know you'd be following me in here? And who knows what a dirty old perv like you would want with a handsome young man like me?"

"Dirty old perv?" repeated Albert resentfully, trying to keep his voice down. "I'm not that much older than you."

"You're ten years older."

"Is that a problem?"

The two men turned and looked directly at each other for the first time. The sexual tension between them was growing.

"Not for me."

"Nor for me," said Albert.

"I like older men."

"Stop it!" said Albert laughing. "And we don't have long. My protection chief gets worried."

"Is he going to break in on us?"

At that moment Graham knocked on the door and opened it just enough to look inside. He was surprised to see Paul there and looked from one to the other quizzically.

"Everything all right, Your Highness?" he asked.

"Everything's fine. Thank you for checking, Graham," said Albert evenly. Looking at them one final time, Graham nodded, then said, "We need to leave for your next appointment, Your Highness," and closed the door.

Albert turned back to Paul.

"Now," he said as he took a small gold case from his breast pocket and opened it. He gave a card to Paul. "This is my private number. Call me. It's safe. It's not bugged. My valet gets me phones at a quick shop and I'm the only one who uses it."

"Is this a date?" asked Paul.

"It's whatever you want it to be," said the Prince casually, too casually for Paul, who angrily reached out and grabbed Albert's arm. Albert returned the anger by abruptly pushing Paul's hand away and pulling back. Realizing his mistake, Paul looked down abashedly at the floor.

"I'm sorry, Your Highness," he said with regretful formality.

Surprised and ashamed of his own impulsive reaction, Albert gently put a hand under Paul's chin and raised it up until they were looking directly at each other.

"Don't apologize," said Albert. "Sometimes the office overwhelms my better judgment. Just call me if you want to meet."

Paul said, "I'll do that."

Albert kissed him quickly on the lips and then left. Graham was waiting for him outside.

"A nice young man with a good voice," was all he said.

"Indeed," replied the Prince, as they made their way to the entrance and then outside, where the headmaster was waiting and, once again, the students crowded the windows to see the Prince leave. This time they cheered as he left. Before getting into the car, he turned back to the school, gave a single, long, broad wave that encompassed the building from one side to the other while grinning widely, then was driven to the cathedral.

Still standing at the loo, Paul looked at the card in his hand and still felt the Prince's kiss on his lips.

CHAPTER 4

The Lord Bishop greeted the Prince at the main entrance to the cathedral.

"Your Highness, it is an honor and a pleasure to have you here today," he said beaming, for he was in his element.

"My dear Lord Bishop, the pleasure is mine," returned Albert with a smile, as he was truly looking forward to the afternoon, after such a delightful morning.

"I trust things went well at St. Giles?"

"Beyond all expectations," replied Albert.

"Excellent! Then welcome to Durham Cathedral."

He led the way inside.

"We are so grateful for Your Highness's kindness in funding the restoration of the organ. It's one of our great treasures in a building of treasures."

"I'm glad we could help," replied Albert. "I realize these grand spaces are difficult to maintain."

"Very expensive," replied the Lord Bishop, "and we prefer to see our limited funds go towards tending our flock. For example, we have extensive programs for education, homeless shelters, food assistance, and language classes for refugees and emigrants. I view the church as a social institution for improvement as much as promoting the faith."

"I couldn't agree more," replied Albert. The Lord Bishop bowed his head, then stopped so the group could look down the long nave.

"Please note, Your Royal Highness, the magnificent rows of distinctive Norman columns, which are among the oldest in the kingdom."

Albert glanced at Sir Humphrey, and they shared a secret smile.

"They are, indeed, impressive," replied Albert, to the Lord Bishop's satisfaction. "I've rarely seen anything like them."

Albert's interest in architecture was well known.

Continuing, the Lord Bishop raised his right hand towards the roof.

"The ribbed and arched ceiling is an early example of Gothic engineering and replaced the original flat ceiling."

Albert looked up.

"An impressive achievement," he replied, which also satisfied the Lord Bishop's pride in the cathedral.

"Earlier structures on this hilltop plateau date back to at least the Iron Age Celts, and there have been numerous archaeological digs both up here and down along the river by faculty and students from the university."

"Excellent," replied Albert. "I'd be most interested in seeing their finds, sometime."

Glowing, the Lord Bishop said, "That can certainly be arranged for a future visit. For now, the organist would like to show you where your money went."

The organist, who was tactfully waiting nearby, stepped forward, greeted the Prince and his party, then took the Prince to see the new keyboard console and pedals, then they went back among the pipes. The organist pointed out specific improvements and explained how the new tracking system worked to regulate the flow of air to the pipes which, complicating things, were placed on both sides of the choir. Standing among the pipes that towered over their heads was like standing in a forest of rounded and smoothed tree trunks. There were also ranks of much smaller pipes, all of which, the organist pointed out, could be combined to create nothing less than a universe of sound.

Albert was indeed impressed. He was interested in such mechanical engineering, things that he could see, and in the way all these elements worked together to create a massive outpouring of harmony when cacophony could happen just as easily, and actually more easily. It was the same way he looked at the workings of the kingdom, and how so many different kinds of people needed to work together to create anything positive, and how easily things could fall apart into chaos. It was amazing that anything positive was done at all, and Albert liked to think that the monarchy played a significant role in harnessing and coalescing his people's ideals in a way that centered and focused the crown as representing the best they were capable of doing and being. Then he remembered the lad at the school who defiantly raised his finger and thought of all those countries that did very well, thank you, without a monarchy, and realized that perhaps the House of Britain was not as secure as he thought.

"Any questions, Your Highness?" asked the organist.

"Oh, none," replied Albert with a start. "You've been most clear." The organist bowed, then they returned to the group where the Lord Bishop was waiting to move to the next item on the afternoon's agenda.

"I believe the choristers are ready for a short concert in conjunction with the organ so you can hear how beautifully the voices and the organ blend together."

"Of course," replied Albert, as he sat on one of the chairs set out near the choir stalls. The cathedral choristers were in their robes and in position. They looked excitedly at him.

"We thought we'd have the boys choir perform for you today," said the Lord Bishop without a hint of irony. "We also have a girls' choir, and a mixed chorus. Many of these choristers come from St. Giles since it is the closest school and has such a renowned music department."

Hearing "St. Giles" made the Prince study the choristers more intently, and so he was pleased to see Paul McGregor among them. He acknowledged the young man's presence with the slightest of nods, which was returned with a smile and a rather disconcerting wink.

The concert began with several short works for organ alone, to show the instrument's range and breadth, both in fast passages as well as lyrical ones. Next, the choristers sang two hymns accompanied by the organ, and then the chorus master faced the Prince and explained that the next hymn had already been performed for the Prince earlier in the day as a solo but now would be performed in its original version for chorus. Then the choristers, unaccompanied by the organ, started to sing, very softly, "I sat down under his shadow with great delight."

Albert was so touched by this gesture that he looked with gratitude at Paul, who was intently staring at the director.

"And his fruit was sweet to my taste."

And at that moment, something changed in Albert, which he realized, to his great surprise, was a budding affection for a lad he barely knew.

"He brought me to the banquet hall, and his banner over me was love, was love."

Albert abruptly looked away from Paul and started studying the carved woodwork near him. Sir Humphrey looked in puzzlement at Graham, who shrugged. From their lusty Prince, this was something new.

The singing ended but continued to resonate moments longer in the vast stone edifice. The Lord Bishop let it die out completely before speaking.

"I trust Your Highness finds the organ to your satisfaction?"

Albert shook himself.

"Yes, Your Grace, most satisfactory."

"Excellent," said the Lord Bishop. "Now, would you like to continue the tour? I believe we have some time left before you must leave."

Albert looked at Sir Humphrey, who nodded.

"Of course," replied Albert. "I'd like that."

The two of them then wandered through the building.

"I understand," said Albert, "that at one time the Lord Bishop of Durham basically ruled Northumberland as a kind of king in his own right."

"Yes, Your Highness. That was our traditional role and responsibility, though our powers were gradually whittled away until now when our temporal powers are basically gone."

"Do you regret that?" asked Albert.

"Not at all," replied the Lord Bishop. "I welcome it. I have enough to do just tending my flock without also collecting taxes and maintaining an army."

"Well said," replied Albert. "I actually find myself in a similar position."

"Then we understand each other," replied the Lord Bishop.

"Quite well," replied Albert, with a smile, and realized this was a prelate he liked. By now the men had gone down a flight of steps to a lower level.

"Here we are at the shrine of St. Cuthbert," said the Lord Bishop. "His body was brought here by monks fleeing the destruction of the Lindisfarne monastery by Viking marauders in the tenth century. Cuthbert was the abbot there until his death. You are perhaps familiar with the story of the dun cow?"

"It's a favorite of mine and I would like to hear it again," replied Albert.

"Then of course," and the ancient story was told once

again.

"Remember that St. Cuthbert appeared in a vision and told the monks guarding his body to take his bier to the top of Dun Holm, 'dun' meaning a fortified hilltop and perhaps of Gaelic origin. Well, the monks didn't know where Dun Holm was, so stopped a passing milk maid who said her lost cow was last seen atop Dun Holm, this very peninsular hilltop surrounded on three sides by the River Wear. Accommodatingly, the milkmaid led the monks here, found her cow, and the monks realized this was the spot foretold by Cuthbert, so they built a shelter for the bier, which eventually became this cathedral."

"Now," continued the Lord Bishop, "Speaking of temporal power, it was your ancestor, Henry the Eighth, who had the cathedral seized and his men were to confiscate Cuthbert's body. The monks had the foresight to hide the true relics and gave false bones to the King's men."

"You mean they lied," said Albert.

"Yes," admitted the Lord Bishop, "but those were difficult times and required unusual measures."

"I well understand," replied Albert with a smile. "And I applaud their ingenuity in saving what was important to them. I am glad Henry let the cathedral stand, as so many churches, abbeys, and monasteries were lost."

"Difficult times, indeed," repeated the Lord Bishop.

"But I promise you now, as I will promise the entire kingdom at my coronation, that I will protect Durham Cathedral and provide for it all the days of my life."

Shocked by this unexpected declaration, and momentarily overwhelmed with emotion, the Lord Bishop could only bow.

At that moment, Albert looked down the corridor and saw Paul McGregor, now in street clothes, approaching from the far end of the corridor.

Thinking quickly about how to have some time alone with the lad, Albert said, "Now, Your Grace, I'd like to spend a few minutes alone in contemplation of the saint."

Surprised yet pleased, the Lord Bishop readily agreed. "But of course, Your Highness. I'll join the others and wait for you at the entrance."

Albert waited as the Lord Bishop left. Paul quickly approached and motioned for Albert to join him in a darkened side aisle. They looked at each other, then Albert pushed Paul against the wall and grabbed him violently. Paul grabbed the Prince with equal force and they kissed each other passionately while loosening their belts and forcing their hands deep into each other's groin. They gasped at the eagerly awaited touch, then Paul started to get on his knees when Albert stopped him and pulled him to his feet.

"Not here and not now," he said reluctantly. "Let's do this right. Call me. That's a royal command."

"And if I don't, will you put me in the Tower?"

"For starters," said Albert with a grin.

"I think you'd like that too much," replied Paul. "Let's start with the call."

"Promise?" asked Albert with a slight tone of desperation.

"Promise," said Paul. "Now don't keep the Lord Bishop waiting. He likes things to run smoothly."

"As do I," replied Albert.

"Let's see how things go," said Paul as he tucked in his shirt and Albert did the same.

"Goodbye, for now," added Paul, taking unexpected command of the situation, "You have things to do and so have I."

They looked at each other, standing close together, breathing heavily. They kissed once more, passionately, then Paul left through a side entrance to take the bus home, while Albert joined the others upstairs.

"Did you encounter the saint?" asked the Lord Bishop.

"Yes," replied Albert, "I believe I did."

The Lord Bishop smiled and nodded, not at all surprised, then led the group outside and watched as the royal contingent left in the waiting limousine, then walked contentedly back inside the cathedral, pleased with the afternoon. He knew he'd developed a positive relationship with the Prince that boded well for the future.

The car soon arrived back at St. Giles and the waiting helicopter. Albert and his party were quickly airborne and headed south towards London and the palace.

After takeoff, Albert basked in a glow of self-satisfaction.

"Well," he exclaimed, "I think that went very well. Don't you?" he asked, looking inquisitively at Sir Humphrey and Graham.

It was Sir Humphrey who replied, "One can only hope, sir," as he looked apprehensively at Graham. But Albert, in his enthusiasm, was unable to see any warning signs. Instead, he looked out the window in the early twilight as the north moors darkened below. All he felt was an erotic anticipation for the future.

CHAPTER 5

As soon as Paul got off the bus, he knew something was wrong. Though still two blocks away, he saw the glow of lights in the vicinity of his house that normally weren't there. In the evening dusk, he slung his book pack over a shoulder and quickly walked to his street. When he turned the corner, halfway down at his house, he saw a jumble of parked vehicles, including media vans with satellite dishes on top, as well as police cars, while the pavement and street in front of his house were filled with media people with cameras, lights, and microphones, while a few had old-fashioned reporters' notepads. He hesitated for a moment, not knowing why they were there, but he knew he had to get inside his house, so he headed towards home. He'd only gone a few feet when someone spotted him.

"There he is!"

The group rushed towards him, and he was quickly surrounded by a sea of jostling hands holding microphones in his face, with the bright glare of camera flashes and bright, steady lights for the video cameras. He had no idea what was going on, but this surge of people terrified him, and he tried to push through as questions were shouted at him.

"How does it feel to be the Prince's new boyfriend?"

"How do you feel about being called the Durham slag?"

"Have you and the Prince arranged for a tryst?"

At that moment a coterie of police reached him, and he was surrounded in a protective cocoon, with two in front as a kind of plow; others, on both sides, grabbed his arms and nearly dragged him through the crowd, while more guarded the rear. The tightly focused group moved through the media like a

Roman phalanx, grimly determined to get him safely inside.

"Not a word!" said one of the police as the group moved along the pavement. Paul was too surprised , too shocked, and even too fearful of what was happening to speak. He noticed a barricade had been set up at the front of his yard bordering the street. With tall hedgerows on either side of the property, only the front was open, so it was easy to cordon off the lot. His mother's car was still in the driveway where it had been when he left that morning. She'd taken the day off from the university lab where she was the director.

The media continued shouting questions at him; the lights blinded him; but finally the group reached the path to the front door. Most of the police stopped there, but two accompanied him right to the door, where a policewoman was standing guard. As Paul approached, she knocked twice, sharply, on the door and it quickly opened. His mother appeared, completely distraught, and shouted "Paul!" The media was in an uproar at the sight of the two of them together.

"Face the cameras!"

"Let's have a smile!"

Paul turned back to look at the yelling crowd in horror, but his mother quickly pulled him inside and shut the door.

"Oh my," she said, gasping for breath as she held him close and finally safe in her arms. They held each other tightly, then she pulled back to see him. "Are you all right?"

"Of course," replied Paul. "Why wouldn't I be?"

In reply, Pauline simply pointed at the door and beyond, to the circus outside, because the answer was self-evident.

"I'm fine," retorted Paul, who was now defensive.

"Good," she replied with relief, "because now I can get angry with you, Paul. How could you be so stupid?" she demanded.

"What?" he asked defiantly.

"Just look outside in case you missed it, and just look at that," as she pointed to the telly, which was on, and whose sound competed with the noise from outside. And when Paul moved to see the screen, there he was, dancing with the Prince of Wales to the tune of "Y.M.C.A."

"But there was no media there!" said Paul.

"There didn't have to be, with apparently every student photographing you two on their phones."

And Paul looked back at the screen and saw all the phones held up high to record the scene.

"You two have gone viral," said Pauline grimly. "You're on every channel."

And she took the remote and thumbed through the channels and, indeed, there he was, and the Prince, on every one of them.

"Wow!" said Paul with a smile. "That's cracking!"

"Ask how my day went," said his mother with feigned sweetness.

He knew it was a trick question, but he asked anyway.

"How did it go?" he asked in a tightened, restricted tone.

"It started off fine," explained Pauline. "I was enjoying a day off from the lab. You know how hard we've been working on that new project."

Paul nodded.

"Then, in early afternoon, Mrs. McCluskey from next door rings up and tells me to turn on the telly. And there you were, already. And it hasn't stopped. I was speechless. But that's when I heard students out front, coming home from school, singing, shouting [and she mimicked them] 'I sat down under his shadow. I sat down under his shadow.' And they stopped outside and continued to sing and shout that horrid verse, and when I went to the door to find out what was going on, the first reporters and media people were already out front and, seeing me open the door, raced towards me shouting questions like, 'How does it feel to be the mother of the Durham slag?' I had just enough time to get inside and shut the door and lock it, when they started pounding on the door and shouting, 'Talk to us! Talk to us!'

"I called the police instead and the first squad car arrived quickly, assessed the situation because the street was already filling with vehicles, even the neighbors were coming over, including Mrs. McCluskey, and the front garden was being trampled down. Evidently the police called for backup because more squad cars arrived, even a police van, and quickly set up the barricade and kept the media and gawkers back. I unplugged the landline because the phone didn't stop ringing, and I wasn't about to answer it. I kept my mobile on, hoping you would call but, of course, you were too busy doing who knows what to call your mother, so that's been my day off. How was your day?"

Paul just stood there, looking from her to the telly and then to the door with the shouting and the lights beyond it.

"Mum," was all he could say. And he looked so dejected, and so frightened and so confused that Pauline realized, at this moment, that he was still a boy in a young man's body. She held out her arms to him, and he rushed to be held. He started crying on her shoulder.

"I'm sorry, Mum. I am so sorry," he said over and over again.

"I know, Paul, I know," she said as she held him and consoled him. "I don't blame you. It's that monstrous Prince who's done this."

"No!" shouted Paul as he defiantly pulled away. "It wasn't him. He was nice to me."

"Because he wants you!" Pauline shouted back. "He wants

your black skin and your black arse and your big, black dick!"

Which made Paul stop.

"How do you know I've got a big dick?"

And that made Pauline stop and smile.

"Well, I know what your father's was like, so actually it's not from my Jamaican side, but from his Scottish side. And I assume like father, like son."

And then both smiled, but the telly was still on, and the media roar was still outside, with shouts of "Come out and talk!" And "Show us what you've got!"

"So, what are we going to do?" asked Paul, looking uneasily at the telly and the front door.

"For now, we can't do anything about that," and Pauline pointed to the television, "Or about that mess out there. This will blow over and they will go on to the next new scandalous morsel if you don't feed them. They are scavengers needing to fill the next news cycle. They would tear you apart just for the ratings and I won't let them do that to you. Your father, even though he's left us, and I worked hard to give you every benefit and every chance to make the most of yourself that you can become."

She sat down on the sofa and motioned for him to sit beside her, then she took both his large yet delicate hands in hers and looked into his face.

"Paul, I've known you were gay for most of your life, and that was never an issue, not even for your father. We both knew how talented you are and how successful you'll be in whatever field you wish to enter – music, teaching, whatever – and we've wanted you to eventually find a good man who will love you and care for you so you can both settle down and do something with your lives. But he [and she pointed to the telly] is not it. For him, you are just the latest number, and a black one this time. You know his reputation. You know his 'once and done' rule. He doesn't have boyfriends; he has conquests; and I won't have you hurt by that royal prick!"

She stopped, and both were surprised by her vehement defiance. And into the silence between them, poised between the noise of the telly and the street, Paul said quietly, "But he wants me, Mum, and I want him."

Then Pauline did something she'd never done before; she slapped him so hard that the impact pushed his head to the side. He slowly turned back and stared at her through tears in his eyes.

"He gave me his number and I'm going to call him."

"Listen to me," she said, with quiet, determined intensity, "He will use you and leave you behind in the dirt. I raised you for better than that."

"He's the Prince of Wales. It doesn't get any better than that. Listen to that, Mum [and he pointed out to the street]. They're calling me the Durham slag. If that's what it takes to get out of this town, then I'll do it. He wants my black arse. Then fine, he can have it. He wants my big black, Scottish dick? Then he can have it. I'm getting out of here, Mum, and I'm using whatever I've got to make it happen."

"Go to your room!" shouted Pauline.

"Gladly!" Paul shouted back and grabbed his book bag and stomped upstairs.

She heard the door slam and wondered if she'd lost him forever. She held her head in a hand, while "Y.M.C.A." thundered from the telly, and the media roar continued outside.

"Well," she said to herself, "I might as well give them what they want, and then maybe they'll go away."

She went to the front door, paused just for a moment, and then opened it. The policewoman outside was surprised to see her approach. Pauline quietly explained she was going to make a statement.

"Are you sure you want to do this?" the policewoman asked doubtfully.

"No," admitted Pauline, "but I'm going to make it anyway."

Then, with great pride, she walked calmly and purposefully to the barricade. The police stood side by side to keep the media on the pavement. She also saw many of her neighbors there, looking at her questioningly, even angrily, at why this circus had invaded their usually calm neighborhood.

Pauline raised her hand for silence, and soon everyone was quiet, waiting for her to speak.

She was live on camera, microphones aimed at her, everyone expectant.

"My son is Paul McGregor, and I am his mother, Dr. Pauline McGregor."

She stood there for an hour, answering the questions she could, honestly about the answers she didn't know. She told them about Paul, about her life in Jamaica, about how she came to Durham to study microbiology, and stayed to teach and do research at the university, about how she met Paul's father from an ancient Scottish family, how they married, why he returned to Glasgow, and how she was currently raising Paul on her own. She admitted knowing little about the Prince of Wales or what happened at St. Giles that day. She declared her support for her son and how she knew he would make the right decision; after all, he was now a man even though he still lived at home.

Finally, all questions were answered; all pictures were taken. The neighbors went back home, and the media started to leave. Pauline turned back and, as she reached the front door, she placed a hand on the policewoman's arm and simply said, "Thank you." The woman smiled and said the police would remain through the night and would reassess the situation in the morning.

Pauline squeezed her arm gratefully, nodded slightly, then went inside, shut and locked the door, then went into the front room where she saw herself on the telly. She turned it off and went upstairs to her own bedroom where she was ready to sleep. It had been a long day.

Paul, whose bedroom faced the front of the house, had watched his mother while standing far back in his darkened room as she calmly and effectively handled all manners of questions, even the most inane. He later realized she had given him his first lesson in how to handle the media, and one he might have to quickly learn. He opened his wallet, pulled out the card with the Prince's private number on it, reached for his phone, and made a call.

CHAPTER 6

Buckingham Palace.
The King's study.

George V, of the House of Britain, is not happy. In fact, he is furious at his wanton son's idiotic behavior. He sits at his desk, then pounds it with a fist. "Damn him! Damn him! Damn him!" shouts the King. "How could he be so thoughtless?!"

George is so nervous and irritated that he stands up and paces the room, waiting for Albert to come so they can talk before tea, a meal he's been looking forward to, but now is too nervous to enjoy and, besides, he has pain in his gut caused by stress. His doctor has repeatedly told him to relax. Easy to say when one is not a ruler! Where is that boy? Damn him to hell. How to make this right? How to make this right? Where is that boy?

"Damn him!" he shouts again as he paces about the room; holding his hands behind his back. Paintings of his mother and grandmother, the second and third Victorias, stare down at him, dour, grim, and judgmental, as though they, too, wonder at how such a simple trip could go so badly. He stops pacing and stares up at the full-length portrait of his great-grandfather, Edward VII, and realizes he's letting them all down by failing to raise a responsible son and a worthy claimant to the throne. Under the withering eyes staring down at him, he really does not know what to do.

He hears the doorknob turn and a footman enters, bows, and says, "The Prince of Wales, sir," then leaves.

George dramatically turns his back to the door so his very

posture will show his displeasure, though Albert seems innocent of any knowledge of the trouble he's caused.

"My word, Pappa," he cries ebulliently after a quick nod to his father, "What a wonderful day this has been. I'm famished. "

With his back still turned to Albert, his father says, evenly, without emotion, "Poached salmon."

Albert rolls his eyes but says nothing.

"Flown in fresh from Balmoral this morning," his father adds.

"You know the Scots don't like us doing that."

Then George's full fury is unleashed as he turns around and shouts, "Damn the salmon. Damn the Scots. And damn you!"

Albert is shocked, speechless at his father's unexpected outburst. He is completely unaware of the chaos he has caused as no one has yet told him.

"What?" asks Albert. "The day was perfect."

"Perfect?" asks his father quietly, then he abruptly changes tone. "Perfect?!" he demands. "You call this perfect?"

And George grabs a remote and turns on the telly. Pictures of Albert dancing to "Y.M.C.A." appear, then George abruptly turns it off.

"It was a triumph," says Albert.

"It was a disaster!" counters his father. "All you had to do was fly to Durham, see the school, your charities fund, then go to the cathedral to see the restored organ, which your charities also funded, and with carefully-chosen media primed for what should have been a good news day, without any prying or embarrassing questions about your wanton behavior, with only an official photographer to provide carefully vetted photos. What could possibly go wrong?"

"Nothing went wrong!" replies Albert defensively. "Each of those students went home to tell his parents what a great bloke the Prince of Wales is. But they know I'm gay, which is why they did the song. Everyone thought it was fabulous."

"Everyone?" asks the King. "What about that lad you danced with so seductively? Was he even of age? Do you even care? It looked like a kind of dark-continent shimmy!"

"Now you sound like great-grandmother."

"At least she was the Empress of India. What will you be?"

"What is there left for me to be?"

The two men glare fiercely at each other, realizing this has gone far beyond a dance at a boys' school to encompass the very nature of the monarchy, and the few lands that still encompasses.

The King continues. "The worst thing that happened today, and a horror that is on-going, involves what you have done to that lad, and since you are obviously oblivious to the chaos you left behind in Durham, let me show you."

He clicks on the telly again and quickly moves through the channels until he soon finds one showing the near-mob scene outside Paul's home. The King angrily points to the screen with the remote. Albert moves closer to see and hear what is happening. His first thought is, "So that's where Paul lives." But he quickly and, finally, correctly assesses the seriousness of the situation as he hears the newscaster say, "I'm standing in front of the Durham home of student Paul McGregor, who lives here with his mother, Dr. Pauline McGregor, the noted microbiologist. As you've seen, Dr. McGregor has just come outside for an hour-long question-and-answer session. This has been the site of one of the most amazing afternoons in Durham's recent history, as a swarm of media people from across the Kingdom have gathered here to learn about young McGregor, who has become the latest object of desire of the Prince of Wales. This was after McGregor sang a hymn to the Prince based on a suggestive passage from the biblical Song of Solomon."

Mobile video of Paul singing to Albert are shown over the newscaster's voice, who continues, "And this is how students at St. Giles School later parodied the hymn."

And Albert watches a group of young men in front of the school singing in a satirical, effeminate, lisping style, "I sat down under his shadow. I sat down under his shadow."

"And here," the newscaster continues, "is young McGregor being protectively led through the crowd outside his house so he can get safely inside."

The King abruptly turns off the telly and faces his son, who is pale and shocked at what he has seen.

"And that is the worst thing you did today," says the King quietly.

"Pappa, I had no idea!" replies Albert defensively.

"I know you don't," says George sadly. "And that's what makes this so difficult, because it exposes your greatest weakness: your apparently complete lack of self-awareness. Can't you see the injury you have so thoughtlessly caused? Can't you see how you have ruined this lad's life? How can he face his mates after this? He's become the laughingstock of Durham. And what must his mother think?"

George pauses. Albert is reeling, completely unaware of these events. Perhaps his father is right about his lack of awareness because, until this moment, Albert really had no idea what was happening, as nothing was said to him on the return flight or after he returned to the palace, although obviously Sir Humphrey had briefed the King.

"Pappa," stammers Albert. "I really am so sorry."

"No," replies the King curtly, "That is not enough. That is not nearly enough and, frankly, I don't know how this can be made right. The magic wand to make this go away was not included with my crown and regalia. But – and this is a command – listen to me carefully, Albert."

And Albert looks directly at his father, who is so angry with him.

"I command you," he repeats, "to never see this lad, this Paul McGregor, again. Do you understand me?"

Reluctantly, yet seeing no way out, Albert agrees. "Yes, Pappa, I understand."

At this point, George makes a father's typical mistake of not realizing that understanding is not the same as obeying.

"One final thing," says a relieved George. "Don't think this is because of the color of his skin, or his social class, or education. I rule a kingdom of all colors and combinations of colors, of all social classes, and of all kinds of education. I am the King of every one of my subjects, without exclusion. No, Albert, this is not because he isn't good enough for you." And George pauses dramatically to emphasize the point he is about to make. "This is because you are not good enough for him, no matter what he is."

Then George abruptly changes tone. "Now, I'm going to eat. I'm famished and I hate cold salmon. I'm going to eat with your sister and Larry and we're not waiting for you because the way I feel right now, I don't want to eat with you."

He leaves the room, closing the door firmly behind him.

In shock at his father's words, Albert sits at his father's desk. He picks up the remote control and turns on the telly. The announcer is still in front of Paul's house and clips of the day's events are being shown yet again. Albert hears shouts of "Durham slag!" and the mocking chant of "I sat down under his shadow," cruelly sung by groups of boys with whom he'd happily danced just hours before. Then Albert abruptly turns off the telly and slams the remote down on the desk with a loud bang that likely broke it. With the eyes of his ancestors looking down at him, Albert lays his head on the desk and says quietly to himself, "Paul, what have I done?"

PART ONE

CHAPTER 7

Albert was purposefully late, and tea was nearly done by the time he entered the dining room. The King continued to eat without looking up at him, still angry, while Lizzie looked up and, with a broad smile, raised her glass and said, imperiously, "Hail the conquering hero!"

"Lizzie," said her father quietly, with just the hint of a threat. Larry – Lizzie's long-suffering yet good-natured husband – looked at his plate, though he'd already eaten everything on it.

"Wow, veni, vidi, vici Durham!" continued Lizzie with a gleeful smirk.

"That's enough!" shouted the King, then he stood up, as did Lizzie and Larry.

"I'll have my brandy in the drawing room. Larry, would you join me, please?" It was not a question.

"Gladly," said the relieved Larry, who nodded and then smiled consolingly at Albert as he followed his father-in-law out of the room.

Albert had always liked Larry who, even after nearly ten years of marriage, still acted as though constantly surprised at finding himself part of the Royal Family, despite Lizzie's abundant fertility, who had already supplied six heirs to the throne. The public joked that she couldn't remember their names. She knew their names; what she didn't know was who they were as people. Perhaps it was due to having lost her own mother at the age of five, and having a father made distant by work, but Lizzie was unsure about how to raise her children. Yes, she had nannies and governesses, but she wanted to take an active role in her children's lives. She wanted to be a positive influence; she wanted to make a difference. But the fact was that she felt more comfortable tending her extensive gardens than tending her children. They were more complicated; and Lizzie found complications to be unsettling. As for Larry, he liked the children; he certainly loved them but didn't have much time for them. Since his youth foundation was world-wide, he was usually spending time with children who were not his own, so he had to emphasize quality time over quantity.

Oddly enough, Albert envied their relationship. They obviously still cared, greatly, for each other; they enjoyed each other's company; and they were each other's best friend. While he would have a kingdom, he didn't have what they shared so easily. Obviously, Larry saw in Lizzie qualities that Albert just couldn't fathom, so evidently it really was love.

For Lizzie's part, while she appreciated the fact that Larry came from one of the wealthiest families in the Kingdom, she didn't need his money. Her annual income from the Royal List was satisfactory; she was as far from being a clothes horse as one could get. Indeed, she depended on her staff to make her look good as she knew she had no taste in clothing and, frankly, didn't want any. But style was expected of her, so she wore what she was told to wear; just another reason she disliked being in public. She much preferred her old gardening clothes.

No, what attracted her to Larry was, first, his remarkable beauty; he'd been called the most eligible bachelor in the Kingdom, and for good reason. She wasn't sure what he saw in her; unlike most of her suitors, it wasn't being a princess. No, when he looked at her, he saw deeper than the potential crown. He appreciated her as a woman, and that she found immensely attractive when that was all most eligible men had seen in her. She had learned early what to look for, and what to listen for, in the way men approached her. Most men were obvious in what they wanted, which made it easy to dismiss them. A few others were more subtle in their approach, but she had a kind of built-in truth radar that eventually penetrated their armor, as though seeing the skeleton beneath the flesh. It was never pretty, and she worried about remaining unwedded, especially as foreign princes didn't interest her. She wanted good British stock, and she got it. The fact that Larry was amusing and curious were also in his favor, though he had the same driven personality she'd seen in other highly successful businessmen. Still, the fact that he had to give all of that up to marry her seemed to come as a relief to him. There were others in the family to carry on with what he'd been doing, and after marriage he finally had time to do something he'd wanted to do for years: create a trust that combined his twin interests in athletics and education.

The Duke of Suffolk Trust started in towns and villages, with the trust putting up half the money to start local youth leagues that emphasized teamwork over competition and required its athletes to attend some kind of vocational or professional training to use when school was finished. The idea was not to train professional athletes, but to create a balance between physical activity and life skills. Now it had spread across the Commonwealth, and always communities were required to fund half of the costs. Still, there were many ways to do that without necessarily putting up cash in hand, and the Trust made sure that any community that wanted to participate was not rejected.

This was why Larry was so frequently on the road and even out of the country, though he insisted on spending at least each weekend at home, either their large London house or the vast Suffolk estate. He covered most of his British appointments in his own helicopter that he took pains to note he paid for himself.

Lizzie was most definitely a working royal; after all, her father had trained her for that role. She did it willingly, knowing it was expected of her; but it was her mother's influence with gardening that she was truly passionate about. She tried to condense her public responsibilities into just a few days each week, so she could still spend time with her children and get her hands in the soil, which nurtured her as she nurtured it. Like Larry, she kept the weekends, whenever possible, open for the two of them. If there were engagements to fulfill, she felt better if Larry could accompany her, and he did so because he knew she appreciated his support. He did joke, however, that he had merely exchanged his family firm for a royal firm. So far, the joke hadn't worn thin, and the love they shared had only grown over time, like the trees she so assiduously planted at Balmoral.

Albert and Lizzie were their parents' only children. Their beloved mother had died when they were five, and both were affected by the loss in ways they didn't realize. That was when Rose Victoria, George's unmarried sister, had moved into the palace to supervise being raised by a caring and dedicated staff, for which the King was forever grateful.

Lizzie and Albert knew early that Aunt Rose was not their mother, but her constant presence provided a security they grew to depend on. It certainly put the King's mind at rest regarding the responsibilities of being a widowed husband and monarch. He loved his children wholeheartedly and without reservation, while not having a lot of time for them. Still, the moments he did spend with them, particularly the extended stays at Sandringham at Christmas and Augusts at Balmoral, were important for the three of them.

Albert finally sat down after the King and Larry left the room and picked listlessly at the cold food on his plate.

"The poached salmon was good, earlier," said Lizzie.

"You know I hate salmon," replied Albert.

"I do know," said Lizzie smiling. By now the twins basically hated each other, as she actually always had, and the reason was the sixty seconds that separated the birth of Albert, as the first to be born and therefore the older, from that of Lizzie, ever so slightly younger, but in the line of succession, those sixty seconds made all the difference, which certainly didn't bother Albert, yet it bothered and tormented Lizzie enough for both of them. But for their respective placements in their mother's uterus, Lizzie would be queen, and her queer brother would play second fiddle his entire life, a reality that rankled her daily. It was her wound that never healed, and she constantly scraped off the scab just to feel the pain.

Lizzie watched her brother listlessly push his food around, and all she felt was contempt and disgust. What a weakling! she thought to herself, a soft, passive, nancy boy weakling. But Lizzie knew she wasn't soft, no, not her. And if Albert died before her, she could still be queen and, even if she died first, she had enough children to inherit the throne, a point she never tired of making.

"So," she said in a derisive tone of voice guaranteed to goad her brother, because she knew his weak spots, "I gather things did not go well today."

"No, dear sister," he replied sarcastically, willing taking the hook she had gleefully tossed before him, "Obviously they did not go well at all. Do you have any other comments you'd like to make?

You've certainly upset Pappa."

"That doesn't take much these days," said Albert. "Not where I'm concerned."

"Throwing yourself at that gigolo slag for the whole world to see. How could you?"

Lizzie was very concerned about appearances, and she knew how this appeared. She didn't care what the world thought about her brother, but she was very much concerned about what the world thought about the Royal Family.

"Lizzie." She was surprised and unexpectedly touched by the pain in his voice. "I was so happy there today, dancing with the lads, and I was so happy dancing with him, that nothing else mattered. It was like all of us were alive there, and the world was gone, and I didn't want that moment to end. I thought that, maybe, even I could be happy. And it wasn't until I met Pappa in the study that I realized I'd made another muddle and not just for me, but for him as well. Oh, Lizzie!"

And Albert reached out with both hands and took hers so gently in his, and his face showed such pain, that Lizzie was shocked and, frankly, did not know what to do. To console her brother was unknown territory. At least she ignored her first impulse, which was to pull away and flee. He held her hands with a kind of wild desperation and continued to search her face as though seeking the answer to a question he didn't know how to ask. Then he bowed his head, and only then was she relieved of the fear that he would ask her for something she really could not give. Finally, he let go of her hands and sat back up. Then his mobile rang. Thank goodness their father wasn't present because he demanded that mobiles be silenced in his presence. He saw them as rudely interfering with his concentration.

In that moment, as the phone continued to ring, the tenuous connection between brother and sister was broken, and Lizzie, relieved to be back on ground she understood, returned to form.

"Maybe that's your Durham slag," she said with a sneer that came so easily to her.

Albert reached into his pocket and turned the phone off.

"Well, dear sister," he said with an equally cutting voice, "You'll never know."

"Shame," she said, "for a slag he did seem like a sweet, innocent kid. Now his life is turned upside down. He must regret this day."

Albert slammed the table with a violence that startled Lizzie, and, for the first time, she realized the depth of his passion.

"Stay out of it!" he warned.

"Or you'll do what?" she asked. "Have me thrown into the Tower? Have my head cut off and put on a spike? Don't forget, dear brother, that it's your life that's at stake here. If anything happens to you, I am queen. And if anything happens to me, then my children rule."

"Those no-neck monsters of yours? Fit to rule a kingdom? Ha!" he shouted, with no laughter in his voice.

"That's right, dear brother, so take care of yourself. I'd hate to have anything happen to you; I'd just hate it!"

The two glared at each other like ancient protagonists with swords drawn, then Lizzie abruptly laughed. "Albert, you are so easy to goad. It's not a fair match. You're just not as smart as I am."

"I'm just not as ruthless, you mean."

Then Albert went back to pushing the food around his plate with a fork, while Lizzie rose, gave her slightly older brother one last glance of disdain, then left.

Albert balefully watched her go, then put down his fork, grabbed the plate and threw it across the room to smash against a wall, leaving a mess for someone to clean up.

"I hate salmon!" he snarled.

CHAPTER 8

Albert sprawled naked, face down, on his bed, waiting, even begging, for the phone to ring again. He checked it when he returned to his room and there had indeed been a call from Paul. Caller ID was such a wonderful invention. But Albert declined to call him back, as he could have, a choice not from any sense of royal prerogative, but simply because he was afraid that perhaps Paul had changed his mind in the meantime and now wouldn't speak to him. So, Albert waited, nervous, doubtful, but then the phone rang again. Albert reached out, grabbed it and immediately answered without checking who it was. He knew who it was, or at least who he wanted it to be.

"Paul," he said breathlessly. "You called!" as though surprised, yet relieved, that Paul might still want him.

There was a momentary pause at the other end until Paul realized that Albert had personally answered, then he cried out, "Make it stop!" Albert heard pain, fear, and anger in those three words, and knew exactly what he meant.

"Paul, sweet man, of course I'll make it stop."

But Paul continued what he had to say.

"The front garden is barricaded. The police are still here, though the media, the neighbors and everyone else have finally gone. Mum is furious with me and, somehow, you must make all of this go away!"

"Paul, Paul," replied Albert soothingly, knowingly, "I'll make it go away; I promise."

"But how?" asked Paul, imploringly. "Do you just command them to leave?"

Despite the seriousness of the moment, Albert laughed,

"No, sweet man. I'm the Prince of Wales, not a magician."

"So, what can you do?" demanded Paul accusingly.

"I have greater power than that," said Albert calmly. "I have the power of diversion."

"What do you mean?" asked Paul, bewildered.

So, Albert explained: "The media is a shark that must constantly feed. It swims in the sea of controversy, 24 hours a day, seven days a week. It never shuts down, but is always searching for the newest, hottest trend of the moment and, right now, dear man, that happens to be you."

"Just make it stop!" pleaded Paul again.

"You are all over the news and the media pursues you like hounds to a rabbit. They mean to eat you alive, my dear, and then, with blood-red eyes, they will look for the next victim to rip apart. And that's the secret, Paul: diversion. I will direct their interest to something new; to something far from Durham, and then they will leave you alone and the police will take down the barricades, return to their station house, and you and your mother's lives will soon return to normal, I promise. It's remarkably easy once you learn how to do it."

"Then do it!" demanded Paul.

"As you command, my Prince," said Albert with a smile. "But I need to say that while it will be easy for me to accomplish, the results will be hard for you to accept. You will read and see things about me, about my activities, over the next few days that you will not want to know and that, indeed, may shock you."

"What do you mean?" asked Paul quietly, so Albert explained.

"To draw attention from you, I will focus attention on myself by playing the madcap royal, the lascivious Prince, once again flitting, like a bee, from flower to flower to flower. The media will follow the scent I want them to follow and will realize that you were just a passing fancy, a sometimes-thing that momentarily caught my eye before I moved on to other, equally passing fancies. But those fancies will be here in London, far from you and, like a magnet pulling iron filings, the media will be drawn to what I am doing, and their interest will move on from you in Durham to me here in London. Then you and your mother will finally be left alone, though I imagine some of the local lads will continue trying to goad you with their mocking version of that beautiful hymn you sang to me – just for me – and that touched me more than I can say."

"Did you really like it?" asked Paul softly. "It was just for you, a last-minute change that caught my accompanist by surprise, but he was a good sport and a good sight reader."

"It sounded like you'd rehearsed for hours," assured Albert.

"Actually, not at all," replied Paul with a laugh, before asking, again, plaintively.

"So, you can really do this? Get my life and my mother's back to normal?"

"Yes, I promise," answered Albert. "But you must trust me. You will hear things about me that you will not like. I must brazenly throw myself around town. I must be seen cavorting, carousing and, believe me, I've done enough of both to know what must be done. Just remember that all of it is meaningless, that the men you'll see pictures of with me will mean nothing to me. I will use them to protect us."

"So, there is an 'us'?" asked Paul plaintively. "I'm not just a passing fancy?"

"My dear boy, there is an 'us', though I'm not sure what that means, or how long it will last or, frankly, anything about what is to come. There is a Noël Coward song that says, 'Maybe a moment; maybe a year.' And, Paul, right now that's all I can honestly say."

"I know," replied Paul hesitantly. "We've barely met. But when you touched me, when you kissed me, I knew I wanted more. I knew I wanted you." And then he stopped before adding, "My mother doesn't want me to see you."

"And my father doesn't want me to see you, either," replied Albert. "We're like a queer Romeo and Juliet."

"Without the tragic ending, I hope," said Paul.

"No tomb scene here," agreed Albert with a laugh.

"Promise?" asked Paul.

"Promise," replied Albert soberly.

Then both men were silent, each listening to the other's breathing.

"Are you hard?" asked Albert finally.

"Of course," said Paul.

"So am I," replied Albert, as he held his firm manhood in a hand, just as Paul held his.

"I want you," said Paul.

"Oh, yes, my beautiful man."

And Albert started stroking himself, as did Paul, and their breathing came faster and faster and neither wanted to wait so they quickly came, gasping for air as their bodies jerked and writhed, each seeing the other before him, then joy turned to its after-glow as each licked his hand clean, and they wiped their bellies, and thought of how the other would taste, and when they would finally have the chance.

They said nothing for a while, to keep the spell alive, until Paul finally spoke for both of them when he asked, "So what happens now? I mean, I understand that you're going to be throwing yourself at beautiful young men. Oh, the pain! The pain!" he said mockingly.

"Stop it!" said Albert with a laugh.

"But when, and how, are you going to throw yourself at me?" asked Paul.

"Give me a couple of weeks to divert the media flood south so they forget all about you. We want you and your mother to be very old news, indeed."

"I appreciate that," said Paul sincerely. "I'm handling this much better than Mum . She's a research scientist, for goodness sake. She deals with molecules, not microphones."

"Well, I assure you that will soon change and you won't have to worry about the media again. In the meantime, I'll call my gay Romanov cousin, Michael, who has an estate in Northumberland. He owes me a favor. Actually, he and his family owe my family their lives, since it was my great-great grandfather Edward who saved the Russian imperial family by sending a ship to bring them to England. Anyway, Michael and I do the odd favor for each other. We both represent the more disreputable lines of our respective families. But his estate, 'Little Russia' they call it, isn't far from Durham, so I'll contact him and see if he can help us. If this works out, let's plan on meeting there in three weeks. I'll text you with the details. And remember, don't take seriously anything you hear or learn about me in the days to come. So, until then, au revoir, Paul."

"Good night, my Prince."

Each, in his respective bed, was quickly asleep after a long, long day.

PART ONE

CHAPTER 9

Paul was surprised, and pleased, at how well Albert's plan worked. The media soon left, like flies to new carrion, though a few curious local onlookers remained to stare at the house, before even they moved on. With no one left to prevent accessing the house, the barricades were removed and the police finally left as well, leaving Paul and Pauline alone again. There remained occasional groups of boys, standing on the pavement and shouting their satirical versions of "I sat down under his shadow," but Paul and Pauline knew better than to go out and confront them, which was precisely what they wanted, and without that reward, the lads returned to checking their mobiles and hanging out until they could find someone, or something, else to torment.

At school, the snickering and mockery continued, but Paul ignored it, hoping it, too, would eventually go away. Besides, the lads, like the rest of the country, were transfixed on what the Prince was doing in London.

One did not have to look far to find out. The Daily Mail, The Sun, and other bottom-feeders printed in bold typeface headlines like "Royal Hunk Seeks Same," over lurid pictures of a gloriously shirtless and sweating Albert dancing apparently ecstatically with other handsome, shirtless men who shamelessly shimmied up against him. The videos of such dancing, which happened nightly at clubs, public and private throughout London, were available on the telly and computer, on YouTube, Facebook, Instagram, and apparently every possible sort of online social media. Google searches for items like "Out-of-control Prince of Wales" brought them all up and everyone, it seemed, was looking. There was Albert as the kingdom's most eligible gay bachelor dancing with a constantly shifting assortment of the kingdom's other eligible young men in a mashup of what the Sunday Times condescendingly described with a sniff as "the salubrious delights of a bare-chested Prince."

So, Durham was forgotten in a media frenzy as the country Cowatched its future King shake his booty from one side of town to the other.

"House of Filth!" was another tabloid headline, over an aerial photo of St. James's Palace, with an arrow pointing to the Prince's apartment, even though Albert kept what he was doing far away from the palace.

Reaction was swift as radio and telly talk shows, as well as internet chat rooms, could apparently deal with little else. Albert was the talk of the country, from Land's End to the River Thyne, from Fishguard to Dover.

"Blimey!" said one caller to The World Tonight. "It's bad enough to have a poof for the next King, but does he have to throw himself at every young bloke in town?"

A telly interviewer standing outside Harrods for responses asked an older matron her opinion of the Prince, but she vehemently shook her head in obvious disgust and stepped inside to shop.

Some republican sympathizers said it was time to abolish the monarchy. Yet there were supporters as well, such as the girls standing in front of their school, shouting the slogan they'd printed on placards held over their heads, "Albert rules! Albert rules!"

Then there was the patron of a well-known Soho gay club who perhaps spoke for many when he said, "We finally have a future monarch worthy of getting on our knees for!"

Buckingham Palace issued a terse "No comment"

statement, as did 10 Downing Street.

However, the parents of Paul and Albert had a lot to say.

Pauline: "Now you finally see what a horrible person that Prince of yours has turned out to be. I hope this shows you what a mistake it would have been to have anything to do with him."

George: "What has gotten into you to drag the monarchy through this filth? I cannot read a newspaper or watch the telly without seeing you disgrace both country and family. This has got to stop!"

Albert remains impassively silent.

George: "I never thought I would say this, but even your sister would be a better monarch."

Albert defiantly says nothing.

Both parents are disgusted at their sons' stubbornness.

The young men talk each night, actually early each morning as Albert gets back late from his evening rounds.

Each speaks to the other from their respective bedrooms, with the doors closed and the lights out.

"Papa is furious."

"Mum is furious."

The two men find themselves being drawn closer each day by the secret they share with no one else. It's the two of them, alone, together, at last, at the end of each day, separated by the length of the country, yet just a phone call apart. Paul alone knows that all of Albert's actions are to protect him.

"How much longer will you be doing this? Haven't you made your point?"

"Yes, I have," admitted Albert, who is exhausted. "No one has come back?"

"No one's been here for days. Even the lads have stopped at school. The headmaster and teachers are too embarrassed by what you're doing to say anything."

"Well, I'm too worn out to keep this up much longer. Besides, my father is so angry he said I would be king over his dead body, but then he laughed because that's precisely how I'll become king."

They are momentarily silent, then Albert asks plaintively, "You aren't jealous, are you?"

"Of seeing you out every night with the most beautiful men in London?" asks Paul. "No, not really. I'm just sorry you have to do it. And I know you're doing it just for me."

"I'm doing it because I – "

And Paul quickly interrupts him. "No, don't say it. We've only just met and, like you told me, we don't know what will happen. Have you got that place for us yet?"

"No, that's the next step of the plan. I'll call Michael tomorrow or rather, considering the time, later this morning, after I get a few hours of well-earned sleep."

"Poor you, dancing the night away."

"For you, my dear, just for you."

The two men have been holding their firmness with one hand as they talk, and each conversation ends with phone sex as they stroke themselves until coming, then they mutually gasp and fall back, spent, as their bodies calm down and their breathing becomes regular once more. And they end each nighttime conversation the same way.

"Good night, sweet lad."

"Good night, my Prince."

CHAPTER 10

Albert did call his cousin Michael Romanov that day.

"Albert, so good to hear from you. I'm surprised you could work me in amongst all the handsome young men who must be crowding your bed."

"I hate to disappoint you, Michael, but regardless of what you see or hear, I sleep alone, chastely, each night."

"I don't think you've been chaste since the age of ten, my dear cousin. But I have a feeling this is not a social call, so what can I do for you?"

"You're perceptive as always. I do need a favor."

"Whatever I have is yours, you know that."

"I need a place, an isolated place on your property, where I can meet someone in secret."

And then everything became clear to Michael.

"It's him, isn't it? Your Durham slag. You're not over him. And these nights of pleasure and lust are just a decoy."

"How dare you think such a thing! That's bloody rude!"

"But accurate, and you can't deny it."

"No," admitted Albert, "I can't deny it."

"Be careful now," teased Michael. "I don't want you growing old and soft on me. Remember your 'once and done' rule."

"Oh, I haven't forgotten. Let's just say I want to reserve some place on that vast Northumberland estate of yours for four weekends and not one weekend more."

"Well, I'm glad to hear it. We lascivious old queers must stick together."

"Indeed, we must," agreed Albert. "So, have you got

something available?"

"I happen to have the perfect solution to your request, and it was designed by a great uncle just for trysts like yours. He converted a small gatehouse into an elaborate place just for a special mistress he kept there. The mistress could come in her own car and park outside the estate walls and go right in, whilst my great-uncle came from the main house and entered from inside the grounds. It's perfectly charming, and I'll tell you the back story sometime so you can tell your slag."

"I wish you'd call him by his name. It's Paul."

"Paul, the Durham slag."

"Michael, you're quickly growing tiresome."

"My dear, it's a Romanov trait, one of many I've inherited, though I'm pretty sure I got my queerness from my mother's side."

"How is the Tsar, by the way?"

"Completely happy, from what I can tell. You know I hate Russia and hardly ever go there. Give me London or Paris."

"And how is the constitutional monarchy going?"

"Well, after being raised in England, he finds it a natural fit. And he's relieved his people like it, too. The pressures that led to the Revolution, and then to the Counter-Revolution, seem to have vanished now that Russia is a prosperous and open society. And that's a miracle."

"Well," said Albert, "My great-great grandfather Edward always said he was proud of three things. First, he maintained the succession, though the deaths of his two sons in the Great War, and his eldest daughter from Spanish influenza after the war, nearly killed him. Still, he realized his daughter Victoria was a capable administrator, which she evidently got from her grandmother, Victoria the First.

"Second, Edward was proud of what he was able to do

during and after the Great War. He couldn't stop it, though he tried, but he did get the Allies to agree to nothing less than the total destruction of the German war machine, and to demand nothing less than unconditional surrender. That's why we kept the Kaiser at Gibraltar for two years. Being half-German himself, Edward knew that Germany's price for the war had to be so steep that it would never consider war again. But he also knew that abject humiliation would cause regrettable consequences for all of Europe, so he, eventually, persuaded the Allies not to penalize Germany with crippling and punitive reparations. This is from a king who had no power but the power of persuasion. As part of that, Edward made sure that low-interest loans were provided by the Allies so that Germany could rebuild its manufacturing and agriculture sectors after the war. People got back to work, and within ten years Germany was a major power again, but this time as part of a truly unified Europe that eventually included your country as well. Which leads me, finally, to the third great achievement of Edward's reign, saving your family. Who knows what might have happened if he hadn't gotten your people out of there?"

"And for that remarkable kindness, my family is forever grateful."

"And I'll be grateful to have the use of your gatehouse, just for four weekends, of course."

"Of course," replied Michael Romanov with a smile. "Of course."

CHAPTER 11

Albert had Gerald, his appointments secretary, set aside four Sundays two weeks apart for two months.

"Very good, Your Highness."

He explained that he would be leaving each Sunday morning, spending the night away, away, and would return by midday each Monday.

"Very good, sir," then Gerald paused. "Away, I suppose?"

"Yes, to Northumberland," said Albert.

"Ah," replied Gerald, as everything became clear to him as well, then added, "I will clear these changes to your schedule with Sir Humphrey."

Albert slammed the desktop with the flat of his right hand. The retort was like a rifle shot that made poor Gerald jump, his eyes wide at the Prince's surprising response to what was a routine procedure.

In a loud, authoritative voice, Albert declared, "You will clear nothing with Sir Humphrey! I am not seeking permission for how to use my one day off. I am telling you what I will do."

Then, shocked at his own outburst and seeing the result on the face of his faithful secretary, Albert continued in a subdued tone of voice. "Of course, you may inform Sir Humphrey of these changes. And Gerald . . . "

The man looked at him with the fearful hesitancy of a slapped puppy, "Yes, sir?"

"I should not have treated you the way I did, and, for that, I apologize," explained a subdued and, in his own way, chastened Albert. Knowing that royal apologies did not come easily, a relieved Gerald merely bowed his head, now understanding just how important these Sundays in Northumberland were to the Prince.

"I'll arrange everything, Sir," he said as he prepared to leave the room.

"Oh," remembered Albert, "And have Graham see me as soon as he can, to provide protection."

"Of course, Sir."

Graham quickly appeared, having been warned that the Prince was particularly prickly that day.

"Yes, Your Highness?" he asked upon entering and bowing.

"I'll be making four trips over the next few Sundays to Northumberland, and I want you and your team to accompany me."

And then the situation became clear to Graham as well, who had been puzzled by Albert's actions since Durham.

"It is him, isn't it, Your Highness?"

"Yes," admitted Albert, "It is him. Paul McGregor, that's capital M - lower case c - capital G - r - e - g - o - r. You'll need the correct spelling when you do your background check to make sure he's not a national security risk who will kill me in my sleep!" he added sarcastically.

Graham was surprised at the Prince's mocking tone because he took his work very seriously indeed. Noticing Graham's reaction, Albert covered his face with a hand and breathed deeply to compose himself.

"First Gerald, now you. I am so sorry, Graham. Obviously, this is very important to me and obviously I want it to go well."

And then Graham realized this situation was different from all the previous ones he'd faced before with the Prince. Even the recent wild nights across London were more in keeping with Albert's playboy image than this unexpected sincerity. Graham realized with a start that the Prince was, perhaps, finally growing up. He also realized, with dismay, that Albert had used him, like he'd used the media, to create a diversion. Graham was surprised not only at the disappointment he felt, but also at the betrayal of the nearly intimate trust the two of them had shared for so long. And then Graham felt a sadness he could not shake off, as he realized that something was changing between them and that, on a basic level, he was being replaced in the Prince's affection, a realization he quickly covered up.

"Naturally, Sir. I understand. And where, in Northumberland, will you be going?"

"To my cousin Michael's estate. You know it." Graham nodded yes. "I'll be staying with Paul in a gatehouse at the edge of the property. I'll get the GPS coordinates from Michael for you, and I'll make sure there is a room for you and the team."

Graham nodded again, hiding his doubt about how he would feel about being in the same building as the Prince and his new, well, whatever this Paul McGregor might turn out to be. Probably just another encounter before moving on but, now, Graham wasn't so sure.

"And how will you get there?"

"As this is a private matter, I can't use the royal helicopter and I don't want anything public, not that you'd let me do that anyway."

"And quite rightly," said Graham quietly.

"So, I'll take the Land Rover and drive myself. You can prepare the details accordingly, but I want this kept small and secret."

"We'll keep protection to a minimum," replied Graham.

"I appreciate that," said Albert. "This is a date. I can't believe I'm saying that. It's not a royal procession."

"Still, it's a long drive up there and back," Graham said,

then added, somewhat hesitantly. "Are you sure it's worth it?"

And, as Gerald before him, Graham was shocked and dismayed at the instant reaction as Albert replied curtly, "What you're really asking is whether young McGregor is worth it. Don't overreach like that again," then Albert returned to the papers on his desk, pointedly ignoring Graham who was left standing there. He bowed and went to the door but stopped and looked back at the Prince he'd served for so long.

"Sir?" he asked plaintively.

"Yes?" demanded Albert, obviously irritated at having the conversation continue. Take aback by Albert's curtness, Graham decided not to ask his question.

"Nothing, sir," then bowed again and left Albert alone with his work.

"Northumberland?" asked a shocked Sir Humphrey. "It's him, isn't it? That boy at the school and then later at the cathedral."

Graham and Gerald nodded in agreement.

"Well, how long will this one last?" he asked rhetorically and obviously did not want an answer.

"No one can know about this," Sir Humphrey added needlessly. "Driving all the way up north four times in two months for a tryst with a boy, even if he is 18 . . . Well, there's nothing to be done except to make sure the Prince is safe. Let's just hope this infatuation ends quickly."

The three agreed about that but, considering how unpredictable the Prince had become, they had their doubts.

CHAPTER 12

The interior of the gatehouse, and that of the boudoir, especially, was magnificent, but held no interest, at that moment, for either man as they only had eyes for each other.

Now, finally, they stood face to face, finally alone, finally each was incarnate to the other, as they had waited so long to experience.

The fantasy, the imagination, the stroking of themselves as they mentally undressed the other while hundreds of miles apart, all of that was past. Now they stood before each other, hearts racing, breaths short, skin already glistening with sweat, yet they didn't madly claw at each other; they didn't rip off each other's clothing to get at what each wanted most. No, they defiantly held in check their impulses to consume the other and, with an outward calmness that belied inner passion, each carefully undid the buttons of the other's shirt and took it off and let it fall to the floor, then each man calmly put a hand behind the other's neck and pulled their heads together until their lips touched, and mouths opened, and tongues searched, and they tasted what they'd longed to taste for so long, and they smelled what they had yearned to smell. And their bodies touched, and each man gasped at the feel of the other and, slowly, each worked at the other's waist until pants fell to the floor, and they stepped out of pants, shoes, and socks, and each was finally naked before the other.

Albert gently took Paul by the hand and led him to the bed. Paul sat on the bed, and then laid back as Albert leaned over him, then Albert crawled onto the bed and gently pulled Paul beside him and laid down on his body, and each continued the exploration of the other for which they had waited so long. They touched each other; they licked each other; they lightly bit each other. They pushed their firmness onto the other's body and gasped at the pressure of the other. Albert took Paul's hands and held them over his head and against the headboard as he licked and smelled Paul's armpits and licked his tongue from one side of Paul's chest, across his nipples, stopping to nibble them as well, to the other. Then he gently rolled Paul over onto his stomach, and started licking Paul's neck, then worked his way lower and lower down Paul's muscular back, down the spine, moving closer to his goal.

"Where are you going?" whispered Paul, then gasped at the knowledge as Albert's tongue entered him and lingered there. Finally, Paul wanted more and asked if Albert had brought any protection.

"Michael thought of everything," he said with a smile, which he knew from having arrived early to check the place out. He'd found what was needed, and more conveniently placed on a bedside table. So soon he began to enter Paul, carefully at first, but he quickly began a rhythmic thrusting that brought each man quickly to a mutual climax as they didn't want to wait. Paul had risen from the bed to arch his back against Albert, and they collapsed in a tangle of arms and legs. They lightly kissed and touched each other, then dozed briefly, then it was Paul's turn to enter Albert and this time they joined with a mutual shout in a frenzied climax that left them both weak.

They laid side by side, tenderly staring at each other, lightly kissing and touching each other, each resting in the other's arms until they started again. There was so much to discover, to explore, and to enjoy. It was only towards morning when they finally slept.

The boudoir had tall, glass doors that opened out onto a

wide stone patio, and beyond that was a well-maintained garden with a large, working fountain in the center. Further out was the great lawn, then the park and its carefully tended trees that ended in a circle of wilder woodland. Mist from the fountain caught the early morning sunlight, softening its sharpness as it streamed into the room in a warm glow that awakened Paul, and he opened his eyes to see Albert staring at him, tenderly, who then said, "When the new god appears, we surrender, wordlessly."

Paul laughed, "Did you just make that up?"

Albert punched him lightly on the shoulder and pretended to be angry. "You'll never know! But I appreciate the assumption that I could."

They stopped playing but continued looking at each other.

"What do you see?" asked Paul.

"The most beautiful man in the world," replied Albert simply.

"Then I must be a mirror of your own reflection."

Paul rolled over and laid his head on Albert's chest, still staring into his eyes.

"I can have any man I want," he said.

"In Durham," joked Albert.

"Well," admitted Paul, "It is a small world there. But the man I wanted above all others came to Durham for me, so that must say something about my power to attract."

"Well, what about me?" asked Albert defensively. "I've had men all around the world, only to find myself here in Northumberland in the arms of a man I didn't even know I wanted until I saw you."

"My powers are formidable," laughed Paul.

"Obviously," agreed Albert.

They looked tenderly into each other's eyes, then turned

away, each confused about what he truly wanted, and each concerned about where this was going, and about where it could go, because it was so unexpected.

Paul abruptly sat up and sat on the edge of the bed. Albert also sat up, concerned.

"Is something wrong?"

Paul slid down to the floor and sat with his back against the bed. Albert sat on the floor next to him, and they both looked out through the tall glass doors to the vista beyond.

"You know so little about me," said Paul softly. "It's time you did."

"What I know," said Albert, gently running a finger along Paul's shoulder, then down his arm, "is how much I love your chocolate skin."

And that simple comment, made innocently if thoughtlessly, ruined everything. Paul pulled away from Albert and abruptly stood up. He turned upon Albert in anger and poured the entire pent-up fury of his 18 years upon the unsuspecting Prince.

"How dare you!" he shouted. "I thought you were different, but you're just like all the others, aren't you? 'I love your chocolate skin'" he said in a mocking tone of voice. "Is that why I'm here? Because I'm a dark African fantasy of yours? Aren't there enough dark-skinned boys in London for you? Must you come to Durham to find a big-dicked nigger to satisfy you?"

Albert was shocked by this outburst and, for the first time, realized both the depth, and the extent, of what Paul had been dealing with for probably all his life.

"Look," he said haltingly, "I'm sorry. I didn't mean . . . "

"So now the Prince is sorry he's revealed his true motive? That you like my black skin and big lips and kinky hair and, of course, my big cock? I can find men like you right in Durham by

86

the dozen, by the hundreds, I don't need you driving up from London."

Albert stood up and attempted to hold Paul who pushed him away.

"Don't touch me! Don't you ever touch me again unless you mean it!"

Albert looked at him quizzically, not understanding what Paul meant. At that moment, Paul felt sorry for him, because he saw Albert struggling to make sense of what was happening.

"I don't trust easily," he explained. "And this is why, because men have always wanted my dark skin and what's in my pants. I was six when I was raped the first time, by a neighbor who wanted some black male pussy. He grabbed me when I'd gone to visit his son, but the son was out and the father and I were alone in the house, and I tried to leave but he grabbed me and pulled down my pants and sat in a chair with me and pushed me up and down on his cock and it hurt so much and I was screaming and crying and then it was over and he set me on the floor, stood, zipped up his pants and said if I told anyone he would kill me. I never went back to his house, but he was still a neighbor so I did see him but he always ignored me after that, with his wife and children around him at block parties, always laughing and having a great time, while I was the one who had to hide my shame in self-loathing and couldn't even tell his son what his father did to me. I was six! And while it stopped with him, it didn't stop with others. Groups of boys would hold me down and, one by one, they raped me, repeatedly, until everyone had their fill of black ass.

"'He's just a slag, a Durham slag'," they said. "And I was too ashamed to tell anyone, but my mother knew something was wrong, and she kept asking until I finally broke down and told her. That's when she had me placed at St. Giles, where there were other openly queer boys like me. Oh yes, she knew early on what I was. Still, I wanted men, and I found them in the woods along the river. There were always men who wanted me, and I wanted them . . . "

Paul sat down again by the bed and, again, leaned back against it. Albert sat near him but didn't touch him.

"My mother came from Jamaica. She got a scholarship in molecular biology at the university. She met my father in Durham, a Scotsman from Glasgow who owned a pub in town that she frequented with her friends. They married after she started teaching, and she didn't mind taking his name. Eventually she became head of her own laboratory. He went back to Glasgow when I was six. That was a bad year for me," he said with a wry smile. "She never found anyone else, so it's just been the two of us, till there was you."

And Paul looked thoughtfully at Albert, and studied his face, probing to take the measure of the man beside him. "You're not a bad man, Albert. Thoughtless, yes. Insensitive, yes. But you're actually a very good man. I just don't know if there is anything between us. I don't even know if there is an 'us.'"

But Albert was sure, and looked at Paul, and started to sing one of his favorite Noël Coward songs.

"Time will tell;
time will show;
whether we shall ever know,
which jealous gods have decided our fate;
what joys and sorrows are lying in wait."

As he sang, Paul leaned back against him, and Albert put his arm around him and held him close until he finished.

"Here we stand,

you and I,
hand in hand beneath the sky.
Will the dawn break the spell?
Time alone will tell."

When he stopped, neither moved, and neither wanted the moment to end. There was the ticking of a clock on the mantel, with birds singing in the trees outside. Finally, Paul broke the silence. "For a prince, you have a pretty good voice."

"I love the potency of cheap music," replied Albert. "That's another Noël Coward line. You know, Coward had a home in Jamaica. I wonder if he knew your people?"

"Only if they worked for him," replied Paul wryly. "But my mother's people are still there. I'll ask them. I've been to the island several times myself, but never to Coward's house."

Then Albert explained that his great-grandmother knew Coward well, and even visited him in Jamaica before she became queen. "She had some wonderful stories, but I doubt she knew the best gay stories about him and the parties he had there and the people he knew. But then, perhaps she did. I was quite young when she told me, and perhaps she wanted to protect my virginal ears."

"I don't think any part of you was ever virginal," said Paul with a laugh.

"That's where you're wrong," replied Albert. "Still, nothing about me is virginal now, except when I look at you and, for some reason, I feel innocent again."

The two men sat silently together, one leaning back against the other, each breathing calmly. And then it was Albert's turn.

"I don't trust easily myself," he explained. "After I was sent to boarding school, there was no lack of sex, but I quickly learnt they didn't want me as a person, but as the Prince of Wales. I'd be asked to spend the weekend at some lad's country house, and it thrilled me to be asked. But then there was always the payback after sex. 'My father wants to know if you could help him with this, that, or the other thing. It's just a small favor, but it would mean so much!' You get the idea. It got to the point where I turned down all such invitations, only to hear I was being snobbish!

"I did have a boyfriend, though, the summer before university. We were at Balmoral and there was a handsome young Royal Marine with a devastating wink who set my heart aflutter. Finding an isolated place to meet there was easy, and we had a passionate affair that continued when we returned to the palace. We continued meeting as we were madly in love, and we thought we were being cautious, but it was Sir Humphrey who caught us in the middle of the act. Well, to him the whole thing was most improper, so he told my father and, I swear, Papa would have thrown my beautiful marine into the Tower and, if this were 400 years ago, he would have had his head chopped off and made me watch."

Albert was bemused at Paul's shock. "I know Papa," he said with a sad smile. Being how this was the late 20th century, and to avoid a scandal, my Royal Marine was quickly transferred to Malta, where he still is, for all I know. I never saw or heard from him again. So, no, I don't trust easily. You worry about my wanting your black skin, while I worry about you wanting me for crown and throne."

"Is that what you think this is all about?" shouted Paul as he broke away and stood up again, looking down at Albert furiously. "That I want your fucking crown and throne? I don't want them or you!"

Then Albert stood up, stared at Paul who was trembling and outraged, then reached for him. Paul pulled back but Albert grabbed his arm and pulled him roughly towards him, putting both men off balance and they fell onto the bed in a tangle of arms and legs as Paul struggled to break free.

"Let me go! Let me go!!" he shouted. "I'm out of here!"

Albert, being stronger, rolled Paul onto his back and forcibly held him there. Both men were breathing heavily and staring into each other's eyes like wounded, frightened animals. Then Paul started crying, and Albert reached over and gently kissed him on the lips. Paul wrapped his arms around Albert's body and pulled him close. Albert rolled to the side and both men continued looking, questioningly, at each other. Albert leaned over to kiss Paul on the forehead.

"I love you," he said gently. And then Paul no longer questioned Albert's motivations, and realized he'd found what he'd always been looking for.

"I love you, too," he said, and each started to heal the other.

Sometime later, Paul asked, "So what happens now? Do you sing another song?"

"No, replied Albert with a smile. "I'm going to tell you about this place as Michael told it to me. It was designed as a retreat by a great uncle for his mistress. He expanded a simple gatehouse into this magnificent boudoir based on a description in a book by Zola called The Sin of Father Mouret. But it sounds much better in the original French," he said with an air of superiority, before bursting out with a raucous, mocking laugh. "Who am I kidding? I don't even speak French, let alone read it."

"Well," replied Paul, "I do speak French, and read it, and Zola is one of my favorite authors, and the book you're talking about is La Faute de l'Abbé Mouret. The priest has a nervous breakdown and is taken to a kind of Eden to recover, forgetting who he was, and falls in love with the daughter of the grounds keeper and they wander the extensive grounds like a new Adam and Eve. But as happens so often in Zola, happiness is destroyed as soon as it is achieved. The priest recovers his memory, and his calling, and rejects his lover, who kills herself by being smothered to death in a bed full of flowers."

"But that's a horrible story!" protested Albert.

"It's art, my dear. And it really is better in the original French."

"Well, I am obviously the slower one of us."

"So, there is an 'us'?" asked Paul tentatively.

"Yes, my darling, there is an 'us'. And you don't blame me for liking your black skin?"

Albert knew he was pushing the envelope, but he wanted to be honest.

Paul momentarily flared up again, but jokingly this time. "Not now," he admitted. "It is a beautiful shade, isn't it?" he said, admiring himself as he held out a long arm.

"Lovely, just lovely," said Albert, as he leaned over and kissed Paul lightly on the shoulder.

"Now, my dear, I must get back to London and you, hie thee to school."

"And when do we meet again?"

"I'll be back in two weeks. Keep in mind that we have three more times together."

"And then that's it?"

"Perhaps," said Albert coyly.

"Unless I drop you first."

"You wouldn't dare, and that's a royal command."

"To hear is to obey, my Prince."

Michael Romanov watched them leave via security cameras while sitting at his office desk. The whole episode had been, literally, quite revealing, and he knew exactly who to tell.

CHAPTER 13

Michael Romanov positively tingled with excitement as he eagerly phoned Princess Elizabeth with his news.

"My dear, you will never guess who spent the night on my estate with his Durham slag."

"No!" shrieked Lizzie.

"Yes!" shouted Michael. "He called and said he needed a place where he could meet someone, and then I knew exactly who it was and that Albert's played us all for fools."

"Even me," she said with a snarl. "I can't believe I didn't see it." She stewed for a moment, then continued, "So what happened?"

"They arrived separately, with Albert's security team as an appendage. I had the most perfect place for his menage, a deux. I must show it to you someday. Such a story it has . . . "

She brutally interrupted him. "Yes, yes, but what about them?"

"Well, my dear, they went inside and weren't seen again until the next morning when they came back out, kissed each other, and then left."

"So my brother fell for that colored bit of arse after all."

"Well, when Albert throws him away, he's mine."

"You're all disgusting."

"Oh Lizzie, you're just so prim."

"No scandal has ever befallen me," she asserted proudly.

"That's only because you've never done anything interesting. In fact, I don't think you've ever done anything at all except marry and breed."

"In my family, someone has to do it and, as they say, my

time will come."

"Well, I believe in having at least some fun along the way."

"Michael, all you do is have fun."

"I know," he said mischievously, "Isn't it wicked of me?"

"So," she said, returning to the subject of her brother, "What happens now?"

"Well, Albert asked to use the House of Sin, as I now call it, for three more Sundays, every other weekend, so it will be another two weeks before the next exciting chapter."

"I can hardly wait! Keep me informed!"

"Ciao."

"Ciao."

Michael smiled to himself after the conversation ended, because he hadn't told Lizzie everything. She didn't need to know the room was bugged and, pressing a button, Michael Romanov sat back in his chair to watch and hear the delicious sounds of love making between the Prince of Wales and his Durham slag. Their moans and groans pleased Michael to no end. He really was a voyeur at heart.

CHAPTER 14

Graham asked to see the Prince of Wales, entered his office, bowed, then stood before the desk as Albert finished some paperwork. Finally, he looked up.

"Yes?"

"We have an issue, Your Highness, a security issue."

"What kind of security issue?"

"I didn't say anything about your choice of location for your . . . assignation with young McGregor as you'd already arranged things and because Michael Romanov is a relative, even if distantly."

Then Graham stopped.

"Yes? Go on."

"It may be nothing, sir, or it may be something."

Graham stopped again, hesitant to continue and Albert, frustrated by the delay, shouted, "Go on, dammit!"

Used to such outbursts and not at all perturbed, Graham continued.

"There were security cameras all around the gate house, on both sides of the wall, meaning both the parking lot from the road and the private entrance from the estate. Now, I didn't see any in the area where the security detail stayed, and it's understandable for an estate that size and with the fame and notoriety of the family that there would be cameras . . ."

Then he stopped again.

"But?" pressed Albert.

"But we cannot be certain that the cameras are solely for security, or that they are not inside the gate house as well."

Graham paused before making his point.

"They could also be used for spying on the occupants."

And with that, Albert put down the pen he'd been holding and considered the implications.

"That bastard," he said quietly to himself.

"Sir?" asked Graham, who didn't catch the remark.

"That bastard!" shouted Albert. "Of course he would spy on us."

"It's highly possible the rooms were bugged."

In anger and frustration, Albert hit the desk with a fist.

"Damn him!"

He clearly saw the image of Michael Romanov thoroughly enjoying what was, in effect, a porn tape that he could play back at will.

"So, what do you suggest?" he asked Graham.

"The question is, will he keep these videos, if they exist, for his own prurient interest, or will he share them?"

"Oh, he's probably already shared them with my sister. They are best chums."

"If these tapes were somehow released to the media and the public, consider the ensuing scandal and how it could be used against you and the Royal Family. They could also be used to blackmail you" said Graham. "Either way, you are compromised."

"Damn him!" shouted Albert again, who now was so nervous that he got up and paced the room.

"Have you told my father or Sir Humphrey?"

"No, sir. I wanted to tell you first."

"So far, most of what we have is supposition and assumption. We don't know for certain what use, if any, these tapes will be put, but we can assume that Michael will tell my sister, so she knows Paul and I are seeing each other. As for the tapes themselves, if they exist, I'm willing to bet that Michael will keep them for himself, at least for now. I know him well enough for that. I also know he's basically a coward at heart, and he would do nothing to compromise his own standing, and he has nothing to gain by compromising his Royal Family or mine. He's aware that he and his family owe us everything they have, their lives, even Russia itself. I think it's safe to say we've reached a stalemate. He'll deny everything if I confront him, and I have no proof to the contrary. On the other hand, he can't really use the videos for any reason other than for jerking off, to put it bluntly. He owns the rarest sex tape in the world."

Albert and Graham looked ruefully at each other, then Albert continued.

"Yet, if he were to release it, everyone would know the source and he, too, would be anathema. And for a man who treasures his position in society, that would destroy him, and his place in his own family, including his stipend. I know how prim his uncle the czar is about things like this. So, I suggest we leave it alone and let Michael cum as much as he wants at seeing what he will certainly never have in person. Does that make sense to you?"

Graham smiled, relieved, at such a positive outcome. He knew his own role at putting the Prince in such a compromising position could still cost him his job, even though the whole affair was against his better judgment. Still, he wanted the Prince to be happy – long-term happy – and realized that young McGregor might be the person to provide that, even though Graham was both ambivalent and apprehensive at the prospect.

"It does make sense, sir, but we also need to think of the future. You can't go back there again."

"Well, I don't think Paul's mother will let us have sex in his bedroom."

"No," agreed Graham with a smile, "Now that you've

pulled the media away, I'm sure she's not eager to see them out front again."

"No; I'm sure you're right. So, what do you suggest? You must have an idea."

"I do, actually, Your Highness. There are royal properties midway between London and Durham, estates that are large enough for you two to meet without worrying about snooping cameras and telephoto lenses. I'll check them out, then you can inform young McGregor."

"Why do you keep calling him young McGregor?" asked a surprisingly irritated Albert.

"Well, sir, he is young, and he is a McGregor."

"So he is," agreed a placated Albert.

Graham bowed and started to leave when Albert called out to him.

"Graham?"

He turned back to the Prince.

"Yes, sir?"

"Could we not tell my father and Sir Humphrey the full details of this mess?"

"Of course, sir."

"And Graham . . . "

"Yes, sir?"

"Thank you."

Graham was caught off guard by the rare compliment. He smiled slightly and nodded.

"You mean a great deal to me."

Now truly surprised, Graham caught his breath, then bowed again and left.

Alone, Albert tried to work, but his anger at his cousin overwhelmed him.

"Bastard!" he shouted at the empty room. But there was

anger towards himself as well because, looking back, he realized he'd let expediency and, frankly, desire, overwhelm common sense. It was a lesson he hated to learn yet again.

CHAPTER 15

The parents are not happy, but they are demanding.

"You will not see the Prince again!"
"You will not see that Durham lad again!"

"Do you hear me?"
"Do you hear me?"

"Yes, Mum."
"Yes, Papa."

"But you're not going to obey me, are you?"
"But you're not going to obey me, are you?"

"No, Mum ."
"No, Papa."

At that point, the parents know they have lost the battle they have chosen to engage. They also know the stubbornness of their sons is part of their own personalities. They are wise enough to realize that if they push hard to keep their sons close, then they will simply push them away, a fate neither parent wants. So, reluctantly, they accept the stalemate and wait for whatever this is to play itself out.

CHAPTER 16

The sons were ecstatic in victory when they spoke to each other that evening.

"You won't believe what my mother said."

"You won't believe what my father said."

"'You won't see him again.'"

"'You won't see him again.'"

There was a moment's pause before each burst out in hysterical laughter. They had won a complete triumph, but they were still unsure what the prize was.

"My mother did say I can't use her car anymore."

Instantly concerned, Albert asked, "Does that mean you can't come to see me?"

"Not at all," assured Paul, to the Prince's relief. "Wherever you are, I'll get there."

"Good," explained Albert, "because Graham doesn't want us to use the gatehouse again. He says it's too close to the public road, and if the media catch on to us, they'll show up again at your place."

"But I love the gatehouse," complained Paul. "It's so beautiful and romantic."

"I know," said Albert, "but he is looking for a more secluded Crown property somewhere halfway between Durham and London, a place big enough that we can be far from any snooping eyes and ears," which was as close as he came to sharing Graham's basic concern.

"I'll text the coordinates of the new place when he tells me. So, a week from Sunday, then?"

Then there was silence before Paul quietly said, "But I

want you now."

And Albert agreed, "And I want you."

Then silence returned as each felt the presence of the other, and both wanted to sustain a moment that was quite fragile.

Paul broke the silence first. "So, signing off from Durham, au revoir. That's French for – "

"I know what it is," interrupted Albert defensively. "I'm not a complete clod."

Then, in a much softer tone, "So, au revoir yourself, my handsome lad."

"My beautiful Prince, good night."

"Good night."

CHAPTER 17

"Something's happened," said Michael Romanov with concern to Lizzie. "Albert called and said he isn't using the gatehouse again."

"What's that about?" asked Lizzie, equally concerned that their masterful plan was shattered.

"I'm not sure," conceded Michael. "He said there were security concerns about being so close to the public road, and I can see that as the road passes right by the gatehouse. Still, I wonder if they're not suspicious. His people must have seen the security cameras."

"I've got to know what's happening!" said Lizzie urgently.

"I can't help you there," replied Michael.

"But I know who can!" exulted Lizzie triumphantly. "I'll hire a private detective to follow the slag to wherever they meet next. I'm not letting up on this."

"Keep me informed," said Michael.

"Later," rang off Lizzie, who quickly made another call to someone she'd hired before and quickly explained the situation.

"I want you to follow the McGregor boy a week from Sunday when he leaves Durham to meet my brother. And you cannot get caught. This cannot be traced back to me."

"I know my job, Your Grace. I've never let you down and I've never compromised you."

"I know you're good," replied Lizzie, "but this is a very delicate matter and nothing can go wrong."

"Rest assured, ma'am," replied the detective. "You'll learn what you want to know."

"Excellent," said Lizzie. "I'm counting on it."

CHAPTER 18

It was a long drive for Paul from the entrance gate to the house; a large Tudor pile set in the middle of a vast estate. Albert gleefully opened the door, and they melted into each other's arms. After a long, sustained kiss, Paul looked around him.

"What is this place?"

"This little cottage?" answered Albert mischievously. "Actually, the site was a Catholic abbey until Henry the Eighth confiscated it, demolished it, and built this country house in its place. The estate is still a Crown property, but now the National Trust operates it as an historic house museum, considered the finest of its kind in this part of the country. But I'm exercising my seigneurial right by reserving it every other weekend for, well, for as long as we want. Do you like it?"

"It's fabulous," agreed Paul. "Of course, I miss the French décor of our last place."

"Well, I'm not the Crown Prince of France, am I?" retorted a miffed Albert.

"Not in the least. It fits you beautifully."

Then he paused before bringing up a delicate subject.

"We're defying our parents to be here together."

"It is like Romeo and Juliet, isn't it?"

"Without the tragic ending?" asked Paul hopefully.

"Without the tragic ending," insisted Albert. "Maybe this is where we break into a medley from West Side Story."

And with that setup, they looked at each other and started singing, "Tonight, tonight, won't be just any night. Tonight, there will be no morning star!"

They stopped singing, but continued looking longingly at

each other, then Albert took Paul by the hand and led him through the house.

"Wait till you see the bed!" he said eagerly. "It's fit for a king!"

"You've waited all day to say that haven't you?"

Albert just turned around and smiled, then they entered a chamber with the largest bed Paul had ever seen.

"Voila!" shouted Albert. "That's French!"

"Thank you," replied Paul with a smirk, but he was suitably impressed.

The bed had four massive, intricately carved bulbous corner posts that held up a massive canopy. The headboard was carved with the Tudor Arms of the red Tudor rose, supported by the well-known lion and unicorn.

"It's one of the finest beds in the Kingdom, and even I had to promise to be careful with it. We can't return it in splinters!"

"Then we'll be careful with it. Or at least we'll try. Of course I don't think copulating elephants could hurt this bed," said Paul after a closer inspection.

"We don't have sex like copulating elephants, do we?" he asked plaintively while removing his clothing.

"I'm not sure," replied Albert with a suggestive smirk as he removed his own clothes. "Let's find out!"

Albert nodded towards the bed with a smile. Paul nodded agreement, then they ran to the bed and leaped upon it. The enormous oak bed shook as they fell onto the hand-embroidered cover and gleefully made love. Only something was different this time, something had changed between them. Now, each man's happiness came from the desire to make the other happy, with a kiss, a touch, a lick, a nibble, each desired to make the other moan and gasp with delight. They were no longer separate individuals; somehow in the two weeks in which they were physically apart, they had become two halves of the same creature, and they knew it. They saw it in each other's eyes, and they expressed it through the mutual tenderness and concern each had for the other's pleasure. The men were growing up, and they were in love, though that word was still very much unknown territory, but it was not one they were at all hesitant to use. The fragile illusion of youth was gone, replaced by each other's reality.

When passion was exhausted, they rested, until aroused again, and they continued like this until finally and completely spent, they slept. Paul awoke to find himself laying across Albert's chest, and said softly, in a dreamlike state, "Je t'aime." Only half asleep, Albert heard the words and held Paul closer.

When they awoke in the morning, overhead on the canopy they saw a vast, embroidered scene depicting the Garden of Eden before the Fall, with birds and animals set in a pastoral paradise of lakes and hills, waterfalls and valleys, with the lion and the lamb calmly beside each other, and the snake and the bird, and Adam and Eve, naked and without shame. It was the first day of the completed world.

The men propped themselves up on pillows against the headboard.

"Do you think Henry copulated in this bed?" asked Paul.

"I think he copulated just about everywhere," replied Albert with a laugh. "He was said to be a great beauty in his youth. Before he grew corpulent and with oozing sores on his legs."

"Promise me that will never happen to you," said Paul.

"I promise," replied Albert. " I want to always be desirable to you."

Paul smiled, "So you plan on seeing me more than four times?"

"I don't know what you mean," said Albert archly. "'Once

and done' was just a vicious rumor promulgated by an earlier, sadder version of me. It has nothing to do with us."

"So, there is an us?" he asked, as he had asked before.

"Yes," replied Albert, as he had before. "There is an us, and I seal it with a kiss."

He leaned over and the two shared a prolonged kiss before pulling slightly apart, still looking deeply into each other's eyes.

"So, what happens now?" asked Paul.

"I want to marry you."

"Then ask me."

So, Albert took Paul by the hand, and they got off the bed and stood before each other. Then Albert got down on his knees and looked up at Paul, but then Paul got down on his knees as well. They held each other's hands, and Albert asked, "Paul McGregor, will you marry me and be my husband?"

"Yes, I will," replied Paul. "And Albert George Alfred Edward, will you marry me and be my husband?"

"Indeed, I will," replied Albert. They leaned forward and gently kissed each other, then leaned back against the bed while sitting on the floor and held each other's hand.

"Now what?" asked Paul.

"Well, now you must ask your mother's permission to marry, and I must get Papa's. This is where it gets complicated. The Prince of Wales does not elope, not if he wants to be king, and I very much want to be king. With you beside me, we can do great things. I know I can be a good king to my people, even within the severely limited powers of a constitutional monarch, which I understand and accept. I think persuasion and example can be very powerful, but I must have you with me. I must convince Papa of that, even though you are a . . ." And he stopped mischievously, which Paul missed because he was instantly angry.

"Because I am a what?" he angrily demanded.

"A commoner, my dear; you are a commoner, while I am of royal blood. Marrying beneath one's station is fortunately not the disgrace it once was, a long time ago. Traditionally I could only have married another prince, even an African one. Are you an African prince?"

"Blimey, no!" laughed Paul. "I was pulling pints in me daddy's pub when I was five, though I had to stand on a chair to do it."

"Well, considering how kings for a thousand years have spread their seed far beyond the confines of marriage, I wouldn't doubt that there is some royal DNA inside you."

"There certainly is now."

"Yes, my dear, there certainly is now, just as your combination of Scottish and African DNA is inside me. And I want it there all the time."

"Your wish, my Prince . . . Besides," continued Paul, "I'm pretty sure I'll be the most uncommon commoner to ever marry within your family."

"Agreed," said Albert, "and, fortunately, virginity is no longer an issue either. Those cherries were popped for both of us a long time ago. Besides, with Lizzie's little no-neck monsters in line for the throne, many traditional issues are simply not relevant for us. Still, Papa must agree to the marriage, and I think he will, once he meets you."

"That, I'm not looking forward to," admitted Paul. "It's going to be like being examined for a promotion."

"That's exactly what it is, a huge promotion, from your neighborhood in Durham to the palace in London. And that's why your mother must agree, because this will also change her life forever. Once the engagement is announced, everything changes and you will never be able to go back and simply pick up the pieces of who you were and what you were doing, either of you. The past will, indeed, be history. So, you and she need to see the changes clearly, and you both must acknowledge and accept them. I'm used to it. I was born into this life, but for you and her it will require a new education as there will be a lot to learn. There will be great demands placed upon you, with high expectations. It's only a glamorous, easy life from the outside. But we can do it; and your mother can do it; if both of you want to."

Albert looked directly at Paul, who unflinchingly returned his gaze.

"Then let's do it," he said.

"And just wait," chuckled Albert, "until you see the wedding. It will amaze you."

"I thought we'd just go before a registrar in Durham," said Paul slyly. "And I have nothing to wear," he protested.

"But you will," assured Albert. "And if I could put a crown on your head, I would. So, I'll talk to my father, and you talk with your mother. Once they approve, which they eventually must, then there will be a lot that must be done, including a background and security check. We must know that you won't murder me in my sleep."

"How do I know you won't murder me? There are all those Jack the Ripper stories after all. Which one of Victoria's sons was it now?" asked Paul mischievously.

"That's a family secret you don't need to know about. Besides," added Albert archly, "at least I could get away with it."

"I can see the headline now," said Paul, "'Durham lad's headless body found floating in river.'"

"Nothing that obvious," said Albert. "People disappear all the time."

"Is that what happens to your ex's?"

"They will never tell, and you will never know. I just never wanted to see them again. I used them just as they used me. 'Once and done,' you know that."

"But I'm different?" asked Paul.

"Oh, my dear, you certainly are."

Still holding each other's hand, they leaned over and kissed, then Albert continued.

"Once the paperwork is done and everything is in order, then an engagement announcement is publicly posted outside the palace, and a Herald, in a fabulous uniform, will read it aloud. Then everyone will know. Until that moment, you can still back out."

Albert looked searchingly at Paul, and with atypical uncertainty and doubt, wondering, worrying, whether the man he loved so passionately would indeed reject his offer.

But Paul gently pressed Albert's hand within his own, understanding his concern, and said, reassuringly, "Never, my dear."

Relieved, Albert continued. "With the public announcement, which should really catch the country off guard considering my reputation as a lascivious rake, then the media will have a field day thoroughly examining your life. 'Deep Dark Secrets of Prince's Fiancé Exposed' will be the mildest, I assure you. Your life, and that of your family here, in Scotland, and in Jamaica will be thoroughly searched for any hints of scandal. And if none are to be found, then they'll just be made up. Details at ten. Not to mention how the web will burn with conspiracy theories and stories of alien abductions. "But," and here Albert took both of Paul's hands in his own. "I promise, in everything that is to come, that I will keep you and your mother safe, and that I will love you and honor you and cherish you all the days of my life."

Paul smiled gratefully, amazed that such a man had

entered his life.

"That sounds like a marriage vow."

"As they say in America, my dear, 'you ain't seen nuthin' yet!'"

CHAPTER 19

When Paul left Durham in a friend's car to see Albert, he didn't realize that he was being followed on the M25 by Lizzie's detective. However, the detective was unaware that he was being followed by Graham and his driver.

The detective, a Mr. Marlowe, was surprised at being pulled over, and even more surprised when Graham stood at his window and showed him his Crown security badge. Graham motioned to Marlowe to unlock the passenger door so he could sit beside him. Marlowe helplessly watched Paul's car disappear down the highway.

"You know why I'm here," said Graham pointedly, "so I don't want any protestations of innocence. Now, I'm going to talk for a few minutes, and I want you to keep both hands on the steering wheel and look straight ahead."

"I'll do no such thing!" protested Marlowe while turning to look directly at Graham. "You have no right – "

"Shut up!" commanded Graham with such force that Marlowe, indeed, shut up.

"Thank you," replied Graham politely. "Now, put your hands on the wheel and look straight ahead."

This time Marlowe did as directed, but with obvious resentment.

"Now," Graham continued, "I'm going to tell you what I know about why you are here, and what you are doing, and then I want you to fill in the gaps on what I don't know.

"First, someone has hired you to follow Paul McGregor as he goes to an assignation with a member of the Royal Family. Whoever hired you obviously wants to know where that place of assignation is. The question is, why does this person want to know something that is none of their business? Will they use the location to plot a kidnapping? Or an assassination? Now you see why I'm involved, don't you? You may think this is just about two poofs having sex, but it involves state security and the security of the Royal Family. Mr. Marlowe, you're in serious trouble."

Marlowe's hands tightly gripped the steering wheel, and his clinched teeth and pursed lips pulled tight lines across his face.

"Needless to say," continued Graham, "Your assignment is ended, and what I want you to do after our little talk is drive back to Durham, forget about all of this and, if you do that, then this meeting never happened. Now, I need to know who hired you."

"I won't tell you. Client confidentiality."

"Oh," replied Graham amused. "So, you find your ethical backbone when it suits. Well, I wouldn't want you to compromise your standards in any way, so you don't have to tell me. Instead, I am going to give you a name and, if I'm right, simply nod your head yes. That way, you really haven't told me. So," said Graham lightly, "Let's try it."

Marlowe said nothing but Graham continued anyway.

"Princess Elizabeth."

Marlowe simply stared ahead, still gripping the wheel tightly.

"Princess Elizabeth," repeated Graham. "Simply nod if she's the one who hired you."

Marlowe did nothing. Now, Graham did not get angry. He simply put things in perspective for Marlowe's understanding.

"Mr. Marlowe, if you do not assist me, then the following will happen: you will lose your license so you will no longer be permitted to work as a private detective in the United Kingdom."

Graham paused for a moment. "Or any country in the Commonwealth. Do you understand?"

Marlowe said nothing.

"Do – you – un – der – stand?" stated Graham coldly and evenly.

Now, for the first time, Marlowe was frightened. This was not the simple job he'd expected. Begrudgingly, he nodded yes.

"I need your verbal agreement," replied Graham.

Reluctantly and slowly, Marlowe said, "Yes, I understand."

"Good, now, once again," as though speaking to a petulant youth, "Is your employer Princess Elizabeth?"

Slowly, and with silent fury, Marlowe nodded yes.

Graham broke into a smile.

"Now, that wasn't so bad, was it?" But he didn't wait for an answer. "You will tell Princess Elizabeth that you have been removed from the case, and you can use my name. She knows me well. And I have a two-word message you are to give her from the palace."

This time Marlowe did turn to look quizzically at Graham.

"The message is simple: Stop it. Have you got that?"

"Yes, I have it," replied Marlowe with a growl.

"Good. Now, we're nearly done. Keep in mind that I expect you to follow through on your agreement. I do not want to find out that you are continuing to follow Mr. McGregor, nor do I want to hear that she has hired anyone else to follow him. At that point, it will be out of my hands and given to MI-6 to follow up on as a case of espionage and criminal conspiracy. The prime minister's office will also be informed and, frankly, you and any others involved will be looking at very long prison terms. Am I clear?"

By now Marlowe was looking forward again through the wind screen, as southbound traffic streamed by on the M25.

"Am I clear?" demanded Graham.

"Yes . . . sir," added a reluctant Marlowe. "You are very clear."

"Good," said Graham lightly. "You and I will not see each other again. I trust you have a pleasant return drive to Durham. It's a lovely day in the country. I also suggest you remove your hands from the steering wheel. They are unhealthily pale."

Graham opened the door, got out, and returned to his own vehicle where he and his teammate waited for Marlowe to leave.

Marlowe's fingers had gripped the steering wheel so tightly that his fingers hurt as he loosened them, and then shook them to restore circulation. He was angry and would remain so for some time. He also had a call to make.

Graham and his security officer watched Marlowe drive away and followed him to the next exit where he turned back north towards Durham.

"How did it go, sir?"

"We'll see," replied Graham thoughtfully. "We'll see. Now, let's catch up to Mr. McGregor."

CHAPTER 20

Albert was exhausted by the time he returned to the palace and all he wanted to do was sleep, so he wasn't pleased when Graham called to say he had to see him urgently.

"What is it?" he asked testily and wearily when Graham entered, shut the door and bowed.

"We have an issue, Your Highness," which Albert knew meant there was trouble.

"Go on," said the now alert Albert.

"Your sister hired a private detective to follow Paul from Durham."

"What?" exploded Albert. "This is too much! So, what happened? Does he know where we met?"

"No, of course not," explained Graham calmly. "We stopped him just outside Durham, and then he returned to Durham, so he has no idea where Paul was going."

"Thank goodness," said a relieved Albert. "I can't believe she would do that."

But then he stopped himself and thought for a moment. "Well, actually I can. So, what did you do?"

"We told him to stop it and to tell your sister the same thing."

"And will he do that?"

"I made a forceful case," replied Graham.

Albert smiled. "I'm sure you did. And I'm sure he'll find other cases that are much less stressful."

The two men smiled at each other.

"Once again, I am in your debt, Graham."

"My pleasure is to serve you."

"And you've always done so with tireless devotion and loyalty. I depend on you, Graham."

Graham merely bowed his head. Such moments were his life's greatest joy, like watering a thirsty plant.

Albert continued. "I told Paul I'd keep him and his mother safe, and I need you to make sure that happens."

And that was the moment when Graham's life irrevocably changed. It was a moment he'd expected, and dreaded, for years, because he realized that what was happening with Paul was unlike any other prior assignation. Graham was startled to realize that Albert, for the first time, truly cared for another man and now Graham would have to share him.

Graham knew his love for the Prince had to remain unrequited; from the time he'd carefully peeled the young, clinging Albert from around his neck. Still, in the only family Graham allowed himself, he saw himself and the Prince as a kind of primary bond, and now that was no longer the case. "Foolish man," thought Graham ruefully to himself. "You knew this moment would come and, now that it's finally here, you stand amazed at the inevitable." It was a weakness Graham regretted. He shook himself.

"Of course, sir. I'd already prepared for this possibility," he said, the first time he'd ever lied to Albert, who was completely unaware of Graham's anguish.

"Excellent, and I will deal with Elizabeth myself, in my own time, and in my own way. Now, I'm knackered and really need to sleep."

"Of course, sir."

Graham bowed and left Albert alone, who fell, exhausted, onto his bed, fully clothed, and was soon asleep, happy to dream of Paul.

Out in the corridor, Graham sat heavily on one of the side

chairs along the wall. He really wasn't supposed to sit there, and he knew the footman would not be pleased, but he was suddenly very tired himself, and overcome by the unexpected change to his life, and yet he was pleased for Albert, amazed that he had found someone he could trust and love. Indeed, Graham realized he was jealous but also knew his responsibility had expanded to keeping both men alive and safe. It was a responsibility he knew he would eventually, perhaps even eagerly, accept. It was part of his job.

CHAPTER 21

"Damn! Damn! Damn! Damn!" shouted Princess Elizabeth after hearing from Marlowe that he was foiled in his attempt to follow that Durham slag to his secret rendezvous with Albert.

"It was Graham!" she shouted to her husband Larry as he was trying to read the morning's papers at breakfast. "Now I'll never know where they are meeting. And do you know what Graham told Marlowe to tell me?"

Larry was well acquainted with his wife's passion for intrigue, though he certainly didn't share it. Still, he put down his paper to show he really was interested and said, "Haven't the faintest."

"He told me to, quote unquote, 'Stop it!' Can you imagine? The gall of that man!" referring to Graham, but possibly her slightly older brother as well.

Larry, a man not without a sense of humor, hid the smile trying to form around his mouth to sympathize with his obviously distraught wife, yet he still felt a need to reply unsympathetically that, "I told you it was a bad idea, with nothing useful to be gained from it."

But then Larry stopped, and Lizzie saw him analyzing the situation with his business-oriented logic, a trait on which she depended, so she kept quiet while he thought.

"So, Graham was there."

She nodded.

"But why is Graham still protecting just another one of Albert's dalliances?"

Well, Lizzie had no idea, so she waited for Larry to continue.

"It makes no sense, unless . . ."

And here Larry broke off again to ponder, and then the dots finally connected, and Larry's face broke into a broad smile as the answer revealed itself.

"Of course," he said more to himself than to Lizzie. "Of course," he continued. "This isn't a dalliance at all: Albert's in love!"

"Bosh!" replied Lizzie instantly, dismissing the idea as absurd. "He doesn't know the meaning."

Ordinarily Larry would agree, but not now.

"But it's the only thing that makes any sense," explained Larry. "This isn't just another of Albert's 'once and done' sexual conquests. This one is different. Graham was there because Albert loves the lad and wants no ill to befall him."

And then Lizzie realized her husband was right.

"That bastard!" she said. "And he's trying to hide it."

"Lizzie, don't you see? Instead of learning the location of two queers fucking, we've stumbled onto a true royal secret."

"Of course!" said Lizzie triumphantly. "So that's why Graham told Marlowe it was a matter of national security."

"Did he?" asked Larry gleefully. "Then we've got it! And it's more than love, as unexpected and atypical of Albert as that by itself is. No, Lizzie," and he paused dramatically so that Lizzie leaned forward in eager anticipation of what her husband would say next – and he savored the moment of triumph – "I hear wedding bells!"

"No!" she shrieked delighted, "Not Albert!"

"Yes!" cried Larry ecstatically, "He's going to get married, and only we know it!"

"Oh, delicious!" she said excitedly, but then stopped, confused.

"But what can we do with this information? How can we

use it?"

Larry thought for a moment.

"I don't know," he admitted. "Maybe we can't, at least right away. But knowledge is never useless, and now we know what almost no one else on the planet knows."

"How delicious!" said Lizzie again. "So, Albert is getting married. Or at least he wants to. I can't imagine Papa approving a marriage between the Prince of Wales and a common, colored boy from Durham. Maybe I should say something to Papa to prevent it?"

"Don't you dare let on that we know anything about this," urged Larry. "I'm sure even your father doesn't know yet. Let's just wait and see what happens."

"But no matter what happens, nothing will change the succession?" asked Lizzie worriedly.

"Of course not," replied Larry. "Even if they marry, and no matter how hard they try, they still will never have children. And even if they decide, like so many queens seem to be doing these days, to adopt, say, a Biafra baby for example, there would be no royal blood, no DNA going back to Alfred the Great and William the Conqueror. Only you and our children have that, and nothing that Albert and the McGregor lad can do will possibly change that. So, no, nothing will change. If Albert dies first, then you become queen. And even if you die first, then our children are still the only legitimate succession. We win either way. So, it makes no difference what Albert and this lad of his do, even if your father approves. We are the only future the monarchy has, and Albert remains a dead end."

"Delicious!" crowed Lizzie with excitement. "And on the wedding day, if there is one, you and I and the children will sit at the front of the Abbey and the world will see just who will follow Albert. You're right!" she told Larry gleefully. "We have nothing to worry about. But we'll have to shine that day, because you know the cameras will be on Albert and his slag. We'll have to look regal!"

"You always do," assured Larry, already worried where this was going.

"New outfits for everyone!" proclaimed Lizzie.

"Sounds expensive," said Larry doubtfully. "And aren't we getting a little ahead of ourselves? There may not even be a marriage."

"It's never too soon to plan," explained Lizzie with her own kind of logic. "Besides, you know I never concern myself with money."

"That's because I pay for everything!"

"Why do you think I married you?" asked Lizzie with a smile.

Larry knew she was joking, but only half joking. In their days of courtship, Larry was under no illusion as to what the world's most eligible princess saw in him: unlimited wealth as he was a modern-day Croesus. But there was more to it than that, as even he was not the only wealthy bachelor in the kingdom. No, he and Lizzie had an agreement that went beyond his money and her title; they did make a team, with Lizzie supplying the drive and scheming ambition while he supplied the thoughtful support that enabled her to succeed. Of course, the problem was that they formed a formidable force without any sense of purpose or direction. All she had to do, all she could do, really, was wait for her brother's eventual death. She, in her way, loved her brother as it had always just been the two of them with their father and no one else, since the death of their mother so many years before, to share their lives or even to understand the isolation of their very narrow world in which they were confined. She hated to use the word "prison," since it didn't sit well with most people who really didn't understand royal life, but it felt like that even though, since her marriage, Kensington palace was no longer her main residence as she, like Larry, now preferred their Suffolk estate. With her husband and her beloved children, her estrangement from Alfred no longer hurt as it once did, even though she and her brother led completely different lives, at opposite ends of the Royal Family spectrum. When their father eventually died, and if Albert died as well, then Lizzie, though queen, would at least have children and husband, so she would hardly be completely alone. Still, being basically insecure, that prospect unsettled her. So, no, she thought, let Albert reign with his Durham slag of a husband, if that's what he wanted, and she would happily stay out of it, at least for now.

Her inability to apply herself to anything truly constructive, in most people's eyes, beyond home and family, was one reason she loved gossip and rumor, which is why she hired Marlowe in the first place.

Which was when Larry conveniently interrupted her chain of thought with the observation that Marlowe had certainly earned his salary, even if unexpectedly.

"Well, actually, he thinks he's failed and is worried he won't be paid at all," she replied.

"I'll take care of it because he's done us a great favor, even if inadvertently," said Larry. "Besides, I'm sure you'll want to use him again for some project or other of yours."

"Well, since I don't have a country to rule, I must do something with my time. You have a business to run."

"You could get more involved with your charities, like Albert does, to keep busy."

"But it's so tedious and not at all to my liking," replied Lizzie, who enjoyed the pomp and ritual of her position, but found the related duties and responsibilities to be remarkably boorish, despite the constant appeals of her advisors to show at least a semblance of interest in the lives of those who could eventually be her subjects. But she was not a detail person, nor was she a big-picture person either. She did like horses, however. And gardening. Especially gardening. She loved simply putting her hands into the soil on a warm summer's day; she loved nurturing things; her plants and her children; those were her favorite things. And Larry, of course.

She would depend on Larry, if she became queen, to deal with the minutiae of being a monarch. His ability to do that was why she had married him. Early in their relationship, there had been lust which, with six children and working on Number Seven, still existed, but it wasn't a major factor in her life. No, the one thing she was really good at was having children, and she recognized her ability in that department. Basically, everything else she left to her husband and her staff. As for love, she did feel affection for him and let it go at that. She also realized that his background in business and engineering, both of which honed his skills in logic and organization, were skills she depended on.

For his part, Larry enjoyed the world of business as it was impersonal. His wife provided enough drama. Still, and even though he really did like Albert and wished him no ill will, when he thought of the scenario where Lizzie became Queen Elizabeth the Second, he had to admit that he liked the sound of Prince Larry. It was certainly a step up from being duke. He was surprised that such things even mattered to him as he had thought himself above worldly vanities, but apparently not.

CHAPTER 22

The parents are angrier than ever at being disobeyed by their recalcitrant and stubborn sons.

The mother: "I told you not to see the Prince again and now you want to marry him? No, no, and no!"

The father: "I told you not to see that Durham lad again and now you want to marry him? No, no, and no!"

The young men are angry and confused themselves as they speak to each other that night.

Paul: "My mother refuses to let me marry you. What are we going to do?"

Albert hears the panic, fury, and pain in his lover's voice, a voice that breaks with tears.

"I hate her! And, I swear Albert, that I will kill myself if I can't have you!"

"Now wait," says Albert trying to sooth the passionate man he loves so much. "My father is equally stubborn, but there is a way through this."

"Then find it!" demands Paul. "I want you; I don't want to kill myself."

"My sweetheart, push such thoughts away. Let me think."

And so Paul waits, an emotional wreck, while Albert deliberates what to do. He understands the ways of court. He'd watched his father in action long enough to know the subtle levers of power, and he wonders what Sir Humphrey, that master strategist, would do. And then it becomes clear.

"My dearest, here's the situation."

"Yes?" asks Paul hopefully.

"Our parents don't want us to marry, but we've been

talking with each parent separately. We're divided and they've conquered. The answer is to get them together. They must meet. The four of us must meet. Our fates are combined, so there must be unity amongst us all. This requires group consensus. We won't win by trying to convince each parent separately. It's all or none."

"So, you want my mother, and me, to meet your father the King?"

"It's the only way."

"But she'll never agree. And even if she did agree in principle, I know what she'd say. Now, understand that she's not vain, not at all, but she takes pride in her appearance so, first of all, she's going to say that she has nothing to wear to a royal audience. And, because she's also practical and frugal, next she'll say she won't waste money on an expensive frock she'll never wear again. So no, Albert, she won't agree."

"For once, you're speaking too far ahead. Let me deal with Papa first. If I can convince him to just meet your mother, then we have a chance with her. Even she can't refuse a royal command to see the King even if she doesn't like it. So do nothing till you hear from me, all right?"

There is silence, then, slowly, acceptance and agreement. "All right, because I simply don't know what else to do."

"You don't have to know," Albert assures him. "I think he will agree at least to a meeting. Beyond that, I cannot say, but at least now we have a chance. At least now there is hope."

"I hope you're right," says Paul softly, then even softer, "Je t'aime. That's French for – "

"I know what it means!" interrupts Albert with mock anger, relieved that Paul can still joke. Then there is silence again, and into the silence, Albert whispers, "Je t'aime, aussi."

Albert met his father for tea. He knew the meal would be poached salmon. He couldn't understand why his father kept an experienced chef, trained in Paris, with a vast and expansive repertoire of, literally, thousands of dishes, when his favorite and most demanded meal could be made just as well by any housewife in Chelsea.

But tonight, the King, apparently, was not hungry. He cut a piece of salmon with a fork but then dropped the fork with a clatter onto the plate, and roughly pushed the plate away.

"I waited all day for this meal," he exclaimed angrily, "so I'm not going to have it ruined by this issue that's come between us. Let's clear the air before it's completely cold."

Albert just stared at him, so George continued.

"You will not marry the Durham lad, ever, and that's my final word. But I respect you enough to hear your opinion."

Then he waited for Albert to speak. Albert knew this was his one moment to change his father's mind. He looked at the salmon on his plate, then looked up, stared directly at his father, and spoke.

"You said Paul is too good for me, and you're right. He's smarter than I am. He's more talented than I am. He's a better per-son – more ethical, more generous – than I am. Which is precisely why I need him at my side. I've never asked you for much, but now I'm asking for this. One day I will be king, and I need some-one beside me I can depend on, who is loyal and devoted to me, someone who will pull me up to his level and demand I become the best king I can be. Someone like Mummy was for you. The two of you were a team; you depended on her. And I know how hard it's been for you since her death. I know how lonely and, yes, how depressed you have been. Frankly, I'm amazed at how you've carried on without her. But I need you to give me the same chance you had yourself. I know how much you needed her; how much you depended on her. She made you a better king. And I need that with Paul. Please, Papa, I'm begging you to give me the same chance you had yourself, to be the best king I can be."

Which was when George realized that something had indeed changed in Albert. He was no longer the lascivious fop of yesterday. There was a thoughtful depth to him that Albert showed to his father for the first time. And the reference to his beloved, and sorely missed, Genevieve, tore his heart, because he did miss her every day and, in his mind's eye, she was still there, beside him, leading him, showing the way forward, which is why no other woman had ever taken her place. George well understood what Albert was saying. He just hadn't realized his son was capable of such self-examination, or that he understood his own needs so well, or the needs of the crown he would one day wear. And the father realized he had his son's male lover to thank for helping Albert to, first, acknowledge this core of his being, and then be able to speak so clearly of his needs. My son is finally growing up, George thought with satisfaction.

"Very well," he said. "I will at least meet the lad and his mother, but no promises beyond that."

He smiled at the relief on Albert's face.

"Thank you, Papa. Thank you so much."

And then Albert did what he'd rarely done in many years. He put his hand over that of his father, who was surprised by the direct contact with another person, which he rarely had. For many years he'd doubted his son's ability to rule. Now, at least there was a chance for him to leave the succession to a young man finally ready for the job.

"One point, though," he said. "We won't meet here. It's far too public and with too much pomp and ceremony. I don't want the McGregor lad and his mother feeling overwhelmed. I'll see them at the country house you two have been using for your trysts."

"How do you know about that," asked Albert completely puzzled. "It's a secret."

"Oh, please," said the King with a smile. "I need to know my successor is safe and stays safe. Besides, I was contacted by the director of the National Trust. Evidently there was some concern about your use of Henry's bed. I had to commit the Crown to cover any damage done to it during your, well, during whatever it is you two lads do there."

"Piffle," said Albert with a smile. "That bed could support copulating elephants."

"Are you calling our ancestor a copulating elephant?"

"Let's just say it's fit for a king."

"You like that joke, don't you?" said George with a smile. "Now, if you don't mind, my salmon is getting cold and colder."

Albert finally removed his hand so both of them could eat. Still, considering how things went, even cold salmon didn't displease him as much as he thought it would.

Pauline sat at the kitchen table, tapping her fingernails on the top. The envelope she'd received that morning was in front of her. Once again, she was angry. Finally, she heard Paul enter the front door. His last year was nearly over; he would soon graduate, and she was concerned that he still had no idea where or what he would study. His lack of planning concerned her.

Paul came into the kitchen, looked at her, knew something was wrong, and that it probably concerned him.

"What?" he asked defensively.

"This came today," and she pushed the envelope across the table so he could see it.

"Did you know about this?"

He picked it up. It had his mother's name and address handwritten in a florid calligraphy style. The return address, embossed in gold, said simply, "Buckingham Palace, London."

He turned away from his mother's stare.

"Albert mentioned something about it."

"It's an invitation for us to meet the King."

"But that's wonderful!" exclaimed Paul. "When are we going?"

"Paul," said his mother reprovingly. "We're not going because I don't need to tell him in person that our sons are not going to marry."

"But Mum!"

"But Mum nothing!" she shouted. "This is absurd: you and I going to meet the King of England."

"And Wales," interrupted Paul, hoping to break the tension. It didn't work.

"Don't be cute with me, son, not now. I don't care if the Prince can convince his father to see us. There is nothing to discuss."

"Just see him, Mum. You've never met Albert."

"And I don't want to meet the man who's stolen my son's heart. I told you not to get involved with that family because it will not end well. Trust me, Paul, they will destroy you."

"But Mum! I don't care! I don't care if I just have a month of happiness with him, or a year, or 50 years, just as long as we are together. Isn't that the way you felt with Da, at least at first?"

Then Pauline looked back at the young McGregor lad she'd fallen in love with. They, too, had been so happy, for a while.

"Do you want you want your heart broken as your father broke mine? And yours?"

"Albert is better than that, Mum. And he needs me."

"He doesn't need you, Paul. All he wants is what's below your belt."

"And he can have it any time he wants, Mum. Yes, he fucks my black body, and I fuck his white body, and it makes us both happy. But that's not why I want to marry him, Mum. It's because he needs me. Yes, we want each other. We desire each other. We love to be inside each other. But he needs me, Mum, and I need him. We're a team, Mum. And the two of us can do great things together. We can change this country, Mum. We can make it a better place. Give us a chance, Mum. Please, I'm begging you."

And Pauline saw the pain in her son's eyes, and knew she was the cause of it, and knew that she could turn it to joy with a single word, and she realized she didn't have the right to begrudge her son that happiness, no matter what the cost.

"Yes," she said.

"Yes?" asked Paul, uncertain she really meant it.

"Yes. We will meet your Albert and his father. But I'm not promising anything else. Just a meeting."

"Oh, Mum! I love you so much!"

And Paul went around the table and knelt down to hold her as she sat, and she held him in her arms. She felt his trembling body, and knew she'd made the right decision. She just didn't want to regret it.

"There is one thing, though," she said as she released him and he stood back up.

"Yes?"

"I have nothing to wear."

Paul laughed.

"I told him you would say that!"

"And I'm not going to buy a fancy, expensive frock just to see the King one time."

"And I told him you would say that as well."

She smiled.

"Am I so predictable?"

"At times," he admitted. "Though I really wasn't sure you would agree."

"And I didn't mean to. I didn't want to. But you are persuasive. And I really can't say no to your happiness, however fleeting it may be."

"But that makes no difference, does it Mum?"

"No," she admitted, "It doesn't."

Into the lingering silence, she said, "Maybe I can justify an expensive dress if there is more than one visit."

"I'm sure you can, Mum," said Paul with a smile. "I'm sure you can."

CHAPTER 23

Paul noticed the increased security as he and his mother entered the estate, then saw more around the house. Still, it was Albert who opened the door himself, and the young men were relieved to see each other. Paul proudly stepped back to let Albert see his mother, who looked radiant in her broad-brimmed hat, lavender formal dress with a tailored jacket, with matching high-heeled shoes and purse. She'd found the complete outfit at the best women's store in Durham. The owner had smiled when Pauline told her she needed an ensemble fit for a king, thinking it was a mere exaggeration, and Pauline did nothing to dissuade her.

Albert was struck by Dr. McGregor's beauty, but also by her poise, her dignity, and her obvious sense of self-worth.

His mother curtsied before Albert. Paul thought of all the times she'd rehearsed before her bedroom mirror, wearing her heels, to make it graceful. He knew how important it was for her not to feel out of place in this very odd situation.

"Dr. McGregor, I am so glad to meet you at long last," explained Albert. "Paul's description doesn't do you justice."

Pauline smiled, despite her resolution to remain officious, and her determination not to give in to what she still considered a youthful whim.

"Your Highness," she said.

"Call me Albert," he urged her.

"Yes, Your Highness."

Then she and Albert both laughed.

"We can have that effect on people," he explained, then added that the King was waiting for them in the dining room at the back of the house.

"You'll love it," gushed Paul. "It's fabulous."

Albert put his arms around Paul and whispered in his ear, "No fear," and Pauline, for the first time, saw them together and, contrary to her intentions, at last recognized their shared tenderness.

Albert led them through the Great Hall, all dark English oak, with a beamed ceiling, carved panels in the walls, and heavy, dark oak furniture. Paul was relieved that the door to the bed chamber was closed. Albert was talking about the house.

"After Henry's death, the Crown retained ownership of the estate and lent it out to various members of the extended Royal Family, mainly dukes. An extension was added to the back in the early eighteenth century designed by Robert Adam and is considered one of finest remaining and untouched examples of his mature style."

Albert stopped at a door, knocked twice, and said, "They're here, Papa."

From the other side came a booming, "Then bring them in!"

Albert opened the door, and the difference between the front and rear parts of the house were striking. Here, everything was light and colorful, with no surface left unpainted. The walls retained their original pale green hue, while the ceiling was a mass of white plastered ornamentation, with more plaster decoration on the walls. The entire effect was rather like an enormous wedding cake. The entire back wall was primarily tall, narrow windows and even the tall, narrow double doors were glass paneled and opened out onto a terrace, with gardens beyond, and the park beyond that. It reminded Paul of the layout at the Romanov gatehouse, and he wondered if all such grand country estates followed the same pattern. Of course, he'd only seen two of them.

An armchair had been moved to face the outside doors, so the King, sitting in the chair, could not be seen. Another chair was placed to one side. The King stood up and turned to the group. He wore a suit of summer-weight wool that Albert had chosen. He looked carefully at Paul and Pauline, taking their measure.

Pauline came forward and gave a deep curtsy, with no unsteadiness, as difficult as that must have been with heels. She rose regally and looked at the King, taking his measure in turn.

"Your Majesty," she said gracefully.

"My dear Dr. McGregor," said the King, "It's an honor to finally meet you. Our sons, it seems, have a great deal in common."

"So, it seems, sir," she agreed, while the two young men looked shyly at each other.

The King held out his hand to shake Pauline's, a gesture that pleased her and which she found surprisingly touching. They looked carefully at each other, each still assessing the other, when the King let go of her hand and faced the sons.

"Now, lads, Dr. McGregor and I have things to discuss, so I would appreciate it if you would be so kind as to go outside to the gardens and enjoy the day while she and I talk. Oh, and leave the doors open as I find it quite stuffy in here."

The young men looked apprehensively at each other as the plan was for the four of them to meet together, but Albert merely shook his head slightly.

"Of course, Papa," said Albert.

He and Paul went out onto the terrace. They stood side by side overlooking the gardens, then held each other's hand as they walked down a short flight of steps to the garden level. Pauline and the King watched them go. Still watching them, the King spoke to Pauline, "I told Albert that Paul was too good for him."

Surprised, Pauline replied, "I told him the same thing. I also told him not to get involved with your family because he will be destroyed."

The King was surprised at her directness and critical tone, so paused to decide how to respond.

"Harsh words, Dr. McGregor, very harsh indeed. When I think of how many people would literally kill to be where your son is now, for whatever gain they would seek, it's refreshing to hear someone warning their child away."

"And can you deny it? Your son promised to keep my boy safe, but how can he?"

The King replied slowly. "I could explain the quality of our security forces and the high-tech protective bubble in which we live, but that's not what you mean, is it? If you're asking about the corrosive effect of the monarchy, well, both my children are examples of that. I think things would have been different if their mother had lived. She would have provided balance that I never had time to provide, so my children basically raised themselves, with results you must be aware of."

He stopped talking, but Pauline remained silent, so he continued.

"Before your son came into my son's life, considering the kind of lascivious, wanton life my son led, remarkable even for a Prince of Wales, I would have agreed with you, and would have told Paul to run away as fast as he could and never look back.

"You see, Dr. McGregor, I have long doubted my son's ability to be a responsible ruler of our people, even recognizing it to be primarily a figurehead position. He was frivolous, with little sense of duty and I thought, seriously, that he might be the last monarch, that the people would finally say, 'Enough!' and just do away with royalty altogether. Albert seemed such a rash, heedless young man, with no center, no depth.

"I thought he needed someone; that the right person could provide the stability and balance that he could not provide for himself. I wanted him to have a partner like I had. Genevieve was more than a wife to me, an accessory, we were a team. We worked together in this goldfish bowl that is the monarchy. She was the person I trusted most to be completely honest with me, to advise me with no other motive than doing what was best for our people. She was always my lodestar, and that's what I wanted for Albert, but he refused to even consider any kind of long-term relationship. 'Once and done.' His rule was well known and frustratingly short-sighted.

"But with Paul," he continued, "everything changed. I mean, maybe he was looking for someone all along but, if so, he never mentioned it to me, and I certainly couldn't see it in his behavior. So naturally I was stunned when he said he'd found someone to love and marry. But how, I wondered, could a boy give him what he needed? How could a boy – "

"A man," interrupted Pauline.

"A young man," the King agreed. "How could any young man possibly understand the needs of the position he would enter, and how could he maintain his own balance while helping my son maintain his?"

"So that's all my son is? A tool to be used to keep your failure of a son on the throne so the monarchy can continue?"

"Harsh words again, Dr. McGregor, but quite honest. And I see I have not made myself clear. A monarch needs a spouse who is dependable, a rock, a place of solace, of inspiration, of devotion and loyalty. It's a lot to ask of anyone, let alone a young man of eighteen. But having met Paul, even briefly, I think he might be the man for Albert, because I also see those same qualities in you."

He said that while looking directly at Pauline, who turned

away.

"I don't want to embarrass you," continued the King, "but we must be clear about what our sons are getting themselves into. It's nearly impossible to rule alone. I only manage it now because I feel Genevieve is still with me, even if I can't see or touch her. Her presence is very real to me."

He paused, then continued.

"I gather your husband has left you."

"That's right, sir."

"It's hard raising a child alone, isn't it?"

She looked at him and simply nodded.

"And we want the best for our children, don't we?"

She nodded again.

"Albert tells me Paul is a young man of many talents. I know he can sing well."

Pauline smiled.

"And I'm sure that when you considered all the possibilities his life could take, you never thought he might marry the future king."

"No, sir, that never occurred to me."

"I understand you are a microbiologist and run your own lab at the university."

"That's right; I do, sir," she said with a hint of pride.

"You are a self-made person. What you have around you has been achieved on your own merit, by your own hard work. Whereas my life, and that of my son's, has been completely planned since before we were born. We are completely predestined. He and I stand on a thousand years of history and never had to think about what to do with our lives. We were told what to do. I envy your freedom, Dr. McGregor, and that of your son. Such limitless possibilities. No monarch ever has that. The only freedom we have is in choosing who will accompany us on our preordained journey. I was very lucky to choose the right person, as she also chose me, and now I think Albert has been equally lucky. What I'm saying, Dr. McGregor, is, if you agree to this marriage, then so do I."

He stopped and looked at her. She took a moment to reply.

"You're right, sir. I never thought of marriage into the Royal Family as an option for Paul, and I'm not sure I do now. And you are right that he is remarkably talented and clever. On the other hand, he has yet to decide what he wants to do with all that talent. He's had no plan for the future, which I've found to be unsettling and frustrating, because I knew early on, even in Jamaica, what I wanted to do and be, and came to this country precisely to achieve what I have done. But Paul had decided nothing, not about university or anything else, until he met Albert, and then it was more than desire, even more than love. It was as though he'd been waiting for Albert all along.

"He and Albert have plans, sir, great plans for what they can achieve together. And I know, now, that if I try and stop Paul, if I try to control his future – if I try to control him at all – then he will resent me, and I will lose him in more ways than one. And I don't want to take that risk. Besides, I want to see what they can do together. I want to see what they can create, like tending a rare flower in a garden. I will not hold my son back. He wants to marry your son. I agree."

The King smiled and turned back to the terrace. He went to the doorway and looked out to the garden.

"Dr. McGregor," he said softly. "Would you mind joining me here?"

She stood beside him and, together, they looked out to see Paul and Albert, hand in hand, walking among the flowers. And the mother to one, and the father to the other, gazed at their children's radiant beauty as each was reflected in the other, and the parents felt they were nearly intruding on the first days of paradise.

"We are going to make them very happy, Dr. McGregor."

"Yes, sir, we are."

The young men heard the King shout down to them. "Join us, lads. We have something to tell you."

Apprehensively, Paul looked at Albert and clutched his hand tighter.

"Now, now, my sweet man," said Albert softly, and gently kissed Paul in front of their parents. As they walked back to the house, hand in hand, Albert leaned over to Paul and whispered, "No fear."

CHAPTER 24

The timing of the engagement announcement was carefully planned so Paul was out of school with one less issue to handle.

Crown security also worked with the Durham police to have barricades and protection at Pauline's house before the announcement was made to deal effectively with the curious and the media.

The biggest problem was how to get Pauline to the lab and back every day with the least disturbance to her regular routine, which was disturbed enough by the presence, discrete as it was, of her new security detail.

Both the Prince and the King were determined to honor what was now a mutual promise to keep her and her son safe. Having security, she grudgingly realized, was essential to that goal.

Access to her house was limited to a list of neighbors and others that she wanted to see, and whose identities had to be verified and then checked against the list. Deliveries and mail were inspected before she got them. Phone calls were screened by an answering service also overseen by security. Requests for interviews were carefully vetted as she made it clear she wanted as little change to her normal routine as possible, and that her work at the lab came first, except for Paul himself.

Pauline understood that colleagues, neighbors, and even shopkeepers would never look at her the same way again. She understood they would be curious about these unexpected changes, and she was resigned to many people basically asking the same questions over and over, such as what it was like to meet the King, to have the Prince of Wales as her future son-in-law, and to become a member of the Royal Family.

She knew also while most people would be happy for her, there would also be the envious, the jealous, those who assumed that, somehow, she was benefiting from all this, rather than the reality of just putting up with the attention and the royal connection just so her son could be happy.

She planned to address the issue at the lab's next staff meeting by thanking the team for their best wishes and then encouraging them to continue with the work they were doing as though nothing had changed, though, of course, everything had changed.

As for Paul, it was decided that he would move to Kensington Palace until the wedding, an event he wanted to help plan, though palace protocol and precedent would dictate most of the ceremony. Still, he and Albert were adamant that, while the wedding at Westminster Abbey was a ritual over which they had little control, nonetheless they wanted a vast, open reception afterwards, in the parks around the palace, to which the entire country would be invited, though how that would work in practice had yet to be considered. The logistical issue of feeding a vast number of people, while providing adequate security, would require most of the six months before the event.

As Albert had explained to Paul, the engagement announcement was printed and posted outside Buckingham Palace, and the Royal Herald, in his traditional and resplendent uniform, read it aloud in his most commanding voice. Beforehand, the palace merely issued a vague statement that an important announcement would be made, and gave the date and time, so there was a curious crowd present who collectively gasped, then cheered the news that the Prince was engaged to be married.

At the same time, a general press release containing the same information was released to the media, causing regular programming to be preempted by the news that flashed around the kingdom.

It didn't take long for the media to realize how it had been successfully and easily duped by Albert's diversionary tactics, which was made clear in the ensuing coverage:

"Albert to wed Durham man after all," was a typical headline, the one that The Times went with.

"Prince makes fools of us all," was a more bitter example.

Across the country, people stopped to assess the news and to react in their own way, with those reactions eagerly sought by reporters.

Those against it were loud and often rude: "No bloody poof and his bloody queer boyfriend are going to rule over me!" said a Bristol man outside a pub. "I'm moving to Scotland where they got rid of the monarchy!"

"I think it's sweet," said an elderly matron in Aldeburgh. "As a girl, I remember dear Mr. Britten and his, well, partner I guess, Mr. Pears, and they were ever so kind to us. And their festival has provided jobs for the locals when most villages are losing their youth to London, so I'm all for it."

Number 10 Downing Street quickly issued a statement congratulating the men, and quoting the Prime Minister as saying she hoped the country would rally around them.

The Archbishop of Canterbury and the Lord Bishop of Durham issued a joint statement congratulating the men and said they looked forward to officiating together at the wedding. They also affirmed the Church of England's recognition of same-sex marriage, whose ramifications continued to reverberate around the world as more countries withdrew from the Anglican Communion.

One radio talk show in Exeter had a man who railed against "the homosexual conspiracy," and whose language grew so vulgar that his call was first bleeped and then cut off.

"Well, we can't say that on the radio," explained the host.

The darker internet chat rooms were studied by security teams who took note of each threat against Albert and Paul, and there were many of them. Still, the vast majority of the general populace in quick surveys said they were excited and pleased with the prospect of a new day for the monarchy, and with the Royal Family finally starting to look like much of the rest of the country.

Patrons of a gay pub in Soho were shown outside in the street with their pints held high and joining in a chorus of "Y.M.C.A."

"Here's to queens all over the kingdom!" shouted one as he took a deep swig that ended with foam all over his face.

"This is our day!" he continued. "May Albert and Paul rule forever! And I'm buying a new frock for the wedding!"

At their country estate, Larry looked over from the telly to his wife and said, "Well, we called that one right."

"Yes," agreed Lizzie, "But what does that sign mean?" She angrily pointed to one of the signs held up by a celebrating group outside the palace that said, "When's the baby?"

"When is what baby?" she shouted at Larry. "You said our succession was not in danger!"

"And it's not," assured Larry soothingly. "That's just talk. We have the bloodline. Remember, they're just two blokes. What's Albert going to do? Use a turkey baster to inseminate one of the maids? Forget about it. Let them have their marriage, and even their adopted baby if that's what they want. We've got the legitimate heirs, and that's all that counts."

Then, seeking to move his excitable wife to another, less

heated and provoking, topic, he continued, "Now, you have six months to plan how you are going to look when you walk up the aisle in the Abbey. And I promise that every straight man in the country, and there are a few of us still left, despite appearances to the contrary, will only have eyes for you."

"Well," said a somewhat mollified Lizzie, thrilled at the prospect Larry presented to her, "If you say so."

"I do, my dearest, I do."

The palace press office was overwhelmed with requests for interviews. Already a family photograph had been released of Albert and Paul seated, with their proud parents standing behind them. While the King and Pauline declined to comment, Albert and Paul had already set aside the next few weeks for interviews, with priority given to the gay press and media, which caused some carping from the others once they figured out what was happening. But Albert and Paul wanted the coverage to be as inclusive as possible as there was a lot to make up for.

"Happy, my darling?" asked Albert.

"Ecstatic," replied Paul.

CHAPTER 25

And so the weeks passed, with Paul in his Kensington apartment, where Albert spent most of his time. They continued giving interviews and posing for photo shoots. They were photographed walking in the gardens, or at a desk reviewing plans for the wedding. Their favorite picture was taken in the drawing room, with Albert sitting in an over-stuffed chair, and Paul perched beside him on a wide, padded arm – both informally dressed in solid-colored sweaters over blue-and-white striped shirts, open necked, with dark slacks and loafers – smiling at the camera, with Paul's hand resting gently on Albert's shoulder. The photo later became the next issue's cover shot for that magazine and, subsequently, one of the most sought-after issues of the year. The men were so taken with it that the magazine company, at their request, made a large version which they had framed for the apartment.

Paul was surprised that there were no requests for them to appear on talk radio shows, as he knew how popular they were with segments of the population they could reach no other way. He found out that the palace rejected all such requests out-of-hand, not wanting to expose the Prince to such spontaneous and, therefore, uncontrollable situations.

"Nonsense," said Paul, "People love these shows so let's do one."

Albert immediately agreed. He liked the idea of responding immediately and directly to his people's questions and issues. The format seemed a modern version of the royal audiences of centuries past when monarchs let any of their people approach with their requests and concerns. It was a way

Albert could get closer to his people. Still, he had to overcome the hesitancy of Sir Humphrey, who insisted the monarchy was not spontaneous.

"Well, it should be!" thundered Albert, while acknowledging that spontaneity was a trait his father avoided at all costs, and who insisted that the very rare media requests he did grant were thoroughly vetted in advance, with no chance for the odd extempore question. "Off the cuff" was an unknown concept to him.

Still, Albert was intrigued by the concept and thought it would be good training for him to think quickly on his feet, even while sitting down. For Paul, it was an opportunity to reach many people in a short time, and to get an idea of what real people, as opposed to reporters, were actually thinking.

Still, because the format was so fresh and foreign, it was decided to start with a program in a small, provincial market first, so if something went wrong and they made a complete bollix of things, then it wouldn't be too widely known. What they hadn't counted on was that the particular program they chose as a test run was also streamed on-line so, theoretically, the whole country could listen. And they hadn't considered just how much interest their appearance on a talk show would generate.

An existing broadcast room at the palace press office was used for the event, with Paul and Albert opposite each other, wearing headphones and with large microphones in front of them.

The program started, the men were excited to be introduced to the radio audience, and the host took the first question.

The men had made it clear that they especially wanted questions from young people, not just adults, and the first question was from a tittering teenage boy who, in retrospect, was likely already drunk or stoned, and his tittering mates could be heard in the background. The initial question was mumbled, so the host asked the lad to repeat it, and this time it was completely clear: "Hey, guv'na, where do you shirt lifters stick it?"

Well, Albert had considered this type of question beforehand, and thought his planned rejoinder of "Wherever we can" was quite witty. Fortunately, however, due to the station's thirty-second delay, the entire encounter was scrubbed and the host quickly moved on to the next question.

"I'm Dylan Jones, Your Highness, and I'm an out-of-work collier, and I've been out of work for twelve years. As Your Highness must know, being our Prince and all, that there's no more mining left in Wales now. So, I'm on the dole, which at least keeps my wife and me in our home, and with food on the table, but I want to work, Your Highness. I'm a proud Welshman and I want to keep busy, not just sitting at home or meeting my neighbors down at the pub. I'm too young to retire. I've got some good years left in me yet. The council said they'd train me for something, but there's no work nearby for what they'd train me for and why, I ask you, Your Highness, should I have to leave home to go to England just so I can have a job? You know Wales, Your Highness, and I'm not going to leave God's own country.

"Now, my wife stays home to raise our grandchildren because our daughter- -in-law works two cleaning jobs and tends a shop as well to make half a living. And our son . . ."

And here the man stopped for a moment, and Albert and Paul realized he was starting to cry, but he continued. "My poor Johnny, well, he couldn't find work either, so he got involved, you know, with drink and the drugs and the painkillers, and that's how he died. Now, it wasn't suicide, I tell you that, Your Highness, not my Johnny bach, but nonetheless he's gone, and my heart is broken, even though I know we'll see him later on. But it's now we are missing him. So, what can you do for people like me? And don't think I'm the only one. There are many the likes of me right here in Llanfynydd, and across the country. Now, Your Highness, you tell me, as our Prince, how we are supposed to carry on? You tell me what we have to wake up for in the morning? How do I look my wife in the eye when I cannot provide? Answer me that, Your Highness. I don't care what you and your lad do in private. That's none of my concern. But I need an answer to what the hell happened to my life!"

And then there was silence. And Paul looked at Albert, who was shocked by the pain and anger and hopelessness in the man's voice. And Albert saw Paul pointing to the microphone to say something because radio hates dead air space. So, Albert spoke.

"Mr. Jones, is it?" Then he continued in Welsh: "Rwy'n falch o'ch cyfarfod. Rwy'n blês eich bod wedi galw. Mae Cymru yn agos im calon. And for those who don't know the glories of the Welsh language, [and here Albert paused and winked at a shocked Paul] I told Mr. Jones that I am pleased to meet him; I'm glad he called; and that Wales is close to my heart.

"Now, Mr. Jones, I could tell you how well the country is doing economically, and it is. For the most part, the cities are booming, as you implied, with work for practically everyone who wants it, which is why we have a related issue of emigration from Eastern Europe and other places where the job situation is so much worse. But that doesn't help you or your fellows or your daughter-in-law working three jobs. And I am sorry for the loss of your son: Mae'n ddrwg gen i ichi golli eich mab.

"But you're right. Mining is gone and it's never coming back. All those windmills on your Welsh mountains producing electricity are both the present and the future. But they don't provide many jobs, as you know. And the question you raise about the need for productive, well-paying jobs in rural areas is one that I know concerns my father, the King, and it's one he frequently discusses with the Prime Minister. The answers are long-term and deal with policy, with education and training, with matching jobs with people, and you're right, you shouldn't have to leave what I'm sure is a lovely town in a beautiful Welsh valley. And if I were a great wizard with a magic wand instead of the sceptre I'll hold at my coronation, I would use it to provide good paying jobs for you, your family and your neighbors. But I won't get that wand at my coronation, just as my father did not get one at his. Yet I can do several things for you. First, I can listen, which may not seem like much, but at least you know Your Prince has heard you. Second, I will tell your story to my father so he can pass it along to the prime minister at their next meeting. Third, Paul and I will be making a tour of the kingdom after our marriage [At this Paul looked at Albert completely puzzled; this was the first he'd heard of the tour] and I will make sure your town . . . What's its name again?"

"Llanfynydd, Your Highness."

"Llanfynydd, then, Mr. Jones. And I promise that he and I will come to your town where we will be pleased to meet you and Mrs. Jones and any others you think we should listen to. And I want you and your neighbors to think of what you would like to see done because, trust me, here in London we don't see things as clearly as you can. You're there, you know the issues, and I think if you put your collective Welsh minds to it, that you can come up with some solutions as well. Will you do that for me, Mr. Jones?"

"I will!" agreed Mr. Jones enthusiastically. "And we will give you a good Welsh meal as well!"

"We look forward to that. Mi edrychwn ni ymlaen iddo. We will not let our Welsh people down. Wnawn ni ddim gadael ein cyd Gymry i lawr. Goodbye for now. Hwyl am y tro."

The call over, Albert looked smugly and triumphantly at Paul, then stuck out his tongue, then motioned to Paul to take the next call.

"Paul McGregor here," he said into the microphone.

"Mr. McGregor, Matilda here, with my friends. [And giggling was heard in the background.] And we wonder just what Prince Albert means to you?"

"Of course," replied Paul, looking at Albert. "You're familiar with the story of Cinderella?"

"We're teenagers, not children," said a defiant Matilda.

"I'm so sorry," apologized Paul. "I didn't mean to insult you, but that story is the frame of reference for my answer to your question.

"Well," he continued. "I wasn't raised by an evil stepmother, and never had step-sisters to use me as a chore girl. But I was also not aware of my life's potential, like Cinderella, until Albert came into my life. He was transformative. And he is my Prince Charming."

And Paul looked at Albert and winked.

"Oh," gushed Matilda and her friends. "That is so sweet. Thank you!"

The next call was from a middle-aged woman, a Mrs. Milnot, who said her first children were nearly grown by the time she had her last daughter, "Who now has become my youngest son."

Paul and Albert looked at each other; this was an unexpected twist.

"Now, I love him just as he is, but he's having a lot of trouble at school. He's being pushed around and beaten up regularly by the other boys who won't accept him for who he is, and I don't know what to do about it. Please help me as I'm not getting anywhere with his teacher or school officials."

Again, Albert motioned to Paul.

"Paul here, Mrs. Milnot, and you're probably aware by now that I went through something similar as a young gay boy. And if my own mother is somehow listening to this show – I love you Mum – then I want the country to know that I literally would not be here today, I would not be alive today, but for her. Because I couldn't take the abuse and violence I faced every day at school – the beatings, the name-callings – and I imagine your son . . ?"

"T," Mrs. Milnot added. "My husband and I named her Tabitha at birth, but now he just goes by T."

"T, then," Paul continued. "I imagine T goes through similar things, and the transgender issue is an added layer of complexity I didn't have to deal with. Anyway, it was my mother who saved me by taking me out of that school and getting me into St. Giles where, not that everything was instantly better, but where I finally met others like me, and also the staff and headmaster were supportive and defended me. I needed that. I needed to know I wasn't alone, and that's what T needs, a safer place where he can find defense and solidarity with others like him. And I want to tell you about an initiative the Prince and I are starting through our new foundation that will, in part, provide support for L.G.B.T.Q. youth across the country with specific resources and options so kids like yours won't feel so alone."

Now it was Albert's time to look at Paul in amazement because he was completely unaware of this new foundation, and so it was Paul's turn to stick out his tongue, then he continued.

"Now that will take some time to set up, but I encourage you to find someplace where T will be supported and can grow into his full potential. We're, all of us, plants, Mrs. Milnot, and we need to find the best soil that provides the nutrients and moisture we need to become the very best we can be."

Mrs. Milnot's voice was shaking with emotion as she said, "Thank you, sir. God bless you, sir."

And that was the end of the show. The host encouraged his listeners to tune in tomorrow when the topic would be the pros and cons of the proposed waste-water treatment facility. Then the host profusely thanked The Prince and Paul for appearing on his show and later, off the air, explained that his guests usually consisted of council members, opinionated environmentalists, and bird watchers.

The red broadcast light went out and the men took off their headphones. Paul asked angrily, "So when were you going to tell me?"

"What? That I speak Welsh? I am the Prince of Wales, not the Prince of France."

"Well, that too," admitted Paul, "It was a surprise. But no, when were you going to tell me that we're taking a trip around the country?"

"It was supposed to be a surprise for the wedding."

"And when were you doing to tell me about the new L.G.B.T.Q. initiative?"

Paul looked sheepish. "Maybe we have too many secrets from each other?"

Only slightly mollified, Albert agreed. "Maybe we do."

Trying to move things along, Paul said, "Then tonight for tea? My place?"

And wanting to move along, Albert said, "Tonight for tea. Our place."

During tea, which wasn't salmon, the two men finally talked about the broadcast.

"Well, there's more than just the trip around the country?"

Suspciously, Paul asked, "Yes?"

"Papa is going to make you a duke after the wedding."

153

"A what?" Paul nearly shouted.

"A duke," replied Albert calmly. "Papa wants it; Sir Humphrey wants it; and I want it."

"But what about me? What if I don't want it?"

"You have to have a title," Albert patiently explained. "You're marrying the future King, and when that happens we can't be introduced as the King and Mr. McGregor. You're marrying into the Royal Family and a title is both expected and required by tradition."

"Even if I don't want it?"

"I know you don't want it, but if you don't have one, then people will suspect something is wrong. And, basically, it's just for formal occasions. No one is going to be bowing and scraping before you," and he paused before continuing, "most days."

Albert smiled to lighten the situation, but Paul wasn't having it.

"I wish we had discussed this first."

"There are many things about being part of the Royal Family that probably should be discussed but never are because, well, it's tradition and traditions are rarely logical, so I've learned it's just better to accept them and move on."

"So that's what you want me to do? Accept my dukeship and move on?"

"Yes," said Albert plaintively. "For me."

Paul sighed in acceptance; the answer he would be giving in many situations to come.

"And the tour?"

"I'm afraid it's the only honeymoon we're going to get, at least for a while. We all have our parts to play."

"So I'm beginning to learn," said Paul ruefully.'

"You're not having doubts, are you?" asked a very concerned Albert.

Paul smiled reassuringly. "Not at all, my Prince, as long as you are with me. But I was hoping for a honeymoon on a tranquil island somewhere. You must own one."

"I'm sure the Crown owns several, or we can rent one if we need to. But right now I want to show you off, and not just to be seen, but to listen as well."

"To everyone," emphasized Paul. "Not just the upper class and politicians."

"I promise," said Albert. "Everyone. And it will be a time when we can show the country that we are a real team. That we work together. That's what we want, isn't it?"

And Albert looked at Paul so questioningly and imploringly that Paul could only agree.

"Yes, my dearest, that's what we want."

They ate in silence for a while, then Paul asked, "Will I be duke of anything, or just Duke Paul?"

Albert smiled coyly."You're going to be the Duke of Durham."

Impressed, Paul smiled, "Ooh, I like that! But Durham already has an earl."

Albert explained, "Yes, Durham has traditionally been an earldom, but we're raising you to a duke now that you're marrying into the Royal Family. Besides, the family in question has been experiencing some, well, some difficulties [about which Albert was purposefully vague], so the title is available. And we'll get you a country estate to go with it so you can be part of the landed gentry you are so suspicious of."

"Trying to buy me off?" Paul said. "Well, it might work if you can get me the Romanov place. It's really nice."

Albert laughed, "Unfortunately Michael thinks so as well. He won't give it away, not even to us. But we'll find something nice. I'm especially thinking of somewhere for your mother. I doubt she can stay at her place much longer; all that unwanted attention must be making her life miserable."

"She tells me it isn't, but I'm going up this coming weekend to see for myself."

"It will be interesting to see how people respond to you now that the word is out. 'Hometown lad makes good.'"

"Stop it!" joked Paul. "I'm taking her out to our usual Chinese place, so it will be interesting."

"I've never been out for Chinese."

"It's probably time you went."

After tea they went into the drawing room, where Albert sat in his large, over-stuffed chair, while Paul perched beside him on the arm. He put his hand lightly on Albert's shoulder, each lost in thought, and looking remarkably like their favorite picture.

CHAPTER 26

Paul had been going to this particular Chinese restaurant his entire life, and his parents by themselves before that. It was a modest affair: lots of food moderately priced and quite informal. The owner always sat at the cash register at the front, and she would direct customers to a waiter or waitress who would then escort them to a table.

Before going to Durham, Paul had received "the talk" from Graham, the talk about the security details now assigned to him and his mother, due primarily to the large numbers of death threats each received on a daily basis.

The number and nature of these threats were kept from Paul and Pauline, but they were aware of them, in general, from the elaborate precautions taken to keep them safe and alive.

"Melissa will head your security unit, while Richard will lead your mother's," Graham told Paul. "The teams themselves will not rotate, and each member has voluntarily taken on the role of protecting both of you. Depend on them fully. If you are told to duck, for example, then duck, without asking why. Because by the time you ask, you could well be dead or abducted. The King has promised your safety, and now I promise your safety. But I can only do that if you follow our commands.

"Now, you can trust Melissa implicitly, as I trained her. She knows her business. When she goes into defensive mode, she is terrifying, trust me on that," Graham said with a rueful smile. "Also, she is one of us," a point Paul didn't catch at first, but then he did.

"That usually doesn't matter, but in this case, I think it does; it provides a common denominator and increases the team commitment. This is not just a job for us, Paul, it's a calling. Remember that each of us is willing to die for you and your mother; but we don't want to die unless we have to. Please don't make our jobs harder by putting you or your mother at undue risk. Don't do anything foolishly. As a rule, there is to be no more spontaneity. By that, I mean you can't just decide on the spur of the moment, to go out for pizza, for example. For your own safety, that cannot happen. Give us two days' notice, at least, so that we can check a place out, a shop, a cafe, a pub; do background checks on the staff and owner; inspect the kitchen; our usual checklist. I know it seems a needless intrusion on your right of movement but, considering what we are dealing with, we can't be too cautious.

"You and your engagement with Albert have stirred up a cesspool of bottom feeders the likes of which I've never seen, and I've seen a lot," he explained grimly.

"In any case, follow these directives and you and your mother can still have good times and long lives. Now, I understand this restaurant is rather good. I assume you will want to drive your mother?"

Paul merely nodded in agreement.

"That's fine," said Graham. "Melissa and her driver will lead the way. Once there, park beside them, then just get out and go inside and enjoy your meal. Other security personnel will be there, but you won't see them. This isn't an American movie with heavily armed troops standing guard. We are British, after all; reserved, discrete. But, if something were to happen, as I said, just do what you're told, don't play the hero with your mother, and we will get you safely out."

Graham understood the look of near despair on Paul's face, as he realized the young man was starting to see his life changing around him.

"Don't worry, Paul," assured Graham. "You'll get used to it. And, once you do, it will all seem very natural. Still, we need to know when you want to eat so the owner will be prepared with a table waiting for you."

"We usually just take whatever is available," interjected Paul. "It's not a fancy place."

"Those days are over," reminded Graham mildly. "From now on, everything is planned. As I said, we are mitigating risks to a minimum."

Paul nodded, wondering just how enjoyable this carefully scripted night could be.

"Oh, I nearly forgot," added Graham. "The cost of the meal will be paid for by the Crown, so have whatever you want."

"But I always pay for the meals," insisted Paul. "It's a treat I give my mother."

Graham looked at him thoughtfully, then smiled.

"Of course," he said, "But it will peeve the Prince."

"That's all right," said Paul, also smiling, "I know how to sort him out."

"I'm sure you do," replied Graham, who paused before continuing.

"He and Sir Humphrey have discussed a regular stipend for you after the marriage. It's actually provided by the government, but until then Albert wants you to have anything you need at his own expense."

"Which makes me sound like a kept man!" replied Paul angrily.

"Easy," replied Graham. "He knows it's a delicate situation. He just doesn't want to see you short in the pocket."

Paul relaxed, but the evening was becoming more difficult than he wanted, though he didn't see any option. This was simply a foretaste of things to come.

"I fear we are making life difficult for you," he said.

"It keeps my job interesting," explained Graham then, staring at his watch, he said, "And your mother is getting 'the talk' right now from Richard."

Paul turned the corner to his mother's house and saw two unmarked cars parked in front of the house, with two Durham police on the pavement. He assumed it was Melissa standing at the door. She knocked on it twice, then opened it for him. As he passed her, she smiled and gave a thumbs-up as he went inside. His mother stood in the hallway, dressed more formally for Chinese than she ever had before.

"You look fabulous!" said an admiring Paul.

"I don't want to dress up; I don't want to think anything has changed; but I know everything has changed, and now people expect me to look a certain way, so here I am. We might as well go, but I'm really not looking forward to this."

"Neither am I," admitted Paul, who opened the door and followed his mother outside. Paul opened the passenger door for his mother. He was glad the crowds of gawkers and the curious were gone, for now, though neighbors walking their dogs or out for an evening stroll stopped to watch them.

Paul backed out into the street and waited for Melissa's security vehicle to pass, with the other vehicle behind them, and so they made their way across town.

"Do they know where we're going?" asked Pauline.

"I'm pretty sure they do," replied Paul with a smile.

"Will they take us right through red lights?" she asked.

"I don't think this is that kind of motorcade," said Paul.

"Shame," she replied. "I've always wanted to go through red lights."

They made it to the restaurant, stopping for all the lights, and Paul pulled in beside Melissa as directed. As he got out, he couldn't see the other vehicle but knew, from Graham's talk, that it, and its occupants, were nearby, which he found reassuring.

Once again, he opened the car door for his mother and she gracefully emerged, now starting to enjoy the evening. Paul looked around and realized that Melissa was also gone as well. He held the door for his mother, and both were glad to see the owner in her usual place at the cash register.

She smiled broadly, not at all surprised to see them.

"Dr. and Mr. McGregor, so nice to see you both again. We've missed you."

The title was unsettling as he had always been just Paul here. But he realized that people wanted to call him something. Being called "Your Grace" would come too soon anyway.

She motioned off to the side.

"Matt will be your server tonight."

This was the one part of eating here that Paul regretted. Matt was the owner's son, working his way up through the business. He came forward, looking stylish and handsome, in the restaurant's uniform of dark shirt and dark slacks, for both its male and female servers. Paul knew Matt from St. Giles. They'd been in the same class. Matt was one of the handsomest boys in school and knew it. He was also straight, which Paul only found out when, desiring the lad, he'd casually brushed against him in the hall one day, but Matt erupted in fury and smashed Paul against the lockers. Matt, a famed athlete, then put his face next to Paul's and snarled, "You touch me again, queer, and I'll kill you."

Now Matt, who recently graduated like Paul, was all smiles and bowed graciously to Paul and his mother.

"This way, please, sir [And then, almost as an after-thought], and Dr. McGregor." Matt then bowed his head slightly, as if to make up for the slight. Paul and his mother looked at other and knew it was going to be a long evening. Still, the game was just beginning, so they followed Matt to their table and the dining room, as they'd both expected and dreaded, was packed with Saturday night diners. Their arrival created a sensation, and it had indeed been many weeks – weeks when so much had happened – since they were last here. As if on cue, the entire roomful of people rose as one and broke into applause for the hometown lad made good.

Paul and Pauline smiled graciously but both wished they had someplace to hide, or maybe the earth would just swallow them up. Matt had pulled out a chair and motioned for Paul to be seated. This was certainly something different, a touch of formality as customers typically just seated themselves.

Still, wanting to win this game, Paul ignored Matt and held his mother's chair for her, as he always did, then went back to his chair where Matt was still waiting for him and smiling. An obsequious smile, rather oily, in fact, that Paul really wanted to wipe off his face, an emotion that surprised him with its violence; it shamed him; and Paul knew the evening was lost. He didn't even know the stakes or who, or what, his opponent actually was.

Paul sat down and Matt helped push his chair in, then leaned over so closely that his body touched Paul's shoulder, and he said softly, "Just let me know, sir, if there is anything off the menu that you want. Anything."

Then he stood back and Paul, remarkably offended, curtly ignored him as Matt set down the menus and described the evening's specials. Paul looked at his mother with despair and anger, but she just shook her head slightly. She knew what Matt had done to Paul before, and she had a good idea what he had just whispered in Paul's ear, which everyone must have seen.

Matt asked if they needed more time to decide, but they ordered the usual, which he noted, bowed again, then left, with a final, knowing glance at Paul, who took a sip of water and looked around for the security team but, as Graham noted, he couldn't tell them who they might be. He did realize, with an inner smile, that they had probably been ready to take Matt out when he touched Paul and whispered to him.

And that was when Paul realized his own new power; how he could have destroyed Matt simply by standing up to proclaim, "How dare you say that to me!" And he could have had Matt removed and possibly arrested, at the least, to the shame of Matt's mother. Though also, Paul knew, to his own mother's shame as well, and that of the Royal Family into which he was marrying. Such a scene was actually unthinkable, and while Paul immediately regretted even thinking such a thing, he also knew it reflected his own unsteady state of mind.

And besides, who was he to judge Matt simply for doing whatever he could, whatever talents he had, to get out of Durham, just as Paul was doing.

He realized, ruefully, that he and Matt were more alike than he wanted to believe. It was just that Paul was luckier. And while Matt could have a very good life here in Durham, Paul did not blame him for wanting more. Without realizing it, Paul had already become a role model. Unfortunately, the availability of princes and princesses was small.

As Paul and Pauline waited for their meal, which usually only took a few minutes, tonight it seemed interminable, as they were surrounded by friends and acquaintances, all of whom had been coming here for years, just as they had, but now everything was different.

"Mr. McGregor [Evidently he was no longer Paul]."

"So nice to see you again."

"Dr. McGregor, hasn't he grown into such a fine young man?"

And Paul and his mother realized while greeting these

well-wishers, that most of them were simply quite pleased, even honored, to see a local lad make good. But beyond this group, there were those who stared at their table, and Paul saw a few were angry, with begrudging, jealous looks. And Paul realized that not everyone was happy at the way things were turning out, and many of the looks came from people he'd known for many years, but now he realized they were upset at the idea of a black man, even a mixed-race man, with a white prince.

Their meals were still not out when Paul saw Mr. Beauregard, the headmaster of St. Giles, and his wife waiting to speak to him. Paul got up and walked over to Mr. Beauregard, who took him firmly by the hand and said, "Paul," before catching himself to say, "Mr. McGregor." While his wife stood at his side, beaming with goodwill. Paul looked at her, smiled, and shook her hand, then moved back and motioned to his mother who stepped forward and warmly shook hands with both of them. It was Mr. Beauregard who had met with her and who personally approved Paul's appointment to the school.

"See what a St. Giles education has done for me?" Paul asked.

"I'm not sure what has happened to you was the result of our curriculum," explained the still smiling headmaster, "but I'm glad we were able to assist in any way we could."

"Without the education St. Giles provided, and the security I felt there, and the encouragement I was given to succeed, I wouldn't be who I am now. Rest assured that I talk up St. Giles every chance I get."

"And it's working," explained the headmaster. "Enrollment applications have skyrocketed. If this keeps up, we'll have to come back to the foundation for funds to build a new wing!"

"And we would be glad to approve it," replied Paul. The

headmaster noted the use of "we," and realized how far his former pupil had come, and how important he was now.

Just then Matt returned with their dinners on a large platter, which he set up on a foldout table.

"We'll talk again," said Mr. Beauregard as he guided his wife back to their own table. "Remember, you're always welcome to visit your old school."

Paul kept smiling as they reached their table and each gave him a quick wave. Then Paul said softly to his mother, and with great disappointment, "Even he wants something," then they started to eat, and it was a most uncomfortable meal. While people refrained from staring directly at them, Paul was well aware of constant, surreptitious glances in their direction. Previously they'd been ignored or, at best, someone from the university would greet Pauline. Now both of them felt on display, and they didn't like it, though they realized it was just a foreshadowing of things to come.

Finally the meal was over and Paul, as he always did, started to reach for his wallet when he finally saw Melissa seated at a nearby table with a pint before her, and she was subtly shaking her head "No." Then Paul caught himself, remembering the recent lesson from one of Albert's equerries that, while he didn't like the idea, still money was no longer an issue and would be taken care of by one of Melissa's team.

Still, he hadn't had time to explain this to his mother, who noticed his hesitation and thought it might be because he didn't have enough money now that Matt would expect a tip worthy of a royal consort. So, she motioned to Matt to come over as she planned to pay for the meal herself. Almost reluctantly, he came to the table, leaned towards Pauline, and spoke softly so only she could hear. Paul saw his mother's eyes widen and look at him in amazement, which she quickly repressed and merely said, "Well then. An excellent meal. Come, Paul." And she waited as he pulled back her chair and stood up. She surveyed the room, spreading a broad smile to the occupants, and then left, with Paul following behind.

As they left, Matt had maneuvered near the cash register, and gave him a wink, that hinted at much else. Paul realized he could have Matt with his strong, athlete's body, if he wanted him; he could even degrade and humiliate him, and Matt would willingly take it, knowing there would be a payoff at the end. But Paul also knew Matt would never really enjoy it, and would always regret it, and would always want to smash him against the lockers.

On the way out, they passed the owner one last time, who was still smiling broadly from her place at the cash register.

"Thank you for coming sir. I trust everything was satisfactory?"

"Perfect," he said with a smile, and she just purred.

"We look forward to your return."

As they went outside, Paul hissed to his mother, "We are never coming here again."

"No," she agreed.

It was a quiet trip back to their house. The issue of money haunted Paul because he could never tell his mother how he made what money he had. He was just as busy as other students who, nonetheless, found time for part-time jobs. Well, Paul made money by providing sexual services for hire, usually down along the river in the woodland below the cathedral. He'd always looked for older men with wedding rings, finding them to be monetarily more grateful. And now he was glad he had because he knew they would keep their secretive and furtive liaisons along the Wear to themselves, even if, seeing him with the Prince of Wales on the telly or in the papers, they could understandably take a deep measure of satisfaction with the thought that, "I've had you as well."

Finally, they made it home and were seated at the kitchen table. Melissa was still outside on watch. Pauline took both her son's hands in hers and looked carefully into his eyes.

"So, tell me," she asked. "Are you really happy?"

And Paul considered the question carefully because he knew his mother truly wanted to know.

"Yes, Mum, I am."

"Then that's all that matters," she said matter-of-factly. "We can put up with the rest of it. I would have appreciated being informed about the money, however.

"I know Mum, but I just found out myself."

"That's fine. Now I know. And at least you won't have to do sex work
anymore."

Paul looked at her in shock.

"Oh please," she said, "I'm your mother. And you never had a job after your father closed the pub; it just took me a while to figure things out. You know I never said anything."

"I know," said Paul gratefully. "And I appreciated that."

"At least you've found someone who truly takes care of you, instead of taking advantage of you."

"They always paid, Mum."

"You know what I mean."

And Paul merely nodded.

"Now I want you to know something."

Paul looked at her questioningly.

"I'm resigning from the lab."

"No! That's your life!" protested Paul. "Why?"

"Because going to the lab now is just like the restaurant. Half the staff expects me to provide a vast, new, and improved building called something like "The King George Institute for Advanced Microbiology," while the other half thinks I'm now incapable of doing any true research on my own since the Crown can obviously buy the finest minds in the world to do it for me. So, I can't take it. I love the lab. It's why I left Jamaica and came to Durham. But it's time for me to move on. Jasmine can run it while a replacement is found by a search committee and, hopefully, she'll get the position herself. I trained her; she knows the place even better than I do; so, it's a good time to leave."

"But what will you do?" asked Paul plaintively. "You're too young to retire."

"Thank you for noting," she said with a smile. "Well, microbiology is out, but I have good organizational skills, so maybe I'll work for some kind of non-profit. Maybe I'll just serve meals at a homeless shelter."

"Or maybe you could run our foundation," suggested Paul.

"Or maybe that," agreed Pauline. "In any case, I'm going to wait to find the right fit. I want to make sure I'm respected for my worth, and not my royal connection."

"From what I've already seen, the Royal Family takes care of its own. It's a family-run business. I think you'll fit right in."

"Maybe there's an entry-level position open, like gardener. I understand there are lots of gardens."

"So, it seems," agreed Paul. "Is it possible for a former microbiologist to actually get her hands in the dirt?"

"I think it's possible for a former microbiologist to do anything she wants," explained Pauline, and her son didn't doubt that at all.

CHAPTER 27

"I've never been out for Chinese," said Albert wistfully upon Paul's return from Durham. They were in Albert's apartment at St. James.

"Trust me," replied Paul, "It wasn't fun."

"I've never even gone out for pizza," complained Albert, then stopped for the thought that was forming in his mind, then he grinned.

"So, let's do it," he said.

"Do what?"

"Go out for pizza."

"Fine. We'll tell Graham in the morning as he said he needs two days' notice to get everything prepared."

"No," replied Albert forcefully. "I mean now. Let's go out for pizza now."

"But we can't. He was emphatic about that."

"But he'll never know," beamed Albert, as he considered the brilliance of his scheme. "We'll sneak out of the palace, find a pizza place, and be back before anyone knows we've been gone."

"That's insane," brushed off Paul. "Security cameras cover every inch of the perimeter. They'll know the instant we leave."

"But I know a blind spot at a service entrance," reassured Albert. "There are no cameras there."

"This is a bad idea that can't end well, and Graham will blame me for not preventing you from going."

"Can you prevent me from going?" asked Albert defiantly.

"Of course not," replied Paul. "You always do whatever you want to do."

"Then you can't be blamed for what you can't control,"

explained Albert triumphantly. "So, let's go."

"No," said Paul. "I gave Graham my word."

"Piffle!" scoffed Albert. "Then I'll go myself and won't even bring you back a slice!"

"You're going out in London, at night, by yourself, to get a pizza?"

"That's right. With or without you."

Paul realized he was trapped and that while he did not want to go, especially after the Chinese restaurant fiasco, he also couldn't let Albert wander through a London night by himself. So, Paul pulled out his phone to search for a nearby pizza place.

"What are you doing?" asked Albert.

"Checking Yelp for the best place around here. Give me a minute."

He went through listings and customer comments before finding one fairly close by.

"Here we are. Ratings are good and it's just a short cab drive away."

"Oh goody!" laughed Albert like a child. "A cab and a pizza. This is going to be fun!"

Paul sincerely doubted that. Albert was already headed towards the door when Paul stopped him.

"At least let's try and disguise who we are," he said, which even made sense to Albert who, anyway, loved dressing up. So, Paul searched through the wardrobe and dressers and found a wide-brimmed fedora that he pulled low over Albert's face, and a silk scarf which he wrapped around Albert's neck and pulled up high, then finished with sunglasses.

"Sunglasses?" asked Albert in disbelief. "Sunglasses at night?"

"It worked for Karl Lagerfeld."

"But everyone knew it was Karl Lagerfeld."

"Just wear them," insisted Paul.

"All right," replied Albert grumpily. "Don't be such a nag."

"Hey, let me see you," said Paul as he stood back. "Well, it will have to do. Let's hope for the best. Now show me your secret door."

Which is how they ended up being seen by a palace security guard watching a bank of video monitors that, indeed, covered the entire perimeter, including the service entrance from which the men exited onto a side street, hailed a passing cab, and were driven off into the London night.

The guard's eyes widened as she watched the men, obviously Albert and Paul, leaving the palace.

"Code Yellow!" she yelled. "The Prince and McGregor have just left by cab!"

Her supervisor was immediately there. "Could you get the license plate?"

"No, sir," she replied. "The camera angle was bad, but I think it was London Minicab."

"Then call their dispatcher and find out which of their cabs was near St. James. We'll be ready to leave once you know where we're going. And I'll call Graham. He won't be happy."

"No, sir."

On that point, they certainly agreed.

And so, palace security moved quickly, and Graham quickly joined them.

"Where could they be going?" he said aloud to no one in particular. He didn't blame Paul. He trusted the lad after their talk and knew he would do whatever he could to protect Albert. No, this was plainly Albert's work; the impetuous Prince heading heedlessly into the dark. Graham just didn't want him to pay too high a price.

The cabby was glad for customers, and cheerfully

asked, without looking into the rear-view mirror, "Where to, mate?"

And then he did look into the rear-view mirror. He'd assumed they were just two gay men probably going clubbing, but he instantly recognized the most famous gay couple in the kingdom.

Albert was looking through his window, like a tourist, while Paul, seeing the recognition on the cabby's face, shook his head, silently asking the cabby not to acknowledge them.

"Going clubbing, then?" asked the cabby, playing along, then Paul gave the name and address of the pizza parlor.

"Good choice," said the cabby, and they soon reached the location. Paul paid the fare, having the foresight to bring cash with him. Albert had no understanding of money and was simply along for the ride.

"Thank you, sir," said the cabby, pleased at the size of the tip. Paul smiled and put a finger to his lips. The cabby smiled back and winked at what seemed to be a royal lark.

At least we're here, thought Paul to himself as he held the door open for Albert who, excited as a child at a birthday party, quickly entered. As the cabby pulled away, he was already calling his dispatcher. "You will never know who I just picked up," he started to say, but was immediately interrupted.

"Where are they?" demanded the dispatcher grimly. "Palace security wants to know."

The small pizza shop, just a store front actually, with only a few tables at the large, plate glass windows along the pavement, also had a serving counter towards the back, lined with stools, with a mirror that covered much of the rear wall, and with a menu sign to one side.

At that late hour, no customers were there, and the sole employee on duty was a Pakistani youth named Rasheed

Patel, whose father owned the business, one of a handful of similar pizza parlors he operated across London, all staffed by the family's considerable number of cousins and other relatives. Rasheed attended university during the day and paid for his tuition by working here at night. Facing the back wall and working at a prep counter, with the pizza ovens at the other end, he didn't really glance at the young men as they came in and a bell rang. He looked briefly up into the mirror and smiled.

"What can I get you blokes?"

Albert excitedly went to the counter and sat on a stool, then took off his hat and scarf and sunglasses, inadvertently eliminating his disguise, as Rasheed turned to face the most famous customer he would ever have. Albert, intently studying the menu, did not see the look of surprise and recognition on Rasheed's face, who then looked at Paul, the second most-famous customer he would ever have, only to see Paul motioning to him as he had to the cabby, shaking his head slightly and silently pleading for anonymity. Rasheed understood this code of silence, and winked at Paul, who winked back.

"So, mates, what'll it be then? Best pizza in town."

Albert, whose knowledge of pizza was limited, looked questioningly at Paul to take care of the order. He quickly decided on a large pizza, extra cheese, all veggies, no meat, to eat there. Which was when Rasheed saw two vehicles pull up, and it was Graham who stepped out of one and then entered the shop. It was his attitude, serious and all business, that made Patel stop and stare at him. He knew it was palace security.

Paul and Albert paid no attention to what was going on behind them at the front of the shop, assuming it was just another customer who had entered. But the look on Rasheed's face made them look into the mirror, and their hearts instantly sank.

Graham spoke, "They will take that pizza to go."

Rasheed nodded and started to pat out a large lump of soft dough to work it into shape. Meanwhile, Graham came up behind the two men, put a hand on each of their shoulders, and whispered, "Leave now and get into the second vehicle."

Paul started to speak, but Graham merely shook his head and watched as the men got their hats and scarves and went outside.

Graham looked at Rasheed and said, "One of my people will wait for the pizza and pay you."

Rasheed nodded. Graham pulled out a hundred-pound note and put it on the counter.

"This never happened."

"It never happened," agreed Rasheed.

"Good," said Graham sternly, then he smiled briefly, and left.

"What were you thinking?" shouted Graham later on after the men returned to Albert's apartment at St. James. The pizza, in its box, sat on a table cooling off.

"It was my idea," said Paul lamely. "Albert just went along to humor me."

Graham looked at him and appreciated his willingness to protect the Prince by assuming responsibility, but he knew Paul would never so foolishly jeopardize Albert's safety. Graham also knew Albert's impetuousness.

"Your Highness," he said staring at Albert, "I think this was your idea and I also think Paul tried to stop you and you overruled him."

Albert hung his head like a child caught taking forbidden candy.

"Sir," said Graham gently. "Albert, look at me."

And Albert did look, hesitantly, at Graham.

"Listen to Paul. Let him be your conscience. He is the best of you. Trust what he says implicitly. Will you do that for me?"

Like the ashamed lad he felt himself to be, Albert looked first at Graham, nodded yes, then looked at Paul for absolution, who gave it with a smile.

"Now, eat up," said Graham. "It's cooling off, and the only thing worse than cold pizza is cold poached salmon. I also brought pints for you."

Rasheed was true to his word. He said nothing to his father about the previous night's customers when he and his father opened the shop the next morning. In fact, the whole ensuing cause célèbre that quickly became known world-wide as Pizzagate would have been avoided if Mr. Patel had not wanted to review the security video tapes, as he liked to fast-forward through them to see the kinds of customers the shop attracted. At first, he assumed the two young men were just another couple out on the town late at night. Despite his conservative brand of Islam, Mr. Patel also realized that he had a significant number of gay customers. As for his son's proclivities, he would deal with that in due time. He knew Rasheed only needed the right girl to settle down and be happy with.

So, he didn't pay attention until the men took off their hats, scarves and sunglasses, and he realized the Prince of Wales had eaten one of his pizzas. Then he yelled out from the back office, "Rasheed. Come here!" This was one of Rasheed's few days when his schedule allowed him to work from morning to night.

Rasheed dried his hands with a towel and went back to the cramped office to see his father standing at his desk and staring at the monitor with the two famous young men frozen in a still shot on the screen.

"When were you going to tell me that Prince Albert and his boyfriend ate here last night?" he asked angrily.

"I promised I wouldn't say anything, Papa. Go further and you'll see why."

So, Mr. Patel advanced the footage and saw the security vehicles pull up, stop outside, and Graham enter. He watched the scene unfold, and saw Graham put the note on the counter, though he couldn't recognize the amount.

"How much was that?" he asked suspiciously.

"A hundred pounds," said Rasheed hesitantly, as he knew what was coming.

"Turn it over" his father demanded, as he held out a hand.

"No! It's mine! He gave it to me!"

"Give it to me, now!" demanded Mr. Patel, even more forcibly.

So, angrily, Rasheed opened his wallet and pulled out the note and practically threw it at his father.

"That was for my tuition!" he yelled.

"Your schooling is here and not in some queer fashion school!"

"It's my life, Papa!"

"No, it's not!" shouted Mr. Patel, who stood up to brutally and forcefully slapped his son's face. Rasheed staggered under the impact, and his mouth started to bleed. He wiped the blood with a hand, looked at it, and then stared at his father defiantly, while his father continued talking.

"And I don't care what you told that security guy, but this is a chance for our place to finally become famous. Pizza fit for a king!"

"Don't do it, Papa," pleaded Rasheed. "It will backfire."

"You just go out front and get things ready for lunch," said Mr. Patel. "I have work to do."

But instead of leaving, Rasheed leaned over his father's desk and stopped the security footage which had still been playing, freezing the two men at the counter.

"Look at him, Papa!" shouted Rasheed. "Look at him!" he demanded. His father turned towards the screen as Rasheed pointed towards Paul.

"His skin is darker than mine! And he's from Durham! He's queer and he's going to marry the Prince of Wales. Who would have believed that just a few years ago? All you want to do is keep me here making pizza. But he shows me there is something more. And obviously you're going to ignore my advice to stay out of this, but I'm not going to take the blame for what you're about to do, which will ruin this place. I don't want this life. It's not for me. Do you hear me, Papa? I'm out of here!"

And he grabbed the hundred-pound note from the desk, stuffed it in a pocket, and angrily left the room. Mr. Patel heard him stomping towards the front. He turned towards the monitor, watched his son take off his apron and throw it on the floor, then he walked out the front door and crossed the street, ignoring the traffic that swerved to avoid him. But before he was out of camera range, Mr. Patel was already on the phone, calling in a nephew to take his son's shift; then he would update the store's Facebook page.

Future fashion historians dated the founding of the fabled House of Patel to this day, when the designer the world would come to know simply as Rasheed left his father's business to make his way to become an international superstar in the world of haute couture.

CHAPTER 28

Mr. Patel was mindful enough of his son's concern to only post video footage from the early part of the men's visit, before security showed up because that would just confuse things.

He proudly explained in the post how Prince Albert and his fiancé had chosen his place, out of all the pizza parlors in London, for their outing. "What toppings do you think they chose?" he asked, hoping to stimulate interest by turning the event into a kind of quiz show.

The video quickly traveled across the web and soon went viral, with more hits than even Mr. Patel dreamed possible. It seemed everyone in the country, indeed, across the planet, wanted to watch the young men ordering a pizza.

Quite soon the first reporter contacted the palace press office for a comment. The spokeswoman was caught completely by surprise but, sensing a problem of immediate urgency, simply said, "No comment" and referred all further inquiries to her assistant while she hastily contacted the head of the office, who quickly contacted Sir Humphrey, who quickly contacted Graham and took him to task.

"How could this happen?" demanded Sir Humphrey as they both watched in shock as the story both unfolded, and unraveled, on the screen. They were appalled because they realized the incident's ramifications. Graham explained what happened, but Sir Humphrey was not his usual, understanding self.

"I know we can't keep them under lock and key, though that would actually be simpler," he explained, "but what bothers me is how you didn't check for security cameras. That's not like you. I depend on your obsessiveness to keep the Prince safe."

"My immediate concern was to get them both out of there, but it's true," he ruefully admitted, "was careless, and I have no explanation."

"Well, I think this is a lesson for us all," stressed Sir Humphrey.

"Still," said Graham, "I don't blame the lad on duty. I'm sure he said nothing. But it's a family-run business, so I think it's the father who's using the security camera footage to spike interest in his business."

"The King is not going to be happy," said Sir Humphrey, and he wasn't.

"How could this happen?" he thundered later to Sir Humphrey. "You know how I hate the idea of anyone using an assumed connection with the Crown to make a personal profit."

"Yes, Your Majesty," said a chastised Sir Humphrey, who had rarely seen the King so angry.

"I won't allow it, do you hear?"

"Yes, sir."

"Shut this down."

"But sir, if we do nothing it will just blow over. From what I can tell, people are mostly amused by it and even delighted to see your son and Paul doing something everyone can relate to."

And, indeed, the country took great delight in watching the men ordering pizza, an interest quickly spurred on by tabloid headlines like, "The Prince and the Pizza," "Let 'Em Eat Pizza," and "Where Can a Prince Find a Good Slice Around Here?"

"Shut this down!" shouted the King again, who was not amused.

"That's not a good idea, and you know it!" replied Sir Humphrey testily, standing up to a man both king and friend. Then the King calmed down, paused, took a deep breath, and, finally, spoke gently to his most trusted advisor.

"I know it, my friend. But we must do something. We must protect the integrity of the monarchy, and this man is abusing that. Please, help me."

And so, against his better judgment, Sir Humphrey called in a few favors.

The next morning, three health inspectors showed up unexpectedly and spent hours checking the pizza parlor from front to back. They came up with a long list of health and safety violations, suspended the food license, and immediately shut it down. Which is how the ensuing scandal quickly dubbed "Pizzagate" began.

Even before the inspectors left, Mr. Patel was angrily, if somewhat gleefully (well aware of the greatly enhanced publicity value), on Facebook, with a post for the shop's rapidly increasing number of "friends" decrying state interference in his business when all he did was provide pizza for a Prince.

The resulting furor over royal overreach quickly turned vicious, with headlines on the order of "Crown Smacks Paki Down." Protesters soon gathered outside Buckingham Palace with signs and chants like, "Let Pakis alone" and "Bake your own pizza next time!"

The Prime Minister's office quickly issued a statement promising a full investigation into what was clearly an abuse of royal power into the sphere of government and into the operation of a private business.

Mr. Patel stood outside his shuttered shop, telling the assembled media his family's story of coming to England as refugees fleeing the Partition and slowly, determinedly, trying to better themselves in a new country they were proud to call home. He held up a photograph of his aging parents, but was non-committal about his son, saying only that he'd gone into hiding for his safety, when actually he had no idea where his queer son was.

The Joint Committee for Pakistani and British Mutual Cooperation and Trade issued a statement supporting Mr. Patel's right to support his family, while strongly condemning what it called Crown support for racist activity. The representative in the House of Commons from Manchester, and whose people were originally from Pakistan, stood and said, in the strongest possible terms, and with loud acclaim from her party, that racist attitudes against people of color by the Crown were completely unacceptable and would not be tolerated.

Albert and Paul, still at St. James, watched in shock as the result of a simple night out embarrassingly unfolded not only on a national stage, but internationally as well, and had no idea what to do about it. But, in any case, Sir Humphrey had told them to stay put and to do and to say nothing.

The Prime Minister called an emergency cabinet meeting and said she would discuss the issue as soon as she could meet the King, an emergency meeting which the palace decided to decline.

"He's afraid to see me," she declared to the cabinet.

And so he was.

"What do we do now?" the King asked Sir Humphrey plaintively.

"The health inspectors will return; they'll find all their concerns have been corrected; Mr. Patel will have his license renewed; he'll reopen; hopefully chastised but, more likely, gloating; and he will sell more pizza than he ever has. And we simply wait for the whole event to pass, as it will. Something will soon enough take its place in the news cycle; it always does."

"I should have listened to you," said the King. At least he was chastised.

"In the long arc of your monarchy," replied Sir Humphrey gently, "this will be just a small blip, a mere footnote to an otherwise illustrious reign."

"I certainly hope so," said the King. "I'd hate to see it end this way."

"There is no question of that, sir. There are many chapters left to write."

The King smiled gratefully at Sir Humphrey, then grimly told him to send for Albert.

"It was purely my idea, Papa," explained Albert. "Paul had nothing to do with it."

"I know he didn't," said the King. "He's obviously the only one with any real sense. You must listen to him as your better half and, trust me, you need a better half." He paused before continuing, "Just as I did."

He smiled ruefully at his son.

"Sir Humphrey assures me this will blow over without leaving a lasting stain."

"Oh, Papa, I am so sorry!"

"I know," said George resignedly. "It was an innocent and understandable miscalculation on your part blown far out of proportion by my own miscalculation and both of us should have known better. There's something to be said about old kings learning new tricks," he said wryly. "Though I admit I'm not looking forward to my next regular meeting with the P.M. Is there such a thing as a royal woodshed, I wonder?"

He and Albert smiled at each other ruefully.

"But there is one thing I need to know."

"Yes, Papa?"

"How was the pizza?"

Albert smiled.

"Cold, by the time we ate it, but even so it was quite

good."

"I wonder, do they offer salmon as a topping?"

"For you, I'm sure they can."

CHAPTER 29

It is 3 a. m. at St. James' Palace, and Albert and Paul are soundly sleeping in each other's arms. Two sharp raps on the outer door awakened them.

"What is it?" asks Paul groggily.

Albert sits up, apprehensively. They hear the door open and listen as footsteps cross the parquet floor, then stop at the door to their bed chamber. Albert gets up quickly and puts on a robe as there are two more sharp raps at the door.

"Come!" says Albert with authority. Paul looks questioningly at Albert, who puts out a hand to prevent him from speaking. Sir Humphrey enters, ashen and grief stricken. He sees Albert, walks to within a few paces of him, then kneels. He stares at the floor, both from form and to hide his tears.

"The King is dead, Your Majesty."

He quickly composes himself, looks up tenderly at Albert and says, "Long live the King."

PART TWO

CHAPTER 30

Paul realized he had just witnessed a ritual of transition and transformation, a continuity that had occurred just a few dozen times in the kingdom's thousand-year history.

Albert walked to Sir Humphrey and gently helped the old man to rise, then held him closely. Sir Humphrey started to cry, as did Albert, and the two stood there for some time, each releasing his emotion at their mutual loss. Finally, Sir Humphrey pulled away and stepped back, bowed, and said, "I grieve for your loss, Your Majesty."

"And I for yours, Sir Humphrey. You were my father's most trusted advisor and truest friend."

A visibly pleased Sir Humphrey replied, "Thank you, sir; so, I like to think. And I trust I can continue to serve you as well."

"For as long as you wish, Sir Humphrey. Your loss must be particularly hard as you two were very close."

"I started serving him when he was still Prince of Wales," said Sir Humphrey. "We had many adventures together, most of which I've, fortunately, forgotten. I was actually not a very good Falstaff, but even I was young once upon a time," he said wryly.

"How did it happen?" asked Albert, without needing to explain what "it" was.

"His footman heard a heavy thud of the King falling, and rushed in to find he'd evidently been trying to get to the bathroom. He was already dead, possibly from a stroke, a heart attack, or an aneurysm. His doctor had warned him about all three, but you know your father. He had access to the best physicians in the world, but refused to take care of himself."

Albert grimly nodded agreement, then looked at Paul, whose expression was something on the order of "And you are the same way." A brief, understanding smile crossed Albert's face, then he turned back to Sir Humphrey, who said, "He was one of the country's greatest monarchs."

Albert replied, "I can only hope to be half the king he was."

Sir Humphrey looked from Paul to the young king and said quietly, "Sir, you have the potential to be even greater."

"So what happens now?" asked Albert quickly. "Should we go to the palace?"

Sir Humphrey caught the plural pronoun, which contained more than the royal form.

"There's no reason to just yet. The medical examiner must finish his work – "

"But no autopsy," interrupted Albert forcibly.

"None is needed, sir, as there is no suggestion of foul play. No matter what killed your father, it was quick and painless."

"Thank goodness for that," replied Albert.

"I suggest you stay here for now," he said, glancing at both men, "and get what sleep you can. Tomorrow, or, actually, today, will be long and busy. It will help if you both are rested. Arriving at the palace later this morning will be fine. He will be laid out by then. In the meantime, the palace press office will issue a standard preliminary statement about the King's passing and your accession. It will also say that you will address the country, and that plans for the state funeral are being developed."

"And the Accession Council?"

"That will be held later today here at St. James. First, the council will meet without you to formally proclaim you as monarch, then you will hold your first Privy Council meeting with them at which time you will make the Declaration regarding the death of your father. After that, you will take the Oath to preserve the Church of England. After the meeting, the Proclamation of you as the new monarch will be read from the balcony here at Friary Court, accompanied by the firing of cannons at the Tower and Hyde Park. The Proclamation will also be read throughout the kingdom, and around the world at our remaining possessions and the Commonwealth nations. Parliament will then convene to determine your title to the throne, and to take the Oath of Allegiance. Everything will follow after that."

"I understand," replied Albert.

He and Paul looked at each other tentatively, nearly overwhelmed by what had happened, and by what was to come. And each was thinking the same thing, "At least we are together."

But before private consolation came the need of the office.

Albert turned back to Sir Humphrey and took his hands in his own.

"I depend on you as my father did."

Sir Humphrey bowed again, stepped back, and said, "My life is to serve."

He left the room, closing the door gently behind him. Paul and Albert heard his footsteps crossing back across the parquet floor, then heard the front door shut to the apartment, and then they were alone again, with everything changed.

Paul held out his hand to Albert.

"Come here, my King."

Albert let Paul lead him to the bed, and soon they were beside each other, the robe on the floor. Albert laid his head on Paul's chest and started to cry. Paul felt the warm, wet tears on his skin, and gently held the crying King in his arms until Albert finally fell asleep.

CHAPTER 31

Albert and Paul woke to the sound of someone entering the antechamber. There was a light knock on the bedroom door, and an equerry entered, bowed slightly, and said, "Tea, Your Majesty."

Paul and Albert put on robes and entered the antechamber where tea was set for two. As they seated themselves, their two valets entered with clothing ready for the day, which they took into the bedroom and laid out on the bed, one man's clothing on each side.

"This is going to be a long day," said Paul quietly.

"But all we have to do is play our parts; tradition handles the rest," explained Albert, and both men were actually relieved that they wouldn't have to make decisions or even think about what must be done. Everything was planned.

Tea was stressful; they didn't talk. There was nothing to be said. Their world had changed, forever, and the innocence of their engagement, and the relatively peaceful life as Prince and Consort, was gone. Now the time was here for decision making that affected an entire country, and both wondered if they were ready.

They quickly finished tea and retired to dress; their clothing was black except their shirts. Then they stood beside each other at the apartment's outer doors, knowing that beyond them was the start of an entirely new life for them both.

Albert hesitated and said, while looking straight ahead.

"I don't think I can do this."

Paul, also looking straight ahead, took his hand. "You have no idea what you are capable of doing."

Albert gently squeezed Paul's hand, then they looked at each other, pleased with what they saw, and Albert nodded to the footman that he was ready, and the doors were opened to their future.

Albert purposefully strode outside, where Graham was waiting, also in black. He bowed, and said, "I am most sorry for your loss, Your Majesty."

"Thank you, Graham," replied Albert.

Graham continued, "Your car awaits, and Sir Humphrey will meet you at the palace."

As they walked down the long corridor to the main entrance, Paul was taken by how things had so quickly changed. The air itself seemed somber, and each staff member wore a black armband and each face was grieved. In a scene that would repeat itself throughout the day, Albert stopped before each person, all of whom he knew by name, and shook their hand or gently touched their arm, and said, "Thank you," as each bowed or curtsied. Sorrow was palpable.

The outer doors opened onto a courtyard, with the largest automobile Paul had ever seen, the King's own Rolls, a relic from another time, probably from Victoria the Third, Albert's grandmother. It was massive and regal. The guards in the courtyard snapped to attention as Albert approached the car. A motorcycle brigade was in front, with another motorcycle brigade at the back, and Graham and his team following behind.

Albert's door was being held open for him. He nodded and got into the car. Paul went to the other side where the door was held open for him by another footman who stared straight ahead as Paul got into the back seat beside Albert. As both doors were closed, Albert took Paul's hand. The driver looked into the rear-view mirror.

"I'm sorry for your loss, Your Highness," he said.

"Thank you, Daniels. My father said he always felt safest with you at the wheel. I hope you'll continue with me."

"With pleasure, sir," said Daniels as he touched the brim of his cap, then looked ahead to wait for the motorcade to leave. The gates to the street were opened, and the lead motorcycle led the way out onto the road. Paul noticed there were many people gathered on the pavement, evidently waiting for a first glance at their new King and, in a gesture that Paul would see continually in the days to come, men with hats had taken them off, and everyone bowed their heads as the King's car passed them.

Albert did not wave or smile at them, but gave a dignified, solemn nod to those along the route. Evidently the procession was expected as people lined the sidewalks, looking somberly at their new king, most were grief stricken, others simply inquisitive, as Albert held Paul's hand and nodded to his subjects.

Paul noted flags were at half-mast. It was a very short drive to Buckingham Palace. Paul saw its flag was also at half-mast, and there was a large crowd of people at the entrance, and there was already a large pile of floral bouquets placed against the fencing.

The Foot Guards stood at attention as the procession entered the courtyard. The limousine stopped inside the portico, and Albert's door was opened first. Albert released Paul's hand and exited the car. Sir Humphrey was there, at the head of a long line of assembled staff members that went into the vast entry and all the way to the broad staircase.

Albert paused for a moment, as he knew everyone wanted to take stock of him and to measure his worth: Would he be a good king, or a bad king?

Sir Humphrey wasn't sure if Albert wanted to proceed immediately up the stairs to the royal apartment, but he was not surprised to see Albert stop before each staff member; again, to mention them by name and to shake their hand or touch an arm as they, too, bowed or curtsied and he said, repeatedly, "Thank you," to each one.

Paul hung back, and he knew that all eyes were on him as well. He realized, with relief, that most of them were sympathetic, and even encouraging, which he appreciated.

As Albert reached the end of the line at the base of the stairs, he mounted two steps and then turned back to the assembly, paused again as all eyes were on him, and then he spoke, loudly and commandingly enough for everyone to hear.

"I mourn twice today, for my King, and also for my father. Indeed, the entire kingdom is mourning the loss of a monarch so unexpectedly taken from us, and far too soon. He was a great King; one of our best; and now I must follow his lead. It will not be easy, but I assure you that, with your help, we can continue my father's work. The palace is a family, and we will work together to continue my father's vision for a just and equitable country where we can achieve our fullest potential; first, as individuals, and then for the kingdom as a whole. Each and every one of you is an essential part of that goal, and I hope that each and every one of you will carry on working with me as you worked for my father. No one is unimportant in that job. Help me as you helped my father, so at the end of my life we can look back together and say, with pride, that we achieved true greatness."

He stopped speaking, and stood there, radiant, nearly glowing, then nodded once, turned, and proceeded up the grand staircase, followed by Sir Humphrey and Paul. At the top, as the group entered the vast corridor that led to the royal apartment, Albert continued to stop before each grieving staff member for moments of mutual consolation. The group finally entered the long row of rooms that comprised the royal apartment, and that ended at the closed double doors of the bed chamber, flanked by footmen on either side.

Albert paused only for a moment outside, then breathed deeply and nodded. The doors were opened, and Albert went inside, followed by Sir Humphrey and Paul.

CHAPTER 32

The King was laid out on his bed in his full-dress uniform, with his hands folded across his chest. Two senior ladies of the court sat in nearby chairs, keeping watch. They rose as Albert entered and curtsied deeply.

"Lady Rose; Lady Margaret; thank you for staying with my father. Now, if you could kindly leave us alone for a few minutes?"

They curtsied again, then left the room. Paul noticed there were four tall lighted tapers on tall bronze sconces, one at each corner of the bed, evidently beeswax from the light scent of honey in the room.

"I thought Your Majesty would want a traditional setting," explained Sir Humphrey.

"Very appropriate," agreed Albert. "My father would have liked that."

Paul hung back, as Albert and Sir Humphrey approached the bed. Albert and Sir Humphrey stood side by side and stared at the body.

"He was a great king," said Sir Humphrey finally.

"Yes, he was," agreed Albert thoughtfully, still doubtful about his own potential. "I don't think I'll ever be able to match him."

Sir Humphrey looked back at Paul and smiled, then turned to Albert. "Sir, as I said before, you have the support you need to be even greater."

Albert smiled gratefully in return.

Sir Humphrey continued, "Your father had his own doubts when he was Prince of Wales, fearing he would not be able to match the achievements of his mother and grandmother, and look what he – "

Which was when Princess Elizabeth forcefully entered the room, followed by Larry, and the mood instantly transformed from one of grieving to one filled with tension.

The men turned to her, and Sir Humphrey bowed.

"My Lady, I grieve for your – "

"Out!" she demanded imperiously as she interrupted him.

Completely unfazed, and all too familiar with royal caprice, Sir Humphrey bowed again and left. Then Lizzie looked at Paul.

"You, too, slag. Get out!"

Surprised and unsettled by her attitude, Paul nonetheless quickly recovered and began to leave when Albert, furious, insisted equally forcefully, "He stays!"

Angered at being thwarted by the only person in the realm who outranked her, Lizzie turned on her brother, "First, why?"

"Because he's family."

"Not until the wedding," she retorted.

"Lizzie," said Albert curtly, "He is family."

And with that, brother and sister squared off.

"So," she said with a sneer. "Has he hypnotized you with that tight black ass and that big black dick?"

Even Larry protested, though feebly.

"Lizzie, not here. Not now."

"Yes, here and now, Larry," she told him angrily, then repeated herself, "Here and now."

Then she turned her wrath back upon Albert.

"When Michael Romanov told me you two were shagging up at his place, I thought this was just another of your passing fancies to fuck and leave. I never thought the nigger would enslave you" she said triumphantly.

"Lizzie," said Albert with barely controlled fury, "You go too far."

"No, older brother," shouted Lizzie to Albert as she looked at Paul. "You go too far, thinking you can demean our family with his colored skin."

Albert, having no idea how Paul would react to this withering assault, and amazed at how Paul just calmly stood his ground and looked at the princess without emotion, decided to defend Paul himself. He approached her for the confrontation, and they were face to face.

"Stop, now," he commanded.

"Oh, I'm just getting started."

"Lizzie, enough!"

"Oh, has older brother finally found a pair? Or is he borrowing a set from his nigger boy?"

"Lizzie," said Albert in a cold fury, "I'm warning you."

"Or you'll what?" replied Lizzie scornfully.

"Lizzie," said Albert, barely able to control himself. "You are entering unknown territory, and quicksand is everywhere."

"What could you possibly do to me?" she demanded imperiously.

Then, quite unexpectedly, Albert's voice dramatically dropped and deepened, and in a dark, low tone more growl than words, Albert leaned forward and said softly into an ear so only she could hear, "You have no idea what I am capable of doing."

And then, for the first time in her life, Lizzie was afraid of her brother. In a desperate attempt to contain the creature she had unleashed, Lizzie abruptly changed the subject.

"Papa is dead, Albert," she said quietly. "Let us mourn him."

Then Albert, as though remembering himself after a deep sleep, shook his head quickly, moved back, and said, in his usual tone of voice, "Yes, of course. Papa's dead. Let's mourn him."

Then brother and sister turned towards the King laid out on the bed, while Paul and Larry, shaken by what was happening, had moved away from the pair to stay safe, so they hoped, in the background, dreading what could possibly happen next. But brother and sister now seemed determined to put enmity behind them.

"I can't believe he's gone," said Albert quietly.

"Nor I," admitted Lizzie.

"He was like an elemental force of nature, and I was often intimidated by him, unintentionally of course, by his sheer size and booming voice," admitted Albert.

"I never was," smiled Lizzie. "He was always just 'Papa' to me."

"You two had a special relationship," said Albert. "I saw it every time we went to Balmoral, where I hated the countryside and just wanted to stay indoors reading, while you and he went fishing and shooting."

"He didn't understand your distaste until you came out, and he finally realized he had a poof for a son."

"An unrepentant poof at that," admitted Albert. "He never understood why I didn't just marry a woman and have children and do whatever I did sexually on the side, with the staff, I guess. Maybe the chauffeur in the garage, or maybe a stable lad in the hay."

"Well," she replied with a laugh, "That's about as close as you'd ever get to a horse."

"They scare me," admitted Albert. "But not you. I think you had your first pony when you were six."

"Four," corrected Lizzie, "When Mummy was still alive."

Then they looked at each other, recognizing that now they were mutual orphans, and the closest blood relatives they had left.

"I still miss her," said Lizzie.

"So do I," replied Albert. "Things were so different after she died. It's as though Papa kept her memory in a secret chamber of his heart into which we were not admitted."

"He raised us as best he could, but it didn't come easily, and he was always relieved when his duties called him away."

"I guess it was at Balmoral where we were happiest. That's where he enjoyed us most," recalled Albert. "And I remember when he read to us, with one of us on each knee, and he encircled us in his arms, and held the books out so we could see the pictures."

"Yes," replied Lizzie thoughtfully, "I do think we were happiest then."

"And now?" asked Albert. "How long will this moment last?"

"Maybe not long after I leave the room," admitted Lizzie, "so let's appreciate the moment while it's here, even if Papa had to die to bring us together."

The twins turned towards their father's body. This was where Paul and Larry both hoped that brother and sister would complete this unexpected reconciliation by hugging each other, perhaps sealed with a kiss, but they were not that kind of family, and touching did not come easily, and kissing, not at all. Still, they stood for a time, side by side, and then Albert reached over to take Lizzie's hand, but she noticed the movement and abruptly turned away, and it was Larry's hand she took as she grandly left the room with him, while ignoring Paul.

Sir Humphrey quickly entered.

"How did it go?" he asked apprehensively, having clearly heard the earlier shouting.

"Better than expected, by the end," admitted Albert.

"Good," replied Sir Humphrey, "because there is an issue."

"What kind of issue," asked Albert apprehensively.

"Princess Elizabeth called the Archbishop this morning and raised the issue of having Paul attend the funeral as a member of the Royal Family."

"What?" cried Albert furiously. "That bitch!"

Reconciliation was now clearly over.

"Unfortunately, the Archbishop agrees," added Sir Humphrey quickly. "Now, he will officiate at your wedding, so that's not a problem, but he agrees with Princess Elizabeth about the [and here Sir Humphrey paused to find the right word] . . . seemliness of having the unmarried Mr. McGregor sitting in the royal pew."

"Absolutely not!" replied Albert. "Paul stays with me."

"But appearances – "

"Appearances be damned," shouted Albert. "Am I king or not?"

"Of course, Your Majesty, and right now the public is on your side as a vast majority approves your marrying Mr. McGregor. Indeed, many see it as a mark of the country's maturity. But you know your sister's connection to the media, which can turn the country against you at a time when we need solidarity, not division."

Sir Humphrey looked at Paul, silently pleading to intervene, which he did.

"Sir Humphrey is right," said Paul quickly, to the old man's relief. "It's not a big issue."

"It is to me," insisted Albert. "I need you beside me."

"But I'll make sure Paul is seated in a prominent place where you can directly see each other," interjected Sir Humphrey. "Please do this," he begged, "for an old retainer?"

Albert could see how much this meant to his most faithful and trusted advisor, and he understood why Paul agreed so easily. It was just another example of Lizzie being Lizzie.

"Well then, I agree," he said with a smile.

"Very good. Thank you, sir," said a visibly relieved Sir Humphrey as he bowed and left Paul and Albert alone. Paul walked forward and stood beside Albert. They looked into each other's eyes, then turned to face the dead King. Neither spoke at first, then Albert asked, "How could you take it?"

And Paul knew what Albert meant.

"Your sister is a neophyte," said Paul. "I was trained by monsters."

Albert looked at him questioningly.

"Not my parents, of course, but kids my age, kids who tried to goad me into retaliating when they called me names, so there was both racism and homophobia. They greatly expanded my vocabulary," he said wryly, "with all kinds of words and phrases just so I would say or do something, anything, so they could justifiably beat me up. They wanted me to retaliate so they could report me for being the troublemaker. Of course, people saw through that. The punks weren't as smart as they thought they were but, still, if they were determined to beat me up, I was equally determined not to fuel their rage at this queer black boy."

"But how did you control yourself," asked Albert in amazement. "I could never do that."

"It was my mother who taught me," explained Paul. "She had to deal with racism when she moved to Durham for school, and then especially after she married my father and they moved to an isolated village they thought would be safer but was actually much worse than anything they experienced in Durham. "My mother liked to sit out on the porch on warm summer evenings, and people would come around, when my father wasn't home, to call her names and goad her into responding so they could come back later and throw a rock through the window or smash her car's wind screen with a bat. But she got through it by remembering the old Methodist hymns she learned as a child back in Jamaica, and she sang them softly to herself while people taunted her, and that got her through. Of course, my parents quickly realized their mistake and moved back to Durham which, in context, didn't seem so bad after all."

"But you're not a Methodist," said Albert.

"No, and she isn't any more either. She's gone back to her African roots in animism, but the Methodists do have good hymns."

They both smiled, then Paul continued, "And I'm not sure I'm an animist either, but my mother did give me something very special."

And Albert looked at him quizzically.

"She gave me a belief in myself. In my own potential, and so when the punks came at me, as your sister did, I think to myself, 'I'm better than this.' Not that I'm better than them, but that I'm better than this situation. I have more potential than this. I saw what happened to those who retaliated, not just in getting beaten up, but who were beaten down inside as well, and who joined gangs for protection but got killed instead or sought escape through drugs and alcohol and died homeless somewhere or tried to live while twisted with hate.

I know what can happen because it happened to people all around me, and I was determined that it would never happen to me."

Albert just stared admiringly at Paul.

"You are amazing."

"And don't you forget it," replied Paul with a smile.

"I am so lucky to have you."

"And don't forget that either."

Then the two turned back to the bed, with the body of the dead king, standing side by side. Albert reached over and took Paul's hand, then moved closer and put an arm around Paul's waist, who put his arm around Albert's waist, and they just stood there for a long time, until Albert finally spoke.

"He wanted me to be a good king. And he knew the best way to do that was through example and practice. So, I must have been five or so when he had a little desk placed beside his large desk, and I sat in a little chair, and I had pens and pencils, and he gave me copies of reports, and papers to look at and to sign as he signed the official documents up on his desk. So, I learned how to write my name with a great, florid "A," which I still love to write.

"As I grew, my desks were changed accordingly. And I always studied him, and Papa explained what he was doing, and why. And I watched him in meetings, even with prime ministers who, I guess, thought it was cute to see a king in training. But it was on-the-job training, and how else could I learn? Even St. Giles offers no courses in kingship." And they smiled at each other.

"That continued until university, and when I came back, he had put a full-sized desk beside his as though we were partners. As a man, he was closed and private, especially after Mummy died, but as King he was open and sharing. Even then, the P.M.'s didn't question my attendance at their weekly meetings with my father.

"So, it's not like I'm untried and unready. He made sure I knew what to do. That's not the issue. It's just – " and here he looked directly at Paul, "It's just that I miss him."

"It's not me you need to say that to," replied Paul gently. "He's right there," he added, while holding out a hand to the bed.

"Tell him."

So, Albert turned to his dead father and said, softly, "Papa, I miss you."

CHAPTER 33

Princess Elizabeth sits on the ground in her garden. She holds a trowel and is working the soil. Her brown dungarees are worn at the knees; her plaid shirt has holes at the elbows; her old head scarf is frayed. She is remarkably happy.

This is not the public image that she so carefully maintains, that of a cultured, elegant woman who enjoys gardens but who would never think of working in one herself. After all, she has people to do that for her. And, indeed, Lizzie does have a large staff to maintain her extensive gardens. But she also has this particular section that is hers alone. This is a side of her that no one outside her immediate family knows about. This is her world.

Lizzie finds it difficult to be around most people because – while it is generally not openly said, but which she nonetheless hears as a faint echo, the aural equivalent of a shadow on a wall, of which she has been aware since her earliest memories – is that she is not Number One. So, while performing her royal duties – such as touring a factory, christening a ship, or attending a charitable function – she understands that people are thinking, "We couldn't get the Prince of Wales, so we had to settle for the other one."

For a woman with a built-in competitive streak, this is nearly unbearable because it's the one thing against which she cannot compete as the race was won at birth. Oddly enough, she blames her mother for somehow not being able to switch the birth order in her womb. In her more rational moments, Lizzie realizes this is bosh, but, still, it hurts.

It's not that she hates her (slightly) older brother, not at all.

She really does love him and would never wish him harm, even if his very existence prevents her from being queen. And he seems to be in remarkably good health, considering his dissipated life. So, she is resigned to never being queen. Still, she credits Albert's choice to live his life as an openly gay man despite their father's futile attempts for several years to convince him to marry a woman simply to provide children for the succession. That was when she realized she had a major role to play, not only within the Royal Family, but within royal history itself, since the succession now runs through her. So, she remains grateful for, and admiring of, Albert's stubborn resistance to their father's cajoling, and his determination to marry a man instead. That was the first, and frankly the last, time she found her brother worthy of admiration.

Before that realization, she'd felt only jealousy, which is not hatred. After all, she didn't get a desk beside her father like Albert did. She was not trained to rule because it was clear that she would not be ruling.

Still, she had a connection with their father that Albert, simply due to his different interests, lacked, especially at Balmoral when Albert sequestered himself in the library or, as in recent years, refused to go at all, preferring to stay in London with his men and his clubs.

Those delicious days in the north were just for Lizzie and her father, as they fished and hunted together.

"Well done, Lizzie!" were the words she appreciated most from him. And she had several mounted stag's heads to show for her shooting skills. At those times, she and her father made a good team, whereas Albert, when he bothered to show up at all, seemed only interested in what was beneath various kilts, to their father's constant dismay. "What am I going to do with the lad?" was his usual admission of frustration, much to Lizzie's amusement.

It was Lizzie's mother who got her interested in gardening. Though she died when Lizzie was just five, the princess treasured memories of working alongside her mother, in the soil, and was so very, very happy. The queen knew her daughter needed something to replace the disappointment of her birth order and so shared her own joy at tending a garden and making beautiful things grow. It is also the one aspect of her life that Lizzie feels she can creatively and constructively share with her own children who, otherwise, remain such mysteries to her. With both her children and her gardens, she is absolute monarch; these are her private realms.

Her mother's love of nature – a trait her father and brother completely lacked – meant she often had her mother to herself. It was her mother who showed her the circle of the seasons, of how even winter was not a time just to get through, but was vital for the earth to rejuvenate itself, and a time with its own unique beauty of ice and snow, something to accept and not control, much like the variable English climate.

In late winter, her mother took her into the greenhouses at Windsor where bedding plants were sprouting and being tended for spring, and it was a time when the two of them studied seed catalogs to decide what they would plant for the coming season.

Before spring's slow reawakening, the two of them eagerly awaited the warming of the soil, and the time to start planting the annuals they'd chosen to grow, as well as pruning the perennials and feeding the soil so the plants would grow healthy and strong.

Some seeds they planted directly in the soil and so, side by side, they made furrows, dropped in seeds, and covered them up, eagerly waiting for the seeds to sprout, or bulb shoots to appear, and leaves to bud on tree branches.

Nurturing came easily to them both, and it remains the

one trait that Lizzie feels comfortable instilling in her own children. She knows she is criticized for not taking a more active role as princess, and for not being a better role model as a modern British woman beyond house and garden, but the fact remains that her one unique contribution to the country is to provide the royal succession.

The historic line of continuity runs through her, and she takes that responsibility seriously indeed. It isn't simply the act of producing children – though her genetic line of royal DNA is essential to maintain the dynasty – it is also in how her children are raised that concerns her, which is why she keeps them at home being taught by tutors. While she often doubts her abilities and skills as a mother, perhaps because her own mother died too soon to help her during those critical teenage years through which she had to make her way alone and confused, Lizzie still wants her children – especially her oldest child, Victoria – to be ready to rule when the time arrives. She wants each of her children to have a wide-ranging and diverse education, which she lacked. She wants them to think clearly and decisively, not just so that any of her children can become a monarch if needed, but so the others can move into whatever pursuits call them in later life.

Lizzie knows her children must eventually move on without her; that they will leave for boarding school and then university, but she wants each of them to have an equal opportunity for future success, which is also her hope for the plants in her garden.

She glances at her watch. Nearly four o'clock, and she momentarily expects to hear her children's voices as they exit the house onto the terrace and, indeed, here they come now, racing each other to reach her first, shouting with glee and leaping into the air as they cross the terrace and down the broad stone steps to where she is in the garden, shouting, "Mummy! Mummy!"

For a moment she is taken back, against her will, to that dreadful day when she and Albert, on either side of their father – too young to be a widower – and fiercely holding onto him while fighting back tears, walked behind the black-draped caisson bearing their mother's casket through the streets of London, with thousands and thousands of mourners, and the city itself one huge dirge. At the rear of the caisson was a large floral display of white flowers bearing a card with a single word, "Mummy."

No, Lizzie evades all mention of that day, as do the people she meets, fortunately, though it remains the most searing event of her life. Nor does she keep any photographic reminders of that day either. Instead, her pictures of her mother show a vibrant, vital woman always smiling at the camera, always smiling at her.

Then Lizzie brushes the memory away and returns to the reality of her children rushing towards her.

"Mummy! Mummy!" they gleefully cry.

"Sweetums, I'm here!" she says joyfully, as they rush into her outstretched arms and cover her face with kisses.

"I love you," she says, glowing with happiness. "I love you all."

CHAPTER 34

The King was reviewing the funeral plans with Sir Humphrey.

"So, are we done?" he asked.

"Yes, sir, I think everything is ready."

"Oh, and Dr. McGregor also wants to attend."

"I've already anticipated that. She will sit next to Paul."

Concerned about the visual implications, Albert said, "I don't want them to appear to be, like that old American saying, at the back of the bus."

Sir Humphrey smiled. "Don't worry, sir. Their prominent position will be the envy of everyone there as they will be in a special diplomatic section reserved primarily for foreign dignitaries."

"I hope they are not intimidated."

"Paul and his mother, or the dignitaries, sir?" asked Sir Humphrey wryly, "because I can't imagine Paul or his mother being intimidated by anything."

"Good point," agreed Albert, who then looked carefully at Sir Humphrey. "You like her, don't you?"

"I haven't had the pleasure of meeting her in person yet," said Sir Humphrey carefully, "but from what I can see, she is smart, gracious and elegant, a real asset to the Royal Family. And, if I may ask, Your Majesty, do you know her plans now that she is leaving her lab?"

"How do you know that?" asked the King perplexed, then he understood.

"Of course; it's your job to know, isn't it?"

Sir Humphrey merely bowed, then added, "Of course, it's

rather like another old saying, isn't it? How do I know what I don't know?"

"Well," replied Albert, "that's true for us all."

He paused, then continued, "Paul and I would like her to move down here into Kensington."

"That would be most wise, sir, as threats against her and Paul continue daily, and now there are concerns that even military-style groups are seeking to assassinate them. It's becoming very difficult to protect her without turning her neighborhood into a bunker, which would not please the neighbors."

"She is coming to understand that" admitted Albert. "We also want her to organize and manage the new foundation."

"An excellent idea, sir," replied Sir Humphrey. "It will be easier to protect her if she lives and works in the same place. Besides, she does bring formidable organizing skills. She took a small university lab and turned it into a world-class research center. She is the perfect person for the job."

"How soon after the funeral can I make Paul a duke?"

"The investiture is scheduled for the very next day and will include others on your first Honors Day. You understood why we had to wait?"

"Of course. It's protocol, and with Papa's death before he could do it himself . . . still, I'll be glad to have it done."

"Of course, sir," agreed Sir Humphrey.

"Well, that's that, then," replied Albert as he glanced at the mantel clock, purchased by George III, and probably his favorite piece in the room.

"I understand the Archbishop wants to see me about the funeral."

"Yes, sir."

"Do you think he's here yet?"

"Knowing the Archbishop, I'd say he's been waiting for some time."

Albert smiled, "I've asked for tea to be served. Kindly show him in as you leave."

"Of course, sir."

Sir Humphrey bowed and left. Albert pushed a button on his desk to signal for the tea, then walked from his desk to an arrangement near the windows of several armchairs and a low serving table. He turned towards the door just as a footman announced the Archbishop, a dignified man older than the late King. The Archbishop beamed on seeing Albert, came towards him, and bowed.

"Your Majesty," he said. Albert held out his hand and warmly grasped the Archbishop's hand in his. He'd known the elderly gentleman all his life.

"Please be seated," said Albert as he motioned to the chairs. "I've taken the liberty of ordering tea. Oh, here it is."

A knock on the door was followed by another footman entering with the tea service on a large silver tray. He bowed, then laid the tray on the table. He glanced at the King, who nodded, and he poured two cups of tea. The Archbishop ignored the cream and sugar as he liked his tea hot and bitter, while Albert liked his with milk and sugar. The footman bowed and left. Each man drank before continuing.

"I understand you want to talk about the funeral," said Albert.

"Yes, Your Majesty," replied the Archbishop. "I wonder if there is anything special you want me to say about the late King?"

"Well, actually I think you probably knew him better in many ways than I did," replied Albert. "At least in a professional capacity. To me, he was a distant but loving father who, as King, trained me to be a King myself but otherwise left me alone, for better or worse. Of course, that did make me self-reliant"

"Of course, sir," said the Archbishop. "It's just that I've rarely had the chance to offer a royal eulogy; there was your mother, of course, and your grandmother before that."

"Ah, yes," said Albert. "Lizzie and I were just babies, so we didn't attend. That was the last thing you needed that day; I imagine we would have screamed the entire time. I can only image the echoes in St. Paul's."

"I imagine you both could have filled it very well," said the Archbishop smiling.

"Still," said Albert, "I'm sure you'll know what to say this time."

"I appreciate your confidence, sir," replied the Archbishop warmly. They took more tea, then the Archbishop continued. "I do apologize, sir, for the issue over seating Mr. McGregor with the Royal Family."

"Damn my sister's interference!" erupted Albert vehemently.

The Archbishop was familiar with the enmity between them.

"But let me hasten to say, sir, that it wasn't only Princess Elizabeth who raised the issue with me."

Albert looked at him quizzically.

"No," he explained, "I've had lay people, rural vicars, even bishops though, I hasten to say, not the Lord Bishop of Durham, all of whom have expressed concern about the propriety of the situation."

"That's quite all right," assured Albert. "We both understand the delicacy of the event."

Relieved, the Archbishop continued. "Sir Humphrey and I worked out what I think will be a satisfactory alternative for Mr.

McGregor and his mother. It's vital that her status within the Royal Family is clear. She is going to be your mother-in-law, after all. Of course, all of this will be resolved by your marriage, which I am looking forward to officiating at."

Albert looked at him gratefully, and the Archbishop continued, "Then all this talk will pass away. I think the marriage marks a great step forward for the Kingdom in many ways, both for church and state."

After having yet more tea, the Archbishop asked a question which concerned him.

"May I inquire as to whether Mr. McGregor is a member of the Church, sir?"

Albert was amused.

"Actually, I don't know what he is as we've never talked about it. I do know that his mother is an animist."

The Archbishop raised his eyebrows in surprise. "Ah, the spirit in everything. Actually, I feel close to that myself."

"Be careful she doesn't convert you," joked Albert.

"If she does," replied the Archbishop with a smile, "We'll have to keep it a secret."

Which led Albert to a delicate issue of his own.

"You know I'm an atheist."

The Archbishop set down his cup and saucer on the table and looked frankly at the King.

"Of course, sir. You've made that clear on many occasions, to your late father's dismay, I must add," a familiar comment Albert still found both distressing and embarrassing, as his father had made his displeasure about that issue known many times.

"How can the head of the Church of England possibly be an atheist?" thundered King George more than once.

"Well, it might interest Your Highness" said the Archbishop as he leaned forward in a near conspiratorial manner, "that even your great-grandmother was what was commonly known as a 'free thinker.'"

"Really," replied a surprised Albert. "I had no idea."

"She confided as such to a predecessor of mine, and the knowledge seems to come with the office simply as something we keep in mind, remembering that varieties of spiritual experience exist even within the Royal Family. To her it was a matter of personal conscience that she kept tactfully hidden."

"Unlike me, for example?" asked a bemused Albert.

The Archbishop hesitated again before admitting, "Yes, Your Highness."

"Will that be an issue for the marriage?"

""Not really," explained the Archbishop. "The royal marriage ceremony is an established ritual, with two people united in the sight of God. Perhaps you could see it as a recognition of a higher power?"

He looked hopefully at Albert, who dashed that hope by shaking his head to indicate "no."

The Archbishop sighed, then continued, "Marriage is a commitment between two people, a sign of mutual declaration and trust, of mutual concern and support. If Your Majesty can see it in that light and take it as a visible sign of what you two clearly mean to each other, and as a public affirmation of your love, then I think the ceremony will be meaningful and significant for you both as well as for the country."

Albert looked at him in admiration.

"Now I see why you are Archbishop," he replied.

With a hint of a smile, the Archbishop acknowledged the praise with a slight nod. The men took more tea, and the subsequent clacking of china in the vast sitting room were the only sounds, except for the ticking of the George III clock and the faint noise of traffic outside.

"Along that line," continued Albert, "I have some ideas for the coronation."

But he was quickly interrupted by the Archbishop.

"Perhaps we can leave that for a future time, Your Highness. I think that, for now, we've reached a point of mutual satisfaction. I suggest we get through the funeral first, then the marriage, before tackling the coronation with issues that could perhaps cause mutual distress."

Surprised and somewhat taken aback by the Archbishop's reply, Albert nonetheless realized its sensibleness and wanted to maintain the current goodwill between them for as long as possible. The other issue, of being both King of a country while head of its faith, which he did not believe, could wait. For now, the tea sufficed as a bond between two men who, despite their mutual affection, might eventually find themselves at odds with each other from their respective positions, and not for the first time in British history.

CHAPTER 35

After the Archbishop left, Albert returned to his office, took off his suit coat, and worked at his desk in his favorite cardigan. Soon, Paul came in.

"How did it go?"

"Well enough. He and Sir Humphrey have worked out a place for you and Pauline in the diplomatic section."

"And the issue of the coronation ?"

"Things were going so well between us that we decided to postpone that for another day."

"Just as well," said Paul. "That could cause some trouble."

"Yes," agreed Albert. "And there's enough to deal with now, with the funeral and the wedding."

Paul went to a window that opened onto the front of the palace and overlooked the street beyond the tall metal fence. He saw the hundreds of people standing there, grieving for the dead King, and the increasing numbers of floral bouquets piled against the fence.

"Albert," said Paul softly, "Come see this."

So, Albert joined him at the window, put his arms around Paul and looked out at the scene and both knew they had to be down there.

"Should I put on my suit coat?" Albert asked.

"No, that sweater makes you look sexy."

"I'm not sure the image of a sexy King is needed right now."

"Trust me, " replied Paul sagely, "Sex appeal never hurts."

So, Albert started towards the door while Paul paused at the desk and picked up the phone.

"Who are you calling?" asked Albert.

"Graham," replied Paul.

Albert was still getting used to the increased security under which his father had lived, so he just nodded his head.

Graham and a security team met them as they started to cross the courtyard. He moved close to the King and said, sotto voce, "This is not a good idea, Your Majesty."

"But you're not going to stop me, are you?"

Graham paused before replying. "No, sir. I admire the thought. I just don't think it's a good idea. Still, we'll keep you and Paul safe. I've had my people undercover and among the crowd all morning."

"How is it you know what I'm going to do before I do it?" asked the King, both amused and surprised.

"That's my job," replied Graham.

"That's what Sir Humphrey said earlier."

"That's both our jobs," replied Graham.

"And I depend on you to keep me safe."

"Thank you, sir."

Graham dropped back as Albert reached the now-opened gate and went through without hesitation, with Paul behind him.

The reaction among the people was instantaneous: "The King! The King is here!"

Graham decided not to control access to him, but to watch how things developed. He was pleased to note how people moved back before Albert and Paul, and created open space around them, unsure what to do.

Paul was taken with the variety of people there, a veritable cross-section of the country. There were obvious business or professional types in suits; others appeared to be geek techies; working class men and women were there; others were in service uniforms; there were young couples with children; and a few who were likely jobless and possibly homeless as well, along with a scattering of curious tourists.

The women curtsied while men removed their hats or caps, if wearing any, which they held before them as they bowed. Parents encouraged their children to bow or curtsy, usually awkwardly.

Albert began approaching individuals, and he started with an older man. He held out his hand and shook the older man's hand. "So good of you to come."

"God bless you, Your Majesty," said the man.

"What's your name then?" asked the King.

"Alfie, sir; here from Blackpool with me missus."

And he turned to show his wife, who hesitantly curtsied with an embarrassed smile at being singled out.

"And so, Alfie from Blackpool, is that souvenir shop with the taffy machine in the window still downtown?"

"Why, blimey, Your Highness, there are many of them, an' it please you sir."

"The one I'm thinking of is where my mother, the late Queen, took my sister and I when we were nearly five, and bought us each a small china souvenir cup with two handles and a picture of the town on it. I must still have it somewhere."

"Aye, sir, they are still available, they are."

"Glad to hear it, Alfie," said Albert with a broad smile, and then he proceeded down what was now a row of people, from one person to another, shaking hands, thanking them for being there and for showing such respect for his father; while Paul stayed near him and started shaking hands and greeting people himself. All the while Graham and his team watched the crowd.

At first, people were reluctant to take pictures with their mobiles, but that changed after one man asked the King if he could photograph him with his daughter.

"Of course," replied Albert, as the child proudly stood by the King and her father beamed as he took the picture. Then it seemed like everyone had their mobiles out, asking for photos, and Albert and Paul patiently waited as shots were set up and taken, then they continued working the crowd like this for over an hour.

The pictures were soon posted on social media and, as people learned the new King and his future consort were outside the palace, more people showed up to see them and to have their picture taken with the royal couple.

Graham knew that soon he would have to let the King know it was time to leave. He was also prepared for the appearance of the media by restricting them to a cordoned-off area so the King could deal only with his people.

"Thank you. Thank you for your kind words."

Albert and Paul made a special point of treating the children present with special respect. They knelt down to be on the same eye level. Many were bashful and hid behind their parents, but one child, perhaps three or four, was obviously frustrated at being restrained by his father, and finally broke free to rush towards the King and grabbed him so tightly and unexpectedly around the knees that Albert nearly fell over.

"Whoa! My young lad!" he said with a laugh. "Let's get you up here."

So, he reached down as the lad let go and picked him up and then held him in the crook of one arm.

"Now then, young man, what's your name?"

Proudly, the lad nearly shouted, "Nelson Mifumee!" to the delighted laughter of those around the pair.

"Well, Nelson Mifumee, do you know who I am?"

"Yes!" said the lad smiling. "You're the King. Can I call you Mister Albert?"

"Only if I can call you Mister Nelson," said the King smiling broadly.

Then the lad, in a completely unexpected gesture, threw his arms around the King's neck, drew him close, and kissed him on the cheek.

And that was the photo that went around the world and which, in a video version, Princess Elizabeth was horrified to see on her telly that evening.

"How does he do it?" she protested to Larry. "Father is dead with a royal funeral ahead and yet it's Albert who gets all the publicity."

"Face it, Lizzie," said her husband, "the people like him and the McGregor lad more than they do you. Whatever it is they have, you haven't got."

"Whose side are you on?" shouted the princess as she turned on her husband.

"Yours, of course," he replied resignedly, having traveled this road so many times he knew every bend. "But I'm also a businessman who faces facts, and the fact is that you are not popular, and they are, even if you were to become Queen."

The princess reluctantly realized her husband was right, and he continued: "So instead of fighting it and stressing you, me, and the children, I might add, just accept it, while keeping in mind that you, and our children, are the succession no matter how popular your brother is. And I suggest that you stick with your gardening and your children to ensure your health and the health of those around you, who love you and who don't want to see you worry yourself into an early grave."

Lizzie understood what Larry was saying.

"But it's hard," she admitted.

"Of course it's hard to admit that you're not popular; that you're not the 'It' woman but, frankly, it makes no difference because, in the long run, Albert will die, the McGregor lad will do something or other, and either you or your children will continue the monarchy, as history books yet to be written will attest."

Lizzie looked at her husband, who obviously loved her, and smiled.

"How did you get so wise?"

"It doesn't seem possible, does it?" he asked. "Now either turn off the telly or at least watch an old movie, or Benny Hill reruns, or something else."

As Lizzie enjoyed the admittedly outdated antics of the comedian who died before her birth, she thought that was a good idea, anything to get rid of the image of Albert holding that boy to popular acclaim.

At the same time, and on her own telly, Pauline was also watching Albert holding young Nelson Mifumee. She watched how Paul and Albert worked the crowd together, like old pros, and she could see how happy they were with each other, and what a capable team they made.

She had doubted that for a long time, but no more. She was also impressed at how easily Paul had adapted to his new role, made easier by his natural dignity, as though born to it. She had just never thought that consort to a king was a career path for him. But there it was, like an unexpected dream of a new world into which they both had awakened.

It was she who was having trouble adapting. She never realized that Paul's life path would demand so much of her – everything, in fact. She liked her work; she liked her house; she liked her neighbors and friends; she liked Durham; and now all of that was falling away.

She was already in her new apartment at Kensington Palace, having arrived to console her son and Albert. It was odd to be paying her respects to a man she had only met one time and yet felt so close to. And she wondered what might have happened if he had lived. But now he was gone, as was her previous life in Durham, all gone.

Her house would be sold, the neighborhood would finally return to its former peaceful state, and she would no longer have to deal with the same unspoken question from her neighbors, "How much longer must we be inconvenienced by you and your son?" Well, not much longer.

Admittedly, her work no longer interested her as it once had, now that she was an administrator and much less of a researcher, which had brought her to Durham in the first place. No, it was time to move on, and she was excited at the prospect of starting an entirely new organization with the potential for doing so much good on a national level. She also looked forward to working with Paul on a nearly daily basis, at least after the wedding when things could calm down.

Until then, she would settle into Kensington and, hopefully, make new friends. The vast complex had long-term residents that she looked forward to meeting, and who could help her learn the ways of a royal household. So, her future was far from bleak as it was an opportunity to reinvent herself yet again, as she had done when she moved to Durham from Jamaica so many years before, and just look at what she had made of herself since then as a woman filled with ambition and promise.

And Pauline realized that, eventually, she would look back upon Durham as she now looked back upon her beautiful yet distant island home, as a place to be from.

CHAPTER 36

The men awoke early the day of the funeral. They were still in Albert's apartment at St. James and would not move into the royal bed chamber until after the funeral.

This was the day for formal funeral attire, and Albert was glad that Wilfred, his father's valet, had agreed to stay on with him, when he could easily have retired to rooms at Hampton Court. The man's knowledge of what was proper and correct for every occasion was encyclopedic.

Wilfred would be essential for those times when Albert would be wearing a formal military uniform, for reviewing the Household Cavalry and such, especially from horseback, for which he and Paul would also need riding lessons, something he had assiduously avoided until this moment in his life.

Unlike his father, who'd gone into the Navy, Albert never entered the military, and it was certainly not a vocational choice for Paul, either. Still, as King and consort, there would be many times to come when it would be essential to be in uniform, and so both men were to be made ceremonial commanders of various regiments so they would have official ranks. And with the uniforms came a variety of badges, medals, and orders, the proper placement of which required a knowledgeable valet.

Albert transferred his own valet, Cunningham, to Paul for the same reason. While both men preferred to dress themselves, they also realized just how useful a valet was to match the appropriate apparel to the occasion.

After dressing, they met Pauline in the dining room. She looked elegant in a long, black dress with a smart coat and a simple but stylish hat. Breakfast was for the immediate family, and dishes were set out on the sideboard so they could serve themselves. As usual, Elizabeth and Larry were late arriving, even though they had spent the night at the palace. When they finally arrived, Lizzie, as usual, didn't even think of apologizing as she swept into the room. She looked surprisingly frumpy, in a rather shapeless black dress. While she loved to shop, it had long been clear that she had no idea what to buy that would enhance her appearance. As the Princess Royal, the idea of enhancing never even occurred to her. She wore what she liked and that was that. Fashion trends were for others. She, frankly, couldn't be bothered.

Ignoring Paul and Pauline, she went to Albert, bobbed slightly, and then air kissed him on each cheek. While she had bowed to her father, she was still aggravated at court etiquette that required her to bow to her own brother. However, she also realized that she'd have to get used to it.

She finally turned to Pauline, who curtseyed, and to Paul, who bowed, courtesies that she appreciated.

"Dr. McGregor," she said with a slightly acidic tone, "so we finally meet."

Pauline curtseyed again. "It's a pleasure, M'am," which Lizzie accepted as recognition of her own royal status, and which also pleased her.

"I just wish our first meeting was in more pleasurable circumstances," said Pauline. "This must be a most difficult time, and I am truly sorry for your loss."

Against her predisposition not to like this woman, Lizzie felt her resolve to be cracking.

Paul enjoyed watching his mother in action. She'd honed her social skills from decades of seeking funding for the lab from university and government officials, as well as a variety of corporate and private donors. She had become quite adept at putting people at ease.

Still, Elizabeth was unwilling to be completely seduced by Dr. McGregor's considerable charm.

"Actually," replied Lizzie, "I didn't think we'd ever meet. Albert's had so many casual dalliances and boyfriends that there's never been a reason to meet their parents."

"Lizzie," said Albert quietly from behind her. He'd already gotten her reluctant promise to be nice to Paul and his mother. Paul felt Albert bristle and touched his back with a hand to prevent a scene while continuing to smile. He had learned many things from watching his mother in action.

Refusing to be baited, Pauline agreed. "I, too, doubted the depth of their relationship on such short acquaintance, but I eventually realized their love was more than mere infatuation, and now I understand how fortunate Paul has been in his choice of a partner."

"He is indeed," replied Lizzie testily. "Very fortunate."

Albert intervened to suggest it was time to eat since they were already standing, so the group went to the sideboard, got plates, and proceeded to help themselves from a variety of platters and bowls.

Pauline was deciding what to eat when Elizabeth came beside her to see what was available.

"Would you like some potatoes, Your Highness?" asked Pauline easily.

Touched by her request, Lizzie said, simply, "Why, yes, I would . . . Dr. McGregor. Thank you."

After placing some on Lizzie's plate, Pauline asked, "And where are your children today?"

With a grieved expression, Lizzie said, "For some reason Albert doesn't like them around, so they are eating by themselves."

Albert overheard this exchange and was about to make a comment about "little no-neck monsters" when Paul caught his eye and, with the smallest of motions, shook his head. Earlier, he'd made Albert agree, reluctantly, to be nice to his sister today of all days.

The group sat at one end of the long table and started eating. They ate in silence for a while, with the only sounds as their water glasses and coffee cups were refilled. Albert sat at the head of the table, with Paul to his right and Pauline to his left, with the Princess Elizabeth beside her and Larry next to his wife.

Pauline turned to Lizzie and said, "I understand you have five children."

"Yes," replied Elizabeth. "They, and my garden, mean everything to me. Larry, too, of course."

He smiled and said, "Still here, darling."

"Paul was my only child," said Pauline, "and we had him late. I didn't know whether I would have children or not."

"I don't seem to have anything else," replied Lizzie with a smile. "And I don't think we're finished yet," she added to Larry's obvious surprise. Paul hastened to touch Albert's shoe with his own, to remind Albert of his promise, which he now regretted making.

"And what are your plans for their education?" asked Pauline, sincerely wanting to know. The three men listened as the women carried on their conversation. No one had ever shown any genuine interest in her children's education before, and Lizzie found herself, again, unwillingly, quite touched.

"Victoria is my oldest child." And everyone, including Larry, recognized the singular pronoun, as opposed to the plural. "So her future is set. She will eventually be queen."

She looked emphatically at Albert, then her look turned unexpectedly gentle. "Our own futures were set the same way.

We never had a choice for careers. We were the only children of our parents, and so Albert was the heir, and I was the spare. Certainly no one ever asked if that was what we wanted, did they, Albert?"

Taken aback by her question, because they never inquired about what each other felt, Albert just, ruefully it seemed, shook his head "No."

Lizzie continued, "So it wasn't like we sat around and asked ourselves, 'Butcher, baker, candlestick maker.' But then there are lots of those, and only one person sits on the throne. And our parents instilled in us from our earliest years to know that while we were not particularly special in ourselves, we did have a unique service to perform for the country. Did it seem that way to you, Albert?"

Surprised at being asked anything by his sister, Albert agreed.

"Yes, completely."

"And while it was clear that Albert would be King, I also knew I had a job of my own to do, even as backup." And here everyone smiled, even Albert, who had never looked at his sister as a thoughtful person.

"So with our children, I – " And here she stopped and looked at her husband and put a hand over his before turning again to the others and continuing. "We – [and Larry was obviously touched by her consideration] recognize the importance of raising our children in the role that any of them may eventually face but, since only one of them will ever likely have that role, then Larry and I have been careful to make it clear that the younger children will have choices that Victoria will never have."

"How do you do that?" pursued Pauline. And, again, Lizzie was taken aback at the realization that no one had ever asked about what was, in essence, her theory of education.

"Early on, I doubted my ability to raise them," she explained, "simply because Albert and I lost our own mother so early. She never had the opportunity to guide our education. What I remember, though, were the many hours she and I spent gardening, when we were so happy together."

And here Albert looked at his sister, who was thoughtful in a way he'd never seen, and realized he was jealous of all the time she'd spent with their mother, while he was with their father.

"There are still times I doubt my ability to raise them properly, I find it helps to think of them as plants in my garden, who simply need to be properly tended, as my mother showed me. I supply fertile soil, proper nutrients, water, and let them grow in the sun as they will. I want them to have a wide-ranging knowledge of the world, of the arts, mathematics, the sciences, history."

Then Lizzie stopped and looked directly at Pauline before continuing, "But I fear your field of microbiology may be beyond them at this point!"

Pauline smiled, "I'm not so sure about that. It's really never too soon to start asking questions about what's going on inside the plants you grow."

And Lizzie was taken aback by Pauline's unexpected generosity.

"I'll keep that in mind," she replied, then continued. "So, the answer to your question as to their futures is that I – that we [and here she put a hand over Larry's] – don't know because our children themselves will answer that. Like many children, they could go into their father's line of work. In addition to the Trust, his family has many and varied business enterprises. And certainly, the military on my side has always been a family career and, with our connections, perhaps something in the diplomatic corps as well."

She stopped to take a sip of coffee before continuing, while her breakfast cooled on her plate.

"Albert?" she asked, who was surprised at being called on. "What do you think you might have done if we weren't royals?"

And he was perplexed at the thought.

"Frankly, Lizzie, I've never considered it. As you say, there was never a choice. Oh," And he paused thoughtfully to consider the possibilities, "perhaps I would have run a souvenir shop in Blackpool!" And he and everyone else laughed at the absurdity of the idea, before he turned serious.

"Actually, I don't think I would have amounted to much. I'm not that bright, original, or creative. Fortunately, many others are. But I knew early on that I, and you as well, Lizzie, had been chosen by fate or call it what you will, by destiny, I guess, to a calling that is literally in our blood, which is why we can't do anything else. And while it's true that, as individual people, we may not be much, but as the monarch and the spare," and he raised a hand to his sister, who returned the gesture magnanimously, "We form a living connection to the country's past and, through your children," and, again, he raised his hand to his sister, who nodded at the recognition, "into the country's future, that no one else can provide."

"Here, here!" said Larry, and with that Sir Humphrey came into the room and said, "We should leave in fifteen minutes, Your Highness."

"Thank you," replied Albert, who turned to the others and said, "Let's finish breakfast as it will be a long time before we eat again."

CHAPTER 37

Afterwards, it was the somberness of the day that Paul remembered most. It started the day before when the family entered Westminster Hall and approached the catafalque with the late King's coffin surmounted by the Royal Standard, on top of which was a single floral wreath, along with the Crown, Orb, and Sceptre. Outside, they had passed the line of many thousands waiting to pay their respects to "Good King George." Inside, the line of people stopped to watch as Albert and Elizabeth placed a wreath with the single word, "Papa," on a large card, at the foot of the bier. Then Larry and the children placed another wreath of white flowers, as did Paul and his mother.

There were four tall, lighted tapers, on tall bronze stands, one at each corner of the catafalque, and with four Officers of the Watch, from various regiments, and four Yeomen Warders of the Tower, standing at constant attention. King Albert himself stood watch for an hour in full dress uniform.

Later, the Royal Family, except the youngest children, received the condolences of thousands: "So sorry." "A great king." "Sorely missed." And the responses: "Thank you." "Thank you so much," repeated endlessly.

Even Lizzie, who was still somewhat uneasy at conversing with strangers, did her part with grace and poise, shaking hands, thanking people whose grief was palpable.

The somber faces continued the next day as the coffin was carefully placed on a special gun carriage by members of the Welsh Guards before it was pulled by Royal Navy sailors the short distance to the Abbey, where the Welsh Guards brought it inside for the service.

Paul glanced at the crowds, grief-stricken, with bowed heads, an entire country in mourning, as military pipers played dirges, and drums kept a steady slow march accompanied by the tolling of bells.

At the Abbey, the coffin was taken in first, and the Royal Family was met by the Archbishop and the Dean, who bowed gravely, then led the way inside, down the long nave, through the massive, hand-carved choir screen that divided the large room into two sections, past the grief-stricken – all people, it seemed, were grief-stricken on this day – assemblage that had risen in the presence both of the dead King, and his successor.

It was a long walk to the Royal Pew, where Albert entered first, followed by Lizzie, Larry and their children. Paul and Pauline were directed to a side staircase and went up to a recently installed balcony overlooking the surprisingly narrow nave, with its soaring columns and ribbed ceiling.

While those on the main floor resumed their seats after Albert sat down, Paul was surprised that the dignitaries in the balcony with him and his mother remained standing until they were shown to their seats at the front and then everyone sat down together.

The music, with the men and boys of the Abbey choir, as well as the organ and brass ensemble, continued to play, and Paul realized he knew all the hymns being sung. What he really wanted to do was to don choir robes himself and join in the singing. After all, he'd sung in the Durham cathedral choir for many funerals, and he knew the ritual today was an expanded version of a ritual with which he was well acquainted.

He looked down at Albert and realized that Sir Humphrey was true to his word in that they could see each other clearly.

Throughout the service, Albert would glance his way, and Paul simply had to nod his head for Albert to smile gratefully and return to the service.

Paul had told Albert several times over the past few hours and days that their love spanned time and distance, that they were bound together no matter how far apart they were, and all it took was a glance to affirm their affection and devotion.

From the Royal Pew, Albert still felt alone. He could tell that Lizzie was gently crying under her veil, while holding her husband's hand. Albert realized that holding her other hand would provide no consolation. He really wanted Paul beside him, and was still angry at being separated from him, though the palace had released a statement explaining that Paul and his mother were sitting apart from the Royal Family for propriety due to the nature of the occasion.

Albert realized that, for the moment, he was the focus of the world's attention, so it was a matter of pride that he looked so frequently at his consort so the world would see how much his beloved meant to him. All it took was a slight nod from Paul, and the briefest of smiles, for Albert to be consoled in his loneliness and loss.

As an atheist, the hopeful message of the service for eternal life held no meaning for him, and certainly no hope. His father was dead in the coffin before him and that was that. Albert knew he would never see his father again in this or any other world. He knew his father remained alive only in his memory, and that, after his death, his father would remain only in books or as images to be viewed on YouTube. Those images of a man that Albert knew as a complicated and complex person, would only present a shadow of the father he had known. Indeed, he was skeptical of the ability of words and images to accurately present more than a fraction of the true presence of any historical personage. He had read many histories of his family's thousand-year connection to the country, and yet constantly felt that even the best of them failed to recreate the essence of what the men and women they attempted to describe were really like. Mere shadows on a wall, better than nothing, but how far they fell from adequately conjuring flesh-and-blood people in the context of their daily lives. And he realized that it would be the fate of his father and, eventually, himself as well.

Albert knew the eyes of all those present in the Abbey, and all those watching around the world, were fully upon him, and he knew their thoughts were the same. As he had wondered so often himself: What kind of king would he be? Would he be a good king, or a bad king?

Well, if someone figures that out, please tell me, he thought wryly. Indeed, the question had consumed him since his father's death.

"Oh, Papa, why did you die so soon? Too soon," he thought to himself. "I know you doubted me, as I doubt myself. All it takes, you said, is for a few serious blunders for the monarchy to come crashing down. Not on my watch, you said. But, surely, not on mine, either. The continued existence of the monarchy depends not on the inertia of tradition, but on choices made daily as king. Make too many of the wrong choices and those who want to see the monarchy abolished will prevail."

Being openly gay, he knew, was not the issue, at least for most, for those whose opinion he genuinely cared about, and Albert did care, very much, about what his people thought of him. He knew that, for now, he had the goodwill of the people behind him. They were willing to trust him because the continuation of the monarchy reflected the continuation of British tradition. Continuing without a monarchy, like the United States, seemed to him to lack the historical thread of continuity the monarchy provided, especially when leaders there changed every four or eight years. Perhaps, he thought, America found its historical continuity in the line of its presidents, or in the White House, the Statue of Liberty, or even Mount Vernon but, in his country, Albert realized, he was the living chain of continuity, and that was a lonely place to be.

If Paul had not come along when he had, Albert knew he would be terribly alone at the very moment when he needed someone most. Which was why he was grateful to be able to look up and see his beloved looking back at him, who, with a slight nod and a gentle smile, made Albert realize he was not alone, even in that vast room filled with people.

After the service, there was two minutes of silence, following by the tolling of Big Ben as the Welsh Guards returned the coffin to the gun carriage for the journey to Wellington Arch, with the Royal Family, including Paul and Pauline, walking behind it, along with Sir Humphrey, the Prime Minister and other dignitaries, and with horse brigades before and after. From the Arch, the coffin was put into a hearse for the trip to Windsor. At the committal service in St. George's Chapel, the Crown, Orb, and Sceptre were removed, and the Lord Chancellor broke his "wand of office" to show his service to the King was done. Albert placed the small flag known as the King's Company Camp Color on the coffin, and George's bagpiper played a lament before the coffin was lowered into the Royal Vault.

CHAPTER 38

"Well, Sir Humphrey was right," says Albert. "This has been a very long day. I thought we'd never eat."

"Or get to the loo," replies Paul with a smile.

Alfred has his hand on Paul's chest. This is their next-to-last night in his apartment at St. James. Tomorrow, the royal bed chamber would be emptied of his father's things, with everything put into storage until Albert and Lizzie could go through them, then Albert's and Paul's things would be moved into the room where King George had slept for so many years, and in which he died. But everything would be fresh and waiting for continuity to continue.

Now the funeral is over, with the coffin in the royal crypt at Windsor. Rather than spending the night there, Albert and Paul both wanted to return, as tomorrow would be busy, what with the move and other things to attend to.

The funeral meal was just for the family, with the children in attendance this time, at Lizzie's request which Albert, without hesitation, had granted. He was particularly interested in observing the young Victoria, his successor, and had to admit that Lizzie seemed to be doing a good job with her as she showed a poise and dignity he thought must be rare for someone her age.

But finally, the meal was over; even the small talk went surprisingly easily, and then Lizzie, Larry, and the children made their "Good nights." This time Lizzie held her brother close and, unusually, kissed him once on each cheek before leaving.

"Let's keep in touch more often," she said.

"I'd like that," replied Albert, to his surprise.

Pauline stayed briefly before leaving for her new

apartment at Kensington and now, finally, the two men are alone, naked, and together in bed. Paul feels that Albert is still tense from the day.

"Would you like something?" he asks.

"No, not really," says a visibly worn-out Albert. "I just want to keep holding." With Paul's arms around Albert, quite soon they were both asleep.

CHAPTER 39

They stood before the bed where they had last seen the body of the late King.

"Are you sure you're okay with this?" asked Albert.

Paul was touched by his concern.

"Yes, I think so," he replied hesitantly.

"Because the sheets have been changed, and we can even change the mattress if you want," explained Albert quickly. "And if you don't like the bed, we can change that, too. There are lots of beds. Not Henry's, of course, but lots of others."

Paul smiled.

"No," he said. "This is the monarch's bed, and now you are monarch. It will be fine. And it really is beautiful."

He knew that would please Albert, and it did.

"Actually, I'm glad to hear that," he said with relief. "I have fond memories of this bed. Lizzie and I used to sneak away from our governesses and come in here early in the morning and jump on the bed just to wake up Mummy and Papa, and find out where they'd been the night before, and who they'd met, and what they had to eat. And they were never mad at us, no matter how late they'd gotten in or how much they wanted another hour's sleep. They'd sit up in the bed, with us around them, and they'd tell us everything; famous people they'd met, foreign princes, we wanted to hear it all.

"Later, after Mummy died, Lizzie and I still rushed in to see Papa, and he was often surrounded by papers and reports and proposals he'd been reading as he fell asleep, and he'd show them to us as we sat on either side of him, and he'd tell us what he was doing and how his meeting with the P.M. went, or else

237

he'd tell us another story from British history. It was all part of our training, so, yes, the bed means a lot to me."

This was the first time Paul had time to see the room. He started with the window side. The chamber was large enough that there were reading areas, and an arrangement of two sofas facing each other, with a low table between them where tea could be served. He saved the most massive object in the room, on the interior wall opposite the windows, for last; the huge fireplace, with its elaborate marble mantle, with robed caryatids on either side so naturally carved they seemed like marbleized flesh. Paul went and stood before it, and Albert followed.

"Does it work?" asked Paul.

Albert was astounded by the question.

"Of course it works! This is a real palace with real chimneys and real working fireplaces!"

"Well," replied Paul, "My mother's house has a fireplace with a gas log in it."

"I can assure you that there are no gas logs at Buckingham Palace!" sniffed Albert, who was careful not to mention other differences between his house and that of Dr. McGregor.

Paul knelt before the vast fireplace and inspected it carefully, then rubbed a finger on the brick floor, looked at it, and said, "There's not a speck of ash. Do you ever recall seeing a fire here?"

Albert paused, then sheepishly shook his head.

"It was never needed for heat," he explained.

"Well," continued Paul, "how would we even get a fire if we wanted one?"

"I have staff for that," said Albert impatiently. "A char girl or something."

"A char girl?" exploded Paul with a laugh. "This place is far more Dickensian than anyone out there [and he pointed towards the windows] would ever believe. And where would this char girl find wood?"

"I guess there's a woodsman who supplies it."

"And does he go to Hyde Park and chop down trees?"

"Look," replied Albert testily. "I don't know, all right? But if you want a fire, I'll get one for you."

"You don't even know how to start a fire, do you?"

"Yes, I do!" thundered Albert. "Your face in my ass."

"That's such an old joke," replied Paul as he shook his head. "Well, I was a Scout, and I can start a fire with flint and steel."

"You were a Scout?" asked Albert dubiously. "You? What, in the pansy division?"

"Of course I was a Boy Scout," replied Paul archly. "We went camping and everything."

"I bet you did," joked Albert. "Do you know that Sir Baden Powell was a pederast?"

"Every Scout knows that" replied Paul. "And we taught ourselves self-defense in case anyone tried anything. A good kick in the balls bends 'em right over. Even you."

"You would kick your King in the balls?"

"I'm just saying, in case it proves necessary," replied Paul. "Besides, I'd love to see you on a royal camping trip. Have you ever slept on the ground, or would you have someone do it for you?"

Eager to change the subject, Albert said, again, that he would find out who was in charge of the palace fireplaces, and then moved on.

"I spoke with Sir Humphrey about a desk for you and he agreed that you can use the one my father had for me when I returned from college."

"I thought you were going to say I could use the tiny

training desk your father first got for you."

"So, you could sit in its tiny chair with your knees sticking up as you tried to work?" laughed Albert. "No, my desk was the one the first Victoria gave to my namesake so they could work together, so now it goes from one consort to another. But I daresay that first, tiny desk is still someplace. Nothing ever seems to be thrown out around here. I'll have to take you up to the attics sometime. They are amazingly full of stuff. Lizzie and I played up there as children. It was a perfect place for make-believe as we pretended to be historical personages. Sometimes I'd be Henry the Eighth, and she'd be Anne Boleyn. 'Off with her head!' Then we'd switch roles, and she'd be Henry, and I'd be Anne."

"That sounds more like your real personalities," said Paul grinning.

"She always was the tough one," admitted Albert, "though that may be changing."

The conversation stopped, and they looked at each other questioningly, then Albert changed the topic again.

"You'll need a security clearance so I can share some of the papers I work with, and Graham has already started that process."

"You mean I'm being investigated and don't even know it?"

"That's how these things work. Need to know, and now you need to know, so I'm telling you."

"I guess they want to make sure I'm not going to kill you in your sleep."

"Partly," admitted Albert, but Paul saw he was only partly smiling.

"Knowing your family, I'm probably the one in danger."

"Jack the Ripper was not part of the family."

"So, you say," replied Paul.

Another pause, then Albert continued.

"The P.M. is not pleased with this arrangement. She's concerned I'll be giving away top secrets, though I imagine she shares such things with her husband, just as I'm sure the U.S. president shares things with the First Husband."

"Look," said Paul seriously, "I don't want to come between you and your advisors or the P.M. I don't need or even want to know state secrets, and I don't want people to think I'm trying to take control of you or anything like that. I have enough to do just with setting up the foundation."

"Well," replied Albert, "Those who really know me know I'm too stubborn to be controlled by you or anyone else."

"But it won't take long, once the public sees our desks side by side, to wonder what kind of nefarious influence I'm exerting over you, and what scheming foreign power is using me to secretly control the throne."

"Like Scotland?" asked Albert with a smile. "From what Sir Humphrey tells me, there are already conspiracy theories spreading on the web, and we haven't even started working together yet."

Paul was visibly taken aback by this knowledge and didn't know what to say.

"Once we're married," continued Albert, "then the security situation changes. Interestingly enough, I don't seem to have a security clearance. I guess they figure if the King can't be trusted, then what's the point of the monarchy? But the P.M. is concerned about the red boxes and the possibility that I might share something that shouldn't be shared. For my eyes only, you see. But asking your opinion is not the same as asking you to make a decision. That's the way Mummy and Papa worked. She had her own office and staff and so they didn't work side by side, but I know he always confided in her; that's the unspoken assumption that governments make about their heads of state, they assume couples talk, at least in bed or at the breakfast table. Papa needed a sounding board, not someone to tell him what to do. He depended on her, as I will depend on you, to listen and to reflect and to show perspectives I may not be able to see because I'm so close to things. And I know how terribly lonely he was, how isolated, after her death because he no longer had anyone with whom he could share, so he ended up keeping it all locked inside him. I saw the cost firsthand – I'm sure it's why he's dead now – and I don't want that to happen to me.

"Still, there will be times, rare, but things will happen, when something comes up, an emergency perhaps, that the P.M. will inform me about that I really can't share. Even I am informed on a need-to-know basis and sometimes I think that Sir Humphrey is the only person who really knows what's going on," Albert said ruefully.

"But the government may be considering a secret military incursion, or retribution for a massive hack by some foreign country, or maybe we've been betrayed by a double agent, or maybe we're even considering going to war, and those things I will not tell you about, not just because you shouldn't know about them, but because it's also better for you not to know."

And that was the first time that Paul understood the weight Albert bore.

CHAPTER 40

They sat before a blazing fire, each with a book.

"What are you reading?" asked Paul.

Albert looked over at him, "Just another history book."

"I don't know why you do that. Here you are, making history every day, yet consumed with the past."

"Papa always said the way to the future is through the past, so I don't want to miss anything."

They continued to read, then Albert put down his book and said, "You know, my grandmother Victoria, as distinct from my great-grandmother Victoria, and as distinct from my great-great grandmother Victoria, had a theory she called, 'the great man of history.' These days it would apply equally to women as well, but she applied it to her prime ministers who were all male at that time. And her theory was that a person, male or female, was made great by their time, and until a moment of challenge, exists only in potential. She mentioned Winston Churchill in that regard. She said he was a fiercely intelligent man who, nonetheless, never reached his potential because there was no significant event to require greatness of him. She said a war, for example, would have stretched him in a way that all those years of peace did not, so he remained just another boring Tory P.M., with a lack of vision to see what the country really needed to transform itself into a land of opportunity for all its varied peoples as the empire fell away. She said he became a kind of dinosaur unable to adapt to changing conditions and fought against the social and technological possibilities that were inexorably coming. In the end, he was destroyed by them or, what is far worse for a politician, made irrelevant. So, the triumph of Harold McMillan, who succeeded him, was to catch the zeitgeist and to put the wind at the country's back, which helped transform it into the economic powerhouse it has become. He had the vision to see how the world was changing, while Churchill didn't, and now McMillan is considered one of our greatest P.M.s, while Churchill is a footnote, an also-ran."

"Well," replied Paul, "You're already more than a footnote; the first openly gay monarch in modern times and the first to marry his same-sex partner."

"There is that" smiled Albert. "Thank goodness for Lizzie and her brood. I'm certainly not the first queer Brit monarch, but I am the first who didn't have to marry a woman to continue the succession. Historically, monarchs had to marry to continue the line, so their wives were used for breeding, while their boyfriends were used for pleasure."

"So where do I fit in?" asked Paul coyly.

"You fit in very nicely, as you very well know."

"You'd think we'd have a baby from all this trying."

"I know," replied Albert. "I guess we need some kind of male ovaries, or maybe a gestating pouch."

"Or maybe we could take turns setting on a nest of eggs, waiting for them to hatch," suggested Paul, which justified Albert's decision to keep Paul close at hand as a sounding board, because it was Paul's off-hand joke about nests and hatching eggs that gave Albert the glimmer of an idea for which he had to seek professional advice.

CHAPTER 41

"So, let me see if I understand this correctly, Your Majesty" said Sir Sullivan, the aging royal physician. "You didn't ask me here because you're ill."

Albert, grinning, shook his head.

"You asked me here because you and Mr. McGregor want to have a child that is fully yours?"

"Cheers," said Albert, now with a full smile. "Specifically, I want to see if it's possible, with our vaunted British medical technology, to remove all the DNA from a human egg and have it replaced with our own, then have that fertilized egg implanted in a uterus, and brought to term so that the Duke and I can have our very own prince or princess."

Sir Sullivan considered his next words carefully to avoid offending the King.

"Your Majesty, just because something can be done doesn't mean it should be done."

"Damn it, man! I'm not asking you to build a bomb!" shouted the King, making Sir Sullivan realize he'd offended the King after all, which was when the old man started to perspire.

Changing tact, he explained the King's request was not his area of expertise, to which Albert said he realized that, but he also knew that Sir Sullivan could get the answer from those who were specialists in the field.

Once again, Sir Sullivan chose his words carefully, making a point that only he, as a long-time observer of the Royal Family, could make.

"There are implications for such a child far beyond the technical ones, sir. Implications far beyond the Royal Family, for the country as a whole. I only ask that you consult with Sir Humphrey before deciding to do this."

"Actually, Sir Humphrey is the next person I'm seeing," explained Albert, which relieved the man who was practically an old family retainer.

"Then I will find out what I can and report back to you, sir," said Sir Sullivan, as he bowed and started to leave.

"Quickly," replied Albert, who noticed the perspiration on Sir Sullivan's forehead and realized that, inadvertently, he'd pushed the old man too hard.

Sir Sullivan wiped his forehead with his handkerchief as he exited the King's study, and saw Sir Humphrey standing and waiting to go in. Sir Humphrey noticed his long-time friend was flustered.

"What's going on?" he asked, but Sir Sullivan passed without even looking at him and merely shook his head. That was when Sir Humphrey knew that what was beyond the door was not good. He was right.

"No, no, no, and no!" he thundered at Albert, then realized, to his shame, that this was the first time he'd ever yelled at a monarch.

"I apologize, Your Majesty," he said softly.

Albert was more perplexed than angry.

"But I don't understand why you are against this. It was obvious that Sir Sullivan is as well. What am I missing? I – [then he stopped to correct himself] – we, want a child."

"He doesn't even know, does he?" asked Sir Humphrey softly. "This is all your idea."

"It's a wedding present!" said Albert defensively.

"On a need-to-know basis?"

Albert sheepishly smiled, "You can call it that."

"Well, at least I'm in the loop."

"So what are the implications of our having a child?"

To which Sir Humphrey brought his formidable powers of persuasion.

"Your approval ratings are high, as are the Duke 's," explained Sir Humphrey. "And I'm sure that most of the country would be pleased to see a royal baby who finally looks like what the country is becoming. Indeed, I've worried for years that the Royal Family is too monochromatic and doesn't reflect the changes the nation is undergoing with immigration and assimilation. The problem is that the succession is set. Your father approved it. You've approved it; and certainly, Princess Elizabeth approves it. And while your approval ratings are up, hers are abysmal. People, for the most part, just don't like her. They find her to be cold, aloof, and calculating, which she is."

"Then what's the problem?" asked an exasperated Albert.

"The problem, sir, is that with her extensive media contacts, she can cause a great deal of trouble. She can raise doubts in the public's mind, both about the legitimacy of the child, but also about your motives for wanting the child. She can say you are being vindictive and vengeful. She can sow the seeds of discord, and then people will feel they have to take sides, either for or against you. And at that point, we are dealing with the fate of the monarchy itself, especially if people see the Royal Family fighting amongst itself. How can people respect an institution of stability and order when brother and sister are against each other? As a student of history, you know civil wars have been fought over this. Five hundred years ago, you would have an army; she would have an army; and you two would fight it out until one was defeated and the other triumphant, either through skill, force, or luck.

"Today," continued Sir Humphrey, "the gravest possibility comes not from people taking sides, but from people turning away from the whole unseemly situation and coming to see the monarchy as completely irrelevant to their daily lives, more concerned with the succession than with the country's prosperity, health, and welfare. And if people consider you and the Crown to be irrelevant, then the monarchy is finished."

"But it's just a child," insisted Albert.

"No, it's not," contradicted Sir Humphrey. "It's much more than a bundle of joy for you and the Duke to hold on your knees and make funny faces at. Because what Princess Elizabeth could unleash might be far worse than she ever intended. Just consider how quickly the dark recesses of the web, for example, would create its own conspiracy theories and play on people's fears. They could link you and the Duke with plots to turn the dynasty, and they would seek to stop you by all means necessary. I know Princess Elizabeth would never do anything to threaten you or the Duke ; she respects the monarchy too much for that. But the dark forces she could accidentally unleash thrive on chaos and would like nothing more than to bring the monarchy down just to see it crumble and the country fall apart in genuine civil war. All it takes is one person with a gun or a bomb to change the course of history."

Albert was genuinely stunned and disconcerted by what he had heard, but resentful as well.

"So you are advising me to live in fear of my own people, and unable to act fearing the consequences? You know me better than that."

"And you know me well enough that I would never suggest that" explained Sir Humphrey patiently. "We need to be aware of the possible ramifications so that we can prepare for any eventuality while creating the story line we want people to know. It's all about getting there first so that, basically, there's no room for anything else. I don't want you to live in fear. I reject that kind of life. If the monarchy is afraid, then the country has no reason to exist. You have to stand for the best we are capable of being, and you are already a role model for how the monarchy can be an example of diversity, and your marrying the Duke will take the country even further along this most necessary path, and then you two having a child together is a natural culmination of the best this country can be, a country united. So, have your child, if that's what the two of you want, and do not live in fear. We will want the country to eagerly await the birth of your beautiful child, the birth of a prince or princess, and that will overwhelm any voices of dissent.

"Princess Elizabeth will not be happy, and she will cause as much trouble as she can, so I urge you, sir, to speak with her privately before she learns about it from some other source, which would make her needlessly, if understandably, angry. Either way, she won't take it well; but we do need to convince her to take it.

"The problem, of course, is that she looks at the succession through her line as being the only way she can ever get over being Number Two, by eventually being, through her children, Number One. With your child, you will take that last hope away from her. At that point, she will be capable of just about anything. I know that you and she have reached a tentative rapprochement, but that is completely based on the succession of her line. Nothing you say or do can replace that. How can she accept that Victoria will not become queen? There are no good answers for a shattered dream. She must accept the thing she will never accept. Will she quietly withdraw from public life to tend her garden? How can she look at her children and tell them the lives she has told them they will have now will never happen? For her, it will be a family tragedy. How can she look at you, the Duke , and the child with anything other than bitter anger and a desire for revenge? These are all the reasons for you not to do what I know you are going to do."

Albert sat motionless; now even more disconcerted by implications he had avoided considering. He finally realized having a child now, with Paul, would be an act of ultimate selfishness, one that could destroy his sister, the monarchy, and the stability of the country itself.

"So, what do you suggest?" he asked quietly.

"I suggest we wait to see what Sir Sullivan finds out, and then you and the Duke need to decide. I do think the country would joyfully welcome a child. It would keep the succession in a direct line from eldest to eldest to eldest. It has been that way since the first Victoria."

"But she became queen only because her uncle had no direct successor, while I already have one."

"But the child of the Princess Elizabeth is not your child, and the country will understand that. But your sister never will."

"Then that's unfortunate for her," said Albert brusquely. "I won't be controlled by my sister's sensibilities and delusions," and with that he turned to the papers on his desk.

Sir Humphrey bowed and left the room. But he paused outside and leaned back against a wall for support. He felt his heart racing and realized, for the first time, that perhaps he was too old for this job.

CHAPTER 42

Later that day, the men were eating dinner together and Paul commented on the salmon.

"I notice it's broiled, tonight."

"Yes," replied Albert with a smile. "I spoke with the chef, and she was glad to do something different."

"I hope it's not from Balmoral, with the cost and everything."

"No, it's not. I learned there's a royal fish monger in town, so that should make the Scots happy as we're not stealing their precious resources, as they call it. It's still English soil, even if it is in another country," he insisted. Then he added ruefully, "As if anything could make the Scots happy."

Paul looked at him with a smile and said, "I'm half-Scottish, and you make me happy. It must be those magic hands of yours."

"Or my magic something or other," replied Albert with a grin.

"Or other," agreed Paul.

They ate in silence for a while, then Paul asked, "Do you think we could ever order out for Chinese?"

"Chinese?" asked Albert in surprise.

"Yes. I haven't had it since that fiasco with Mum back in Durham and we used to have it regularly. I miss it."

"Well, I'll ask Graham to see how that would work. I don't know if they would believe it was the King ordering General Tso's Chicken."

"And would they just drop it off at the front gate? Is there a royal credit card to pay for it or would they only take cash?"

"I'll check on that, too," replied Albert with a smile.

"I bet you've never even had Chinese, have you?"

"Actually, Papa and I had a wonderful banquet at a palace in the Forbidden City a couple of years ago when we made a new trade agreement with China."

And Paul stopped eating, put down his fork, and realized, yet again, how different were the worlds they were from.

"And you used chop sticks?"

"Of course. Our ambassador taught me before the banquet, and the premier's wife complimented me on my proficiency."

"She probably says that to all the princes she meets," said Paul wryly, and Albert laughingly agreed, "She probably does."

And while the moment was light, Paul felt oddly oppressed, as though visiting a giant gas planet and being crushed by the force of its gravity.

Albert caught the doubt in Paul's eyes.

"What is it?" he asked with concern.

"Just another lesson in how different we are. My mother taught me how to use chopsticks at the Chinese buffet in Durham, while you're eating in the Forbidden City with the premier and his wife. Oddly enough, there was a picture of the Forbidden City at the restaurant. I never thought I'd know someone who's been there."

"But we can both go there, and the premier's wife will probably complement you as well."

"You would arrange a state visit just so I can eat with the premier's wife?"

"No, not just for that. But would you turn down the opportunity?"

"No, of course not. I love Chinese robes."

"Then we'll get you a dozen."

But while Albert was amused at the thought, he noticed Paul wasn't.

"What is it?" he asked again, confused at what could be bothering Paul, because it was clear that something was wrong.

Paul hesitated to speak.

"Tell me," persisted Albert.

"No," said Paul. "It's embarrassing."

"Just tell me. Anything you want, you can have."

Which was when Paul flared up.

"That's the problem, Albert, right there. You will give me anything I want."

"Of course, darling," said a confused Albert.

"But I have no money of my own!" shouted Paul unexpectedly, and Albert, for the first time, realized just how troubling this situation was for Paul, who went ahead and explained it.

"You live in a world where you don't need money because everything's paid for you. And I know I will be on the Royal List after we marry so I'll have an income. But being given money like that is not the world I come from; I earned my money, even if it was on my knees." Albert smiled weakly, not sure where this was going, but feeling he wasn't going to like it. There's a classic American blues song that says [And Paul started singing the Billie Holiday standard], "God bless the child that's got his own; that's got his own.'

"And there's another song that goes, 'Diamonds are a girl's best friend.' Well, I have no diamonds in case the marriage goes potty. I have no money. And I don't want to start soliciting men again; it wouldn't look good for the monarchy to have the King's fiancé arrested for solicitation by a copper in some men's loo."

And Albert could only agree with that.

"But darling, just wait because, as you've already said,

you'll have money after we're married," he said in what he hoped was a soothing tone of voice.

"But I have nothing now!"

"Then I'll get you some money. That's not a problem."

"But it is, don't you see?" asked Paul plaintively. "I already feel like your kept boy, and I know people look at me and think, 'Gigolo. Gold-digger.'"

"Who says that?" demanded Albert. "I'll fire them!"

"That's the problem," explained Paul despairingly. "You can hire people. You can fire people. Whatever you want, gets done, whereas I've always had to work for what I have, and no one works for me."

"But you'll have your own staff," explained Albert in confusion.

"What I'm saying, my darling, is that it's hard for me to adjust to your world."

Unhappily, Albert looked at him. "Are you saying that our love is not enough to bridge the gap between your world and mine?"

"Oh, it is," assured Paul, "Of course it is. But you speak of getting me a wedding gift, and I can't even get you a ring."

"But I can get us both rings," said Albert. "There are lots of rings available."

"Of course," cried Paul despairingly, "You have lots of everything. That's another problem. I want to buy you a ring with my own money, even if it's just gold plated."

"Plated?" asked Albert, in a mock serious tone, until he saw Paul's crestfallen face and realized this was no time for humor.

"Look, my darling, I didn't realize this was such an issue. And I promise that you won't have to wait until we're married to get some money. Let's go ahead and put you and your mother on the foundation payroll so you can start earning money you can keep and that will make an honest man out of you. Will that be all right?" he asked pleadingly.

Gratefully, Paul looked at him and nodded.

They continued eating in silence, then Albert asked, in a tone of surprising despair.

"Why did you say our marriage could go potty? Do you doubt my sincerity? Do you doubt my love?"

And Paul saw the distress he'd caused, clearly evident on Albert's face.

He put his hand on Albert's and smiled with that joy that was healing rain to Albert's parched soul.

"Not at all, my dearest. But if something happens to you, I don't want to end up having to turn tricks in my middle age along the River Wear just to survive."

"No," agreed Albert with a smile. "We don't want that. But I dare say you could tell your story for enough money to make up for a lot of tricks along the river."

"I didn't think royal memoirs are allowed."

"Actually, they aren't and, frankly, I'd hate to see our story turned into a book or, heaven forbid, a BBC mini-series. Maybe we can get an insurance policy on my life."

"Then I hope you reign forever."

"As do I, my dear, with you beside me. Now let's see what's for dessert."

As the dishes were changed, Paul continued his concerns.

"You are difficult to buy anything for," he said. "I want to buy you a wedding present, but it's like you already own everything and in multiple quantities. Even if I had the money, you don't really need another Rembrandt or another copy of the Magna Carta."

"Actually," explained Albert, "I'm pretty sure I don't own a copy of the Magna Carta, but I understand what you're saying. Frankly, there's very little I do own. It's like I'm the recipient of a vast lending program. So much of what I have is owned by the people, or by the Crown, which is not me, even as King. If I had to raise money, I couldn't go out and sell that Rembrandt you mentioned. I'm far from broke. I'm quite a wealthy man, but everything is tied up in different ways and not easily converted to cash. But solving your quandary about what to get me is easy enough because all I really want is you," he said with a smile.

"Which you've already got," pointed out Paul.

"Then give me something you've made yourself. You're creative. Give me something unique. Give me something I can't buy with all the royal treasury, or that even Larry couldn't buy with all his billions. Give me something from you. And hang Rembrandt and the other Old Masters. I never look at that stuff anyway. I must make appointments to see most of it, curators get involved, and it's just a hassle. And so, my darling, give me something of you, something by you, that I can keep right here and not in a vault or gallery someplace."

Touched by Albert's unexpected request, Paul said simply, "I can do that; let me give it some thought."

As they finished dessert, which turned out to be chocolate mousse, Albert said, "Do you know what I think to myself when I hear people say, on the telly or someplace, that they want to be happy as a king?"

"No," replied Paul with a smile, "What do you think?"

"I'm reminded of Benny Hill's old line, when he'd look at the camera and say in that stentorian voice of his, 'BIG --------DEAL!'"

"Benny Hill?" retorted Paul sarcastically. "He's so last century."

"Okay, smarty pants, what young Brit comics do you

like?"

Paul thought for a minute, then sheepishly replied that he didn't know any.

"I spent my time studying and practicing."

"And tricking down along the river," added Albert.

"And tricking down along the river," agreed Paul.

"Well, my grandmother loved Benny Hill and had him appear at several royal galas, and even my parents and Lizzie and I watched him on the telly. Reruns, of course. He was before my time, you know."

"So, you say," replied Paul.

"I'll tell you what," said Albert. "At our first benefit gala, we'll invite a roster of upcoming, young Brit comics and we can decide for ourselves which ones we like best. Besides, I have the Royal Box at Covent Garden. Best seats in the house, and it will be so much fun to watch the ladies with their opera glasses turning from the stage to watch us instead. That's a show in itself."

"You can't deny you live in a different world," explained Paul. "Anyone else wanting to compare Brit comics would just go to YouTube to watch them, whereas you bring them all together for a gala."

"It's a great life, isn't it?" asked Albert grinning.

"It's certainly a different life," admitted Paul. "And it's one I'm trying to adjust myself to, I really am."

"But it's a world I want to share with you. And the reason I mentioned Benny Hill's 'Big -------- Deal!' is not that I don't recognize or appreciate just how incredibly lucky I am, and I'm certainly not going to go on about being just a bird trapped in a gilded cage. See? I know old American songs, too," Albert said archly. "But you already know how lonely and isolating my life is."

Paul just nodded.

"But what makes the crown bearable, my darling, is you, my beautiful man, with whom I can share my life. I know fully how lonely Papa was in his widowhood, but at least he had years of companionship with Mummy to remember and savor. I wondered if I would ever have anyone, and then you came so unexpectedly into my life. If I hadn't gone to Durham that day, you probably would have found a nice boy there and settled down with him and made a life together and enjoyed your Chinese buffet and we never would have met. We never would have shared the thrill of sneaking out for pizza, or a gala with British comics, or simply looking at each other across the table. You bring me so much joy that, at my coronation, I will willingly put on the crown because I will be able to share it with you. I owe you so much that, frankly, I wish I could give you a copy of the Magna Carta right now."

And with that, dinner was done, and they went to bed, but not to sleep. Later, as Paul lay in the arms of the already dozing Albert, he looked around and realized, with great finality, that he wasn't in Durham anymore.

CHAPTER 43

And so, the weeks went by, as the palace was officially in mourning for a month, and Albert restricted his public appearances, and the family and household staff wore black armbands. But much was going on behind the scenes to plan and prepare for the royal wedding, the coronation, and the royal tour of England and Wales.

Very little was released about the wedding, and what little was known was parsed and dissected by the public and media alike, and what wasn't known was filled with gossip and speculation, and by none more so than Princess Elizabeth.

"The wedding will be bigger than ours."

"Of course it will," calmly explained Larry. "He's the King, while you were . . . ." And his voice trailed off.

"The also ran," filled in Lizzie.

"Still, your father went all out for you. There was the procession, the horse-drawn carriage, people lining the streets, the Abbey was full."

"I think they papered the room to do that."

"Well, I did have to pull in some favors from business associates," he joked feebly then, seeing her crestfallen face, he hastily added, "Not at all, my dear. Trust me, no one must cajole people to attend a royal wedding. They showed up from everywhere. And your father footed the bill, which must have cost a not-inconsiderable fortune.

"Besides," he continued, "This wedding is special. Monarchs are typically already married when they ascend the throne. The first Victoria was the last monarch unmarried at her coronation, and before that it was probably Henry the Eighth, and he's certainly not the comparison the palace will want the people to associate with Albert."

"Did I tell you I used to play Henry while Albert was Anne Boleyn?"

"Yes, dear," replied the ever-tactful Larry. "And I can just imagine you standing with feet apart, hands on your hips, and with a magnificent beard."

"You mean like this?" and Elizabeth stood and struck the Holbein pose.

"Except your beard's a little scraggly."

"Hormones will cure that."

"You mean I must be married to the country's first transgendered queen? If so, then I'll ask you to shave before I kiss you. That may appeal to Albert, but not to me. And tell me again why he, Paul, and Pauline are coming here this afternoon?"

"It's like I told you, he called himself, not his appointment's secretary, and said they'd like to visit us [Larry had already noted with relief that Lizzie had finally stopped referring to Paul as 'the Durham slag.'] and the children, if you can believe that, for a picnic, of all things, and Pauline specifically wants to see the garden, which touched me."

"I never thought of you as the picnicking type."

"Oh, certainly not after Mummy died. We only tried it once and the three of us just sat there on our plaid blankets, just looking at each other, and thinking of what we'd lost. It was dreadful, and we never did it again. But we used to picnic all the time when Mummy was alive – at Balmoral, of course – but also at Sandringham and even at Windsor.

"Sometimes it was just the four of us, but often there were cousins and, once, they even invited the Romanovs. That was a horrid experience. They brought their own servants and even their own food and drink. I guess it was borscht and vodka. They even brought their own china, with that emaciated eagle on it. And while we were all supposed to be together, they kept to themselves, except for a moment when they trooped over to see us and just sniffed. It was a disaster, and they were never invited back. I was too young, of course, to pick up most of this, but Papa talked about it for years. He was dreadfully insulted, especially as they owe their lives and their throne to us."

"So why are you and Michael such good friends?"

"Well, he's the gay brother I never had. We're catty, opinionated; we love to gossip and talk on the phone. Next to you, he's my best friend."

The picnic went better than anyone thought possible. It was held on the vast lawn beyond the gardens, beside the lake. There was a large blanket for the adults, and another nearby for the children. There were immense wicker hampers for food, drink, plates, glasses, and utensils.

The children gobbled their food and soon were playing on the grass. Paul joined them, and somehow a rugby ball was found. Though he had little time for athletics in school, rugby was the one team sport he enjoyed. He showed the children some of the more esoteric aspects of the game. Lizzie showed Pauline the gardens, and Larry and Albert watched from their blanket.

Pauline was most impressed with the gardens, which were not well known as they weren't open to the public for much of the year.

"You've done an amazing job here, Lizzie" said Pauline, who had dropped the formal "Ma'am" as the princess had dropped calling her Dr. McGregor.

Lizzie loved showing the gardens to those who were truly interested in them, particularly the area tended by her and the children. She was impressed at the thoughtful questions Pauline asked, and with how she actually listened as Lizzie explained her experiments with soil nutrition and her theories of garden design through similar and contrasting arrangements of annuals and perennials, flowers and shrubs.

Eventually the children joined them, and Pauline started to tell them about how plants absorbed nutrients and water, and how they responded and adapted to changes in the environment. The children were fascinated, and Lizzie realized Pauline was a natural teacher who got right down in the soil to make her points, and how she made a point of addressing each child on her or his own level, and not just showing respect for Princess Victoria, as so many did, while ignoring the others.

Later, when they were alone, Lizzie told Larry how much she had enjoyed the day, especially the time with Pauline.

"I invited her back," said Lizzie. "And you know my idea to set up a foundation to bring gardens to inner-city schools? Well, I think she's the one to start it. Yes, I know she is working with Paul to set up some kind of foundation with Albert, but she said she would be pleased to help with the initial organization and then to continue as a consultant."

This was an idea that Lizzie had considered offhandedly for years without doing anything to make it happen. Inwardly, Larry smiled at the idea of sibling rivalry having such positive benefits.

At the end of the day, as Albert, Paul and Pauline were preparing to leave, brother and sister stood awkwardly at the front door, while the limousine was waiting. They looked at each other, these two people who were not the touching kind, then Lizzie stepped forward and surprised Albert by kissing him tenderly on both cheeks.

"Come back," she said. "You know where I live."

"I'd like that," he said with a genuine smile. Then there were hugs all around and soon the car was speeding across the

Suffolk countryside.

At first, the three of them talked about the day and how well it went, especially to Albert's surprise, and Pauline mentioned Lizzie's surprise offer about organizing the foundation, which she hastened to assure Albert and Paul she could manage to do in addition to their own.

"It's a matter of priorities and good staffing," she said, and, besides, doing both would keep her constructively busy, which she needed, with her energy level. But then Paul and his mother noticed how preoccupied Albert was as he stared at the passing scenery, turned golden in the soft evening light, and they started talking softly between themselves to leave Albert with his thoughts.

He hadn't seen Lizzie so happy in many years and, frankly, this was the first time he'd even seen her gardens or spent any considerable time with her children, most of whom, he reluctantly realized, did have necks after all. And, once again, he was struck at how mature Princess Victoria was for her age. Lizzie was training her well. The succession, he realized with dismay, was in good hands, which made the idea of him and Paul having a child together needlessly redundant. Even now, when she was still just nine years old, Albert saw in Victoria the makings of a monarch, so how could he entertain the idea of having a child of his own when he knew that would destroy the tentative rapprochement, the tender affection, brother and sister now felt for each other, and had obtained with such difficulty? Indeed, it could possibly destroy Lizzie, who staked her happiness on her children's succession, if not her own.

How could he do it to her? It could shatter the Royal Family, as Sir Humphrey predicted, by forcing people to take sides in what could easily become a modern kind of civil war that would shake people's faith in a stable monarchy and could even topple it.

What was he thinking? He's just become King, after years of training for the position, and now could he be the one to end a thousand-year tradition? Was it simply vanity and ego? Another sign of incurable self-indulgence? And how could a child possibly add to the love that he and Paul already shared?

Everything, absolutely everything, warned against the folly of such an act. Why bring a useless, needless child into the world? One whose existence could destroy everything Albert stood for.

He continued to stare through the window at the passing countryside, and saw his own reflection in the glass, along with the reflection of Paul and Pauline beside him. He felt the presence of Paul's body next to him. And at that moment he realized he loved Paul so much that he wanted his child regardless of the consequences. He wanted a tangible representation of their love. Otherwise, at the end of a lifetime together, all they would have was fading memories. But wasn't that all anyone ever really had? Why should he be any different? And at such a ghastly cost, which, possibly, could be not less than everything.

Finally, he realized there was no rational point to be made, no logical connection, that would justify what he wanted to do. All he knew was that he loved Paul so much that he wanted to have his child. He hoped that would be enough to convince Paul this very night when he planned to finally broach the subject.

CHAPTER 44

It wasn't. The men were in bed, sitting up and facing each other. Paul was angry, and this was the first argument they'd had.

"No! I won't have it! What a stupid idea!"

Albert was shocked at this unexpected vehemence and, frankly, did not understand it.

"It will destroy your renewed relationship with your sister, so tenuously achieved; it will destroy the Royal Family; and it could bring down the monarchy. Besides, we don't need a child! What's the point? The succession is set. Changing it now would only make people question your sincerity. It would make you appear vindictive. They would turn against you and that loss of trust is the one thing a monarch cannot afford to lose. People would question the very value of the monarchy and, at that point, it's a very short distance to abolishment. Is that the legacy you want to leave? The King who abolished the monarchy? Because that could easily happen. There are many just waiting for the slightest scandal to press the case that the monarchy is a useless institution, completely unconcerned with the needs and concerns of the people and having this child would just feed into that. You don't realize how fragile your base of support really is.

"Besides, Albert, I'm a nineteen-year-old gay man. What do I want with a child? And what kind of parent could I possibly be?"

Paul finally stopped talking as he saw Albert's ashen, perplexed face, and realized he'd said too much. He relented, leaned back against the headboard, pulled Albert against his shoulder, and brushed Albert's hair with his fingers. In a much more conciliatory tone, he said, "Oh, my sweet, sweet man. I know how much you love me. And I know you see a child as the consummation of our love. But we don't need a child to prove anything. At the end of our lives, after, hopefully, many decades together, think of the memories we'll have and all we will have achieved together, the good you can do, the foundation, and so much more. Let all of that be our many, many children. That will be all the legacy we need."

Then he stopped talking but continued holding Albert until Paul fell asleep. Albert was unable to sleep, but kept his head against Paul's chest, listening to its calmly beating heart. He knew Paul was right. He'd already heard and thought all those reasons not to go where he wanted to go. He understood everything.

"And yet . . ." he thought. "And yet . . . "

CHAPTER 45

Two weeks later, Paul found Albert collapsed and unconscious on the same bathroom floor where Albert's father had died less than two months previously. Paul quickly knelt beside him and ripped his shirt open. The buttons skidded across the tile floor. Paul pressed his ear to Albert's chest, and heard a heartbeat, though faint and irregular.

"Help! Help! The King!" he shouted.

Soon, an ambulance was dispatched to the palace, and, upon arrival, the emergency team raced up the stairs with a gurney. Word had quickly spread through the palace, and staff watched with concern as the King, strapped to the gurney, was taken back down to the ambulance and carefully, but quickly, put inside. Paul tried to enter but was stopped. "Against policy, sir." But at Paul's look of despair, and knowing who he was, the emergency technician stepped aside and said quietly as Paul entered, "Just keep out of the way."

With sirens blaring, the ambulance headed to the hospital. Graham was somehow already there and working with his staff. Knowing Albert was alive, Graham worked on the assumption that he would recover, just as Sir Humphrey did, who was being driven to the hospital and was already on his mobile with the palace press secretary crafting a brief, non-committal statement to the effect that King Albert had collapsed due to stress from overwork and would spend two days, at least, in hospital for observation and recovery.

He next phoned Princess Elizabeth, wanting her to hear the news first from him and not from the media which, he knew, would soon have the story. He quickly explained the situation and assured her that Albert was alive and would be thoroughly examined in the emergency room.

"I'm coming in," said Lizzie.

"No need," assured Sir Humphrey. "Everything is under control," with an assurance he really didn't have.

"I'm coming in," she insisted, speaking from her country home.

He didn't want this as he fully understood how it would appear to the nation to have the successor attending to the King in hospital. It wouldn't look good.

"Albert's had some kind of attack," she told Larry, who was standing beside her during the call. "Paul found him and now he's being taken to hospital. I'm going in. Stay here with the children until I see what's going on."

Next, Sir Humphrey called the Prime Minister to inform her of what happened. She said she would await developments.

En route, Albert was quickly hooked up to monitors and diagnostic equipment that sent his information to the emergency team already assembled and waiting for the King's arrival, so the doctors on duty had some idea of what they would face. Sir Sullivan was also on his way and expected to arrive shortly after the King.

Paul was impressed with the team's cool efficiency as they went through the check list of procedures, and in constant contact with the emergency room. Albert remained unconscious and pale, though a drip had already been inserted through a needle in his arm. Paul said nothing; asked no questions; and, as ordered, kept out of the way as best he could in the cramped space. His worried presence was not questioned. One of the crew looked at him reassuringly, so Paul was cautiously optimistic.

When the ambulance reached the emergency room entrance, the doors were flung open, and Albert was quickly taken inside. As Paul exited and followed him in, he noticed barricades were set up to contain the expected crowds of media and spectators. Sir Humphrey was already in the waiting room. He nodded to Paul, and both wanted to follow Albert into the emergency room but were stopped by a physician who crossed his arms and blocked the way.

"But I must go in!" thundered Sir Humphrey. "It's the King!"

"I know who it is," explained the physician calmly and patiently "Our team knows what it's doing. And since you cannot help, we're taking you to a private waiting room and someone will be with you just as soon as we know exactly what we're dealing with."

He already had a good idea based on the information he'd received, but he wasn't going to say anything until he knew more.

Sir Humphrey was a man unused to being thwarted, but he looked at Paul, who nodded acceptance of the situation, then smiled grimly, and nodded in agreement. As an orderly led them to the private waiting room, they noticed Sir Sullivan in hospital scrubs heading into the emergency room. He glanced at them and gave a "V for Victory" sign, which reassured them both.

By now the media had made the first announcements about the King's collapse, and reporters and TV crews were already outside awaiting developments and repeating for the cameras what little information they had. While the web was already rife with rumors that the King was dead, most people were content with waiting to hear the expected updates, and Sir Humphrey awaited the arrival of the press officer who would deal directly with the media.

Meanwhile, he and Paul were both too agitated to sit down. Paul explained how he had found Albert, how the emergency team had entered the bathroom, quickly checked the King's vital signs while strapping him to the gurney, and how he'd followed him to the ambulance and the subsequent trip to hospital.

Both men kept staring at the wall clock, with its slowly moving second hand and its even slower moving minute hand. Five minutes . . . ten minutes . . . Then Pauline came into the room and glanced quickly at Sir Humphrey, who nodded to reassure her. Paul said, "Mum!" and rushed into her arms and, for the first time since he'd met Albert, started crying. She held him comfortingly and said, "My baby. My poor baby." But her consolation was quickly over as she held him out at arms' length, then took a handkerchief from her purse and dabbed his tears. In some ways he was still a child, but now he was also consort to a king.

"Paul, look at me," she said, so he did.

"Albert's alive, isn't he?" which she said as a statement and not a question. He nodded. "Then he's going to live and thank goodness you found him when you did. Now we are going to wait until the doctors tell us what happened, and what must be done so this doesn't happen again. Do you hear me?"

"Yes, Mum."

Sir Humphrey looked at her and mouthed, "Thank you." She just smiled at being more knowledgeable about handling young people than Sir Humphrey. She then sat in a chair and pulled Paul into the chair beside her, held his hand, and the three waited, with Sir Humphrey stepping outside frequently to keep in contact with the press office.

The second and minute hands continued going around. Fifteen . . . twenty minutes . . . The three were relieved that Albert was alive but stressed at not knowing the details.

Twenty-five minutes then Sir Sullivan came into the room

and looked at the three with a smile.

"The King is awake and conscious," he announced to general relief, as no one, least of all Paul, wanted to deal with a second royal funeral in less than two months.

"He's had a mild heart episode, not a heart attack," he insisted. "Likely brought on by stress, and the same arrhythmia that killed his father."

"I thought he died of an aneurysm," said Paul.

"He did," replied Sir Sullivan, "which I think was caused by his arrhythmia, which affected his heart in such a way that blood was not completely pumped out of his lower ventricles, which caused blood clots to form, one of which lodged in his brain to cause the aneurysm. Both the arrhythmia and potential clotting were controllable with medicine, which I prescribed to him for years, but he started taking them irregularly and I don't think he was taking them at all by the end. If the queen were still living, she would have made sure he followed his prescribed regimen. As it was, without her, he became willfully stubborn, which seems to be a genetic trait."

"But you, young man," and he looked directly at Paul. "I expect you to make sure this King follows his medication promptly and in the prescribed amounts. Can you do that?"

"Oh, can I!" said Paul with a smile.

"I'm sure you can," agreed Sir Sullivan. "So, you can see him, briefly," he said to all three. "Then he'll stay in the emergency room for a couple of hours to monitor his condition before he's taken to the royal suite. And yes," he said, anticipating Paul's question, "You can stay there as well."

All three were relieved at the good news, and Sir Humphrey let Paul and Pauline see the King first, while he stayed to talk with the press officer about how to explain the heart issue to the media.

The press officer wanted to stay with the original story, that the King had collapsed from overwork and exhaustion, but Sir Humphrey overruled that on grounds that any attempt to cover up the truth would ultimately be revealed, and to the discredit of the palace, which would only fuel media and web speculation that the King's health was worse than it was. Being open now would save a great deal of trouble later, reasoned Sir Humphrey.

Meanwhile, Paul and Pauline were led in to see Albert, who was lying back in bed with his head raised, and with a host of monitors and various I.V. drips attached to him, while breathing through an oxygen tube in his nostrils.
He was smiling, but obviously weak, and still pale.

Paul leaned over and gently kissed his forehead, and then admonished him, "Don't ever scare me like that again!"

"I promise," said Albert abjectly. "I think another royal funeral would bankrupt the country!"

With his paternalistic air, Sir Sullivan, who had also entered the room and was carefully hovering over his patient, admonished the King that he would need to take the same medicines prescribed for his father, and probably for life.

"Promise me you'll always take them. Always!" insisted Paul with an urgentness that both confused and touched Albert.

"For you, anything," he said. "Yes, of course I'll take them."

The attending physician entered and said the King needed rest, but the group could wait outside for him to be moved to his private suite. As Paul reached the door, he looked back at Albert and mouthed the words, "I love you."

Albert merely winked, then closed his eyes to rest.

Princess Elizabeth arrived shortly after Albert was moved to his suite. She was so relieved to see Pauline that she went to her first and both held each other tightly before she turned to Albert, who replied with mock jealously, "But I'm the one who collapsed. And I'm still alive so you're not queen yet."

"Well, I'm glad you are and, frankly, I'm relieved," admitted Lizzie honestly. "And this is a good time to tell you, all of you, what I've been thinking about since your visit, particularly after talking with Pauline," who looked at her quizzically. Lizzie turned to Albert and spoke to him directly.

"I want you to live a long life and to rule for decades. I finally realized I'm not Queen material. I can do the job, but my heart's not in it. I'll continue as a working royal, and especially with my . . . our [and she looked gratefully at Pauline, who smiled and nodded back] foundation but, most of all, I want to be home, cultivating my garden and raising my children, and I can't do that as monarch, so I'm stepping out of the line of succession and Victoria will follow you, Albert. I can already tell she has the bearing, and the ability to thrive in your position. I just don't want to lose what I have. "How odd," she mused softly, "that for all my life I've wanted to be queen more than anything else, or so I thought, until I started talking with Pauline and asking myself what is truly important in my life. And now I know, and being queen isn't on the list. Frankly, Larry is relieved as well as he wants to stay with his own foundation. So, if that's all right with you, Albert, that's what I want to do."

The others, including Albert, were shocked at Lizzie's announcement as it went against everything, they'd thought about her, for years in Albert's case. For Pauline, it signaled just how far her new friend had come in, knowing what she genuinely wanted to do and not just leading the life that was expected of her. For Sir Humphrey, the decision meant an end to the often-rancorous conflict and verbal squabbling of the siblings who, for too many years, seemed little more than unruly children ruled more by short-term emotion than by long-term duty and responsibility. As for Paul and Albert, it meant . . . Well, they weren't sure what it meant.

As Lizzie prepared to leave, she told Albert that she would be staying in town for a few days, and that Larry and the children would be coming down as well.

"They're looking forward to seeing both their uncles," she explained. "Albert and Paul." Then she kissed Albert gently on the forehead, as Paul had done, much to Albert's surprise. She held Pauline once again, said goodbye to Paul and Sir Humphrey, then left.

A nurse came in, bowed to the King, and stood beside the opened door, making it clear that the visit was over. Sir Humphrey and Pauline bowed to Albert, then left. Sir Humphrey had already directed the palace staff to bring appropriate clothing for both men during their stay and for their eventual return. The nurse showed Paul the spare bedroom where he would spend the night though she also agreed, when Paul asked, that he could just sleep in the armchair beside the bed.

"Just don't bother him," she quietly insisted. "He needs to rest."

Paul nodded as he settled into the chair, but he was in no mood for sleep.

When he had so curtly rejected Albert's idea for a child, that was when Paul still believed that, basically, the two of them would live full lives. Now it was shockingly apparent that that might never happen. Albert could well be dead now, he thought to himself, "And what would happen to me? What would I be left with? A few memories, shattered hopes and dreams. Nothing, really, to show for what could have been: a shared life, achievements; all gone. And what could I do? I can't go back to Durham. What would I be good for? What has he left me good for? No. My old life is dead. Better to go into seclusion, like Dietrich or Garbo; then people could say, decades and decades hence, that 'He was a great beauty once. He was the consort of a King.'

"How could there be so little to show for such great passion?" he asked himself. "But a child – our child – would make everything different. Part of him would remain, part of our love would remain. I cannot let that go. I must have his child."

Only after making that decision was Paul able to sleep.

The night was filled with nurses and doctors coming in to check on the King, who remained in a sedated sleep, while the constant intrusions didn't bother Paul, who was aware of them, but whose concern was only for Alfred, so he kept looking at each person who came in for reassurance, and was relieved at simply a smile or a nod.

The next morning there was another round of visits. Sir Sullivan, for example, now dressed again in an elegant suit, pronounced himself satisfied with the King's recovery; again, emphasizing to Paul the importance of Albert taking his medicine regularly and, if so, he would likely live a long life.

Finally, during a rare moment of quiet, Paul reached over from his armchair to take Albert's hand. Now awake and alert, Albert appreciated this moment of affection, while wondering if Paul was going to say something. Paul hesitated, then said what he'd planned to say.

"You asked me a question some time ago and, though it's odd to say after what you've just been through, I know my answer broke your heart. It seemed right at the time, but since you collapsed on the floor, and not knowing if you would live or die, I've changed my mind. I want to have your child, regardless of the consequences."

Albert was overjoyed, and tried, unsuccessfully, to hold

back unkingly tears. He pressed Paul's hand gently to his lips and said quietly, "That makes me the happiest man on earth."

Sir Humphrey arrived at the hospital and, in consultation with the doctors, decided, since Albert was recovering so well, that he would return to the palace the following day, though with a greatly reduced workload.

The departure was a photo-op for the media to see the King walk outside the hospital and thank those who had cared for him, the hospital and emergency room staff, as well as the ambulance squad for their quick response and subsequent expert care. He waved to the press and public before entering the car, informally attired, for the drive back to the palace. He ignored shouted questions, but a release from the palace, in his words, thanked the responders and hospital staff for their attention that facilitated his recovery. He also thanked the British people for their good wishes.

For his first day back, Albert stayed in bed, with Paul beside him, who was hesitant at first to even touch him.

"I'm not going to break," replied an amused Albert.

A nurse in attendance was asked to stay outside the bed chamber, much to her dismay.

"That's not procedure, Your Majesty," she replied curtly. "I'll have to report this to Sir Sullivan."

"Of course," said Albert gently, "And I realize this makes your job harder, but the Duke and I want to be alone."

She nodded, resignedly, and left.

He wanted Paul to himself, without feeling constricted by any kind of social protocol. Paul carefully got into bed next to Albert, but they had only a few moments left before they heard the shouts of children racing through the royal apartment, then the doors were flung open and Lizzie's brood rushed into the room.

"Uncle Albert! Uncle Paul!"

And they gleefully jumped onto the bed, while Paul rather ineffectually said, "Careful now!" Two squeezed in between them, the others on either side. Lizzie and Larry followed in and sat on the edge of the fortunately large bed. The nurse rushed in and was prepared to scold but demurred at the King's look asking forbearance. She bowed and left.

"The children insisted on seeing you, now," explained Lizzie. And they demanded to hear all about what happened, how Paul found Albert on the floor, and how much blood there was. They were greatly disappointed to learn there was no blood. Then they demanded to see the scar and to hear all about the surgery; and were disappointed again to learn there was no surgery and no scar.

"Then what's the point of hospital at all?" asked one.

"Your Uncle Albert's heart went off a little and had to be corrected," explained Paul.

Not to be put off, they insisted he tell them all about the ambulance ride and the siren and the dash to the hospital.

"If you'd died, then I would be queen," said Victoria excitedly, who had already been told of her mother's decision to step aside.

"Well," explained Albert, "Actually your mother would serve as queen regent until you were old enough to be queen in your own right.

"Oh," said a crestfallen Victoria. "I thought I'd be queen right away."

"Not quite, darling," explained a slightly embarrassed Lizzie. "But when you were ready and old enough, then you'd be queen."

"I see there's already competition for my job," said Albert with a smile. "At least I know the Crown will be in good hands," as he and Paul exchanged a glance that Lizzie caught but didn't understand.

At that moment, Pauline came into the room.

"Aunt Pauline!" shouted the children as they rushed from the bed to her and held her about the legs. By this time Lizzie was standing and came over to greet Pauline as well. They held each other over the kids and kissed each other warmly. Pauline had heard Lizzie, Larry, and the children had come to visit.

Victoria told Pauline proudly that "If Uncle Albert dies soon, then Mummy becomes queen regent until I'm old enough to rule."

"Well, it's a relief to know things are in good hands," said Pauline with a smile, who caught another glance between Albert and Paul that she didn't understand either, as though they shared a secret.

Now the nurse entered again, grimly determined, bowed, and stood with her arms folded over her chest to signal the King needed to rest. The children weren't ready to leave, but Larry and Lizzie gathered them together and herded them out, under the nurse's watchful eye.

Pauline followed them, but turned back to stare at the men, who stared back at her innocently enough, so she relaxed, smiled, bowed, and left.

Some days later, after Albert had returned to work on a reduced schedule, Pauline came into the King's study to see Paul leaning over Albert and studying some papers. They looked up, startled to see her, and she noticed Albert covered the papers over as he greeted her fulsomely.

She studied them both and realized something was going on that they were keeping from her.

"What are you two up to?" she asked with a smile.

They looked at each other sheepishly, having been found

out. Then Albert nodded to Paul, who looked at his mother and said, "Mum, we have an announcement to make."

"That's what people say when they are expecting a baby," she replied, then the truth suddenly dawned on her.

"No!" she said vehemently.

"Oh, but it's possible! The child will be from both of us," replied Paul eagerly, if disconcerted by his mother's obvious displeasure.

"You misunderstand me," explained Pauline coldly. "I know it's possible, but just because it's possible – "

"Doesn't mean we should do it," interjected Albert angrily. "Yes, we know that."

"Well, if you know that, then I assume you're equally aware of all the reasons not to do this, especially the harm it will do to Lizzie."

"Yes. Yes. We know all of that," replied a furious Albert.

"And you're content to go ahead with this madness anyway?"

By now, both men were frustrated with her not understanding their side.

"You don't realize just how fragile your sister is, Albert."

"Fragile?" he sneered. "She's always scared me. She's always been stronger than me."

"That's her act to cover up her deep insecurity. So why do this now that she's basically renounced the throne in favor of her daughter?"

The men stubbornly looked at each other, then glared back at her.

"She's the first true friend I've had here, and I already love her," explained Pauline pleadingly. "If you go through with this, she will blame me for duplicity and she will never trust me or talk to me again. There is no way she would understand that I haven't been part of what she will, understandably, see as a plot to deprive her children of their legitimate right to the throne. How can you do this?"

"Mum!" said Paul in a strained voice. "When I saw Albert laying on the floor unconscious – "

"Let me guess," interrupted Pauline. "You decided your love for Albert was so great that you just had to have his child. Am I right?"

Paul just nodded, sullenly.

"But he didn't die. And you're going to make sure he doesn't die from here on by seeing he takes the medicine that will prevent this situation from recurring. So you two will have long lives together, creating memories for decades, and achieving great things for the country with the foundation and all the other accomplishments you will have, and those will be your children."

"That's easy for you to say," replied Paul curtly. "because you at least have me, after your marriage failed."

If the words were meant to hurt, they didn't; Pauline simply continued.

"But your father wasn't King," she explained curtly, as to a child. "It was just he and I, and then there was you, and when he left, it was just you and me, the two of us. But now this involves the monarchy and the kingdom, so much is at stake, beyond your own selfish desires. You can't possibly do this."

She looked at the two defiant, stubborn men before her.

"But you're going to do it anyway, aren't you?"

Their silence was their answer.

"So, this is the moment when, if I were a stronger woman, I would leave, go back to Durham, and never see you again."

"No, Mum!" pleaded Paul, and Pauline finally broke, and realized she could never leave her son and Albert alone.

"But I'm not that woman, unfortunately," she admitted.

"But this will cost me my friendship with Lizzie. I will stay, not because I want to, but because the child will be my grandchild, and despite having the best governesses and teachers in the world, I won't let the child be raised without my support and love because I, frankly, don't know what kind of fathers you will make."

She smiled briefly, for the first time, which gave the men hope, but she quickly grew serious again.

"This is a mistake, and I know it will not end well. But I will stay. I will stay."

Paul got out of bed and rushed to hold her tightly.

"Thank you, Mum. I love you so much."

Then she put her arms around Paul and held him close, but she turned to Albert with a look of such unhappiness that he finally turned away.

The nurse came in again, bowed, and said, reproachfully, "The King must rest."

"Of course," replied Pauline as she let go of Paul, bowed to Albert, and then left. The nurse stared at Paul, then at the King, accepted the situation, then turned and quietly closed the door.

"Come here, my handsome man," said Albert gently as Paul returned to bed and laid his head against Albert's chest, hearing the beating heart that brought the man he loved so close to death. Albert enfolded him with his arms and held him close. Paul was upset, and it took a long time for him to sleep, whereas the King was so troubled he couldn't sleep.

"This will end badly. This will end badly."

Pauline's words haunted him. He realized she was like the Sibylline prophetess sought by kings before making a momentous decision to know whether their choices were favored by the gods and fate. He knew this was the defining moment of his life, the most important decision he would ever make, one that would draw a line between what happened before now, and everything to come.

This was that moment in classical tragedy when the choice a King made would steer him away from the abyss or hurl him, screaming, into the depths as the world collapsed around him. He could still turn back, and no one would be harmed. Or he could continue on this path and defy the gods and fate and taunt them until he was broken.

"So, you understand that?" asked the goddess, who appeared before him beyond the bed.

"You know I don't believe in you," said Albert with a smile.

"You pathetic man, as though I need your validation and belief to exist. I'm here to make sure you understand your choice, and the foreseeable consequences of that choice."

"You mean there may be unforeseeable consequences?"

"There are always unforeseeable consequences."

"But if you know them, and I assume you do, then tell me so I can make a more informed decision."

"You don't need to know more than you already do about the consequences of the child you want. And nothing will change your mind, will it, Albert? You are determined to have a child. But beware . . . beware."

And then he woke up, not even realizing he'd been asleep. He touched his forehead. He was sweating. But he looked down at Paul, sleeping peacefully on his chest, and thought to himself, "I love you so much. Our child will be so beautiful."

CHAPTER 46

The weeks leading up to the wedding were busy as plans were checked and rechecked. The military units, the bands, the pipe corps, everything needed for the procession through the city, was organized. The state carriage was cleaned and polished. The matched horses chosen to pull it were carefully groomed. The silver and brass bits and other metal parts of the harnesses were polished. The city was in an increasing state of excitement as an event unique in British history approached: the marriage of a King to his male favorite.

The Archbishop met with Albert and Paul to review their vows, part of which he let them write themselves as a nod to the occasion. He wanted to make sure they were not caught by surprise during the actual ceremony by its traditions and rituals.

The irony of an atheist King and, well, whatever it was that Paul believed in or, probably more to the point, did not believe in, was not lost on any of the three.

The Archbishop made it clear that, as the event was a sacred ecclesiastical ritual in which the King, as official head of the Church of England, despite his personal beliefs, – which were quite well known – he, the Archbishop, could not and would not alter the idea of marriage as a commitment sanctioned by God. However, in his homily he would recognize that these two men brought the strengths of their own, unique understandings to the relationship as well.

He also recognized that the commitment to "obey" was out of step with the times and, indeed, it had already been replaced in many other marriage ceremonies at which he had officiated with the idea of trust or fidelity.

Still, he emphasized to Albert that while the wedding ceremony could be tailored in some aspects to the personal expectations of the participants, that would not be allowed during the forthcoming Coronation , whose ritual was set by precedent and would take place without alteration.

Albert curtly said it was best to leave that discussion until after the wedding, and the Archbishop gladly agreed, while noting the King's unexpected tone of defiance.

He did ask about Paul's religion and was not surprised – considering his mother's animism – when Paul said he was spiritual, but not religious. So, the Archbishop was in the odd position of marrying two people in one of the major rituals of the Church of England, neither of whom believed in it. He realized he needed to take a "big picture context" of yet another unprecedented aspect of the current monarchy.

He explained to Albert and Paul that some conservatives within the Church, even some bishops – though not, he hastened to add, to Paul's relief, the Lord Bishop of Durham – were already deriding the marrying of two men, let alone two unbelievers, as a mockery that would not stand in the eyes of God.

"That is not my position, of course," he said. "Nor is it current Church policy, which has finally accepted, at least within the European and American branches, the marriage rite as a commitment between two people of any gender," especially two people obviously so much in love with each other, he thought to himself while looking at them both. He avoided mentioning the resultant schism among certain conservative branches in other parts of the worldwide organization that had fragmented the church, probably irreparably.

The wedding rehearsal at St. Paul's went reasonably well. Sound and light checks had already been done to ensure there was adequate lighting for the cameras that would broadcast the event worldwide, and to make sure that the exchanges during the ceremony could be heard throughout the vast space, as well as for broadcast.

Albert had asked Sir Humphrey to be his best man, a role he had filled at his father's wedding as well. The old man was touched at the honor and repeated his own vow to serve the monarch in whatever capacity was needed, for which Albert thanked him, and resolved to give Sir Humphrey a special commendation at the next honors.

Pauline would give Paul away, as it were, and she realized that maybe it was time for another formal dress, in addition to her Durham dress in which she had met the late King.

After the rehearsal, there was a family dinner to which Sir Humphrey and the Archbishop, and their wives were also invited.

Paul, noting his mother in deep conversation with the Archbishop, pointed them out to Albert beside him, who leaned over and quietly said, "I wonder how long it will take before she converts him?"

Paul added with a smile, "I don't think he has a chance."

Princess Elizabeth, Larry, and the children were stretched out along the table. Like Albert, Paul, and Pauline, Lizzie had been asked for interviews by the media, which were particularly interested in her thoughts on the marriage. She gave precedence to gardening magazines and was careful to arrange her children close to her when photographed working in the gardens. However, she was disturbed to find that the photos were frequently cropped for publication to show just herself and Princess Victoria, as the child the public was most interested in seeing. In the interviews, Lizzie took care to always mention how Pauline [always "Dr. McGregor" in these formal settings] would be helping her set up her own new foundation.

That was a point Pauline also emphasized when she was interviewed. As the King's soon-to-be mother-in-law, she found herself to be in great demand to talk about her son but, also, about herself. Her Jamaican roots were considered exotic, but she regretted articles on the order of "Poor emigrant Black girl makes good."

She tried to emphasize Paul as much as possible; while not denying the conflicts he faced as a mixed-race gay boy in the North, without getting specific. She came across as a mother fiercely proud of her son's accomplishments, and eagerly anticipating working with Paul on the foundation that he and the King were starting, in addition to her organizational work with Princess Elizabeth, and it became apparent to palace watchers that Dr. McGregor was already a member of the Royal Family to be reckoned with, and appreciated both for her intellect and her judgment.

Still, the bulk of the media interest was in the marrying men, continuing the frenzy that surrounded the engagement announcement, which seemed so long ago now. They were photographed in gardens, in drawing rooms, or at their side-by-side desks. They recognized the unique opportunity to represent a more inclusive Britain, and understood that photographs of them, in love, side by side, spoke more to their goals for the country than any words they could say.

They made a point of being open to a variety of media opportunities, not just professional media outlets, but, for example, to the student newspaper at St. Giles, and to its female counterpart in Newcastle. There was a grammar school class in Wales that interviewed them via Zoom, and a Progressive Workers paper in Liverpool, as well as the gay press from around the world. The two of them seemed to be on the cover of every magazine, as well as news shows, newspapers, and across the web, in the days before the wedding: "Royal Poof Marriage Mania" according to one headline. The media wasn't always kind.

Paul and his mother were especially amused by enterprising reporters who sought out former classmates of his who, to a man, swore their school days had been filled only with acceptance and encouragement for the obviously talented young man. No, never any trouble, they agreed, as Paul, somewhat bitingly, pointed out to Albert that those who had violently abused him years before now, ironically, had no recollection. Nor, to their mutual relief, did anyone mention any encounter down along the river.

"That would be hard to see on world-wide television, and I wouldn't want to read the online comments," explained Albert. "What's being said is far better than what could be said," to which Paul could only agree.

Both he and his mother had side-stepped questions about his father, her husband. Just the facts, nothing else. So enterprising reporters went to Scotland to find the elusive Patrick McGregor, though with little success. They did learn that after leaving his wife and son to fend for themselves, he headed north where he bought a pub, lost that, then worked as a bartender, got fired, then drove a beer truck, only to be fired again, and then a host of odd jobs, menial in nature, and then he dropped out of sight. There was some indication that he may have died a homeless vagabond in Glasgow, and possibly buried in a pauper's grave, but no one knew for sure. Well, Graham and Sir Humphrey knew for sure, but kept it to themselves, knowing that Paul and Pauline had put the wastrel in their past and wanted nothing more than to forget him.

Graham was busy coordinating security between his teams, police, the military, and domestic intelligence. The wedding was viewed as a run-up to the coming Coronation, now only a few months away, and what was decided now would be a blueprint to be used then. Of greatest concern was, naturally, the increasing number of threats, mainly in the dark recesses of the web, including potential assassination plots to create panic and chaos, in addition to possible riots. The wedding route was checked and rechecked for weak spots, places where snipers could find clear aim. The wedding, like the Coronation, was to be a joyous day, and Graham and Sir Humphrey were working diligently to keep them that way. Police would, naturally, line the route's barricades, but the regimental horse forces were mainly for show. The true strength would be present, but not obvious. What was below ground was also a worry, what with the city's vast subterranean array of tunnels, sewer and water lines, transportation tubes and shafts that ended in manhole covers to which bombs could be attached.

Graham wanted to make sure that the words of the old Noël Coward song came true: "Long live the King, if he can. And if he can he'll be a most remarkable man."

Commercial enterprise was having a field day. London hotels were already booked to capacity, and people even seemed to be listing little more than closet space for those desperate to attend. Indeed, rooms in the Midlands were being booked for those who didn't mind the commute by train or road. Airline flights into the city were also booked for days on either side of the wedding.

Souvenirs, ah, souvenirs. Take your pick: plates, mugs, scarves, towels, buttons; each with some version of the royal couple, both those officially registered, and the inevitable and unavoidable cheap knockoffs as well. Production lines were busy at every price point.

Souvenir shops were sprouting up all over town, and

pavement vendors would be out as well. One of the most popular items, especially on various home-shopping channels, was Albert's now-famous blue pullover sweater. The high-end versions were hand-knitted cashmere or merino, while cheaper versions were machine-knitted acrylic. Whatever the material, it didn't seem to matter as everything was selling.

Finally, it was the evening before the wedding. Finally, Paul and Albert were alone after a busy and heavily scheduled day. Paul was tired and just wanted an early bed, knowing the stress the morning would bring, which was when Albert looked at him and asked, "Where's my bachelor party?"

CHAPTER 47

"Your what?" asked Paul.

"My bachelor party. I'm the chief bachelor in terms of age and rank, and I want my party."

Paul was dumbfounded because that was the one thing he'd never even considered.

"Get our friends together and give me a party," demanded Albert.

"First, we don't have any friends," explained a tired and frustrated Paul. "Second, are you expecting a giant cake with some beefsteak nude model popping out of it?"

"That would be nice," said Albert grinning. "Let's start with that and see where we end up."

"If I can't come up with that within the next five minutes, do you have a backup plan?"

Albert thought about it, then said he'd rarely been to a pub, rarely had fish and chips, and had never pulled his own pint.

"That would make a perfect party for me."

"Don't forget that I was raised in my father's pub and was pulling pints by the age of five," explained Paul, "though I had to stand on a chair to reach the handle."

"Does that mean we can't go?" asked Albert perplexed.

"No," replied Paul. "It's just clear, once again, that there were significant differences in our respective younger years. What's novel to you, in this situation, is old hat to me."

"So, make me happy. Let's do this. How do we make it happen?"

"First, I tell Graham."

"Really?" asked Albert in a pique.

"I promised him after the pizza fiasco, and now that you're King it's even more important."

"All right, all right," said Albert resignedly. "Do what you must."

Paul pulled out his mobile and held it so Albert could see what he was doing. He pulled up the number for palace security to make a text call, and then simply pressed the number eight.

"That's it?" asked Albert in surprise.

"That's it," replied Paul with a smile.

"You mean I've been reduced to a code?"

"Yes."

"Am I that predictable?"

"Yes."

Albert was perplexed and angry.

"So, what does Number Eight stand for?"

"Going out the rear."

"You're kidding," said Albert in disbelief.

"Not at all. That's your plan, isn't it? Slipping across the back lawn, then over the fence?"

"I know a place where we won't be seen."

"You said that before. There are cameras everywhere. This is London. You're the King. We will be followed, but discretely. Graham assured me we won't even be aware of it."

"So much for freedom of movement," groused Albert.

"Again, you're the King. You have no freedom of movement."

"Well, I'm still leaving. What kind of disguise should I wear?"

"Considering we are now the most recognizable men on the planet, I say you could wear a full hijab and still be known. So, let's just go as we are. Let me get some money."

Paul finally had some of his own, and soon they were making their way across the Great Lawn.

"This is so like 'The Prince and the Pauper'," said Albert enthusiastically.

"I loved that book as a child," replied Paul.

"When was that? Last week?" asked Albert sarcastically.

Paul unceremoniously stuck out his tongue at Albert, who just laughed. "Actually, it was one of my favorites as well."

When the text was received in the palace security center, an on-duty team member called out, "Number Eight. Alpha and Little Dog are headed out the back."

The staff was instantly alert as the officer on duty made sure the planned arrangements were in effect.

"Plain clothes team out back?"

"Check."

"Can the new cameras pick up the license plate if they go by cab?"

"Yes, ma'am."

"And a van to follow the cab?"

"It's getting into place now."

"Once Little Dog texts specifically where they are going, I'll let Graham know so he can get there first and begin surveillance."

Then they waited for Paul's text.

Paul was waiting for the reaction of the cab driver when he recognized his new fares, and he wasn't disappointed. The cabby's eyes widened in disbelief in the rear-view mirror.

"Your Majesty. Your Majesty." And he awkwardly tried to bow while in the driver's seat and nearly hit his head on the steering wheel. Finally, he regained his composure and asked, "Where do I have the great pleasure of taking His Royal Highness and the Duke?" in, once again, a distinctive Pakistani accent.

"My good man," said Albert ebulliently, "We are looking for a pub with the best fish and chips in town. Where would that be?"

"Only one place for you, Your Majesty, and that would be the Cock and Bull."

"You're joking," exclaimed Paul.

"Not at all, sir. It's famous."

"Then take us there, my good man," replied Albert magnanimously.

The driver bowed again as best he could, and said, "With pleasure."

Paul hid his mobile as he texted the pub to security.

"Ma'am, they're going to the Cock and Bull."

"So," said the security officer to her assistant, "He wants to see how the rest of us live."

Graham and his team were already on their way.

There was no small talk in the cab as the driver couldn't think what to say and Albert was occupied with the sights of London.

Graham and his team stopped in the alley behind the pub. The backdoor to the kitchen was open on this warm, humid summer night. He stationed one there and took another inside with him. They passed a storeroom at the back, then the wash station, and finally they entered the kitchen.

One of the kitchen staff saw them enter and asked curtly, "Who are you blokes and what are you doing here?"

Graham already had his royal security I.D. out and showed it to the man, but another member of the kitchen staff, thinking they were immigration officials, took off his apron, threw it on the counter, and started to make his escape to the front.

Graham called out, "We're not immigration officials. You're fine."

The man stopped, hesitantly turned, then sheepishly put his apron back on and returned to work.

"The manager?" called out Graham as the entire kitchen staff had stopped working and were looking at the two.

"Here," said a young woman. Graham quickly filled her in, explaining he and his team were providing security for a pending visit. He didn't need to explain who was coming as the royal security I.D.'s said it all.

"Now just return to work and we'll stay out of your way."

They found a darkened recess from where they had a good view of the crowded, noisy pub out beyond the open serving counter that separated the kitchen from the front, without being too noticeable to the patrons who were talking loudly, and eating and drinking on what was basically a party night for the entire city.

Meanwhile, Graham arranged that one of the team following the cab would stay out front while another would stay inside near the front door. He directed the King's car to park a block away until needed. Albert and Paul would not be taking a cab back to the palace.

The cab pulled up outside.

"Thank you for an excellent trip," said Albert.

"My gratitude, Your Majesty, at choosing my humble vehicle," said the cabbie, who got out and opened the door for the King. Despite the pub being crowded, the few people out front were so occupied with their own affairs that they ignored the unexpected royal couple standing on the pavement. Over the front door was a large, old-fashioned wooden sign with a carved rooster and bull.

Paul knew the driver expected a royal tip and was pleased

at the man's profuse thanks as he pocketed the sum he was given.

As the cab drove away, Paul and Albert paused for a moment at the door.

"This is going to be quite an experience," said Paul.

"That's precisely what I want," replied an eager Albert.

Paul opened the door and Albert entered. Despite being crowded and noisy, and with loud music playing, Paul and Albert were quickly recognized.

"The King! The King is here!" ran through the crowd. The music was abruptly turned off; those seated at tables stood up, men doffed their hats and caps, and the men and women awkwardly bowed or curtseyed, not quite understanding what was happening.

"My good people," proclaimed Albert. "As you may be aware, the Duke and I are getting married tomorrow."

At that, the patrons broke into applause and cheers, then Albert held up his hand for quiet.

"And when the Duke asked me what I wanted to do for a bachelor party, I said I wanted nothing less than the best fish and chips in London, so here we are!"

The crowd again began cheering and applauding, and a pathway opened to the bar, where a barmaid awaited them, while Graham and his assistant watched carefully from the back of the kitchen.

As Albert and Paul approached her, the barmaid turned back to the kitchen and said across the counter, "Two fish and chips, and make 'em special."

Then she turned back to the King and Paul and asked, "Now, what would Your Majesty and the Duke like to drink with your meal?"

She was already holding two mugs by their handles.

"Actually," replied Albert rather sheepishly, "I was

wondering if I could pull my own pint?"

Another cheer went up.

"Let him pull it!" yelled several patrons.

"Of course, Your Majesty, seeing how's it's your wedding tomorrow and all. You two just come 'round 'ere."

And she directed the King around the end of the bar, so he could stand beside her as she gave him a mug, and handed the second to Paul, who had followed and wondered doubtfully just how this was going to go.

Albert had never pulled a pint in his life, but he took the mug, held it directly under the spigot, then pulled the handle. Soon there was a pool of stout on the floor, and his mug was filled primarily with foam.

"Cracky," said a man, "He can't even pull a pint!"

To save the situation, Paul stepped forward, gently moved the surprised Albert to one side, expertly tilted his mug under the spigot, and filled it with only a thin head of foam. He drank half of it down, wiped the foam off his lips with the back of a hand which he then rubbed on his pants. The pub erupted in cheers.

"Ata way, lad!"

"That's how we do it in Durham, mates!" cried Paul gleefully.

Albert was relieved at escaping an embarrassing situation, but also felt a twinge of jealousy, and wanted to prove himself at something else. He looked around the pub and saw a dart board on a nearby wall. He went to the dartboard and people tactfully backed away as he approached. He pulled the three darts out of the cork and stepped behind the line he saw marked on the floor. Now the crowd's attention was on him again, and Paul wondered, and dreaded, how this would turn out.

As with pulling pints, Albert had never thrown a dart in his life. He wasn't even sure how to hold it, and the intense scrutiny of the crowd didn't make it any easier, nor did the number of phones held up recording the moment. Still, he prepared himself, took a deep breath, and threw the dart at the board. He'd obviously held it the wrong way because the dart missed the board, hit the wall, and fell, clattering, to the floor.

"Blimey," said one man into the ensuing silence. "He throws like a girl!" And many agreed as the mood in the pub darkened. Rattled, but undeterred, Albert aimed again, and this time the dart at least stuck into the wall. There were groans again, and a few titters, from the patrons, who were not pleased with what they saw.

Once again, Paul stepped forward. He took the remaining dart from Albert, then pulled the dart from the wall and picked up the third off the floor. He moved to the line but then took four paces back to be even farther away. A few cheered his bravado, and a man said, "Now we're going to see summat!"

Paul took careful aim and threw his dart, which hit the exact center of the target. A cheer went up, and Albert was visibly impressed.

"That's why we brought him from the North," he explained. "To teach us a few things."

And several people laughed, which Albert appreciated.

Then Paul tossed his second dart, placing it slightly to the right of the first dart, and then put the third dart close to the left. The pub erupted into cheers, and Paul raised both fists high into the air.

"That's another for Durham!" he shouted.

By now, he and Albert just wanted to eat and leave, but as they made their way back to the bar, a tall, burly man blocked their way, who was obviously deep in his cups.

"So, Your Majesty," he said with a sneer, "You can't pull a pint. You can't throw a dart, and you use our tax money to live in those grand palaces of yours. So, tell me . . . Your Majesty . . . just what are you good for?"

Now Albert was not a short man, but he had to look up into the face of the man who towered over him. But Albert wasn't afraid. He just wasn't sure, yet, how to respond. And then the man stepped even closer and roughly tapped his finger on Albert's chest.

"I want to know, exactly, what you're good for?" the man repeated, this time with a threatening growl.

"Back off, Georgie," said a man.

"Yes, Georgie, back off," said another. "It's the King."

And Paul stepped forward to get between Albert and the man, but Albert put out his hand to stop him. At the back of the kitchen, Graham's assistant started forward, but Graham held her back, whispering softly, "The King wanted to meet his people, so here they are. If we pull him out now, he'll always be afraid of them. And they will, forever, lose all respect. And not just here in the pub but look at all the mobiles recording this event. The whole world will laugh at this. Let him figure out how to deal with it."

So, his assistant waited with Graham to see what would happen.

"What's your name, mate?"

"I'm not your mate."

The King looked at the man kindly.

"I'm Albert," he said, and then held out his hand and continued to look until the man turned away and said, almost shamefully, "George. Named for your father. I was born two weeks after him."

And then George turned back and shook Albert's hand.

"And a very good name it is, too, George. And you are correct. I can't pull a pint. I can't throw a dart, and I have very little real power. So, you've asked a very good question: just what am I good for? What use is the monarchy? And I ask myself those questions all the time."

The pub was silent, with everyone staring at the King; and so that everyone could see him, he stood on a chair.

"The most common answer," continued Albert, "is tradition, that a thousand years of royal blood flows through my veins. But that's not as exclusive as it sounds because those monarchs had so many bastards along the way that probably half of you in this room are my cousins," a comment that brought a chuckle from most of the people, and from the back someone called out, "Cheers, Cousin Albert!"

"And cheers to you, my cousin," said Albert with a smile, before turning serious again.

"But tradition is the past and doesn't help you now. It doesn't get you a job or keep a roof over your head. So, what can I, who has so little power, do about those issues so critical to your everyday survival and well-being? Not much, directly."

"So what good are you?" shouted a woman.

"Not much at all, in practical terms."

"Then get the hell out!" shouted a man, "And give us your money so we can do something with it!"

And many of those present agreed with an undercurrent of assent.

"You're right, again," replied Albert easily. "I do live in a palace, several nice palaces, actually; and the monarchy itself is immensely wealthy; so what can I do to deserve all that wealth since it seems only a matter of luck that I will shortly wear the Crown whilst none of you ever will? And I can't simply snap my fingers and give you [And he pointed to a man in the pub not far from him] a job or see that your child has an adequate education [And here he pointed to a woman]. No, in our society, it's the politicians – the Prime Minister and Parliament – who have the power to formulate policy and to allocate funds. The thing about politicians, though, is that they are elected, and I'm not. I was born to the job. And it is a job. I have an office and sit at my desk, as Paul [And Albert held out his hand to him, and Paul nodded slightly] can attest since his desk is next to mine. So now you know that I have a hereditary job with very little power, a complete waste of money, you could say."

"A complete waste!" yelled someone along the wall.

Albert smiled, then continued. "But not being political means, I stand outside the electoral process, with no need to run for office, to curry favor from you, the voters, no need to compromise. It gives me a very different perspective, which is clear when I meet the P.M. every week. Her eyes are on the polls and the party and the next election, whilst I'm here for life, or until you overthrow me or abolish my office [There were only a few chuckles as no one could see where this was going]. That gives me perspective to take a long view and to see what can be done for my people – for you – which I know sounds very paternalistic, and no one needs a father-figure, especially not one who is a relatively young poof like me, when what you really need is a hand paying the bills. Am I right?"

And there was a murmur of agreement.

"We also don't need a father-figure because most of us want to stand on our own two feet and make some- thing of our lives. But it's hard, isn't it, to see someone like me who starts life with so much, with so many ad-vantages, and the obvious question is how we can level the playing field to give everyone an equal opportunity, an equal start so that at the end of our lives we have really accomplished something."

Albert paused, then continued.

"It's true that I have been given much; indeed, more than

anyone in the country. So, you can rightly expect more from me than from anyone else as well. And you know that I'm not the only member of the Royal Family. The Princess Royal, my dear sister, Elizabeth, maintains a full schedule of activities and events; she has her royal duties to fulfill. But after doing those, what she enjoys doing most of all is spending time in her garden and with her children. My sister is a nurturing person. She nurtures and trains her children so they can reach their full potential and, eventually, succeed me to the throne. And she nurtures and tends to her garden, so all the plants she cultivates there can also reach their potential.

"Now, I don't have her green thumb. I hardly know which end of a plant goes in the ground [And Albert was encouraged by the number of those who chuckled at his attempt at humor]. But I look at myself as a kind of gardener, only my garden is the entire country. Like my sister, I want to nurture my garden so every tree and shrub and flower can reach its fullest potential.

"I'm always asking myself, how can our country achieve its greatest potential for everyone, not just a lucky few who, like me, are born with a nice roof over our heads. I'm reminded of Dr. McGregor, Paul's mother, who came to this country from Jamaica with basically only her talent and her ambition and has achieved preeminence in her field by building one of the country's premiere research centres. And she is going to help Paul and I establish a new foundation whose goal is to recognize and to support outstanding and important programs around the kingdom, from both urban and rural areas, that provide unique educational opportunities and help create that level playing field we want, so everyone has the chance to reach their fullest potential. And every week, when I meet with the P.M., I ask her how many jobs have been created this past week. How many educational opportunities have been provided? How many homeless people have been sheltered? How many seniors are getting the health care they need? And she shares my concerns.

"Together [Now Albert was getting even more enthusiastic], yes, together we can make this island, minus Scotland, of course [He smiled broadly, and there were a few hoots and catcalls] into a verdant, bountiful, beautiful garden where everyone can have a satisfying job, where children are given the educational skills they need to succeed; where everyone has decent housing and good medical care. And now, here at the Cock and Bull, I, Albert, King of England and Wales, give you, George and everyone else, my solemn oath that I will work for you and your children and your children's children all the days of my reign. And George, if you or any of you others decide I am not true to my word, I want you to let me know. I'm in the phone book under 'B' for Buckingham Palace!"

He stopped talking. There was complete silence in the room, then it erupted into cheering. Graham caught his assistant's eye and smiled, as if to say, "See? I told you so."

Albert smiled in the victory he had achieved and then looked down at Paul and winked. He got off the chair and stood beside Paul, then raised his hand for silence. He put his arm around Paul, then leaned forward and kissed him full on the lips. Paul returned the kiss, and the room erupted in cheers again. And that kiss was seen around the world as it was captured by many in the pub with their mobiles. It went viral within the hour.

Still with his arm around Paul, Albert said, "You may have heard that we are getting married in the morning."

More cheers.

"And if that's not a lead into a song, I don't know what is. You may be aware that Paul, the great love of my life, has a great singing voice. [There was scattered applause], while mine is more of a croak. We are now going to sing you a song that is quite appropriate to this place and moment."

Paul looked at him dubiously.

"Now we haven't planned this. In fact, you can tell that Paul doesn't know the song I have in mind, but you'll see how quickly he catches on."

Knowing he was trapped, Paul knew the best thing to do was to accept the situation and make the best of it. "You lead," he said, "And I'll follow."

Albert, with the words alone, no melody, said, "We're getting married in the morning."

Then stopped so Paul could repeat them. Then, still speaking, "Ding, dong! the bells are gonna chime."

Then he stopped again while Paul repeated them. Then Albert started to sing and quickly realized that Paul knew the song after all.

> "Pull out the stopper!
> Let's have a whopper!
> But get me to the church on time!
> I gotta be there in the mornin'
> Spruced up and lookin' in me prime."

Then Albert continued by himself.

> "[Lads], come and kiss me.
> Show how you'll miss me.
> But get me to the church on time!"

By now it was clear that many of the patrons also knew the song as they joined in, and those who didn't caught on as best they could, even just humming the tune.

> "If I am flying

Then shoot me down.
If I am wooin'
Get [him] out of town!"

Unseen by Albert, Graham and his assistant started making their way through the crowd and towards the front door, where the King's car was now waiting outside, with a van for Graham and his team behind it.

Meanwhile, the song continued as everyone by now joined in. Albert saw Graham at the front door, who motioned to him. Albert caught Paul's eye and motioned towards the door, and they slowly made their way towards it through the crowd while continuing to sing.

"For we're getting married in the morning!
Ding dong! the bells are gonna chime.
Feather and tar me.
Call out the Army
But get me to the church,
Get me to the church,
For Gawd's sake, get me to the church on time!"

By now Albert and Paul were at the door and turned back to face the pub's patrons who broke into boisterous cheering. Once again, Albert held up his hand for silence and looked across the room to the barmaid and said loudly, "Set 'em up, me darlin'. Drinks all around!"

The crowd cheered again and rushed to the bar. Albert turned to leave, but said to Graham first, "Pay the tab, and make sure we get our fish and chips. Order enough for your team as well."

Graham smiled and nodded but, standing in the doorway and holding out his hand to prevent Albert from leaving, he leaned over and said softly so only the King could hear, "Never do this again without checking with me first."

Albert raised his hand in a vow.

"My salad days are over."

Graham nodded, relieved, then stepped aside so Albert and Paul could get into the waiting car, and they headed out into the London night.

Future historians looked back upon the visit to the Cock and Bull as one of the defining moments of Albert's reign.

Seeing Albert on the telly later that night brought back Lizzie's incipient sibling rivalry that she thought had been completely buried.

"It's the night before his wedding and he's everywhere!"

"People love him," said Larry. "It's a public relations coup."

But her jealous anger remained unabated until she watched her (slightly) older brother mention her, her garden, and her children, with such kindness, respect, and obvious love that she was genuinely touched, and realized how much she had wronged him for so long.

CHAPTER 48

The men awoke early on their wedding day and were dressed by their valets in their respective clothing, with Albert wearing the scarlet uniform of a colonel-in-chief of a Welsh regiment, and Paul in formal morning attire. When ready, they looked at each other in the mirror.

"You look good enough to eat," said Albert.

"That's for tonight," said Paul with a grin.

Albert noticed the two valets looking at each other, trying not to smile.

"That's fine," he told them, smiling slightly himself. "You may go."

"Very good, Your Majesty."

They bowed and left.

"I've heard that, historically, kings and their consorts had to consummate the marriage with officials and courtiers looking on."

Albert looked at him with amusement.

"Have you seen a court around here?" he asked. "There are no courtiers; hardly any equerries; and not a lady-in-waiting. My grandmother had two ladies-in-waiting, and my mother had two. I liked Lady Margaret. She used to bounce us up and down on her knee."

"Were you sixteen at the time?" goaded Paul.

"That's a state secret," replied Albert archly. "And as for people watching the consummation, you've seen too many BBC costume dramas. We're not back among the Tudors and the Stuarts."

"So, I guess the issue of whether or not I'm a virgin is a

moot point."

"Very moot, my dear."

"But I thought members of the court watched to ensure the King did his royal prerogative and actually copulated with the queen, just so there were no substitutions."

"Again," said Albert with a smile, "I don't think that's an issue with us."

"And wasn't the royal birth also observed, to make sure there were no changelings, for example, and that the child was truly of royal blood?"

Albert stopped smiling and looked directly at Paul.

"Just what is your point?" he asked.

"My point is that I'm concerned about this upcoming gene splicing where your genetic material is combined with mine."

"I still don't follow."

"What if there's a substitution?"

Albert just looked questioningly at Paul, who explained, "Let's say a male lab technician decides to substitute his own genetic material for yours or mine."

"But why would he do that?" asked a puzzled Albert.

"Just think about it," persisted Paul. "What lab technician could resist the opportunity to insert his genetic material into the royal line? Even if he never told anyone, he would know he'd interfered with the hereditary link you're always talking about that makes you and your sister so unique and would alter the line forever."

"But who would do such a thing?"

"Who could resist?" countered Paul.

"You're remarkably suspicious this morning."

"I just want to make sure that our child is indeed our child."

"But it's being done at Oxford!"

"As you keep quoting Benny Hill: BIG . . . DEAL! Are they no longer human at Oxford? Are they on some supra-human moral plane of existence?"

"So what do you want done to prevent this genetic substitution that worries you so much?"

"I want Sir Sullivan and my mother present at the mixing of our genes. I want them to verify that the child will be wholly ours."

"But neither of them are geneticists."

"No, but they are both doctors and they can make sure my fears are not confirmed."

"And that will satisfy you?"

"Yes. This procedure and the resulting child have now become very important to me."

"Then it's done, my dear. Have no fear. They will attest that our child is indeed ours. Now, our wedding breakfast awaits."

They kissed each other briefly on the lips, took one last, lingering look at the handsome, well-dressed men in the mirror, then went to the wedding breakfast.

The meal was attended by those who'd attended the rehearsal dinner, with the addition of the Lord Bishop of Durham, sharing, at Paul's request, the duties of the ceremony with the Archbishop, who had gladly agreed. However, earlier in the week there had been a testy meeting between the two prelates regarding the respective religiosity, or lack thereof, of King and Duke. The Lord Bishop was surprised to hear what the Archbishop had learned during his meeting with the men, that Paul was more of an animist, like his mother, than anything else.

"I can't believe Paul is a pagan!" he thundered. "After all these years of singing in the cathedral choir, I assumed he was Church of England. He sang for all the services."

"And he told me he respects the Church and its sacraments, and he specifically asked for your participation. He admires you tremendously."

"And I was delighted to accept. I like the lad, and he was one of our best singers: disciplined, never missed a service that I recall, did extras like funerals and weddings." He grimaced. "And now I find out that he was lying. A non-believer?"

"Did you ever ask him , or were you making the error of assumption? Lying is when you're asked and then deny. Besides, do you require that choristers be Church of England?"

"No," admitted the Lord Bishop, "but it is presumed."

"Ah," said the Archbishop with a smile. "There you go. So who knows what variety of beliefs and non-belief you have represented among the choristers?"

A thought that the Lord Bishop found suddenly disconcerting.

"Besides," continued the Archbishop blithely, "It's the harmony of the voices that matters and, these days, I find it amazing that young people of any persuasion still want to sing in church choirs. That says much for the strength of tradition. And I told the King that he would not be the first royal atheist to lead the Church."

"You said that?" asked the Lord Bishop in disbelief.

"You know it's true," replied the Archbishop.

"I thought his atheism was just part of the role of the roué he played for so long. You know this will cause trouble for the Coronation."

"He knows that, but we've agreed to put that off for now as we both want the wedding to be a time for unsullied joy. Don't you agree?"

And he looked almost defiantly at the Lord Bishop, who

replied skeptically: "By uniting two non-believers in one of the Church's most sacred sacraments?"

"I find them both to be earnest in wanting to be married under the auspices of the Church. It is a sacrament they are both vowing to uphold."

"A sacrament neither believes in?"

"A sacramental consecration in which they both desire to be recognized by the Church. They are setting an example to the country when so many these days have no desire at all to be married in the Church."

"But how can it be valid if they don't believe in it?" persisted the Lord Bishop.

"I believe they honestly want the Church's blessing on their union. And can't the arms of the Church open wide enough to embrace them? Where is our compassion? Where is our mercy?"

"I'm not sure I want to be part of this mockery," said the Lord Bishop with finality, which made the Archbishop carefully consider his next words.

"The Duke wants you to officiate with me. He specifically asked for you. It's been announced. For you to back out now would cast a shadow over the whole ceremony. It won't look good for you, and it won't look good for them. People will question what's wrong and could doubt the validity of the marriage itself. Please don't let that happen as it would color the King's entire reign. Do this for me, as an old and dear friend, and do it for Durham as well. What an honor this is for you and the city. Would you really like to see this honor pass to Salisbury or Chester?"

The Lord Bishop thought about this for a long time, as the Archbishop worked at his desk. Finally, he spoke.

"For you, and Durham, and Paul, I'll do it."

"Well done, my old friend. This will make the King, as well as Paul and I, very happy. It's good to do the King a favor because you never know when you might need one from him."

But all of that was now behind them as the two men sat cordially side by side and shared the breakfast table's general conviviality. The children were particularly excited at the idea of riding in horse-drawn carriages and had pestered their mother to take them to the stables to see the horses being curried and primped for the occasion. Already, at the age of nine, Princess Victoria loved to ride more than almost anything and was thrilled to mount bareback several of the large horses who would pull the various carriages.

Lizzie looked around the table with satisfaction she thought she'd never feel again in the family. She realized it was practically a miracle that Paul and his obvious love for Albert had changed her brother in ways she never dreamed possible. He'd actually turned into a mature man, surprisingly caring and thoughtful, and she realized that Albert could make a greater monarch than their father.

For her part, Lizzie felt only relief at stepping out of the succession. She had never considered the stress she had imposed upon herself for years and that now was completely gone. She credited that not only to Albert's change of heart, but also to the advent of Pauline into her life who, almost unconsciously, had shown her options she never knew she had. Her jealous obsession with Albert's status as the older sibling and first in line for the throne, had blinded her to the reality that she no longer wanted the monarchy. And with the idea of a foundation made possible with Pauline's organizational skills, Lizzie realized she could make a lasting and worthwhile contribution to the country without being trapped in a largely ceremonial role as queen. With Pauline at her side, and as a friend which, she belatedly realized, she'd never had before, Lizzie felt finally ready to take her own place, and to make her own way, within the Royal Family.

She looked benevolently around the table, and smiled contentedly at Albert and Paul, at Pauline, at Larry and their children, and realized that she had much to be thankful for and that, for the first time, her position within the Royal Family actually made her happy. She looked forward to the coming day, to seeing Albert marry a man he genuinely loved, and knew that Victoria would be a worthy successor.

She stood up.

"A toast," she said, and raised her glass. "To my dear brother, Albert, and to Paul; may their love grow through the years."

"To Albert and Paul," said the company as they also raised their glasses.

"And to my beautiful, darling Victoria, the future queen," she added.

"To Victoria," agreed the company.

But Lizzie noticed another glance between Albert and Paul that she didn't understand; neither did she understand why Pauline was looking down at her plate. And she nearly panicked right there as dark specters of doubt and fear came to reclaim her, but they quickly passed like a summer squall. The anticipatory joy of the approaching wedding swept away all other possibilities, and she smiled broadly at those looking so eagerly at her.

"To life!" she said gaily.

"To life!"

Then it was time to descend the great stairs and greet the assembled staff, to enter the waiting carriages, and then pass through the gates to the waiting day beyond.

CHAPTER 49

One did not need the perspective of history to realize that with the wedding of Albert and Paul, the British monarchy entered the modern age. Commentators around the planet tiresomely pointed out that, as of this day, the Royal Family finally started to resemble the diversity of its subjects.

And so, the many weeks of planning began to unfold as the wedding procession started from the palace. Motorcycle units of the Metro police were followed by the mounted cavalry of the Household Brigades resplendent in their uniforms and shining, plumed helmets. Albert sat alone in the 1902 State Postilion Landau, then another group of the Household Brigade preceded Paul and his mother in the Glass Coach, separated by another regiment of the Household Brigade from Princess Elizabeth who, with Larry and their children, followed in an open landau. More mounted brigades followed them, and eventually street cleaners came to pick up the horse dung before it was crushed into the roadway.

From the palace, the procession entered the Concourse and went around the Queen Victoria Memorial, whose steps were crowded with media photographers, then along the Mall, past St. James's Park, through the Admiralty Arch to Trafalgar Square, where it entered the Strand to make its way to Fleet Street, then Ludgate Hill, and finally to the steps in front of St. Paul's Cathedral to be met by the Archbishop, the Lord Bishop, and the Dean of St. Paul's.

Along the way were stationed detachments of Foot Guards of the Sovereign's Escort, along with members of the Metropolitan Police, who faced the throngs of spectators standing behind thousands of steel barricades.

Military bands, including a kilted bagpipe unit from Northumberland – now that Scotland was independent – were also located along the route.

What members of the Royal Family later remembered most about the procession was the sheer, physical sensation of the sound of the crowd, the pressure of its exuberant roar against the eardrums, that lasted all the way from the palace to St. Paul's.

It was a day for smiling and the royal wave, which Paul and his mother had already practiced, so their hands would not be worn out during the nearly half-hour procession.

Graham and the Royal Wedding Office at New Scotland Yard had carefully planned security, as the number of bomb threats and assassination attempts had swollen to a tidal surge. Overhead were camera drones keeping an eye on the buildings along the route, while underground tunnels were securely guarded. The route was closed the night before as a security measure, and plainclothes police were in the crowd. Their job was not to watch the procession, but to watch the people watching the procession.

Albert, alone in the lead landau, was most exposed, but he was determined to show his people that not only was he fit to rule but fit to love as well.

"How was I so lucky to find Paul just at the moment when I needed someone most?" he asked himself as he waved and smiled to the crowd.

"He saved me by allowing me to mature into a king from the brash hedonist I was as the Prince of Wales. How could I have survived Papa's death without him? And after this day we'll start the procedure for having a child of our own and announced after the Coronation so people can see the entire Royal Family, perhaps one last time in this configuration, as a symbol of continuity and solidarity."

Meanwhile, Paul and Pauline found it odd to be enclosed in the covered Glass Coach, which made it seem as though they were on exhibit in a kind of moving goldfish bowl, which they were. Both looked resplendent, with Paul in his morning coat and top hat, and with Pauline in purple silk, with a matching hat. She tightly held Paul's hand while both continued to wave. Yet even here, even on this day when the world was watching, there was still the occasional shout of "Poof!" and "Queer!", and Pauline would grasp his hand even tighter. But those short, hateful words lost their power to hurt in the vast, supportive cheering of so many others who had looked forward to this day without equal in British history. Paul and Pauline were also encouraged by the frequent shouts of "Go Durham!", at which both always laughed.

Yet Paul himself was haunted by his very position in the procession, between Albert and Lizzie – too symbolic, it seemed to him, of coming between brother and sister – while acknowledging that it was the marriage, and the addition of his mother into Lizzie's life, that had led to the current reconciliation. What tore at Paul was knowing the reconciliation was temporary, and that what was coming would permanently rip the family apart. And all because of a child.

Pauline was amazed at how quickly her life had changed. She'd thought that coming to England had been her life's defining moment, yet here she was, riding in a glass coach beside her Cinderella of a son and recognized around the world. But all of that was meaningless next to the approaching tragedy of the loss of Lizzie's friendship, and how the change of succession would destroy the family. That reality made each interaction with Lizzie – and now they were daily – so unbearable, and yet she could say nothing. Pauline knew Albert would not tell his sister until the procedure and implantation into a host mother was successful.

Until then, she would enjoy Lizzie's friendship as best she could, until it ended forever.

Princess Elizabeth was completely happy, riding in an open royal landau pulled by beautiful horses, with her beautiful family around her. Yes, in a different world she would have been in the lead carriage as queen, but the relief she now felt at never being queen surprised her after a lifetime of wanting it so badly, and at hating Albert for taking it away from her.

Now that she was no longer stressed, she found herself capable of achieving more than she'd ever dreamed possible. Instead of constantly chafing at her fate and feeling thwarted from her rightful place, now she was, in fact, capable of amazing accomplishments, and for that she had Pauline, in large part, to thank. Her first true friend, her only friend, who, somehow, unlocked, unleashed, Lizzie's long-simmering potential in ways that surprised not only herself but her own family, especially Larry, who had watched, helplessly, as she'd been consumed with envy.

Now that was behind her as she was glad to see Albert settle down with Paul. She knew her brother would make a great king, just as she knew her Victoria would make a great queen.

Sir Humphrey waited at St. Paul's, on the extended chancel constructed specifically for the occasion, where the Royal Family would sit to one side as Albert and Paul said their vows to the Archbishop, with Sir Humphrey to the side of Albert as his supporter, and Pauline to the side of Paul, as his.

Sir Humphrey was touched that Albert had asked him. He knew this would be his last royal wedding, as the upcoming Coronation would be his last as well. Sir Humphrey had been pleased to lead a life of service to three monarchs, and while he wasn't sure how much longer he could continue to serve Albert, he knew the time was coming when he would finally step aside for someone younger, with the energy and zeal he once had and that still made their occasional appearance, as they had today, in the vast, surprisingly bright space of St. Paul's, ringed with lights for the cameras that would both record and broadcast the ceremony. He thought of his friend, the Archbishop, another man with a lifetime of service, but lifetimes, it seemed, come to an end.

The Archbishop was waiting just inside the cathedral, in all his finery, for the moment when the procession arrived and he, the Lord Bishop, and the Dean would greet the wedding party at the top of the steps. He was pleased to feel himself genuinely happy. He'd known Albert all his life. Indeed, he'd performed the christening. And he realized early on, though not as early as Albert himself, that he was same-sex attracted and realized that, with tact and diplomacy, he could facilitate his friend, the late King, into seeing Albert's homosexuality – especially when the lad was so open about it – as a unique contribution to expand what the monarchy was capable of being, and especially with Elizabeth handling the succession, which freed Albert from any act of hypocrisy.

Despite the unique and royal nature of this wedding, and even though the King himself would officially become head of the Church and, therefore, the Archbishop's superior, at the upcoming Coronation, he still looked upon his role as one of pastoral care which reminded him of his own humble beginning as a country vicar. His many administration duties as Archbishop kept him from most of the day-to-day functions that were ably done by the Dean of Canterbury and his assistants. Fortunately, the Dean had readily acceded to the Archbishop's desire to do at least a few weddings, funerals, and christenings each year, and for a cross-section of parishioners, not just the wealthiest or most well-connected ones. Still, the Archbishop found this wedding to be especially gratifying to his concept of an inclusive church. He recognized the difficulty of being a national church when the nation itself comprised so many different flavors of belief and non-belief. Still, with Albert and Paul joining together in Holy Matrimony, one of the Church's most sacred sacraments, the Archbishop recognized that his vision of the Church of England as a force for positive change in the country was finally coming true. He also recognized that his tenure as Archbishop was coming to an end, though only his wife knew his true interest at seeing Albert crowned before he retired, perhaps in favor of the Lord Bishop beside him, but he also realized that Albert's atheism could be an insurmountable stumbling block to that very Coronation.

What the Archbishop wanted to do at all costs was to prevent a schism that would force Albert's abdication and push the young Victoria to the throne before her maturity and make Princess Elizabeth regent. Fortunately, that was a conversation for another day. For now, he had a marriage to perform. The litany variant eliding the vow to obey was not the issue. No, what upset the Lord Bishop and many other conservatives was how he'd approved shortening the service at the King's request, including the versicles and responses sung by the choir, as well as the lessons and subsequent prayers. The Lord Bishop accused him of changing the ritual, whereas he had merely edited it. He explained to the Lord Bishop that the King and Duke wanted to emphasize the vows and the sacred ritual that bound them together in the eyes of God. Fortunately, that seemed to mollify the Lord Bishop, though criticism continued from other traditionalists. Still, if he couldn't make changes as Archbishop, then the power of the position wasn't worth much. Perhaps we are all trapped by our offices, he thought. He certainly knew the King was, and both men felt the chaffing of the harness.

His reverie was broken by the Dean, who said, "The

procession has entered Ludgate Hill."

"Ah," replied the Archbishop. "Then, as they said in vaudeville, it's showtime, folks."

Seeing the shocked look on the Dean's face, the Archbishop replied, "Never forget that what happens here is simply sacred theatre. After all, look at the set!"

Soon, the three were standing just outside the great wooden doors. The cheering was getting louder and already the lead elements of the procession were approaching the cathedral. The press photographers were taking pictures, and the final band, stationed near the Cathedral, was playing an Elgar march. The three men looked at each other.

"Let history begin," said the Archbishop, as the King's landau approached, stopped, and the door was opened. The cheers were deafening as the King stood, then stepped down to the street and walked up the steps to greet the three clergymen, who bowed. It was only then that Albert turned to acknowledge the crowd, looking resplendent in his scarlet uniform. He raised one hand, the cheering somehow grew even louder, then he turned to follow the three inside.

A trumpet fanfare announced his entrance into the nave; the congregation stood, and the organ and massed choristers started a Purcell processional as the King started the long walk to the chancel where he would await, first, the entrance of Princess Elizabeth and her family, who would sit to the right of the extended chancel platform, and then Paul and Pauline, who would join him on the platform, in front of the three clergymen.

Albert walked with smiling composure on this day he had eagerly awaited. The eyes of the 2,500 people in attendance were all on him, as well as the eyes of the broader world outside these walls who were watching it live.

The three clergymen stepped up onto the chancel

extension, then turned to face the King as he joined them, and then Sir Humphrey came and stood beside him. Princess Elizabeth and her family had arrived by now and were awaiting the cue to start walking down the long aisle as well. Though practically playing no role in the ceremony itself, Lizzie was keenly aware that her presence, and the presence of her daughter Victoria, showed the world that, while the marriage dealt with the present moment, the future of the monarchy resided with her line, in full attendance, and in full view. She could not be happier.

Finally came the climactic moment as Paul and his mother awaited the cue to begin the procession that, until this moment in history, had always been taken by a woman marrying a prince or king, or a man marrying a princess or queen. Now, for the first time in British history, a king was marrying another man.

The moment was here. With a flurry of trumpets, then the peal of organ and choirs, Paul and Pauline walked to the glorious sounds of a march by the German-born yet so English-identified Handel. It was the moment for which the world had waited as Paul with his mother, who rested her hand lightly on his arm, walked side by side, and the world gasped at their beauty. They awed the room with their elegance as they passed pew by pew, and all eyes turned to watch their progress as they finally joined Albert and Sir Humphrey. Paul and Albert smiled at each other, then the matrimonial ritual began. They knelt side by side before the Archbishop, whose voice echoed throughout the vast space of the cathedral.

"Dearly beloved, we are gathered here in the sight of God and in the face of this congregation, to join these two men in Holy Matrimony, which is an honorable estate instituted by God himself, signifying unto us the mystical union that is between Christ and His Church, which holy estate Christ adorned and beautified with his presence, and first miracle that he wrought, in

Cana of Galilee, and is commended in Holy Writ to be honorable among all men, and therefore is not by any way to be enterprised, not taken in hand, unadvisedly, lightly, or wantonly; but reverently, discretely, soberly, and in the fear of God.

"Therefore, if any persons can shew any just cause, why they may not lawfully be joined together, let them now speak, or else hereafter forever hold their peace."

This opening of the service to possible public dissent was the riskiest moment of the ritual because it was unknown whether anyone present would object to the marriage, so the Archbishop didn't wait but moved quickly on. Waiting was only inviting trouble.

"I require and charge you both, as ye will answer at the dreadful day of judgment when the secrets of all hearts shall be disclosed, that if either of you know any impediment, why ye may not be lawfully joined together in Matrimony, ye do now confess it. For be ye well assured, that so many as are coupled together otherwise than God's word doth allow are not joined together by God, neither is their Matrimony lawful."

This time he did pause, the men were silent, so he continued.

"Albert George Alfred Edward, wilt thou have this man to thy wedded husband, to live together after God's ordinance in the holy estate of Matrimony? Wilt thou love him, comfort him, honor, and keep him, in sickness and in health, and forsaking all others, keep thee only unto him, so long as ye both shall live?"

Albert, turning to look at Paul, said, simply, "I will."

Then the Archbishop turned to Paul.

"Paul McGregor, wilt thou have this man to thy wedded husband, to live together according to God's law in the holy estate of Matrimony? Wilt thou love him, comfort him, honor, and keep him, in sickness and in health, and forsaking all others, keep thee only unto him, so long as ye both shall live?"

And then Paul, turning to look at Albert, said simply, "I will."

Next, the Archbishop asked, "Who giveth this man to be married to this man?"

"I do," said Pauline, then the Archbishop received Paul from his mother and Albert took Paul by the hand and repeated after the Archbishop: "I, Albert George Alfred Edward, take thee, Paul McGregor, to my wedded husband, to have and to hold from this day forward, for better for worse, for richer for poorer, in sickness and in health, to love and to cherish, till death do us part, according to God's holy ordinance; and thereto I plight thee my troth."

Then they separated their hands, and Paul took Albert's hand, and repeated after the Archbishop: "I, Paul McGregor, take thee, Albert George Alfred Edward, to my wedded husband, to have and to hold from this day forward, for better for worse, for richer for poorer, in sickness and in health, to love and to cherish, till death do us part, according to God's holy ordinance; and thereto I plight thee my troth."

At this point, the ceremony was again altered so that each man could give the other a ring. Albert had Garrard, the Crown Jewelers, make a gold wedding band engraved with the initials A and P intertwined within a lover's knot.

It turned out that Paul needn't have worried about the money to buy a ring for Albert because his mother gave him the wedding band she had placed on her husband's hand when they married. He had given the ring back at their separation. She told Paul that despite the apparent failure of her own marriage, the ring signified its success through the subsequent creation of her son. What she didn't say was something that, nonetheless she sincerely felt, that Paul and Albert didn't need a child to make their marriage a success, though she understood that was not their reason.

Then the Lord Bishop continued the service.

"Bless, O Lord, these rings, and grant that he who gives one, and he who shall wear one, may remain faithful to each other, and abide in thy love and favor, and live together in love until their lives end. Through Jesus Christ our Lord, Amen."

And the Lord Bishop looked sternly at each man, to emphasize the specifically Christian nature of the moment. Then he took one ring and gave it to Albert to put upon Paul's left hand, who responded, "With this ring, I thee wed; with my body I thee honour; and all my worldly goods with thee I share."

And by stopping there, and by not continuing the expected and traditional ending of "In the name of the Father, the Son, and the Holy Ghost," Albert made it clear that this was not just a Christian ritual for him. Thus began the trouble with the traditionalists, including the Lord Bishop, who strove mightily to contain his anger, knowing the eyes of the world were upon him, and feeling the tension from the Archbishop beside him. He would save that issue for another day.

Then he took the second ring and gave it to Paul to put on Albert's left hand, and Paul repeated, "With this ring, I thee wed; with my body I thee honour; and all my worldly goods with thee I share."

Then the Archbishop continued the service.

"Let us pray. O Eternal God, Creator and Preserver of all mankind, giver of all spiritual grace, the author of everlasting life; send thy blessing upon these thy servants, these two men, whom we bless in thy name; that, living faithfully together, they may surely perform and keep the vow and covenant betwixt them made, whereof these rings given and received are a token and pledge; and may ever remain in perfect love and peace together, and live according to thy laws, through Jesus Christ our Lord, Amen."

The Archbishop joined the hands of the two men together and said, "Those whom God hath joined together, let no man put asunder."

He then looked beyond the men down the long nave of the cathedral to speak to those assembled: "For as much as Albert George Alfred Edward and Paul McGregor have consented together in holy wedlock, and have witnessed the same before God and this company, and thereto have given and pledged their troth to each other, and have declared the same by giving and receiving of ring, and by joining of hands, I pronounce that they be husband and husband together, In the name of the Father, and of the Son, and of the Holy Ghost. Amen."

Then he added a blessing: "God the Father, God the Son, God the Holy Ghost, bless, preserve, and keep you; the Lord mercifully with his favour look upon you; and so fill you with all spiritual benediction and grace, that ye may so live together in this life, that in the world to come ye may have life everlasting. Amen."

Chairs were provided for the newly wedded couple to sit upon while the Archbishop gave his address based on the quote, "Where love is, the spirit dwells."

After that, the couple followed the Archbishop to the altar, where they knelt in silent meditation and for another blessing by the Archbishop.

"Almighty God, the Father of our Lord Jesus Christ, pour upon you the riches of his grace, sanctify and bless you, that you may please him both in body and in soul, and live together in holy love unto your lives' end."

Then the choirs and the congregation joined in singing "I vow to thee my country." With the service over, the Dean led the grooms to the Dean's Aisle where they signed the Register. Then they returned and made their way back down through the congregation, this time as husband and husband, to the music of Mendelssohn's "Wedding March," the only music Albert insisted on, as he noted that not only was Mendelssohn the favorite composer of the first Victoria and her beloved Albert, but also it was a family story and point of pride that Mendelssohn himself had taught her how to sing.

Albert and Paul proudly walked hand in hand down the aisle and then exited the building into bright sunshine and roaring cheers, while the press corps frenetically photographed them.

They stood at the top of the steps, then someone started a chant which was quickly taken up until it became a vast command, "Kiss him! Kiss him!"

So they looked at each other, embraced, and gave each other a long, long kiss to cheers that echoed from the stone facades around them. And that was the royal wedding image that quickly went viral. After lips finally separated, the men walked down the steps to the waiting open landau, and started the long procession back to the palace, again accompanied by the tremendous roar of the crowds. But, even then, at the height of their happiness, there were those who could just not leave them alone, for there were still scattered cat calls of "Bloody poofs!" and "Queers!"

And while the men continued smiling, Albert said, sorrowfully and resignedly, to Paul, "Even now. Even as King."

He and Graham had previously discussed what to do in such a situation, which they knew was likely to happen. While apprehending and arresting those responsible was a possibility, both men knew it was better to ignore the hecklers rather than calling attention to them. Besides, the crowds around them took their own action and drowned them out. Albert knew it was a matter of free speech, as well as not wanting to recognize hatred. They represented such a small part of public opinion, but one he also knew would never go away.

Finally, the procession reached the palace gates and the carriages pulled up to the porte cochere. The men were tired, but also eagerly awaited their balcony appearance before taking an hour to rest and change for the reception to be held out back on the palace grounds. They received the best wishes of the staff before ascending the stairs, followed by Princess Elizabeth and her family, and Pauline and Sir Humphrey, all of whom made their way to the balcony to make their public appearance as a united family, waving to the crowds beyond the fence. And, again, to shouts of "Kiss him! Kiss him!" Albert and Paul kissed each other again. Finally, they returned to their bed chamber where the waiting valets, after congratulating them, helped them change into less formal clothes – plain suits and ties this time – with only a few minutes to themselves, before it was time to head out back to the reception.

The 2,500 people from the wedding were invited to the reception, set up near the lake behind the palace on the broad lawn. It was a long afternoon because everyone wanted to meet the King and his husband, and they made themselves available. There was the cutting of the cake, and the sharing of a slice between them. It wasn't until late that night when they were finally in bed together.

"You were right about the icing. It was fabulous. I asked to have a section of the cake saved for us to enjoy this week, but it seemed there was plenty for everyone," said Albert, as he cradled Paul in his arms as they sat back against the headboard.

"Did you see how much cake Victoria put away? She's a girl who likes her sweets."

"I fear she'll have lots of time for them after learning she won't be queen."

"Yes, she may be the size of her namesake before she's twenty."

"Do you regret having a child, then?"

"No, not the child. I regret the results of having the child on your sister and her family. Did you see how happy they were?"

"Yes, she's mellowed admirably now that she's no longer frustrated at not being queen."

"But her frustration will return, enhanced, at having the succession so unexpectedly taken from her children."

"I know, and that doesn't please me, to see her life, and the lives of her children, so shattered, if not destroyed. And that will be completely on me."

"And me."

"And something we will have to endure."

"It's a terrible price to pay."

"At least that price we can foresee."

And they looked at each other, and that part of their future stretched out darkly before them, so Paul abruptly changed the subject.

"It was nice seeing the Durham contingent. People I'd never met, like the mayor herself, suddenly have known me for ages and are so proud of my achievements."

"You are Durham's most famous son."

"I'm Durham's most famous poof, you mean."

"That, too."

"Still, it was nice seeing the headmaster and his wife, and so many teachers and classmates who showed up."

"Durham has become one of the most talked-about cities in the kingdom."

"Now, if that could just translate into jobs and opportunities."

"Give it time. Give it time," replied Albert soothingly. "Your mother seemed pleased at seeing so many of her former colleagues."

"I know she misses the lab, but starting two foundations is keeping her busy."

"She's working with Lizzie almost daily. I understand she has her own rooms now."

"They are best friends. Mama's never had that. Lots of acquaintances, lots of neighbors, but never a friend."

They both looked at each other, foreseeing yet another casualty from their actions, then another change of topic.

"I think the reception can be used as a prototype for the larger one after the Coronation," explained Albert. "I'm thinking the Strand can be closed off and the reception area expanded into Green Park, if necessary. Sir Humphrey will work with Graham to figure out exactly how many can be accommodated, with a kind of royal enclosure just behind the palace where people can come see us in some kind of organized fashion."

"But it will be for everyone, right?" asked Paul concerned. "I mean, all they have to do is have their name placed in the lottery and everyone whose name is drawn can attend?"

"Yes, everyone."

"And they won't have to wear some kind of required formal attire?"

"Not at all; they can dress as best they can, with no stigma attached to how they look. I want a butcher from Leeds to have the same chance to get in as the Leeds mayor, though there will be a list of people who must be invited, such as church leaders, Commonwealth officials, foreign dignitaries, Parliament, the cabinet, and the Prime Minister, who must be invited. Still, everyone else, the vast majority, will be a cross-section of the country, everyone and anyone who puts their name into the lottery: factory workers, factory owners, those who sweep the factories, as well as those laid off from the factories, and even the homeless who sleep outside the factories. The people's Coronation: that's what I want to see."

"Well, my idealist, what I want to see right now is you undressed so we can begin the nuptial consummation. I understand I'm supposed to be an innocent virgin."

"My dear, you are neither innocent nor a virgin," said Albert grinning. They undressed hurriedly, got into bed, and had just started to touch each other when there was a sharp rap on the door.

"Bloody hell," said Paul angrily. "Who can that be?"

Instead of answering, Albert called out with a commanding voice, "Come!"

A man entered looking as though he'd stepped out of an Elizabethan play. He knelt before the bed, bowed his head, and spread out his arms.

"Your Highness," he said while looking down at the floor. "Your courtiers are here to observe the royal consummation."

"Crikey!" yelled Paul, looking at Albert. "What's going on?"

A dozen men and women in Elizabethan costumes entered and solemnly stood around the bed, intensely looking at the pair in bed.

Paul had pulled up the sheet to completely cover his naked body, and looked at Albert in consternation for an explanation, when the King and all the others started laughing.

"Cheers, mate!" cried the leader, which was when Paul finally realized he was the butt of a practical joke. He took his pillow and beat Albert with it, who simply continued laughing.

"I couldn't pass it up," explained Albert while still laughing. "Ralph's an old acquaintance I've known for years, and it just so happens that his theatre company is doing 'Dr. Faustus' now, so it worked out perfectly."

"Good friends," he told the group. "You've done well. Now, wedding cake, a grand repast, and a bountiful fee await you."

The actors roared their approval as they bowed and left, with Ralph giving a deep, grand bow before winking at Albert. Albert turned to a questioning Paul and explained, "He and I had a brief but torrid affair years ago and we've kept in touch."

"Now," he said as he gently pulled the sheet from across Paul's body. "Where were we? No interruptions this time."

"We were discussing consummations," explained Paul. "Who wants to be consummated first?"

"Me, first," said Albert eagerly. "How do you want me?"

"Let's start on your stomach, and we'll see where we go."

So Albert rolled over, with his buttocks fully exposed. Paul looked at them with delight and said, "The perfect end to a perfect day."

CHAPTER 50

With just four months until the Coronation, the Royal Wedding Office at New Scotland Yard was simply renamed the Royal Coronation Office, with much of the security work to be a duplication of the earlier event. Much of the planning was also a duplication, with the same regiments, the same regimental bands, the same cleanup crew, and the same horses that had to be made ready for another procession, though this time to Westminster Abbey, the traditional coronation site where the King would ascend the Coronation Chair. However, now with Scotland independent, the King would no longer sit over the famous Stone of Scone to show England's domination, which had been returned to Scotland at the time of separation in a ceremony attended by his father. Indeed, Albert was determined to return Balmoral itself to the Scottish government with the understanding that the vast estate would be opened to the public, in addition to whatever uses the property and buildings could be put. He had no good memories of the place, though he knew his sister would miss it.

Concerning the Coronation preparations, Graham and the security office had to contend with something new that the King and Paul insisted on, a subsequent "Parade of the Nation" which would pass in front of the palace, where the Royal Family and selected guests would sit in a grandstand erected in front of the fence with room for thousands of spectators along the circular route that would include significant buildings in the city's history, such as St. Paul's, Guildhall, the Tower, and the Houses of Parliament along the Embankment, and would cover both sides of the river.

This time the military would stand down as the parade would be led by the Mounted Branch of the Metropolitan Police, followed by what Albert insisted would be a representative sampling of the entire kingdom. He insisted that he wanted those watching, either in person or on the telly, to see someone like themselves, regardless of color, ability, social class, sexuality, gender identity, or anything else.

He was adamant that a significant LGBTQ contingent be near the front,

"So it will seem like a Gay Pride parade," he explained, followed by community bands and contingents from Welsh and English mining communities. He wanted school bands from throughout the country, with school children from all areas included as well, and with a special place for Paul's St. Giles School. There would be trade unions; arts and sports groups; political and environmental organizations; manufacturing, tech, and business groups; religious organizations of all kinds; non-religious groups such as the British humanist and atheist clubs; as well as contingents from rural and urban areas, from hamlets to villages to towns and cities. He wanted the kingdom to converge on London that day as he wanted the country to celebrate itself, with the Coronation as the catalyst for the event.

"If they live in Britain, I want them to see themselves in this parade," he declared. He wanted the parade to go on for miles, and for hours, with all the music groups that could be found, from community choruses and bands to all manner of the performing arts, as well as representatives of all the ethnicities that comprised the country's diverse population.

Britain's few remaining possessions, as well as the Commonwealth countries, were also invited to participate in the parade, as it was a celebration not just of the homeland, but of all the areas around the world who shared a connection to the monarchy. However, Albert also made sure that it was clearly stated in the invitations that each government was expected to include a delegation from their respective LGBTQ communities. Without that inclusion, the invitation would be withdrawn.

This requirement rankled leaders of the few Commonwealth countries where homosexuality was still illegal. They saw it as an unwarranted intrusion into their country's internal policies and made their opposition clear. One leader, who had recently gained power through a remarkably bloody coup, and whose sexual practices with under-aged females was well documented, thundered against "the perverted King who dares to undermine the sanctity of our country's cherished foundations of family and home." He said this on national television while dramatically ripping apart the royal invitation, and promptly withdrew his country from the Commonwealth, and did two other leaders.

"Let them go," was Albert's only comment, as he was greatly relieved at not having to greet these gentlemen at the upcoming Commonwealth meeting.

The Prime Minister, however, was not pleased at what she saw as the King's meddling into her own arena of foreign policy. She made her displeasure tactfully known at her next weekly meeting with him, and she was surprised at Albert's frosty rebuff. For the first time, she realized there was a stubborn streak in him that had been lacking in the late King's more malleable personality. The idea of a possible rogue monarch had not yet occurred to her.

On the day following the parade, participants and spectators were to be invited to what was to be billed as The Nation's Party, to be held at the palace grounds, as well as the nearby Green Park and St. James's Park. There, groups would provide food for free, reimbursed by the Crown, and with pavilions, stages, and performing spaces set aside for dances, craft displays, dramatic and musical events, information booths, and everything would be free.

Albert and Paul would greet the crowds in a covered enclosure just behind the palace, and while Graham was worried about the forces needed to provide security for the parade and the party, he assured the King that it was possible, though always with some degree of risk.

CHAPTER 51

Princess Elizabeth was happier than she'd ever been. Indeed, unbeknownst to her, she was happier than she would ever be again. And she credited her happiness solely to the presence of Dr. McGregor. Each woman found in the other her first and only true friend. For Lizzie, it was due in large part to the respect that Pauline paid her by seeking her advice on issues surrounding the organization of the foundation.

To her great surprise, she had fulfilled her royal duties for years without ever being asked her opinion about anything of substance. Now, for the first time in her life, she felt activated by the knowledge that she could contribute something more worthwhile than just her name and title. Pauline wanted to know what she thought, and Lizzie responded to those requests by growing into the role of a decision maker. It was as if she'd been transplanted into fertile soil after being seeded among sterile rock. She blossomed, like a plant in her own garden.

Pauline realized her friend's understanding of how the world worked was restricted by her privileged upbringing, so what she did was to go through the possible options for any question for which a decision was needed, and to review likely outcomes, then Pauline stepped back while Lizzie made her choice, and then Pauline worked to implement it.

In this way the women forged a bond as a team, with the eventual goal of formulating the foundation's objectives while devising the organizational structure so that an executive director could be hired to run it.

Pauline was now spending much of her time at Lizzie's country estate and being in such close proximity daily, and beginning to know her friend as well, Lizzie soon realized that Pauline was keeping a kind of secret sorrow to herself. She noticed Pauline looking far away at times, with a distinctive melancholia, so Lizzie decided to find out what was bothering her.

Fortunately, Pauline had another issue that was bothering her besides the creation of Albert's and Paul's child, so she felt relieved that she could present a true issue without dissimulation.

"It's my family," she explained. "They're all back in Jamaica and I haven't seen them since I moved to England 25 years ago. Oh, I keep in touch – I write and call them often – but I haven't seen any of them for so long that many are old and increasingly infirm, while others are grown with up with children of their own. I'd like to see them, and I'd like you and Albert and Paul to see them since they are now a large part of our extended family. I thought about having them here for the wedding, but I think the Coronation and its surrounding events would be even more amazing for them to experience. I just don't know how to do that."

Pauline had hesitated in bringing up the Coronation because she still wasn't sure how hurtful it might be, especially if Lizzie regretted the fact that it wasn't her Coronation. But Lizzie had, remarkably, moved on from the issue and could deal with it objectively now that she no longer wanted to be queen. In fact, she was looking forward to it, so she looked upon Pauline's concern as just another problem to solve, and a rather easy solution it was.

"Just ask Albert," she said. "He can handle everything. And if he's too cheap to foot the bill for the airline tickets, I'll get Larry to pay for them. I want to see your family, too."

"You're amazing," said Pauline, genuinely moved. Yet

despite this moment of closeness, she knew the Coronation would also mark the coming divide that would separate the two friends forever. She was aware that Albert and Paul, based on how the preparations went for splicing their genetic codes together and inserting them into an egg, planned to make a public announcement about the impending birth soon after the Coronation, and then Pauline knew her relationship with Lizzie would end, and not nicely, as she realized it would end in recrimination and anger, with feelings of betrayal at why Pauline, her friend, had not told her in advance but had kept the secret to herself. But Pauline knew she also could not betray the trust that Paul and Albert had placed in her, and that only Albert could tell Lizzie, before the public was made aware that a direct heir would soon be born. Pauline admired Albert for his willingness to accept full responsibility for what was about to happen, and that understanding caused the melancholia that she could not explain to Lizzie.

CHAPTER 52

Albert was working at his desk when a sharp knock was heard at the door.

"Come," he said, looking up as Gerald entered, bowed, and said, "Your Majesty, Dr. McGregor wishes to see you."

Albert immediately smiled.

"Of course," he said. "Show her right in."

As Gerald bowed again and left, Albert stood and walked towards the door as Pauline entered. They warmly embraced and kissed each other on the cheek. Pauline was still surprised at how physically affectionate the King was. Unlike her own family in Jamaica, for whom touching was normal behavior, she realized the Royal Family was well known as rarely showing affection, at least in public.

Albert led the way to a sofa and patted the area next to him for her to sit beside him.

"Now," he said gaily, "We don't see you as much anymore, as though Lizzie is holding you captive in Suffolk."

Pauline laughed easily.

"Not quite, but she did inquire about something that has been bothering me about the Coronation , and so I'm here to ask a favor."

"Anything within my power to give," he said. "And, considering my situation, that's quite a lot. So, tell me what I can do."

But she felt a need to explain herself first, before dealing with the actual issue.

"You know, I find it hard to ask for anything for myself. It's part of my self-reliance, I guess."

"I do know," replied Albert. "And I find the same confounding attitude in your son! It makes it difficult to do anything for either of you."

Pauline smiled and felt better at making her request.

"I haven't seen my family in Jamaica since I left for England a quarter of a century ago. I'd like, somehow, to bring them over for the Coronation as a family reunion."

Albert lit up.

"That's a smashing idea! I'll take care of everything."

He rose abruptly, went to his desk, and pushed the intercom button.

"Gerald, when Dr. McGregor leaves, she'll give you the contact information for her family in Jamaica. They are now an extended part of the Royal Family. I want you to arrange their travel to London for the Coronation . First Class all the way. You'll need to go through the Foreign Office, who will contact our embassy in Kingston to get the paperwork completed so they can be here in time. And no hotels. They will stay at Clarence House or St. James. Also, arrange some kind of shopping day for them all. I'll cover everything. Keep me informed. Also, I always want cars available for them. No cabs. Plus, security. Add this to Graham's already extensive list of things to do."

"Of course, Your Highness," replied Gerald crisply.

Pauline was always amazed at how easily Albert handled the levers of power. He returned to his place beside her.

"This is so exciting!" he exclaimed enthusiastically. "I'm especially looking forward to meeting . . . is it your great aunt? To hear about working for Noël Coward."

"She's quite elderly and infirm now," explained Pauline, "so she may not be able to make it."

Seeing Albert's disappointment, she quickly added, "But having some idea about what you want to know, I think it's my

Uncle Teddy who will have the most interesting stories, and I'm sure he will definitely come."

Albert looked at her expectantly to explain.

"He was just a teenager then, but he paid for college with what he made . . . um . . . how can I put this politely?"

As she considered different words, Albert interjected in a smile, "Servicing?"

"Yes," she agreed, returning it. "Servicing Coward's friends and visitors."

Albert laughed.

"I doubt he serviced my grandmother, who, when still a princess, visited Coward at his Jamaican home. But I've often wondered where my own wild streak comes from, and it may have been her. It certainly wasn't from my rather prudish father."

Slightly uneasy at the tone of the conversation, Pauline hastily said, "Well, thank you, Albert. This is so generous of you."

"Not at all," he explained. "Meeting your family will be a pleasant relief from the formalities of that week."

And then they were silent, as the presence of the unspoken hovered around them. Finally, Albert asked, softly, "And how is my sister?"

Relieved to finally be able to deal with the issue, Pauline said, "Radiant. I've never seen her happier. She is blossoming, as though she's discovered a new world. She's more than just a figurehead for the foundation. It's her vision. I'm merely helping her flesh it out. Things are moving so quickly that we'll soon be advertising for the executive director. I want to have as much in place as possible before the Coronation ."

She might as well have said, "By the time everything collapses," because both were fully aware that would be the result of the child whose conception was moving ever closer. Soon, Pauline and Sir Sullivan would go to Oxford to observe the actual gene-splicing procedure. Even then, the project could still be stopped at any moment right to the implantation of the fertilized egg into the uterus of the host mother, who still had to be chosen by Paul and Albert in coordination with the medical team.

But both Pauline and Albert knew that would not happen. They knew the project was going ahead regardless of what, in military terms, was called "collateral damage." And both were fully aware of just how extensive that damage could be, how far it could spread like shock waves from an epicenter. Yet now even Pauline accepted the need for a child, despite the consequences, a price she was still reluctant to accept as, indeed, was Albert. But the decision was made and would be seen through to its conclusion. So Albert and Pauline, facing the situation while sitting on a silk brocade-covered, gilded wood, mid-eighteenth-century sofa under a life-sized portrait of George III, had nothing to say because words, in this instance, were useless.

CHAPTER 53

Michael Romanov is calling his favorite cousin.

"Lizzie! What's happening? I never hear from you. You never call or write. I fear Dr. McGregor has possessed your soul like Rasputin. And the stories I could tell you about him that didn't make the history books!"

Princess Elizabeth is appalled to hear Michael's high-pitched, shrieky voice. It's an echo of a world she has left behind and of which she does not wish to be reminded. She has become a different person, in which creative action has replaced bitterness. She now has something to live for, instead of to fight against, so she replies frankly, with a disdainful tone she hopes he, sensitive man that he is, will understand. He does.

"So good to hear from you, Michael. I can tell you haven't changed at all."

"But why should I, ma Cherie? I enjoy life. You, on the other hand, seem determined to become Saint Lizzie of the Teeming Masses. I hear you and the good doctor plan on bringing the healing benefits of nature to the truly unwashed gangs in inner city of Leeds and Manchester. Do you really think they'll do anything but mock you? Beware of the proletariat. That's the lesson of my family. They need to be ridden hard until broken with a whip."

Lizzie doesn't deign to take up the challenge, knowing Michael will simply continue until he draws blood, which he counts as success. And he does continue.

"Instead of giving them carrot cake, I suppose you'll be teaching them to grow carrots."

"And what could you possibly know about carrot cake?"

asks Lizzie incredulously. "Have you ever even tried it?"

"Of course not!" laughs Michael disdainfully. "The name alone is simply appalling. I don't have to try something to know I won't like it."

Lizzie decides it's time to make Michael face certain unpleasant truths about himself, in a bid to change a cousin she really does love.

"Do you want to know what's wrong with you, Michael?"

He is so surprised at this unexpected dive into his own psychology that he bursts out laughing.

"Oh, do tell! I can't wait to find out!"

"You're vain. Indulgent. Intolerant. And you're incapable of loving or being loved."

"My dear Lizzie. Tell me something I don't already know!" says the man who is quite self-aware and reflective.

Lizzie is taken aback by his nonchalant reply. She expected defiant claws instead of calm reproach.

Michael decides to explain.

"You say I'm incapable of loving. That's not true. I simply choose not to love or to be loved. To me both are weaknesses I can't afford. You see, my dear cousin, I am a Russian Buddha. I know that love leads to attachment, and attachment leads to suffering. And I choose not to suffer, and here's why.

"In the early days of the Revolution, when Edward presciently and fortunately decided to send that battleship to save my family, it wasn't just for the immediate family – Nicholas, Alexandra and their children – but for all the extended family as well. All the uncles and aunts, nieces and nephews and cousins. And one of them was my namesake, Prince Michael, a known homosexual, who for years had been lovers with a handsome young officer in the Imperial Guard. Of course, not only could they not live together, but such relationships were condemned by state and church, so they could only meet clandestinely, but they met regularly, and their passion and love were so consuming that they swore neither would live without the other.

"And so, with the British ship on its way, Prince Michael developed a plan to bring his lover with him, disguised as a minor and distant member of the Royal Family, quite removed. Now Nicholas could approve this so the lover would have the necessary papers, but Nicholas, as head of church and state, and strongly influenced by the Holy Patriarch of the Russian Orthodox Church, was offended by his relative's sinful and most unholy liaison and so he refused. It was Prince Michael alone and no one else.

"The British ship docked at St. Petersburg; the Romanov family went onboard; and the revolutionaries were relieved to see them leave as that was one less thing to worry about as they seized control of the country, but Prince Michael refused to leave his lover, knowing full well the consequences.

"Nicholas, naturally, was also relieved at leaving the stain of perversion behind, and so the ship sailed away. And before it was out of sight on the horizon, the entire Imperial Guard, along with Prince Michael, was lined up against a wall and shot. The lovers' death pact came true.

"But Nicholas didn't consider the force of the love that Michael's sister, Princess Irina, had for her brother. He was everything to her – best friend, companion, confidant – though she, also, did not understand his perversion and blamed it for killing the deepest love of her life. She determined to keep his memory fresh by naming her first son Michael in his honor. But she also recognized the danger of loving neither wisely nor well, and so she turned against love completely, her love for her brother notwithstanding. She herself married well but not for love. And she taught her son, Michael, the error of love, using her brother's affair as the primary object of her lessons, which she repeated day after day, year after year, until he, too, grew up to recognize the folly of love. Ironically, he, too, was homosexual, but never acted on it, and eventually married a woman to carry on the line, but not for love. And he named his first son Michael and taught him the family lesson. He, too, learned it well. He, too, ironically, was homosexual, who refused to act on it, married, had a homosexual son he named Michael, who learned, by now, the old family lesson, and so it came to me, the first open homosexual Michael Romanov and also the first not to marry, but I also learned the lesson handed down by my great-great-great-grandmother, who was known as the Ice Princess within the family.

"Now understand that I have all the sex I want with all the men I want, but no one spends the night – like Albert was once famous for doing, before the Durham slag – and I never, ever, see them again. So, the family lesson stops with me. I think it's time for something else or for nothing at all.

"But I don't regret the family lesson. And I certainly don't want you to pity me. Pity is useless, like giving water to a corpse who died of dehydration. No, I'm perfectly happy in my perfectly loveless life. Unlike you, I have no desire to win the affection of the masses or to improve their lot or whatever it is you want to accomplish with Dr. McGregor. I live the life I want. You have crossed the moat of your life to explore the world. Cheers. I have pulled up the drawbridge, perfectly content on my island of beauty, untainted and unspoiled by love."

He finally pauses, but Lizzie has nothing to say. He has one last point to make.

"Now, I'm going to tell you something you need to know."

Lizzie waits, dreading what is coming without not

knowing what it could be.

"Albert will destroy you. I don't know how, but he will. You think he has changed, but he hasn't, not at all. One thing I know from my family's history is that personality is buried deep into our psyche. It's like fate; you think you can avoid it or evade it, but you can't, and it's folly to think otherwise. Right now, you spurn me because I remind you of who you were, when I'm reminding you of who you are. Right now, you are basking in the arms of a loving, accepting family. You see an affectionate, even nurturing side of Albert you never knew existed, and you are glowing and growing in that moment. Fine, enjoy it for as long as it lasts. But remember my distant uncle Prince Michael and his lover, crumpled together at the foot of a brick wall covered with their blood. Don't think it can't happen to you. Do you think you can magically evade the bullets coming your way? They will pierce your body and shatter your flesh. And don't ever think they can't. Now, after Albert betrays you, and your perfect world falls apart, remember me. You have my number. And I'll be here, waiting. Cheers."

Then he hangs up.

In her prior life, this call would have shattered Lizzie's fragile sense of self. But, contrary to Michael's dire predictions, she is no longer that woman. With Pauline beside her, Lizzie can valiantly face the future with hope.

CHAPTER 54

Sir Sullivan and Dr. McGregor felt put upon by Albert's demand that they oversee the gene-splicing procedure. They knew they were not qualified, and the medical team also knew it, and resented their presence with the inescapable realization that the King did not trust their professionalism. However, Sir Sullivan and Dr. McGregor did trust it, implicitly, and went out of their way to assure the team that they were present to merely affirm that the procedure was carried out in accordance with the King's wishes, which was understandable to the staff.

The two also admitted their lack of understanding of the specific processes and techniques involved in the procedure, and explained how they wanted to understand it, so it could become a teaching moment. The team readily agreed and then the work went smoothly. However, quite soon it was necessary to have actual human eggs to work with from the host mother, several of them to perfect the technique as well as for storage in case future children would be sought. And the choice of the host mother was up to Albert and Paul.

It was solely up to Albert because Paul declared himself to be useless at finding someone; indeed, his only suggestion was an advertisement on the order of "Host mother wanted for royal child," which Albert quickly dismissed. He knew that protocol required the prospective bearer to be from within the extended Royal Family for the child to legitimately accede to the throne, that, in effect, the child had to come from royal loins, and Connie fit the bill.

Besides, with so many loose ends to deal with, he wanted someone already familiar with how things worked, rather than

347

trying to teach protocol and customs on top of everything else the situation would demand. And he knew exactly who he wanted: Cousin Constance, Connie, the Duchess of Essex. They shared the same great-grandmother, Victoria the Second, who had two daughters, his own grandmother, Victoria the Third, and Alexandra, Connie's grandmother, who herself had a girl, Louisa, and a boy, Henry, who was Connie's father.

Albert didn't know her very well, as he had usually only seen her briefly in their youth during Christmas holidays at Sandringham and summer holidays at Balmoral. Such fleeting moments continued after she married an abstract painter named Basil Worthington. Still, he could tell they loved each other very much, and he could tell she was a patient and nurturing mother to their two young children. None of that was important to the role of being a royal host mother, whose requirements, basically, centered around her ability to bear a healthy child. Still, those qualities were important to Albert as she would also be raising the child, at least initially, after the birth. So, he had invited her to visit him and Paul.

For her part, Connie could not figure out why she was asked to come alone to the palace. She liked her cousin Albert, what little she saw of him. It was Lizzie she had problems with, whose disdain and scorn had been obvious for years. For example, it was Lizzie who organized the family portraits taken at Christmas, and Connie always found herself at the far end of the family grouping, usually beside a potted palm. She would not have been surprised to find herself behind a porcelain elephant. She knew what Lizzie thought: "Connie the cow" was how Lizzie usually described her, even to her face. Connie realized she was probably the most minor of the minor royals, so far from the line of succession that most royal watchers, those who made a living commenting on the ins and outs, the who's and what's of the Royal Family, usually completely overlooked her. In terms of the Royal Family tree, Connie thought of herself as a minor twig, far out on a useless branch. Indeed, she rarely thought of her station as even a minor royal. Early on, she was determined to make her own way and turned a passion for books into a passionate career as a book designer for a major London publishing house.

It was at university where she met her future husband, a struggling painter studying commercial art so he could have an income while pursuing his own passion in creating huge abstract canvases. The quality of his work was deeply respected by a few cognoscenti, at a time when mainstream public opinion preferred figurative art, so his work was admired, but not popular.

Basil soon realized that designing ad layouts and product packaging was not for him and considered himself lucky to land a teaching position at a rural university in the Midlands, where he was able to commute from home while helping to raise their children. Home was a small country estate given as a wedding present from Connie's parents. It provided privacy and, with its ancient manor house, also suited their aesthetic tastes. However, maintaining the property was difficult on two entry-level salaries, and money was always an issue.

"So why am I here?" asked Connie to herself, as she ascended the staircase to the main drawing room.

As she entered, both Albert and Paul rose from the sofa. Albert greeted her with open arms and a kiss to both cheeks, as did Paul. She was touched by the affection and realized how much Albert had matured from his hedonistic younger years, which she attributed both to the crown and to Paul. Besides, she liked gay men. Knowing many of them from her work and from Basil's position in the art department, she appreciated the fact that they didn't judge her on her weight and size, as most straight men did automatically, so it seemed.

She had only briefly met Paul at the funeral, and then again at the wedding.

"So why am I here?" she asked herself again, as she sat down in the armchair pointed out by Albert as he and Paul sat again on the sofa. She was touched at how easily Albert took Paul's hand.

Albert started by asking the obvious question, "How are you doing?"

"Fine," said Connie. "Better than fine. One of my books just won the Man Booker Prize."

"Well done!" exclaimed both men simultaneously.

"And did that bring a salary raise?" asked Albert, familiar with Connie's constant money woes.

"Yes, it did," proclaimed Connie proudly.

"And Basil?" continued Albert. "Didn't he have a gallery show in Chelsea?"

"Yes, but they dropped him. It seems only the Americans like abstracts these days. But a gallery in Los Angeles has taken him on, so we're hopeful."

"You know I've wanted one of his paintings for the Royal Collection for ages."

"And you know," replied Connie, "he thinks that is just a polite way of giving us charity and that you're not genuinely interested in his work."

"That's not true at all," protested Albert. "My curator showed me photos of his work, and I admire it immensely."

Flattered more than she cared to admit, Connie said she would keep after Basil to eventually sell something to Albert.

"And while you're at it, give him our love," said Albert, and she agreed, though still confused about why she was at the palace.

"You know," continued Albert, "I've never been to your house. Why don't you invite us out some time? I understand it's lovely country Tudor."

"Well, it's not Hampton Court," she said, somewhat defensively.

"Connie," said Albert without taking offense, "I'm not like that."

Abashed, Connie replied, "I'm sorry, Albert. We would be honored to have you and Paul visit."

"And how are the children doing? Still the two of them?"

"Yes, and they're doing well, thank you. The older one starts school next year."

"My, my," said Albert. "And any plans for a third?"

Now Connie was puzzled.

"No, not at present. Children, Tudor houses, and even small country estates are expensive to maintain."

And with that, the small talk was over. Albert and Paul looked at each other, and Paul nodded at Albert for him to proceed. They liked what they saw so far.

Albert still hesitated, then broached the subject.

"Connie, what I'm about to tell you cannot be divulged to anyone else except Basil. Do you agree?"

Connie was surprised, and even concerned, at this secrecy.

"Are you sending me on a spying mission for MI-5? I don't understand."

But she saw both men still looking at her and awaiting her answer.

"Yes, of course. I agree."

Relieved, Albert proceeded.

"Paul and I want you to be the host mother for our child."

Connie could not have been more surprised than if she had been asked to spy. And she really didn't understand. Her puzzled look was Albert's incentive to explain.

"Paul and I have decided to have a child, a true child from each of us, and we need a host mother to supply an egg that will be filled with our combined DNA and then placed in the uterus where it will grow into a child that will be born and, eventually, become the future monarch."

Connie's puzzlement continued.

"But Lizzie," countered Connie. "She's relying on Victoria to succeed you."

"Yes, yes," replied Albert quickly. "But after Papa's sudden death, Paul and I realized that if one of us were to die early, the other would have nothing, there would be no continuity. We don't want that to happen, so that's why we want a child, and why we want you to be the mother."

Connie didn't know what to say.

"I'm greatly, greatly honored that you would even consider me. It would be a unique privilege, wouldn't it?"

Both men nodded affirmatively.

"We haven't thought about a third child," she added. "We've thought two were enough."

She looked at the men, who were staring expectantly at her.

"Do I have to answer now? I'd rather discuss this with Basil first."

"By all means," assured Albert. "Take your time. Just please don't talk to anyone else about it. Even once you accept and, see, we're confident that you will," Albert said with a smile, "we want your identity to remain a secret through the pregnancy. In fact, we want you and the children to move here for the length of the term, for security. Now, after the child is born, boy or girl, and we're letting nature decide the gender, then your identity will be revealed and your life will change forever, as mother to the future monarch.

"If you agree, there will be a lengthy contract you'll have to sign that you and Basil need to review with your solicitor. Keep in mind that Basil is basically out of this as he will have no rights over the child. This is between you and us. Now, there is one point that I hesitate to mention, but I'd rather you heard it from me first rather than from reading the document and possibly becoming upset. If you do get upset, then take it out on me."

Connie looked at him puzzled.

"You will have complete control over whether to do this or not right up to the moment when the fertilized egg is planted in your uterus. However, from that moment you become fully committed to giving birth. Now, if there is a problem with the pregnancy, meaning if something goes wrong and your life is physically at stake, then the pregnancy will be terminated. Your health comes first. But the pregnancy cannot be terminated for any other reason."

Albert realized from her anger that perhaps he'd said too much too soon.

"That offends me," she said curtly.

"I apologize," Albert replied contritely, "but, as I said, it's in the agreement and, if you and Basil approve it, that is one of the conditions. Now, following the birth, you'll be free to give all the interviews you want and I'm sure you'll be inundated with requests as public interest will be enormous, both in the procedure itself and in you as the host mother. Just prepare yourself."

"All right," said Connie, who wasn't used to any interest in her or her life.

"Also, we'd like you to stay here with the child until weaning. After that, you can have as much or as little involvement with the child as you want, but the child stays here, to be raised as part of our family, not yours. Now, you and Basil can still have future children of your own, but it's also possible that, if the first child works out, then [And Albert looked at Paul who nodded agreement] we may want another, the traditional heir and spare routine, you know."

Then he and Connie both smiled.

"Finally, you will always be the mother. You can have as much access to the child as you want, or as little. But you will always be known as the mother to a new line of monarchs. That's a great honor, and we would be honored if you would accept. Now, I've done all the talking. Paul, do you have anything to add?"

"Only that this is much better than my idea of an advertisement," he said grinning. "And, Connie, [And he looked at her with disarming directness] we would be privileged and honored to have you as the mother of our child and I, for one, will just be crushed if you don't accept."

"Then how can I say no?" she said with a smile. "But Lizzie?"

"She'll just have to accept and adapt," explained Albert calmly. "It will be hard, but I know she can." Or, rather, he hoped she would.

"Well then," said Connie, who pushed away her own feeling of skepticism, "then I will ask Basil, but I'm pretty sure he'll agree."

"Excellent!" said both men at once, then Albert continued: "There is one more thing you need to know, one that will also be included in the agreement. At signing, in the presence of our mutual solicitors, you will receive a check for fifty thousand pounds, with another fifty thousand pounds after the birth. It's our way of saying 'Thank you.'"

"It's his money," said Paul with a smile.

Connie was stunned, as the idea of money had never occurred to her; she had seen the surrogacy not as a family obligation, and certainly not as any kind of paid job, but as a way of helping Albert and Paul, both of whom she found herself deeply caring for. Still, the men saw in her face that she would gratefully accept the money.

"Well then, that's it," said Albert as he rose, followed by the other two. They looked at each other, fully aware of the significance of the moment in royal history. Then Albert held Connie, kissed her on the cheek, and said, softly, "We love you."

Once again, she was surprised at Albert's new affection. Then Paul held her and kissed her cheek, adding, "We love you."

And, in return, and in all honesty, she said to them both, "I love you as well."

Then she left.

Albert looked at Paul.

"What do you think?"

"She's perfect. Absolutely perfect."

"I agree."

And while driving back to her Tudor house in the Midlands, Connie kept seeing the headline, "Connie the Cow Gives Birth to Royal Heir."

She knew Basil would agree. He did.

CHAPTER 55

Albert and Paul were working side by side at their respective desks. Albert put down his pen and looked at Paul.

"I'm concerned about this meeting with the Archbishop concerning the Coronation. We've put it off this long, but the Coronation is coming up, and we can't put it off any longer."

Paul, who had turned to look at Albert, put down his pen in turn and said, "You don't think he will change the ceremony to accommodate your atheism?"

Albert laughed without amusement.

"The ceremony recognizes my assumption as God's representative on earth, a god I don't believe in. I'll be the Protestant equivalent of the Pope as the Vicar of Christ, in whom I also do not believe. How does one get around that except by abdication? This is the role for which I was created. A thousand years of monarchs are in my blood. And now, because I'm a non-believer, I throw it all away? Papa would only feel shame and disgust. But he must have seen this coming. Surely, he spoke to the Archbishop about this. And the Archbishop must also know. Everyone knows. Yet plans are proceeding accordingly. Do they expect a conversion the night before? 'Not bloody likely', as Benny Hill would say. So then does Lizzie find herself on the throne after all? Do I place her there myself? Or next to the throne as regent to Victoria? I have no idea what will happen and, frankly, my darling, I'm scared."

Paul quickly got up from his chair and went to stand behind Albert. He put his hands on Albert's shoulders. Albert, in turn, put his hands on Paul's, and leaned his head back against Paul's chest.

"My dearest Albert," said Paul. "Your royal blood is safe. You have a destiny to fulfill, a great destiny to make Britain a better place, more accepting of diversity, more equitable, more caring, more just. The monarchs of history are with you. Your father is with you. Whatever forces there are that are guiding your fate and destiny are working to ensure you will be crowned King and assume your rightful place on the throne and in history itself. Never doubt that. And I know the Archbishop himself can work miracles on your behalf, so when you meet with him, you will not be alone.

Greatly relieved, Albert said, "You are amazing. Do you know that?"

"Of course I do. Now go to your meeting and let me know what happens. I can't wait to hear."

They met in the drawing room and sat across from each other.

"So," began Albert, "This is the meeting we've kept putting off."

"Yes," replied the Archbishop, almost with sadness. "And let's be frank. There is a certain element within the Church, small but vocal, that is ready to support Princess Elizabeth as the rightful heir to the throne, and who adamantly rejects the very possibility of a non-believer on King Edward's Chair. If the Princess Royal were to give any credence to these efforts, any hint of support, then the country would be split by civil war, at least amongst the most adamant factions for and against you, because you remain remarkably popular, especially amongst the younger generation, who see you as the only hope for the monarchy to remain at all relevant into the future. And I must say that many older people, including myself, agree. As a figurehead, regardless of her private views, Princess Elizabeth appeals to a reactionary group that prefers Britain to not only remain where it is, but to regress into the past, into some kind of idealized Camelot of knighthood and chivalry that never really existed. They want to make Britain great again by living in a world of illusion and delusion.

"Four hundred years ago this would have been settled on the battlefield between your army and hers, and the winner of that bloody contest would assume crown and throne. Today's civil wars are fought in internet chat rooms and the dark web and on the field of public opinion. The danger is that we will succumb to hand-to-hand fighting, and that faith in the institution will be shaken with the inevitable result that, instead of taking sides, people will just turn away and deem the monarchy itself to be irrelevant to their daily lives.

"Yet it is the monarchy that is supposed to be above the fray, to stand apart from turmoil. That's the realm of politics, to divide and conquer, as the Prime Minister would be the first to admit. Politics rarely unites. Only the monarchy brings the country together. But if the monarchy itself is divided, then it becomes useless and, what is worse, irrelevant, and all your plans for a glorious British future will vanish.

"On the other hand, a last-minute conversion, even if it were to happen, would be seen as a desperate and cynical attempt to hold onto power and simply would not be believed. There would always be a lingering doubt as to your actual sincerity. No, if you are to rule, it must be as you are, as everyone knows you to be. You can rule as a non-believer protecting the Church of England because you will swear, by all that is holy – carefully left undefined – to uphold, to defend, and to protect the Church from all her enemies, domestic and foreign, to the best of your ability. And that's it. We cannot ask more of you than your willingness to lay down your life for Church and State which – for purposes of the Coronation – are one and the same. The people know you are a non-believer, but if you are willing to sacrifice your life for an ideal in which you do not even believe, then that can be seen as positively heroic and worthy of a monarch."

He paused.

"Do you understand?"

"Yes," replied Albert solemnly.

"Good," said the Archbishop. "Now, the religious nature of the Coronation ceremony can be altered but not eliminated. Historically, the British monarch is head of Church and State since Henry the Eighth seized church power from the Pope and gave it to himself. Effectively, you are a figurehead, but an important one that is both recognized and celebrated by the Coronation . Still, I cannot and will not ask you to take an oath in the name of a deity in which you do not believe. In those instances, the Apostles Creed, for example, will be sung by the choristers and not said by you, so you do not have to compromise yourself. You can remain silent during the prayers. In this you can adhere to the form, and you can be seen as the British St. Michael publicly defending the faith, while your private conscience remains your own. This is the only solution I see, Your Majesty."

"And worthy of Solomon," replied Albert, impressed at the tightrope the Archbishop was prepared to walk on his behalf.

"And will this assuage my critics within the Church?"

"My goal is simply to have them remain silent if they cannot fully acclaim you as King."

"That's all we can ask, if we are to accept their own claim to conscience."

He looked at the Archbishop and said gratefully, "I've caused you so much trouble, and yet you have stood beside me. I will not forget this."

The Archbishop himself was pleased with the result.

"Your father worried about this moment. He wanted more than anything to have you wear St. Edward's Crown. He and I decided on this solution years ago."

"And will it work?" asked Albert.

"I swore to him that I would see you as King. Yes, sir, it will work."

"Then I am forever indebted to you. I realize this must come at some personal cost for you."

"That, as they say, comes with the territory. For my part, it is both an honor and a privilege to serve you, Your Majesty."

And the meeting was over.

Paul was working at his desk when Albert returned.

"How did it go?"

"He's taking the risk of schism within the Church to see me on the throne. And he did use the A-word. Still, it went well."

As the Archbishop returned to Canterbury, he worried that perhaps he should have been more open about the true breadth of dissent within the Church of England at having Albert on the throne, and especially as the church's titular head. Still, there was no need to unduly alarm the King. Now that he knew Albert would swear to uphold, defend, and protect the Church in good faith – such an ironic term in this case, he realized – it was time to release his pastoral letter to the faithful, assuring them that Albert would fulfill his duty and rule to the utmost of his abilities, and that, therefore, he was a worthy successor to throne and crown. The letter would be read from every Anglican pulpit so there would be no mistaking the Church's allegiance to the new monarch. That should be enough for most of the faithful to enthusiastically support Albert, and to at least silence the rest. At such a delicate moment, even quiet muttering could undermine the support of some, while he knew that on Coronation Day the country needed to be unified. Well, he was a firm believer in the power and efficacy of prayer to perform miracles, and now it was definitely miracle time.

CHAPTER 56

"Great news!"

The men are at lunch. Paul looks at Albert expectantly.

"Connie's eggs have passed the test!"

"Cheers!" exclaims Paul enthusiastically.

"She has signed the contract. She has her first payment of fifty thousand pounds. And now Sir Sullivan and your mother can see the procedure through to its end, with the implantation of the fertilized egg. Once it becomes viable and starts to divide and multiply, and a birth date can be determined, then the public announcement will be made sometime after the Coronation ."

"And when will you tell Lizzie?"

"The night before."

"And do you want me there?"

"No. This will be just between brother and sister."

"I'd wear protective clothing, just in case she decides to rip you apart like a defensive and vengeful lioness."

"I can just see the headline now: 'King Mauled by Maddened Feline Sister!'"

Paul smiles, but neither one is happy at the thought.

"You need to be careful," Paul warns. "She might be capable of anything once she understands the line of succession has been irrevocably changed."

"My hope is that, after she calms down – "

"If she calms down," interrupted Paul.

"That after she calms down," continues Albert, "she accepts the situation and continues her outstanding work with Pauline on her foundation, which can help so many people. She is capable of a lifetime of benefit to the country. I just want her to continue that. After all," he says with a smile, "I am a cockeyed optimist."

"That's one of the things I love most about you."

"Anything else?"

"Your armpits."

"I would hope so since you spend so much time in them."

"Let me enjoy my simple pleasures."

"Any time, my love. You do know how to make me happy. Your investiture as Duke will make me especially happy because you will be provided for in case anything happens to me."

The two men look solemnly at each other.

"Thank you," replies Paul quietly. "I appreciate that."

"Now," says Albert as he recovers his jocularity. "What's happening with the Coronation ?"

"Ask me tonight because I'm going to the Abbey this afternoon."

"Well then, cheers."

"Cheers."

CHAPTER 57

Later that night, the two are in bed.

"I spent all afternoon at the Abbey, and I can tell you with authority that things are cracky great, as we say in Durham."

"That's good news!"

"Do you know the Duke of Norfolk well?"

"Not well at all, actually; I only see him a few times each year. But coronations and other royal occasions are part of what he and his ancestors have traditionally done in terms of planning and organizing. So, how is he doing?"

"I am so impressed!" enthused Paul. He has the Abbey and all the workshops absolutely humming with remarkable efficiency. Everything is just about ready. He reeled off bucket loads of facts to me, such as the Abbey usually holds twenty-five hundred people but, with the addition of scaffolding, platforms, and balconies, it can now seat some seven thousand. They've taken out many of the side windows so people can enter on ramps and get directly to their seats. The pipe organ is being restored, and I can't wait to hear it. There's a special royal box for Lizzie and Larry and the children, and Mama who, I can tell, is getting really excited. Well, the whole city is excited and, from what I can tell, so is the entire country and all the ships at sea! Albert, it seems to me the whole country is behind you or else, if they aren't, at least they are keeping quiet."

He enthusiastically continued: "The music will be fabulous, with a chorus of four hundred from cathedrals throughout the country, an orchestra of seventy, with a special trumpet section, all preparing to acclaim you as King. It will be a glorious spectacle. The Abbey will be positively smothered in flowers. At the moment you are crowned, the Abbey bells will start peeling, as a signal for bells to be rung across the city, then across the country, then in every Commonwealth country around the world. It's going to be indescribable. I know you've already had fittings for the crowns, and that you are practicing to wear them. Five pounds, I believe, for St. Edward's Crown. Make sure it doesn't fall off! Your Coronation robes look spectacular. I am highly envious. Now, I'll be sitting in the Recognition Chair, to one side of the platform, where you'll go to face the four directions after being crowned. There is even a special carpet that was woven in India from Australian wool – "

"How I miss not being Emperor of India," said Albert with a sigh. "And I know we had to give the Koh-I-Noor back, but it was an amazingly beautiful stone."

Rather than wade through the errors of colonialism, Paul just moved on: "The carpet is one hundred and seventy feet by twelve feet wide. I saw it being rolled out across the Abbey floor, which is now covered in wood to protect the original stone. "Anyway," he said almost breathlessly, "the carpet is blue with your initials woven in gold letters, and those are the Coronation colors as well."

Albert interrupted: "Can't the carpet be made in this country?"

"Evidently the last broadloom capable of that size is in Scotland."

"Ah," said Albert resignedly, "Say no more."

Paul continued: "The Duke coordinates everything from a kind of central control room. The Annexe in front of the Abbey is completed, which you'll enter first for the final preparations, and where the peerage will gather for the entrance into the Abbey. There is even a committee overseeing officially recognized souvenirs, headed by some duke or duchess. Hotel rooms are booked. In-bound flights are full. Diplomats are coming from all over the world, even the Tsar and Tsarina, so Michael can have his own family reunion. I can say, in all honesty, that this is a very big deal, and the only one you will ever get."

"I'm worn out just hearing about it," admitted Albert. "And wearing St. Edward's Crown is tricky. I really don't want to stumble."

"Oh, they are also checking the raised platform on which the investiture takes place to make sure it's completely smooth and carpeted so there's no chance that you'll stub your royal toes on anything, and nothing will snag your royal robes."

"There's a lot to consider, isn't there?"

"You have no idea. And where do all these officials come from, anyway? There's the Hereditary Usher of the White Rod, the Gold Stick of England, even the King's Champion, of all things. I've never seen them hanging out here."

Albert laughed as he explained, "Nowadays they are purely ceremonial in nature, primarily just for the coronation, though centuries ago they usually had other roles to fill as well. After the coronation they go back to their everyday lives, as we all can.

"Also, after the coronation is when Sir Humphrey thinks it best to have my first Honors Day, when you will be formally invested as Duke of Durham. He knew it would be better to wait until I'm crowned and anointed King, in case someone raised the issue of legality later. It seems these days one can never be too sure. Also, I'll have several knighthoods to perform, which I'm looking forward to; I just love the idea of wielding a sword. Now, that's entertainment! There will also be several OBEs and Dames of the Empire, what's left of it."

Which was when Paul said he'd rather be a dame than a duke.

"I know," agreed Albert, "but we're already pushing the envelope as it is. Push any harder and the whole edifice might shatter, so let's just let things go for now. And, anyway, what were you saying about armpits?"

But Paul was already there.

CHAPTER 58

The Lord Bishop pays a surprise visit to Princess Elizabeth. She receives him in her drawing room. He enters, bows, and she motions him to the chair in front of her. They both sit.

"And to what do I owe this pleasure? You are far south of Durham."

She is puzzled because she barely knows him. Why is he here? she asks herself. He is dour and taciturn.

"Unfortunately, this is no social call, Your Majesty, if I may be the first to use that phrase."

Its inappropriateness worries her, and she feels a tinge of dread, but shows nothing and says nothing. The Lord Bishop is confident and continues without hesitation. He knows his talking points, and the end he wants to achieve.

"I represent a small but powerful group [Most assuredly all men, she thinks to herself, and instantly dismisses whatever it is he is about to say], of highly reputed clergy and laity, of influential peers, politicians, members of the House of Commons, well-connected bankers, industrialists, media owners, and even high-ranking military officers. [Yes indeed, all men, she thinks scathingly]

The Lord Bishop mistakes her silence for assent and so continues.

"Our goal is to prevent your brother from ascending to the throne at the Coronation so he can be replaced with you as Queen, or [since he understands she has rejected the crown] you as Queen Regent until your daughter Victoria comes of age."

She remains silent; her face impassive; so he goes on, confident of success.

"We consider your brother anathema to the goals and values of this country and of the monarchy. He is an open homosexual – "

"Whom you helped to marry," she points out.

"And which I now sorely repent and regret. He has married a multi-racial boy."

"Who is legally a man and whom, I understand, you have praised as the finest singer in your own cathedral choir."

This unexpected resistance starts to unsettle the Lord Bishop.

"Yes, well, in his place he performed admirably. But I am not here to discuss young Mr. McGregor."

Back on task, he feels confident again.

"Your brother is an avowed and even proud atheist. And how can an atheist be head of the Church of England?"

By now his anger has brought him to the point of shouting at the startled woman.

"It is folly! It is immoral! And it must be stopped!"

Suddenly the Lord Bishop realizes he is yelling at the very woman he wants as queen. He stops abruptly, takes three deep breaths to calm down, and proceeds in a far less emotional tone.

"For these reasons, Your Majesty, [How shameless, she thinks. She already has an aversion to this man and his mission which, unfortunately for him, she can see all too clearly], we have concluded that your brother is mentally unfit to rule. We consider him to be psychologically unbalanced, and we suggest, instead of seeking the crown, that he should step aside and seek treatment instead."

There is still no verbal response from the Princess Royal, just a slight narrowing of the eyes. The Lord Bishop is too obtuse to understand what he's unleashing, and so he continues.

"Therefore, we propose, once you give your word of

consent, to immediately make public our support for you as the only legitimate monarch, the only choice to follow your father, whom we deeply revere. Your brother is not that person. You are. We can change public opinion so the country understands the danger into which Albert is leading us: a world where tradition is not only cast aside but ground under foot, and we will not have it!"

Once again, his voice rises in anger.

"Albert must abdicate to you and, if he will not go peacefully, he, nonetheless, will go. All we need is your word and the deed is done!"

He finally stops talking and looks expectantly at Elizabeth. He knows she must accept what he and the group have so carefully planned. However, she makes him wait while she continues to stare at him, until he actually begins to sweat and to squirm. Finally, she speaks.

"You want my word?" she asks in a toneless voice, which itself is a warning he chooses to ignore.

"Yes, Your Majesty."

"Little man!" she says with a tone of authority that he, in his admittedly confined world, has never heard from a woman and from very few men.

"You vile worm!"

She speaks with an icy hauteur that shows her complete contempt, utter disdain, and absolute repugnance of him. He knows all is lost. He also realizes that he is confronting a queen.

"You come into my house, and you dare to threaten my family, the Royal Family, with a cabal? A putsch? You know nothing about me and even less about my father and his ideals. My word to you and your gentlemen, and they are all white males, aren't they?"

His downcast silence confirms her suspicions.

"I thought so. Once again men are telling us [And she does not need to clarify who this 'us' is] what to do. I will not have it! Boys. You are just boys in your boys' club playing at being men. You are the pretenders. You want my word? Here it is: No! No!! No!!!"

And the power of her voice pushes the sound of the word into the very walls of the room. Now the Lord Bishop is shaken and clearly trembles.

"My brother Albert is our father's rightful heir, and he is your rightful King. He lives by our father's ideals. He has a vision for Britain that is not crippled by your narrow prejudices, the detritus of the past. Yes, he is openly homosexual, but he has found a man he genuinely loves and, together, they will make Britain worthy of the best of its past. And he has publicly affirmed my eldest daughter as his successor, so the line is assured. And I hope Albert reigns for many, many years before Victoria ascends the throne.

"And, yes, he is an avowed atheist, but he is also a student of history, and he knows and acknowledges the intimate connection between Church and State. And at the coronation, he will publicly affirm the oath, and will sign the document as well, giving his word, as King, that he is prepared to die to defend the Church of England as it, and the monarchy, have defined our country's history, paid for with so much blood. That is his ideal, despite what he privately thinks, and that was our father's ideal as well. Is that not an admirablc, and expected, goal for a monarch?"

She does not wait for an answer but continues.

"I understand, Your Grace, that at one time you participated in a hunger strike to force the creation of a Palestinian homeland?"

He looks at her in surprise and merely nods.

"Am I not correct in thinking that the purpose of a hunger strike is a willingness to die for a cause? And, in that instance, for a people in whose religion you did not believe?"

The Lord Bishop is moved to protest.

"Your Majesty, I hardly think the two can be – "

"Silence!"

He submits and says nothing more.

"You disgust me with your hypocrisy. I thought you were a different man. What has happened to you? It's like you've been through some kind of re-programming camp. Why have you changed?"

He sullenly says nothing.

"I don't understand it," she admits. "But I will give you one chance, and only one, to regain your footing from this lapse into which you have fallen."

He looks at her skeptically.

"Attend the coronation. Bend the knee. Swear fealty and devotion on your life to my brother, as sole and rightful monarch; pledge to him your honor, fortune, and obedience; and nothing you have said here today will leave this room. But if you cannot do this, then I cannot answer for the consequences. Do you understand   me?"

He merely nods.

"Say it!" she commands.

Silence, then, very softly, "I understand."

"Good. Now leave. You bore me."

She picks up a small gold hand bell on the table beside her and rings it. Immediately a staff member opens the door, enters, and bows.

"The Lord Bishop is leaving," says the Princess Royal in a curt, business-like tone.

"Accompany him to his car and make sure he takes

372

nothing on the way out."

The Lord Bishop gives her a look of hatred, but she has already turned away to study a Gainsborough on a nearby wall. She already regrets that last remark as the one time during the entire confrontation when she let her anger override her reason, but she also admits just how much she enjoyed saying it. A simple pleasure after a most distasteful afternoon.

Steaming and hurt, the Lord Bishop bows his head, says, "Ma'am," and leaves.

And that is how Princess Elizabeth single-handedly stopped what would literally have been a palace coup. She was also true to her word that she never told anyone, not even Larry, what happened that afternoon in the drawing room. As it turned out, she didn't have to.

CHAPTER 59

The Archbishop is working at his desk when the man who doesn't yet know he is already the former Lord Bishop of Durham is announced by his assistant. The Archbishop continues to work and doesn't recognize his entrance. The man stands before him, not understanding the lack of acknowledgment, when the Archbishop, a man of great civility, would normally rise to greet him with a smile, firmly grasp his hand, and lay his other hand warmly on his shoulder. So, the man knows something is wrong.

This is two days after his meeting with Princess Elizabeth, and he can only surmise that the Princess Royal lied to him, and he assumes the Archbishop knows about the meeting. For his part, the former Lord Bishop has already informed the others in the plot that their mission has failed, totally and abysmally, and there is no backup plan.

The Archbishop continues to ignore him, and now the once Lord Bishop of Durham is starting to perspire, which he does easily when stressed, and now he is certainly stressed. He doesn't know whether to continue standing, or if he can sit in the chair facing the Archbishop's desk. He decides to sit, and then continues to wait, and he perspires even more as he glances around the room with its oak paneling and beamed ceiling and hardwood parquet floor. This could have been his, he thinks, except for that cursed woman.

Finally, the Archbishop's anger overwhelms him, and he slams his fist onto the top of his desk. The loud retort vibrates through the wooden desk and bounces around the wooden room like being inside a kettle drum when struck. The Archbishop finally looks at the man with the intense ferocity he'd last seen in Elizabeth. He knows, again, that the game is over.

"How could you be so stupid?" demands the Archbishop, and it is not a question.

"You could have had everything if only you'd been content to wait. You were to be my successor," he tells the startled man, who actually hadn't known that at all.

"This," and the Archbishop, with a forefinger pointed to the ceiling, waves his hand in circles to encompass the entire room. "This," he repeats as he lowers his forefinger to point directly at the now-profusely sweating man, "could have been yours."

He glares at the man before him with disgust and contempt.

"Did you really think you and your group could plan a putsch and we wouldn't know?"

He does not need to define "we," as the now former Lord Bishop clearly realizes it includes Church and State.

"We knew everything from the beginning. Fortunately, there were loyal men among you justifiably horrified at your plot to overthrow the rightful King, and who have informed on you since then and have spied on you like moles in a Le Carré novel. You thought your silly, Masonic-like oaths of secrecy would override loyalty to King and England? Now you've lost everything. Everything!"

And once again, as he had with Princess Elizabeth, the now former Lord Bishop takes out a linen handkerchief to wipe his forehead beaded with sweat. His eyes have the horror of a hog who knows it is going to be slaughtered.

"So, you repudiate the marriage vows of a doctrinally sanctioned ceremony which you and I performed side by side? What's happened to you? Why have you changed so much as to be unrecognizable to me? What did they offer you? I cannot figure it out. I am completely baffled."

But the answer comes as he sees the man in his own office, and he triumphantly smiles with the knowledge. He holds up a hand.

"This is what they promised you, isn't it? The Archbishopric itself. And you just couldn't wait, could you? You have ambition I didn't notice before, and I pride myself on my understanding of human nature, but I see I've made a terrible mistake. And that is completely on me. And so that is why you've repudiated the marriage, despite its being in accordance with church doctrine."

"It was wrong," said the former Lord Bishop for the first time.

"Oh, so now you're putting conscience above doctrine, like a Free Thinker? Will you be the next George Fox? No, I think Machiavellian duplicity is more your style. But I don't condemn your questioning of doctrine. You know I've always said that if doctrine cannot be justified, then it becomes arbitrary dogma that kills the spirit. So let's look at what you have repudiated to see if it truly does contradict fundamental Christian principles.

"Did you truly see how the King and Mr. McGregor looked at each other as they stood before the high altar at St. Paul's? Their love is so deep and so intense it's clear that each is willing to die for the other. Each man would sacrifice his life to ensure the survival of his beloved. And what you clearly do not understand is that the King is equally ready to sacrifice himself for country and church to defend them, for he correctly understands that one is the reflection of the other. The King is a man of principles and ideals, like his father before him. For both, their duty is life itself. Albert would lay on the high altar, raise the knife himself and cut out his still beating heart if it would save his people, his country, and the Church of England. Duty, with honor, above all else. That is a true monarch, and how few of them have we really had in our country's long, long history? So it makes no difference what he personally believes. Even I have come to recognize that, because that is solely between him and his conscience. What we as a country and as a church can rightfully demand is that he does his duty; and the oath to that effect – to be paid for with his life if need be – he will give at the coronation. He will lead by example, as a good monarch must. Your example, however, is treason."

And here the former Lord Bishop feels he must justify himself and his own actions.

"It is not treason to replace a false king with the rightful monarch."

"Albert is the rightful monarch!" countered the Archbishop. "He is the first born of the previous King and that is how we define the succession in this country. Anything else is a lie, deception, and treason. Five hundred years ago, and if Albert's name were Henry, your head would already be separated from your body and placed on a spike above the Tower gate. As it is, Albert has requested leniency. I had planned to dismiss you without pension, but the King has decided, instead, to forgive you, which, ironically for a man without faith, proves himself to be a better Christian than either of us."

"So what will happen to me?"

"First, you are no longer Lord Bishop of Durham."

The former Lord Bishop looked resigned.

"Instead, you have a reassignment. For some years now I have been petitioned by the good people of Durban – "

"South Africa?" interrupted the startled man.

"Of Durban, as I said, who have patiently been waiting for a bishopric. Now, I've finally found the right man. Your new church is easy to find, just go south, cross the Channel, cross Europe, cross the Mediterranean, and continue south until you run out of land, and there's Durban.

"To make sure you arrive in Durban, you will be escorted from the time you leave this office by a security detail who will follow you back to Durham, where you will pack whatever suitcases you can take on the plane. Your passport and ticket for tomorrow's flight are ready. Whatever else you want will be shipped later, at your expense. You will also pay the entire cost of the security detail. Whatever is left of what you have managed to accumulate these past years will be given to the poor.

"As for the others of your cabal, all the clergy will be reassigned, out of the country. I looked at a map of the world and even I was surprised to learn just how far flung our missions are. As a church, we've ended up in some remarkably remote places. Oh, and these appointments are for life. Meanwhile, the laity involved will be removed from all church offices and from the church rolls as well, as though they never existed. They will not be able to take Holy Communion or to partake in any other church ritual.

"The career politicians are dismissed from their offices. The peers are removed from committee assignments and while, of course, they cannot be removed from the House of Lords, they will be advised, strongly advised, to retire from public life and find solace in their country estates. Members of the House of Commons are removed from office. Bankers and financiers will find all their personal monies invested in their institutions removed at the direction of the Lord of the Exchequer. Military officers are dishonorably discharged without pension. Industrialists and media owners forfeit all government contracts. I believe that about covers it, but you get the idea. And the best part is that the general public will never know what has happened, certainly not before the coronation, which is to be a joyous event of national pride, without worrying about how a small group of discontents who cannot adapt to the present, let alone the future, tried to stop a legitimate succession. Now, I've spoken long enough. Do you have anything to say?"

"What if I refuse?"

"Immediate dismissal without pension, with no chance, as they say, of ever working in this town again. I really wouldn't suggest it."

"And how long have I got to decide?"

The Archbishop looks at his wristwatch, then back at the new Bishop of Durban. "Until you exit this room and stop at the desk of my assistant who is expecting your answer."

The bishop stands, and takes a long, long look around the room that could have been his. The Archbishop pushes a buzzer on his desk and his assistant opens the door.

"Our meeting is over," he explains.

As the bishop turns, nearly painfully it seems, to leave, the Archbishop has a parting thought.

"There is one benefit to your reassignment," he explains. "It adds a nice alliterative touch to a title for a memoir," and the man turns wearily yet quizzically back to the Archbishop, who explains, "My Life as a Traitor, from Durham to Durban."

He smiles icily.

"I won't buy a copy."

Then he returns to the paperwork on his desk.

Summarily dismissed, the Bishop of Durban looks longingly around the room one last time, then leaves, but he does stop at the desk out front, ignoring the security guards waiting to take him to Africa.

CHAPTER 60

Albert gets up from his desk and goes over to sit on the sofa by the window. He calls out to Paul.

"Come here, my darling, and sit beside me."

Paul looks up from his work and misunderstands what Albert has in mind, as he gets up.

"So, you want an afternoon treat?" he asks tantalizingly, until he approaches Albert and sees the seriousness on his face. No, no treat is desired; that's clear.

Albert pats the sofa cushion beside him and Paul sits, puzzled and now concerned. Albert takes his hand and holds it.

"I must tell you something disquieting about the Lord Bishop of Durham. I know you like him."

Paul continues to look at Albert questioningly.

"He is part of an attempted coup to prevent me from being crowned King at the and replaced with Lizzie as Queen."

"What?" shouts Paul, blindsided by this totally unexpected news about a man who not only helped to marry them, but was also a religious man he deeply respects.

"I'm afraid so," continues Albert. "He was one of a small group of men who, it now turns out, took it upon themselves to judge me unfit for the crown because I am both a homosexual and an atheist which, to them, indicated psychological instability. It turns out that the Lord Bishop himself had personally asked Lizzie to either be queen or queen regent until Victoria comes of age."

"And her response?" asks a still shocked Paul.

"Total rejection, of course; after that, the putsch fell apart. She single-handedly saved my throne, which makes the future even more awkward."

He stops talking for a moment, and Paul remains silent, then Albert continues.

"There will be consequences, of course. The Lord Bishop has been transferred and, at this very moment, is on his way to a new post in South Africa."

Despite his horror at this turn of events, Paul bursts out laughing.

"Well, that must be a surprise."

"Yes," agrees Albert with a smile. "I didn't realize the Archbishop had such a delicious sense of irony. And all the others are receiving similarly measured consequences for what is nothing less than treason. And the general public will not know anything, at least not before the Coronation. And while some may speculate at the timing and context for all these changes, there will be no official explanation."

"But you're all right?" asks Paul urgently.

"Of course, darling. I'm fine. And so are you. Graham makes sure of that."

"Because I can't live without you," continues Paul. "I refuse. I would willingly, gladly, die for you, my love."

Albert sees the passionate commitment on Paul's face and hears it in his voice. He takes Paul's hand and brings it to his lips to kiss.

"You know, my dear, that many will bend the knee to me at the Coronation, and pledge fealty and devotion, and their lives and honor, not really to me, but to the crown. And that is as it should be. But you, my darling [And here he kisses Paul's hand again] only you say it to me personally, not as Albert the King, but as Albert the man. And that means more to me than I can say. And in return, I pledge myself to you, to defend and to protect you with my life."

"No, you can't do that, sweet Albert. For as I am a man, so you are the King. And no matter what happens to me [And here Albert tries to protest, but Paul refuses to let him speak] . . . No, my darling, let me finish. If anything happens to me, you must continue. Your duty is to your country. And whether I live another day, a week, or a year, it doesn't make any difference because if I do die, remember, always remember, that I will wait for you. And when you are a very old and a very smelly old man, know that I will be there at the moment of your death so we can cross the river together."

"You promise?" asks Albert softly.

"I promise," reassures Paul. "So what we need to do is to treasure every day we are together, so that no matter what happens, or when it happens, our lives will be full, with no regret."

"How did you get to be so wise?" asks Albert, genuinely in awe of the man before him.

"Let me tell you a story, a personal story of transformative love," says Paul. "And it involves, of all things, a squirrel."

"Is this a La Fontaine fable?" asks Albert.

"No, it actually happened to me. I was in our backyard when I saw a baby squirrel, just this short [And he spreads out his thumb and forefinger]. I don't know how or why he got out of his nest. Maybe he was just adventurous. Maybe his mother knew he was going to die. And maybe he was actually a she, I don't know that either. But I saw this young, confused little creature with no idea where it was, with two neighborhood cats approaching to kill and eat it. So I snatched it up and brought it inside and found a box for it that I lined with cloth and then found an eyedropper, warmed some milk, and fed it. It took the milk, not a lot, but some, and that's how the squirrel I named Little Scrappy came into my life.

"He was so innocent, so trusting, so needy. I immediately took the place of his mother. I held him in a hand and gently touched his forehead. He just relaxed. And he was so tired that he went to sleep in my hand. After that, we were inseparable. It was summer so I could spend all day with him. He loved to crawl on me. He liked to find his way up my arm to lay on my shoulder, next to my neck where he'd just go to sleep. Maybe he felt my heartbeat or liked my warmth. He found his way into my shirt pocket and liked to crawl in there and sleep some more. And he kept taking milk. Never a lot, but enough to keep going. When he was hungry, he would squeak to be fed and, in the middle of the night, he would go, 'Squeak! Squeak! . . . Squeak! Squeak!', so I'd get up and warm some milk and feed him.

"I knew he needed solid food, so I started pulverizing nuts and adding them to his milk. My goal was to eventually get him big enough – and eating solid food like nuts – so he could live outside on his own. One day I had him on the kitchen countertop as I was preparing some nuts, and I decided to give him a large piece of walnut, and he grabbed it with his tiny fingers and held it to his mouth and started nibbling it. He had never done that before. He'd never been taught to do that. He just did it. And I knew then that he could make it on his own. After that, I broke up nuts and put the pieces on a plate. He ate some, but then he stopped eating and all he wanted was the milk. That was when I realized that every moment with him, every hour, every day, was a gift. I knew he was weakening. I knew I could no longer save him. But those moments, when I held him in my hand, or he slept against my neck, or in my shirt pocket, became moments to be treasured because I knew, all too soon, that they would be gone.

"One day I put him on the counter as I prepared his milk, and then he just leaned over and died. I guess his little heart just gave out. And he passed from being a living, vibrant, joy-filled creature to become just a thing, an unmoving thing."

Paul paused, looked away, and Albert said nothing. Then he continued.

"You know, Durham is Viking country, and I loved Vikings. I read all I could about them. So, I gave Little Scrappy a Viking funeral at the back of our garden. I dug a square hole, put a flat stone on the bottom, and lined the sides with other stones, then carefully wrapped my child in a beautiful, patterned piece of Indian silk. I covered him with costume jewelry. I didn't have access to the Crown Jewels at the time. [And he and Albert smile] But he had rings and bracelets, broaches, and a necklace for his very own Viking horde. Then I covered the tomb with another flat stone, and put soil over that, and my baby was gone. But I prepared him to cross the river, and he wasn't alone. And that's how Little Scrappy taught me the transformational power of being thankful for every moment. And you and I, dearest Albert [And Paul looks directly into Albert's eyes, which are surprisingly moist], you and I must do the same, so that when I go [And Paul notices Albert is already protesting] . . . if I should go before you [And Albert doesn't protest now but looks at Paul as though experiencing a kind of apparition], then give me a Viking funeral, and know that I will be waiting for you."

Albert pulls Paul towards him and Paul leans onto Albert's shoulder. If this were a movie, the camera would pull back at this point until the two are in a distant shot, then the iris would close with a slow fade-out to black.

But it's not, as Paul abruptly sits up.

"Besides," he continues, "You must live for our child, whether prince or princess; it must be taught by you alone how to be a monarch. Out of all the people on the planet, only you can teach what he or she must learn. That will be part of your duty to your country, and to me. Now, how is our child doing, by the way?"

Albert, eager to change the subject anyway, abruptly stands up.

"I don't know. Let's go ask the mother."

Soon they are in Connie's apartment.

"We've come to feel our child!" Albert says enthusiastically.

"What is it about men who want to feel the stomachs of pregnant women?" asks Connie in mock indignation. "Well, boys, you're a month too soon. Your child is still a blastoid."

"A what?" asks Paul.

"A blastoid. A small but growing clump of cells."

"But aren't we all just clumps of cells?" asks Albert.

"Yes, but we're fully grown. This little one is still really little. But we do have a prospective birth date.

"Ooh!" say both fathers simultaneously.

"Sometime six months after the Coronation."

Albert turns to Paul.

"So now we can decide when to make the public announcement."

"And when we destroy Lizzie's life," says Paul grimly.

"Unfortunately," agrees Albert, and the three of them look at each other, fully aware of the consequences of their conspiracy.

"You know," says Connie sadly, "She will later look back upon all these times we've interacted with her, visited her, laughed with her and her children, even worked with her, as times of calculated deception. And she would be right. And she will blame your mother most of all."

She says this to Paul, who averts his eyes, and speaks.

"Mama says this is possibly the most difficult and challenging time of her life. She loves Lizzie and the children. She hates to dissimulate, but she also understands the confidentiality involved. She's pulling back from her direct involvement in working with Lizzie and the foundation. The statement of purpose and master plan are done; the board is in place, and the executive director has just been hired. When the split comes, and she knows it will, her hope is that, eventually at least, Lizzie will find solace in the work of the foundation and all the good it can do."

He stops, and Connie continues.

"Our betrayal will break her heart. How could she possibly forgive us?"

"I don't think she ever will," admits Albert. "By creating new life, we're going to destroy an existing one."

"It's like Shiva," explains Paul, as Connie and Albert look at him. "Shiva, the dancing Hindu god who destroys and creates simultaneously. He destroys old worlds while calling new ones into being. He is wreathed in the cosmic snake and the sacred river, while dancing on one foot inside a ring of fire. Now that's a god!"

"What would England be like today if Henry the Eighth had turned Hindu instead of Protestant?" asks Albert.

"It boggles the imagination," says Connie, and the others agree. But they turn silent at the realization that, like Shiva, they, too, are living at the uneasy intersection of creation and destruction, of birth and death, and they sit in silence for a long, long time because there are no good solutions. A baby will be born. A relationship will die. Finally, Albert speaks.

"Our child is a blastoid."

"Trust me," replies Connie wryly. "We've all been there."

CHAPTER 61

Despite the total collapse of the coup following its rejection by Princess Elizabeth, and despite the subsequent retaliation of various kinds against all known members, there remained concern that various pockets of resistance to the King and his Coronation, or even independently acting lone wolves, might still seek regime change. One obvious way would be through assassination, and Graham and his security team, along with MI-5 and various units within New Scotland Yard, were tracking all known suspects. Another, more legal but equally disruptive possibility, was someone using the upcoming hearing of the Court of Claims, before the Coronation, to press a case in public that the King was somehow unfit or unsuitable to be crowned.

This was a distinct possibility, though the Court of Claims typically handled mundane issues such as who was eligible for various titles, duties, and offices regarding various aspects of the tradition-bound and complicated day of ceremony that comprises the Coronation. Still, as the hearing was open to the public, anyone could press a claim, and it was the open-ended nature of the process that worried the government and the palace.

The members of the Court who reviewed and judged the worthiness of the claims were presided over by the Lord High Chancellor, and included the Lord Chief Justice, the Duke of Norfolk as Earl Marshall, the Lord Chamberlain, and several other high-ranking officials of the peerage.

Typically, the agenda dealt with such prosaic items such as the Dean of the Abbey and his staff asking to, as their written request put it, "instruct the King in the Rites and Ceremonies, and to assist the Archbishop of Canterbury, and to retain the

Robes and Ornaments of the Coronation in the Vestry of the Collegiate Church of St. Peter in Westminster, and to have certain allowances and fees."

Another claim made before every Coronation came from the Lord Great Chamberlain, a role which alternated between three notable families of the kingdom, was compensation for a number of items, including "Forty yards of crimson velvet for his robes", as well as the right to dress the King on the day of the Coronation, and that "he or his deputies would carry the royal robe and Crown, the Sword of State and scabbard, and the gold to be offered by the King at the High Altar." He also offered the more prosaic claim to provide both silver and other basins, and for fine damask linen towels for the King to ritually cleanse himself before the Abbey procession began, and with the right to keep the silver and the fine damask linen towels, along with other stated items, as his fee.

There were also historical claims that the current Lord Great Chamberlain decided not to press, including "That he may have livery and lodging in the King's Court at all times" and that he could keep, also as his fee, "the bed wherein the King lays the night previous to the Coronation, with all the valances and curtains thereof, and all the cushions and clothes within the chamber; together with the furniture of the same; and also the night robe of the King wherein His Majesty rested the night previous to the Coronation."

The specific nature of these items provoked the following incident late one night when Albert attempted to explain this claim to Paul.

"He's not taking our bed!" shouted Paul.

"No, my darling, of course not," countered Albert smoothly. "It's just that, historically, the Lord High Chamberlain, since he was responsible for the monarch's chambers, was granted both clothing and lodging near the King at all times, and – "

But Paul wasn't listening and insisted again: "He's not taking our bed!"

Paul really liked the vast size and opulence of the royal bed.

"If he insists on a bed, I'll go buy a cheap one at a Salvation Army thrift store – there must be one somewhere in London – as well as some cheap cotton printed towels with pictures of the Tower and London Bridge on them, and he can have those."

By now, Albert was so annoyed with Paul's persevering about an issue that was not an issue at all that he decided the easiest reply was to take one of the bed's feather pillows and hit Paul with it, who was so startled that he grabbed another feather pillow and hit Albert. Soon, they were battering each other so fiercely, though laughing, that the pillows eventually ripped open and the entire room was covered in a falling snow of white down that had been carefully plucked from the flock of royal geese at Sandringham. Finally, the men stopped and looked ashamedly around the room at the mess they'd made.

"How will I ever explain this to the chambermaid?" asked Albert.

"My dear," replied Paul, "You're the King. You don't have to explain."

Nonetheless, the men spent two hours picking up most, but not all, of the feathers. The chambermaids kept finding stray bits of down for days but never asked any questions.

Cleaning up the room gave Albert and Paul a burst of energy, which they relieved with torrid sex, then, just as Paul was going to sleep in Albert's arms, he mumbled softly, "He's not taking the bed."

Albert just smiled.

The solution of how to handle any untoward claim that the King was unfit for office came from the procedures of the Court of Claims itself, and specifically in the person of Mr. Solomon Pembroke, who pressed his family's historical claim to be the King's Champion. Traditionally, this involved physically defending the King from challengers to his own claim to the throne.   The proudest moment in this regard in Pembroke family history was at the 1821 Coronation Banquet held in Westminster Hall, when the Pembroke at that time entered through the hall's vast wooden doors in armor and on horseback, accompanied by three other gentlemen in their regalia, and also on horseback, as well as sergeants-at-arms, various equerries, and a herald. Then Pembroke, the King's Champion, waited for trumpet fanfares to announce his presence, and the herald proclaimed that "if any person, of what degree soever, high or low, shall deny or gainsay our sovereign lord . . . to be the right heir to the imperial crown of this realm, or that he ought not to enjoy the same; here is his Champion, who saith that he lieth, and is a false traitor, being ready in person to combat with him; and in this quarrel will adventure his life against him on that day soever he shall appoint."

Then Pembroke threw down his gauntlet to the floor and waited for any challenger to pick it up. If none did, the gauntlet was retrieved and the ritual repeated in the center of the hall, then a third time before the King on his throne. Next, the King drank to his champion's health from a special gilded cup and presented the cup to Pembroke in appreciation for his service.

It was Sir Humphrey who decided that a similar strategy might be usefully incorporated into the proceedings of the Court of Claims to, hopefully, dissuade, and even intimidate, any would-be resister to Albert's right to the throne from even presenting a claim which, considering the media who would also be in attendance, would provide an unfortunate disruption just before the Coronation and which must be avoided at all costs considering the event was supposed to be a moment of national unity.

Sir Humphrey decided to present the plan to Solomon Pembroke before the Court convened to make sure he was up to the task.

"So good of you to see me, Mr. Pembroke, on such short notice," said Sir Humphrey.

"Not at all," explained Mr. Pembroke, "My pleasure. Whatever I can do."

"I'm glad you feel that way," smiled Sir Humphrey.

"As the King's Defender, I serve His Majesty with my life."

"We do hope it doesn't come to that," assured Sir Humphrey smoothly, but in a way that made Pembroke question the true nature of the meeting.

"Your family has a long history as the King's Defender."

"It's been my family's privilege to serve the King in that capacity for many generations."

"And then there was that remarkable bit of pageantry in 1821," continued Sir Humphrey,

"The high point of my family's history," said Mr. Pembroke proudly.

"Of course, now the office is purely ceremonial," began Sir Humphrey.

"We bear the Standard of England in the procession," added Mr. Pembroke.

"Quite so," said Sir Humphrey thoughtfully, "but this time the King requires more of you than that."

"It would be a privilege," exclaimed Mr. Pembroke, enlivened at the possibility of greater honor for his family.

Now Sir Humphrey has turned solemn.

"You understand, no doubt, that there are those who say the King isn't fit to rule."

"Scurrilous treachery!" shouted Mr. Pembroke boldly.

"Our thoughts exactly," said Sir Humphrey with a smile. "However, there are concerns that someone may appear at the Court of Claims to petition for the King's removal and, naturally, we cannot allow that to happen."

"Of course not," replied Mr. Pembroke quickly.

"Then you agree that, as the King's Defender, it is your responsibility to make certain of that."

"Of course," asserted Solomon Pembroke, then he paused. "But what can I do?"

"We've decided to use the 1821 ceremony as a precedent."

"But," protested Mr. Pembroke, "I don't have a horse and don't know how to ride."

"That's not an issue because the chamber is too small for a horse anyway," assured Sir Humphrey. "No, we do want you to use the gauntlet however."

"But I haven't got a gauntlet," protested Mr. Pembroke again, not at all sure where this was going, but becoming more convinced that he didn't like it.

"Not a problem," explained Sir Humphrey. "There are many in the Royal Armory Collection. Our plan is to have the Court of Claims approve of your reappointment as the King's Defender as the first item on the agenda. At that same time, the gauntlet will be ceremonially brought into the chamber on the same pillow used to carry St. Edward's Crown in the procession. You know the one, crimson velvet with three lions rampant embroidered in gold thread. The gauntlet will show your authority, and the pillow represents that you are supported by the authority of the crown itself. We hope this show of royal power will be enough to dissuade any would-be resister from pursuing any claim against the King."

"But if it doesn't?" asked Solomon Pembroke quietly.

"Then we have prepared a short speech for you, based on the 1821 speech of your ancestor, in case anyone does proceed with a claim. Here it is all ready for you. Please review it now to assure us that you can memorize it."

He handed a paper to Mr. Pembroke, who read it, then looked up at Sir Humphrey and said, "Done."

"With barely a glance?" asked Sir Humphrey skeptically. And Solomon Pembroke lowered the paper in his hand and quoted it back perfectly, then smiled.

"I have a photographic memory."

"Most impressive," admitted Sir Humphrey. "You do seem the best person for the job. If, after making your challenge, the resister continues to present a claim, then it must be formally considered by the court and a decision made, and I can assure you that the claim will be rejected, but by that time the damage will be done as the media will quickly understand the significance of the claim and will report it to the nation. It's common knowledge that there are pockets of dissent to the King but bringing it to the Court of Claims gives it a kind of legitimacy that must be avoided at all costs. If public approval were to turn against the King, and with Princess Elizabeth rejecting the crown and her daughter too young to rule, who knows what might happen? Indeed, the goal of some resisters is the very abolition of the monarchy, and that we cannot allow."

"No, of course not," agreed Mr. Pembroke.

"At any cost," said Sir Humphrey, while looking directly at the King's Defender. "Because it's possible, if a claim is pressed and rejected, that violence could erupt, and so I need to ask you, Solomon Pembroke, are you prepared to defend the King's honor with your life? As the King's Defender, you swear fealty and honor and your life, but do you mean it? Many will bend the knee to the King at the Coronation and pledge their lives, but I wonder, if it comes to that, how many would actually defend their King to the death?"

Then he paused dramatically and stared piercingly at Pembroke as though weighing his very soul before quietly asking, "Would you?"

And now Solomon Pembroke faced the major existential crisis of his life: would he put that life on the line to defend his King? He thought of his wife, whom he loved and adored; he thought of his grown children; and of the grandchildren he wanted to have. Could he die before even seeing them born? But could he live with himself as an honorable man knowing that he had not been true to his word to defend his King with his life? It was the age-old question of a death with honor or a life in disgrace. How could he face his family? How could he face himself?

Sir Humphrey was glad to see Pembroke taking time to consider a question of such importance. He distrusted those who gave quick, facile answers, knowing they would not hold up under fire. So, he waited while Mr. Pembroke contemplated his future. Finally, he asked again, so softly he could barely be heard: "Will you defend the King with your life? Or must I find a true subject to take your place?"

"Not at all," replied Solomon Pembroke. "Please assure the King that my answer is yes. I will defend him with my life."

"Excellent," replied Sir Humphrey with a smile. "I knew I could count on you."

That evening, as Solomon Pembroke entered his London apartment, his wife was waiting.

"How did things go with Sir Humphrey?"

"He asked if I would truly defend the King with my life."

"And you said . . . ?"

"Yes, of course."

"Cracking good!"

And despite the solemnity Mr. Pembroke felt, he had to smile at a phrase he'd never heard his wife use before.

"He said there might be physical danger from these groups that don't want the King to be crowned. But my oath is to defend the King with my life, and I will do that."

"Well," replied his wife, "if you do die defending the King, know that I will be the proudest widow in Britain."

"I just hope it doesn't come to that," he replied honestly.

"Neither do I," she said. "Neither do I,"

Later that night, in bed with his wife, and just as he fell asleep, Solomon Pembroke thought to himself with a smile, "Cracking good, indeed."

Mr. Pembroke arrived early at the Court of Claims and noted that Sir Humphrey was already there. Gradually the room filled up as the starting time approached. He'd been told that metal detectors were not used for those in the room, so as to not offend the sometimes-touchy sensibilities of the peers in attendance. Pembroke looked around the room and knew most of the people already there from his work in government. However, there was one middle-aged man who stood out, obviously a working man, perhaps a tradesman or shopkeeper. Now Pembroke realized that the man could just be interested in the workings of the Court itself, but he decided to keep an eye on him, nonetheless. He noted that members of the media were already in the press section. Soon, everyone rose in the Privy Council Office as commissioners of the Court, led by the Lord High Chancellor, took their places at a long table, and the hearing was called to order.

The first item on the agenda was indeed the petition of

Solomon Pembroke to be assigned to his family's traditional position as the King's Defender. But before the petition was discussed, the Lord High Chancellor nodded to a bailiff standing by the main doors, who opened them to admit a peer wearing full regalia and carrying, with both hands, the crimson velvet pillow with the three gold-embroidered lions rampant on which laid the royal gauntlet. The peer walked carefully with noble demeanor and carefully placed the pillow with the gauntlet on a table before the commissioners, then bowed to them, turned, and left the room. Neither the Lord High Chancellor nor anyone else made any note of the gauntlet, as though its presence was a traditional part of the Court's ritual proceedings and nothing out of the ordinary. Then the commission addressed the issue of Mr. Pembroke's petition and quickly approved it without comment or question.

Then the Court continued working its way through the day's agenda, beginning with the request by the Dean and Chapter of the Abbey to instruct the King and to perform their other traditional duties. The petition was approved. In each case, the basis for consideration and approval was whether the applicant or the applicant's family had performed the same duties in prior coronations, especially those of Victoria the Second, her daughter Victoria the Third, and her son, George V, Albert's father. Petitions of those who could not provide such a pedigree were rejected.

Based on precedent, the Court affirmed the right of the Duke of Newcastle "to provide a glove for the King's right hand and to support His Majesty's right arm while he is holding the Sceptre"; the right of the Bishops of Durham, Bath, and Wells "to support His Majesty at the Coronation, and to have certain privileges"; and the right of the Mayor of London "to attend the King within Westminster Abbey during the Coronation and bear the Crystal Mace."

The Court also approved the request of the Marquess of Cholmondeley as Lord Great Chamberlain, with the right "to dress the King with all his apparel". The Marquess wisely chose not to request the King's bed, bedding, or room furnishings.

Four petitioners from the same family requested the right to carry the Royal Spurs. Rather than trying to disentangle the conflicting claims, the Commissioners deferred the matter to the King to decide.

Because there was no longer a Coronation Banquet at Westminster Hall, the Court was spared deciding who should be the Grand Panettiere, in charge of bread, salt and carving knives and who, literally, was entitled to the crumbs from the banquet table; the Chief Lardiner, who supplied the meats and whose fee included "all the meats left in the larder after the guests had been fed"; the Napier, in charge of the table linen; and even an office of Herb-Strewer, "who with her attendant maidens scattered flowers on the dais." That position, along with the others related to the coronation banquet, was last filled in the time of George IV. None of those, and others besides, fit the modern conception of the Coronation and their loss was only known, and perhaps even mourned, by traditionalists and historians.

After a break for lunch, the Commissioners continued their work through the afternoon until the very last item came up for consideration, when the Commission accepted any remaining claim from the public at large. By now, few remained in the seating area, and Solomon Pembroke carefully searched each one, wondering if one of them, including the tradesman, might be the person to raise the issue of the King's suitability and thereby activating his own position as the King's Defender.

The Lord High Chancellor called the question: "Are there any other claimants to be heard today?"

And, at that moment, Mr. Pembroke made one of the most important decisions of his life. Rather than waiting for someone to approach the Commissioners and request them to consider the King's suitability, at which point Mr. Pembroke could only react from a weakened defensive position, when the media still present would be aware of dissension and turn it into the main story of the day and, possibly, of the entire Coronation, Solomon Pembroke decided to act peremptorily and head off the opportunity for protest before it could actually be made. So he stood up, strode to the table, turned to face the remaining audience and, with stern countenance and forceful authority, slowly, and with dignity, reached out his hand and placed it on the gauntlet; then glared at the few remaining people in the room.

The Lord High Chancellor repeated the question: "Are there any other claims to be made today?"

Then Solomon Pembroke made another adroit decision to prevent anyone from speaking. He spoke the lines he'd quickly memorized at his meeting with Sir Humphrey, the lines spoken when his ancestor had ridden into Westminster Hall in 1821. In a voice thundering with unexpected power, and though he hardly considered himself a public speaker, he proclaimed, as this time there was no herald to do it for him: "If any person, of what degree soever, high or low, shall deny or gainsay our sovereign lord to be the right heir to the imperial crown of this realm, or that he ought not to enjoy the same; here is his Champion, who saith that he lieth, and is a false traitor, being ready in person to combat with him; and in this quarrel will adventure his life against him on that day soever he shall appoint."

When he began the speech, Solomon Pembroke glared from person to person of those still in attendance but, halfway through, he concentrated his baleful stare at the tradesman, who stared angrily back. When finished, Pembroke did something so unexpected and inspired that those who saw it later spoke about it with near reverence: he raised the metal gauntlet from its crimson velvet pillow and threw it to the floor, where its ancient iron crashed against wood and the resulting boom was magnified by the oak-paneled walls until it seemed like the roar of cannon fire. Even Sir Humphrey jumped. And in the subsequent silence, the Lord High Chancellor made his third appeal, with careful deliberation: "Are there any other claims to be heard today?"

Solomon Pembroke continued to stare at the man he had picked out as the one most likely to disrupt the proceedings of the Court, of the Coronation and even of the very stability of the monarchy with an unwarranted claim, and the man continued to stare angrily back. There was no movement in the room. Everyone was staring at the contest between the two men.

"You will not dishonor my King," thought Solomon Pembroke to himself. "I defend him."

And then the man looked away; Mr. Solomon Pembroke had won the day. The man quickly left the room. The media was completely unaware of what had just happened, and a few attempted to follow the man to ask questions, but a bailiff stood in front of the doors and refused to let them leave.

Sir Humphrey looked at the Lord High Chancellor, and both breathed a sigh of relief. Only they knew how close the meeting had come to creating a crisis for the country.

Mr. Solomon Pembroke was sweating profusely.

That evening, when his wife asked how the day had gone, Solomon Pembroke said, proudly, "I threw down the gauntlet!"

"Cheers!" she replied with pride.

The next day, Solomon Pembroke went to see Sir Humphrey in Whitehall.

"Topflight job, Mr. Pembroke," said a pleased Sir

Humphrey.

"Thank you, sir. A pleasure to serve the King. In the back of my mind, a thought did occur that perhaps the man was innocent and simply interested in the workings of the Court."

"Then you'll be relieved to know," explained Sir Humphrey, "that he was taken into custody immediately after leaving the chamber and, when searched, officials found a loaded handgun, and he said he planned on killing as many as he could before he was killed himself. By staring him down the way you did, you saved not only a bloodbath but possibly the monarchy itself. A good day's work, Mr. Pembroke, a very good day's work indeed. And, best of all, whilst the media knew something was happening, they were never sure what it was, and no one enlightened them. That moment will be swept away by the pageantry of the Coronation. Again, thank you. One of the most astounding acts of courage I've ever witnessed."

Mr. Pembroke was humbled by the acknowledgment.

"It was an honor to defend the King."

Sir Humphrey continued. "His Majesty is well aware of what he owes you, Mr. Pembroke. Sometime after the business of the Coronation is over, you and your wife can expect an invitation to the palace."

And, for the first time, Solomon Pembroke allowed himself to realize he really had done something splendid.

In telling his wife about the meeting with Sir Humphrey, he decided not to mention the upcoming invitation just so she would be surprised.

She was.

They were admitted first to the drawing room, where the King and Paul McGregor were seated on a sofa, and both rose to greet them as they entered. Mr. Pembroke bowed; Mrs. Pembroke curtsied, and the King motioned for them to come forward and sit in the armchairs on the other side of a low table that separated them from the sofa. But as they came forward, the King held out his hand and said, "I'm proud to shake the hand of the man who, single-handedly, saved the crown and possibly even my life. Mr. Pembroke, you are truly the King's Defender!"

Then he did the unexpected and pulled Mr. Pembroke towards him and embraced him in a hug. Both Mr. Pembroke and his wife were surprised. Then Paul stepped forward and hugged her as well. Finally, when they were seated, Albert said he had a present for Mr. Pembroke as a token of his appreciation. He nodded to the footman standing at the door, who left but quickly returned with a large gift box which was set on the table.

Mr. and Mrs. Pembroke looked at each other quizzically while the King smiled like the Cheshire Cat.

"Open it," he urged.

Mr. Pembroke lifted the lid, set it aside, and gazed into the box. There, laying on a crimson velvet cloth, was the gauntlet he'd thrown to the floor.

"This is yours as long as your family remains the Monarch's Defender, which I hope will be as long as there is an England."

Mr. Pembroke raised it out of the box like a holy relic, and showed it to Mrs. Pembroke, who gazed at it as though it were indeed a piece of the true cross.

"And one other thing," said Albert as the gauntlet was placed back in the box.

"At the next Honors List, you will receive an hereditary peerage, not only for you, of course, but for your family, forever. You will be Lord Pembroke, not just Sir Pembroke."

The couple looked at each other in amazement, and, before they could thank the King, he said, "Trust me, my friend, you have earned it."

What he did not say was that the peerage had come open when the previous holder, one of the major conspirators, had renounced it, saying he would never live in a country ruled by a homosexual atheist, nor would he live in any Dominion or Commonwealth country where he would have to see the King's visage on currency or stamps, so he decided to move to America.

"Ah," said Paul when informed of the foreign exile, "the ultimate sacrifice."

"Now, let's eat," said the King, so they did.

That evening, in bed, the King's Defender leaned over to his wife and said, "Quite a day, eh, Mrs. Pembroke?"

"Quite a day, indeed, Mr. Pembroke."

"The Royal Gauntlet, an hereditary peerage, and lunch with the King and his husband."

"Yes, Mr. Pembroke."

Then he paused to consider another idea.

"I suppose a horse would have been too much?" suggested Mr. Pembroke hesitantly.

Mrs. Pembroke, familiar with her husband's tendency towards what Americans call pushing the envelope, just smiled.

"Yes, indeed it would have been, Mr. Pembroke."

"Ah, pity," he replied as he switched off the light.

CHAPTER 62

It was after midnight, and Albert couldn't sleep. His coronation was in a few hours; no longer tomorrow, but today. He tossed; he turned; he tried sleeping on his stomach; on his back; on his side. Nothing worked, while Paul slept soundly beside him. Well, it wasn't Paul's coronation. Albert didn't even try counting sheep. Some of his favorite childhood memories were being with the flocks at Sandringham and Balmoral. The royal shepherds let him into the stalls when the lambs were born. He liked to dry them with a towel. The mothers didn't seem to mind as they still licked them clean, as their genes told them to. As they grew up and gamboled across the fields and meadows, he would run with them. This was one of the few things he appreciated about Balmoral, while Lizzie and Papa were off killing things, and one of the few outdoor activities he actually enjoyed there. He watched, amazed, as the sheep dogs carefully rounded them up and drove them into a paddock each evening for safety.

No, sheep would not put him to sleep, so he rehearsed, yet again, the ritual at the Abbey. The Dean had been thorough in his instruction. Albert knew where to sit, when to stand, when to approach the High Altar, when to kneel, when to rise, what to hold, what to put back, what to say, and when to say it. He was a quick learner and memorizing the ritual and the words came easily. He only resented how often the Dean made him repeat prayers that Albert wouldn't even be saying, as though by repetition he would become a believer. The Dean, now old, had, years earlier, provided the same instruction for Albert's father and, as his father was a conforming, traditional man who

403

believed easily, it had been simpler and much less stressful for the Dean, who now rejected the advice of the Archbishop to ignore the prayers and go easy on Albert who, in turn, realized the Dean knew he was preparing an apostate to be head of the Church of England. Albert had enough people against him; he didn't need the Dean as well, so he patiently repeated the prayers and supplications, still without believing in them, but equally determined to spend his entire life defending them, and even to die for them if necessary.

And yet, Albert was finally coming to realize that it was too easy to say he was simply a non-believer. After long and numerous discussions with both Paul and Pauline, he now realized he wasn't an atheist after all. He recognized that while he was not religious, he was most definitely spiritual. It was just that in rebelling against the dogma and beliefs of the church of his youth, he had done the typical trajectory of going in the exact opposite direction to loudly proclaim he was a complete atheist. The truth was, and this was something he had discussed with the sympathetic understanding of the Archbishop but not yet with the very dogmatic Dean, that while he refused to be told what to believe, unlike his father, he was, nonetheless, very open to the subtle experiences of his own intuition, which is to say that he recognized a spiritual unity, a foundation that underlies, well, everything, like a creative fire from which everything comes and to which, eventually, everything returns. It was this reality of the creative and ever-creating spirit to which he responded, which was why the most important moment of the service, the only one that really spoke to him personally, was at the actual anointing, during which the choir sings the "Veni, Creator Spiritus" – "Come, Creator Spirit" – to which he responded in a non-Christian way as being the closest statement of his own personal belief.

He eagerly anticipated the moment when the sacred oil was poured from the beak of the Ampulla – the gold bird – that didn't just represent the spirit but actually contained the spirit in the very essence of the oil itself, which was given to Thomas á Becket during a visitation by the Holy Mother when he was in France. The oil was then secretly protected for two centuries until first used at the Coronation of Henry the Fourth.

The oil for Albert's Coronation was pressed from olives grown in monastic groves on the Mount of Olives and were pressed outside Bethlehem. Essential oils of sesame, rose, jasmine, cinnamon, neroli, benzoin, amber, and orange blossom were then added in proportions according to an ancient church receipt.

Finally, it was consecrated in a ritual at the Church of the Holy Sepulcher in Jerusalem by both the Patriarch of Jerusalem and Jerusalem's Anglican Archbishop.

From the beak, the oil was poured into the gold Anointing Spoon, with its handle inlaid with four pearls. The Archbishop would touch the oil with a finger, and then touch the oil onto Albert's chest, his palms and, finally, to his head. The oil would be absorbed into his body as the spirit entered him and he would be transformed, as though glowing from within.

Albert thought it was rather like his father's woodworking, the closest thing the late King George had to a hobby. He loved to carve wood, and he had his own woodworking shop at each royal residence. He carved figures – animals and birds mainly – but also utilitarian objects like spoons, ladles, and bowls. When an object was done and the King had sanded it smooth, he would coat it with linseed oil, and Albert loved to watch the dull, opaque wood – be it cherry, oak, or walnut – and see it change with the simple application of oil that soaked into the wood and made it glow as though it were alive. It gave a depth to the wood, and a kind of fire that completely transformed a prosaic object into a kind of jewel. It was a running joke that any newborn within the extended Royal Family could expect its own spoon and bowl set as though being prepared for its first meal of porridge, despite the fact that, even at Balmoral, oatmeal porridge was never on the menu. Albert's own spoon-and-bowl set was still in his room at Balmoral, proudly displayed on a Regency bureau.

The Anointing was a similar, though internal, kind of transformation, and Albert knew he would never be the same again. The spirit in the sacred oil would, somehow, make him glow in a way similar to his father's spoons and bowls. It was an actual sign of a preexisting internal reality that was true for all people, as each person comes to recognize a particular destiny provided by fate, or by the equally inscrutable workings of the spirit. It was just that, in his case, his destiny would be observed today by, potentially, a billion people.

This was why, as he had explained to the Archbishop, the English religious tradition to which he most responded to was not the dogma of the Church of England or, indeed, any similar Christian church, but to the Inner Light as described by George Fox, the remarkable founder of the Society of Friends. Yes, Albert was unquestionably ready to follow that light wherever it would lead. Unfortunately, the Archbishop refused to change the traditional words of the ritual to incorporate any more than just a hint of Quakerism, as it had remained anathema to the official Church of England for many years, to the point where its adherents were persecuted, jailed, and even tortured as being dissidents. Yet Albert was content to conceptually acknowledge the state religion with his head, while his heart led him someplace else. And so, on some level, the Dean was aware of this split within Albert and it concerned him – though certainly not the Archbishop – which meant the Dean simply did not trust Albert, as he had his father; which was why, in one last, desperate attempt, he hoped that by repetition something of church dogma would sink into his recalcitrant royal student.

Yet, the way Albert saw it, the official church could have his body, but not his soul; that he reserved for his own conscience, and his own spiritual experience. And he understood that by protecting his own belief, he was protecting the diversity of belief and non-belief of his people as well, for many of whom the Church of England was simply no longer meaningful.

And with that, Albert finally felt ready to sleep. He rolled over and put an arm and leg across Paul's body, who was facing away from him. Then he laid his head against Paul's shoulder, and pushed his face towards Paul's neck, until all he smelled was Paul.

They were awakened by a sunrise salute of twenty-one cannons firing from a battery in Hyde Park.

"Now we're awake," said Paul as they got out of bed and put on dressing gowns for a private breakfast with Pauline.

Her people, now also his, had arrived from Jamaica and were staying at St. James Palace, while Lizzie and her family were staying at Kensington, and Connie and her family were at Buckingham Palace where they'd been for some time.

The Jamaican contingent had already had its day of shopping on the town and returned with so much stuff that Albert was considering leasing a private jet just for them and their luggage. Many of their purchases were souvenirs, and Paul and Albert were surprised to see themselves packaged as royal bobble heads, and with their faces on tee shirts, plates, football jerseys, pennants, and even on the sides of plastic replicas of Durham Cathedral and the Abbey.

He and Paul hosted a large dinner for the extended Royal

Family, followed by a remarkably pleasant evening in the Great Hall, where the children of Lizzie and Connie, as well as those of Pauline's family, ended up playing together and running and yelling up and down that vast corridor that was half sitting room and half hallway. Pauline was embarrassed but Albert was delighted, saying the palace hadn't rung with the sounds of children since he and Lizzie were children themselves, and even then, their father required them to behave with the decorum expected of future monarchs.

It was only at Sandringham and Balmoral where the twins could run outside and yell with the abandon that most children take for granted.

It was while seated together in the Great Hall that Lizzie realized Connie and her family had been living in Buckingham Palace for weeks. This surprised her as she knew Connie worked from home and just assumed, if she needed to be in town for work reasons, that she would have a place of her own, an apartment at Kensington, for example. Still, she knew how strapped Connie and her husband were for cash and thought it considerate of Albert to let them stay in the palace while Connie was evidently working on a new book project.

It was also that night that Albert finally got to hear the stories which he'd eagerly awaited: the experiences that Paul's great uncle had while working at Noël Coward's house in Jamaica, which was how he put himself through university to become the family's first professor. Paul's great-grandmother had indeed not been able to come due to age-related health issues, but the great uncle had amazing stories to tell about Coward and his guests, and Albert said he'd never look at Lord Olivier the same way again.

Breakfast was eaten in silence as all three were aware of the immense preparations that had been taking place for weeks to ensure the day's events would proceed faultlessly. They were also aware that, literally, millions of people already lined the direct and short processional route to the Abbey, and the much longer return trip that would take them on both sides of the river. The very weight of the occasion seemed to prohibit speech.

As breakfast ended, a footman entered to announce the entrance of the Lord Great Chamberlain to help Albert prepare. All three stood up from the table. Paul would dress separately as the preparation for Albert required its own specialized routine of ritual bathing and being dressed. Albert looked at the two of them with just a hint of melancholy, and said, "And so the great work begins," freely quoting from one of his favorite plays.

Paul watched Albert return to their bed chamber to prepare for the day, then went to the room where his valet helped him dress. He regretted not having time to speak privately with Albert after breakfast, at least for a few minutes, but the two of them were already captured by the rituals of the day and were no longer capable of volition, having already surrendered to the fate that moved them along according to the checklist of an inviolable agenda.

But what would Paul have said to his husband? "I love you," naturally. "We'll meet at the other side of this day." That would be odd to say because they were going to spend most of the day in the presence of each other, though they would be together in the presence of millions along the processional routes, of seven thousand in the Abbey, and a billion or more on the telly. But what made Paul remarkably sad was knowing that Albert, the man, would be irretrievably different the next time they met in private, late tonight, and, for that reason, things between them would never be the same. It was as if all these months together were the only honeymoon they would ever have, a time they would later look back upon with regret, because today Albert would change, and be changed, forever. Today he would be entered by the spirit and transformed into something more than the man he had been until now. Paul realized that from today he would be sharing the bed not of a human being, but of a god; not a Christian god of perfection, but more like a Greek or Norse god whose strengths, and frailties, are magnified by their divinity. This new reality filled Paul with uneasiness because, frankly, he did not know who he would be sharing his bed with. Albert, by virtue of what he would undergo today, will not be the same Albert he was this morning. Like a butterfly emerging from its chrysalis, he will undergo a metamorphosis. The body will be the same, but not the person inside it. The spirit will enter and consume the Albert he knew and nothing – Paul understood regretfully, and a point he could only repeat – would ever be the same again. By virtue of his consecration, Albert is to become an offering to his people, and the prior relationship between Paul and Albert that had been at least somewhat carefree to this moment, has already ended. For months Paul had looked forward to this day, not knowing the full meaning of the sacrifice it entailed. He could not stop it. Yet he would stand by Albert and protect him and love him until their lives were over, but he also knew, with a wistful melancholy, that their innocence was gone.

The Lord Great Chamberlain was waiting for Albert in the bathroom. The large, porcelain tub was half filled with mildly steaming water. He was assisted by two other chamberlains; all called into being for this particular moment. Albert stood by the tub and held out his arms so his dressing gown could be removed. He stood there, naked as he had been born, for this was a day of rebirth. He wanted the three to see him naked in the flesh, so they could later vouch, if need be, that, indeed, he took nothing with him from his previous life. Then he stepped into the warm water and sat down in it as it rose to his stomach. A chamberlain hung the dressing gown on a metal hanger on the wall. Beside the tub, a chamberlain held a gold tray, with a gold cup on it, a new bar of the finest Castile soap in a porcelain dish, and an actual sponge. Albert wondered where on earth one could still find a real sponge these days – Harrods, perhaps – but then he banished that speculation as unworthy of the moment and simply blanked his mind of all thought so he could be completely mindful of an experience not to be repeated in his lifetime.

The Lord Great Chamberlain knelt on a plush white rug beside the tub, took the cup, lowered it into the water, filled it, and poured it over Albert's head, who stared straight ahead as rivulets of water streamed down across his face. The Lord Great Chamberlain continued pouring water across Albert's body, then set the cup back onto the tray, and then took the bar of soap, dipped it in the water to wet it, and rubbed it gently across Albert's skin so it lathered into bubbles. He returned the soap to its dish on the tray, and then wiped the sponge across Albert's shoulders, then his back, then his chest. Albert, in a moment of vanity, was pleased his body was in such good condition, even if it was pale.

The Lord Great Chamberlain lifted Albert's right arm to wash it, and then his left. He stood, and asked Albert to lower his head so he could pour liquid Castile soap from a small ewer on an adjacent table onto his hair and wash it. He gently rubbed Albert's scalp and the soap lathered up under his fingers. He then stood aside as an assistant chamberlain poured several pitchers of warm water over Albert's head and torso to completely remove the soap.

"Would Your Majesty please stand up?" he was asked, so Albert stood as water flowed down his body. The Lord Great Chamberlain took the bar of soap again and gently rubbed it over Albert's genitals, and then his buttocks, and then up and down his right leg, and then his left. More pitchers of water were used to completely rinse the lower part of Albert's body, and the soapy water was drained from the tub so Albert's feet could also be washed and rinsed.

The Lord Great Chamberlain held out a hand, which Albert took to steady himself as he stepped out of the tub onto the soft, plush rug, then towels of the softest pile Indian cotton [Not Egyptian, mind] were used to wipe Albert's head and body dry.

Albert realized similar rituals of cleanliness were used in ancient times to prepare both human offerings and their attending priests, and he felt himself to be both offering and priest. He was ready to sacrifice himself for his people, and to serve them as well. The entire Coronation was simply a public announcement of these twin commitments.

A wooden-handled bristle brush was used to comb Albert's hair, and then he stood there, arms slightly apart from his body, hands facing outward, to show he was purified, then he walked back into the adjacent bed chamber to be clothed for the day.

Linen was the cloth of choice, mentioned in the Bible as worn by the Hebrew priests in the Temple in Jerusalem. While using a plant fiber requiring a sedentary farming life might be seen as an odd choice for what had been a primarily nomadic and herding people who followed their flocks of sheep and goats, the Hebrew people, it is said, learned the sacred significance of linen while in captivity, from their Egyptian rulers, because the finest linen clothed the pharaohs, and so the fabric achieved sacred purity when the pharaohs, as gods on earth, were clothed in the cloth of the sun, from plants that grew along the sacred waters of the Nile.

The linen cloth, of the purest white, used for Albert's

Coronation, came from flax fields at Sandringham to be hand-processed into fiber, and then hand spun and hand woven into cloth that, if not quite as fine as that worn by the ancient pharaohs, was still an outstanding example of modern-day craft. Each of Albert's garments was hand tailored, and even the linen stockings were hand-knitted to his dimensions of foot and leg and were tied in place by silk garters made especially for the occasion at Lullingstone Silk Farm in Kent, which had long supplied silk for royal occasions.

The garments Albert would wear were laid on the bed. The Lord Great Chamberlain started with the drawers and knelt at Albert's feet while Albert stepped into the drawers, which were then pulled up to his waist and tied, again, with a silken cord. Next, the linen shirt, that was similar to an old-fashioned night shirt and reached nearly to his knees. Over that was laid a kind of linen surplice, which also hung low. Lastly, Albert was dressed in a crimson royal stole and a cloth Cap of Maintenance, which he would wear in humility until it was replaced with the crown.

Finally, he was ready and looked at himself in the mirror. He was pleased but merely said "Thank you" to the three chamberlains, who bowed in gratitude, and perhaps in relief, as their first part in the day's ritual was over. Under their ministrations, Albert was now cleansed and purified and ready to face the world, so he left the bed chamber to meet Paul waiting outside, looking quite distinguished in his formal morning clothing, and Pauline, elegant in a long lavender dress, with matching hat, coat, and handbag.

They smiled at each other, then Albert entered the Great Hall where he was met by the Lord High Chancellor and Sir Humphrey, both men looking majestic in their robes of state. Albert followed them. The staff, in their liveried best, kept their heads bowed in respect as the King passed. The group stopped at the top of the staircase; Albert paused to catch his breath and then descended to the day.

CHAPTER 63

Along the stairs stood uniformed members of the Household Brigade. At the bottom, and making a double file to the entrance doors, more of the household staff was lined up, immaculately dressed. This time, unlike the wedding, there were no smiles or greetings. Albert passed them somberly as they bowed or curtseyed.

The Royal Family was assembled at the porte cochere: Lizzie, Larry, and their children, except for the youngest ones who stayed at Kensington; Connie, Basil, and their children; plus, descendants from the first two Victorias and Edward the Seventh.

Albert greeted them all with a nod, then he and Paul entered the State Coach of 1761, with its gilded Baroque carved woodwork and large glass windows, all four tons of it pulled by four matched cream-colored horses. The coach was preceded by a battalion of the Royal Horse Guards, resplendent in their highly polished and plumed helmets that gleamed in the sun, along with highly polished breast plates over their crimson coats, tightly fitting white trousers, and highly polished black leather boots.

The Household Brigades, in their distinctive bearskin "Beefeater" hats, crimson coats, and black trousers, were already stationed along the route, as were thousands of Armed Service members and squads of police, each one in front of a steel barrier to keep the millions of people present from rushing onto the road as the royal procession passed. Also, in front of the State Coach walked high-ranking members of the Armed Services – generals and admirals – as well as various service divisions, practically an entire army on the march, with seemingly every horse in the kingdom used for the event, hundreds, if not thousands, of them.

The State Coach started forward with not even a lurch, with Albert and Paul sitting impassively side by side. As the coach exited through the gates, the waiting crowd, pressed against the barriers, started to cheer, and the cheering remained constant along the route all the way to the Abbey. "Long live the King! Long live the King!" was the cry, in constant repetition.

When the State Coach moved out, an open landau pulled up to the porte cochere and stopped as Princess Elizabeth and her family approached. The door was opened by a footman, and the family mounted the steps and took their seats. The door was closed, but these horses started ahead with a jolt that made the children laugh. It was preceded by its own escort of Royal and Household Brigade mounted troops.

A third open landau pulled up for Connie, Basil, and their children. No one knew she was pregnant with the future monarch. These children were also caught off guard by the starting jolt as the horses pulled the carriage forward. As with Lizzie and Larry's children, the children of Basil and Connie were excited by their horse-drawn carriage and the cheering throngs of people. Regularly spaced, tall steel masts were hung with blue and gold banners featuring the royal arms, and each mast was capped with a gilded imperial crown and lion. The buildings along the processional route were covered in so many banners, bunting, and floral arrangements that it seemed London was wearing a spring frock. The children, beaming, waved to those along the route, and were enchanted to see the people waving back to them. This was the fun part of the day for them; while the arcane and rather tedious ritual itself, though spectacularly beautiful, would be something for the children to plod through until fun was regained on the extended return procession.

Their parents were also smiling, nodding to the crowd,

and constantly holding up a hand to acknowledge the cheers. Everyone was caught up in the exuberance of the day, though Elizabeth still wondered at the unexpected prominence of Connie and her family. Well, they were the closest relatives to her and Albert, but something about their presence still unnerved the Princess Royal; she just couldn't figure out why. She was already unnerved by jealous feelings kept in check until this moment, of wishing that, somehow, she could have been in the State Coach instead of Albert.

And so, the procession, with its carriages between battalions of mounted horse guards, made its slow way to the Abbey.

Most of the more than seven thousand members of the audience had already been in their places inside for more than two hours, with the doors closed. The Jamaican contingent had also arrived and was seated in the Royal Box to one side of the raised wooden platform – the theatre – constructed before the High Altar. Foreign dignitaries were in place: government leaders like the President of the United States, the head of the European Union, as well as heads of the Dominions and the Commonwealth countries. Representatives of many of the world's remaining royal families were also present, including the Tsarina of Russia, who sat between her sister – Michael Romanov's mother – and her son, the Tsarevich of Russia, with his cousin Michael beside him.

The Tsar had made a point of not attending, letting his people, and the Patriarch of the Russian Orthodox Church, know he would not acknowledge the legitimacy of a homosexual atheist to the throne of the United Kingdom, no matter how grateful he was to the British Royal Family for saving his own family from death by firing squad. In a note that Michael Romanov had sent earlier to Albert, he explained this single act showed how glaringly conservative his great uncle the Tsar really was.

"Your family saved mine from popping its clogs and all they can do is send the next in line," he wrote scathingly.

Riding in the Royal Coach, as it swayed on leather straps that cushioned the box from the pounding of the massive wooden wheels on the pavement, Paul found it hard not to smile and acknowledge the crowd, but Albert remained passive, doing little more than nodding to the multitudes, many of whom were holding up mobiles to photograph the event.

Finally, the procession reached the Abbey, after passing along the Mall, through the decorated Admiralty Arch, along Whitehall, and then to the front of the Abbey where the coach stopped at the newly constructed, if temporary, Annexe, with its special entrance reserved solely for the King and his consort, and a second entrance for peers and peeresses. As Albert and Paul exited the coach, Albert stopped and turned back to the crowd, whose cheers became even louder as, with just a hint of a smile, he nodded slightly, then went inside for the final preparation before the procession through the Abbey to the High Altar.

Those who sat in the grandstands erected specifically for the Coronation all along the route had paid dearly for the privilege, but none more so than those who sat before Westminster Hospital. Observation places on rooftops and in buildings along the route had also been sold for the privilege of seeing the royal couple from better perspectives than being at street level among the teeming throngs.

Expecting a most profitable day were the souvenir dealers, both high end – with their porcelain portrayals of King and consort, or engraved silver sets, to the more prosaic – and much cheaper – felt hats, pennants, mugs, bobble heads, lapel pins, brooches, watches, spoons, tee shirts, even candy bars, basically anything on which the images of the royal couple could be placed. There were official souvenirs required to be made within the kingdom, or at least the Commonwealth, and unofficial souvenirs made wherever labor and materials were cheapest. Everything sold briskly – regardless of price – because so many people wanted to be part of – and to remember with keepsakes – this Coronation unique in British history.

The layout of the Abbey itself posed issues. It was long but quite narrow, three times as high as it was wide to provide a feeling of soaring up through the air to the ribbed ceiling. The normal seating capacity of barely two thousand people had been creatively expanded to accommodate seven thousand, though most of them were prevented from seeing much of the ceremony by the rood screen that separated the nave from the quire to provide a more intimate ritual space.

In front of the transept, with the Royal Box to one side, was the Coronation Chair. With the Stone of Scone now back in Scotland, Albert's father had it replaced with the even more hallowed Coronation Block, said to have been the seat for Coronations of the country's Anglo-Saxon kings. The replacement had been carefully done to avoid damaging the seven-hundred-year-old oak chair.

Near the Coronation Chair, and closer to the High Altar, there was a raised throne for Albert, where he would receive the obeisance of the Peerage, as well as the Chair of Recognition, where he would sit for the opening part of the ceremony, with another Chair of Recognition for Paul as his consort. Overlooking the theatre were temporary balconies for the peers and peeresses, as well as other members of the nobility, and members of the government, including the Prime Minister and the cabinet, plus areas for the media, foreign dignitaries, and foreign royalty, for a total of about five hundred. Mainly what everyone else – the more than six thousand seated on the other side of the rood screen – would see were the processions to and from the High Altar.

Albert, followed by Paul, entered the Annexe for his final preparation, while the peers and peeresses prepared themselves, with their robes, coronets and other accoutrements of the occasion. In a vestibule adjoining the Abbey, a table covered with crimson cloth held the Royal Regalia – the crowns, maces, Orb, Sceptres, swords – all the objects that would be carried in the procession and to be used during the ceremony. The gold Ampulla – filled with oil – and the gold Spoon were already on the altar.

The Lord Great Chamberlain made the final preparations for Albert's entrance, replacing the stole he wore from the palace to the Abbey with his Coronation robe. Then, precisely at 11 a. m. , the procession through the Abbey began with a vanguard of church officials, followed by peers with the Regalia, including the Sword of State, which the King would wear, and clergy with the Bible, Chalice, and Paten.

Next came the King's Defender, Solomon Pembroke, bearing the Royal Standard; followed by the Lord High Chancellor, the Lord Great Chamberlain, the Lord High Constable, the Earl Marshall, with other dignitaries according to their rank, all wearing the elaborate and ornate robes of their offices. And so, the procession – the "Great Proceeding" – entered the Abbey and worked its way towards the High Altar to trumpet fanfares and cries from Westminster School students of "Vivat! Vivat Rex Albertus!"

Albert stared straight ahead as he walked the long distance from portal to High Altar, where he and Paul knelt first, before sitting in their respective Chairs of Recognition. As Paul was not of royal blood, he did not have the designation of Prince Consort that Albert's namesake had to the first Victoria, but having Paul beside him during the ceremony, and taking part in it, even to a limited extent, showed the world – as the ceremony was both televised and streamed – the important role that Paul played in Albert's life, and the high esteem in which he was held.

The Archbishop awaited them and smiled as they approached. Members of the clergy stood ready to assist the Archbishop, and the age-old ceremony began.

First was the Presentation, in which the Archbishop loudly proclaimed, "Sirs and ladies, I here present unto you King Albert, your undoubted [the Archbishop paused to emphasize the word] King: Wherefore all you who are come this day to do your homage and service. Are you willing to do the same?"

Then everyone in the Abbey said, "God save the King" to the accompaniment of a trumpet fanfare. This happened four times as the Archbishop and the King turned to face the four directions.

Then the Bible, the Chalice, and the Paten were placed on the Altar, following by peers carrying the Regalia, except the ceremonial swords, which was presented one piece at a time to the Archbishop, who took each one and passed it to the Dean, who then placed each piece on the Altar.

Next came the Oath. The Archbishop said to the King: "Sir, is Your Majesty willing to take the Oath?"

"I am willing," replied Albert.

"Will you solemnly promise and swear to govern the peoples of England and Wales, plus all your other possessions and territories, according t o their respective laws and customs?"

"I solemnly promise to do so."

"Will you to your power cause Law, and Justice, in Mercy, to be executed in all your judgments?"

"I will."

"Will you, to the utmost of your power, maintain the Protestant Reformed Religion established by law; And will you preserve unto the Bishops and Clergy of England and Wales, and to the Churches there committed to their charge, all such rights and privileges, as by law do or shall appertain to them or any of them?"

"All this I promise to do."

Then, assisted by the Lord Great Chamberlain, and preceded by the Sword of State, Albert went to the Altar and, laying his right hand on the Bible, said, "The things which I have here before promised, I will perform and keep. So help me, God."

Then Albert kissed the Bible and, taking an old-fashioned dip pen, placed its nib into a small bottle of ink and, with a great flourish, signed his name to the Oath printed on linen paper.

The Archbishop turned to face the nave.

"Let us pray."

He paused a moment, then began, "Oh God, who providest for thy people by thy power, and rulest over them in love; Grant unto this, thy servant, Albert, our King, the Spirit of wisdom and government, that being devoted unto thee with all his heart, he may so wisely govern, that in his time thy Church and people may continue in safety and prosperity; and that, persevering in good works unto the end, he may through thy mercy come to thy everlasting kingdom; through Jesus Christ our Lord, who liveth and reigneth with thee, and the Holy Ghost, ever one God, world without end. Amen."

Then came the Anointing. The King and Paul knelt at their kneeling stools, and the choir began the "Veni, Creator Spiritus."

Veni, Creator Spiritus,
mentes tuorum visita,

[Come, Creator Spirit,
and in our souls take up
       Thy rest,

imple superna gratia   come with Thy grace and
                                          heavenly aid

quae tu creasti pectora.   To fill the hearts which
                                          Thou hast made.]

Afterwards, the Archbishop led another prayer: "Oh Lord, Holy Father, who by anointing with Oil didst of old make and consecrate kings, priests, and prophets, to teach and govern thy people Israel: Bless and sanctify thy chosen servant Albert, who by our office and ministry is now to be anointed with this Oil [And the Archbishop laid his hand on the Ampulla] and consecrated King: Strengthen him, Oh Lord, with the Holy Ghost the Comforter; confirm and stablish him with thy free and princely Spirit, the Spirit of wisdom and government, the Spirit of counsel and ghostly strength, the Spirit of Knowledge and true godliness, and fill him, O Lord, with the Spirit of thy holy fear, now and forever. Amen."

Then the Lord Great Chamberlain removed Albert's Cap of State and his crimson robe, and he solemnly walked to King Edward's Chair and knelt before it. This part of the ritual had in previous Coronations been conducted out of sight of most of those in attendance by taking place under a canopy of Cloth of Gold suspended on silver poles held over the monarch by four Knights of the Garter. However, Albert wanted his people to see this most sacred part of the ritual and the Archbishop agreed.

The Dean took the Ampulla and Spoon from the Altar, went to King Edward's Chair, poured the holy oil from the Ampulla into the Spoon, which he held out to the Archbishop, who dipped a finger into the oil and turned to the kneeling King, who held out his hands before him, palms up. The Archbishop made the sign of the cross, in oil, on each palm, and said, "Be thy hands anointed with holy oil."

Then he dipped his finger again in the oil to make the sign

of the cross on Albert's chest.

"Be thy breast anointed with holy oil."

For the third time, the Archbishop placed his finger into the oil, with perhaps at least a trace remaining of the holy oil given by the Holy Mother to Thomas á Becket so many centuries before, and made the sign of the cross on Albert's bare head, saying, "Be thy Head anointed with holy Oil, as kings, priests, and prophets were anointed: And as Solomon was anointed King by Zadok the priest and Nathan the prophet, so be you anointed, blessed, and consecrated King over the Peoples, whom the Lord your god hath given you to rule and govern. In the Name of the Father, and of the Son, and of the Holy Ghost. Amen."

Then the Dean returned the Ampulla and Spoon to the High Altar, and the Archbishop said the following blessing over the King as he sat on King Edward's Chair: "Our Lord Jesus Christ, the Son of God, who by his Father was anointed with the Oil of gladness above his fellows, by his holy Anointing pour down upon your Head and Heart the blessing of the Holy Ghost, and prosper the works of your Hands: that by the assistance of his heavenly grace you may preserve the people committed to your charge in wealth, peace, and godliness; and after a long and glorious course of ruling a temporal kingdom wisely, justly, and religiously, you may at last be made partaker of an eternal kingdom through Jesus Christ our Lord. Amen."

And so the spirit entered Albert and stayed with him all the days of his life.

The King rose while the Dean placed two ritual, tunic-like garments on him, the Colobium Sindonis and the Supertunica, and girdled his waist with ceremonial cloth-of-gold, then the King sat again for the presentation by the Lord Great Chamberlain of the Golden Spurs, which he touched to Albert's heels [Being no longer tied on to his feet, as in olden times]. Then the Spurs were returned to the Altar. Next, a Sword of State was brought from the Altar and Albert stood while its scabbard and belt were tied to his waist by the Lord Great Chamberlain, then the King sat while the Archbishop prayerfully exhorted him to do justice to his country and his people. Next, the King rose to remove the sword, scabbard and belt, placed them himself on the Altar, and returned to the Chair. The Sword was then redeemed by the peer who carried it into the Abbey, for one hundred silver shillings, which he gave to the Dean, who then handed him the Sword, which he removed from its scabbard to carry before the King for the rest of the ceremony.

The King stood again as the Dean put the Royal Robe on Albert with the Lord Great Chamberlain fastening the clasps. Then the Dean brought the Orb from the Altar and gave it to the Archbishop, who placed it in the King's hand, saying, "Receive this Imperial Robe, and Orb; and the Lord your God endue you with knowledge and wisdom, with majesty and with power from on high; the Lord embrace you with the robe of righteousness, and with the garments of salvation. And when you see the Orb thus set under the Cross, remember that the whole world is subject to the Power and Empire of Christ our Redeemer."

Then the Orb was returned to the Altar, and the Archbishop placed the King's Ring on the fourth finger of Albert's right hand, saying, "Receive this Ring, the ensign of kingly dignity; and of defense of the One True Faith; and as you are this day solemnly invested in the government of an earthly kingdom, so may you be sealed with that Spirit of promise which is the earnest of a heavenly inheritance, and reign with him who is the blessed and only Potentate, to whom be glory for ever and ever. Amen."

Next, a white glove was put on the King's right hand by the peer approved for the act by the Court of Claims; then the

Archbishop placed the Sceptre with the Cross in Albert's right hand, and said, "Receive the Royal Sceptre, the ensign of kingly power and justice."

Then he placed the Sceptre with the Dove in Albert's left hand, and said, "Receive the Rod of equity and mercy: and God, from whom all holy desires, all good counsels, and all just works do proceed, direct and assist you in the administration and exercise of all those powers which he hath given you. Be so merciful that you be not too remiss; so, execute justice that you forget not mercy. Punish the wicked, protect and cherish the just, and lead your people in the way wherein they should go."

Now, with Albert sitting on King Edward's Chair, it was finally time for the moment perhaps a billion people were waiting for. The Archbishop took King Edward's Crown, laid it on the Altar, and said, "O God, the crown of the faithful: Bless we beseech thee and sanctify this thy servant Albert our King; and as thou dost this day set a Crown of pure gold upon his head, so enrich his royal heart with thine abundant grace, and crown him with all princely virtues, through the King eternal Jesus Christ our Lord, Amen."

Albert bowed his head, indicating that, as King, he bowed only to God. Then the Archbishop went to the King, while the Dean brought the Crown from the Altar and handed it to the Archbishop, who, carefully, placed the nearly six-pound Crown, made of gold and set with rubies, diamonds, sapphires, and pearls, upon Albert's head. Now, he truly was, in the eyes of the world, King Albert. The people shouted repeatedly, "God Save the King! God Save the King!" Trumpets blew a fanfare, combined with the peal of bells from the Abbey towers known as a "fire." There was cannon fire from the Tower for a minute. Finally, the great throng in the Abbey grew quiet again and the Archbishop said, "God crown you with a crown of glory and righteousness, that by the ministry of this our benediction, having a right faith and manifold fruit of good works, you may obtain the crown of an everlasting kingdom by the gift of him whose kingdom endureth forever. Amen."

Then the choir sang, "Be strong and play the man: keep the commandments of the Lord thy God and walk in his ways."

Next, the Bible was presented to the King by the Archbishop, who said, "Our gracious King, we present you with this Book, the most valuable thing that this world affords. Here is wisdom; this is the royal Law; these are the inspired Oracles of God."

The King handed the Bible back to the Archbishop, who had the Dean place it on the Altar. [Sometime later, when looking at this edition of the Bible with its spectacular sixteenth-century engravings, Albert found the Archbishop had inserted a letter that Quaker founder George Fox had written to a questioner in which he presented the basic tenants of the Society of Friends. Albert never asked the Archbishop how he came to have the letter, but it remained, to the end of his days, one of his most treasured possessions.]

Finally, it was time for the Archbishop to give the Benediction.

"The Lord bless you and keep you: and as he hath made you King over his people, so may he prosper you in this world, and make you partake of his eternal felicity in the world to come. Amen [Also pronounced by the bishops and the peers.]

"The Lord gives you fruitful lands and healthful seasons; victorious fleets and armies, and a quiet Empire; a faithful Parliament; wise and upright counselors and magistrates, a loyal nobility, and a dutiful gentry; a pious and learned and useful clergy; an honest, peaceable, and obedient commonality. Amen."

Then, facing those in the Abbey, the Archbishop said, "And

the same Lord God Almighty grant, that the Clergy and Nobles assembled here for this great and solemn service, and together with them all the people of the land, fearing God, and honoring the King, may by the merciful superintendency of the divine Providence, and the vigilant care of our gracious Sovereign, continually enjoy peace, plenty, and prosperity; through Jesus Christ our Lord, to whom, with the eternal Father, and God the Holy Ghost, be glory in the Church, world without end. Amen."

Then Albert rose from King Edward's Chair and went to the Throne slightly behind it, for the "Lifting Up," when he was to be placed on the Throne by assembled clergy and peers. What once had been a literal and physical lifting of the King to the Throne was now symbolically done. Gathered around the Throne were all those who had helped in the service thus far, including the peers who carried the Regalia, while the Archbishop said, "Stand firm, and hold fast from henceforth the seat and state of royal and imperial dignity, which is this day delivered unto you, in the Name and by the authority of Almighty God, and by the hands of us the Bishops and servants of God, though unworthy: And as you see us to approach nearer to God's Altar, so vouchsafe the more graciously to continue to us your royal favour and protection. And the Lord God Almighty, whose ministers we are, and the stewards of his mysteries, establish your Throne in righteousness, that it may stand fast for evermore, like as the sun before him, and as the faithful witness in heaven. Amen."

Next came the Homage, in which the Archbishop, speaking for all the bishops, pledged to honor and to serve the King by kneeling before him. Before accepting the Homage, Albert handed the two sceptres to a peer who returned them to the Altar. Then the Archbishop kissed the King's left cheek. Next, Paul knelt before Albert, and made his pledge, then kissed the

King's left cheek while Albert stared solemnly ahead. Then, in a break with tradition started by his father, rather than have the leaders of the peers and the nobility give oaths of allegiance and service, a general statement of support for the new King was read from the programme by everyone in attendance.

When the Homage was over, drums were beaten, the trumpets sounded a fanfare, and the people shouted, "God save King Albert! "Long live King Albert! May the King live forever!"

The long service ended with a Te Deum, and not, in a much discussed and, by some, bitterly contested break with tradition, a Communion.

Finally, Albert, with the Sceptre with the Cross and the Rod with the Dove once again in his hands, and with peers going before him with the four Royal Swords, helpfully assisted by the Lord Great Chamberlain as he had much to bear, proceeded, with Paul behind him, into the adjacent St. Edward's Chapel, where the Sceptre and the Rod were given to the Archbishop, who placed them on the Chapel's Altar; then St. Edward's Crown was removed, replaced with the lighter weight Imperial Crown, and the heavy and lengthy Royal Robe of State was replaced by the lighter weight, and significantly shorter, Robe of purple velvet. Then the King was given the Sceptre with the Cross in his right hand, and the Orb in his left, and returned to the theatre, faced the High Altar, then turned to face his people. The Recessional followed, as Albert, with Paul behind him, and accompanied by the Archbishop, the Dean, and other bishops, with royal officers, peers and nobility after them, started the long walk back, through the Choir, past the massively carved rood screen, then out into the nave, where most of the seven thousand in attendance had their first good look at Albert since he was actually crowned King.

Shouts of "God save the King! and "Long live the King!"

rang through the Abbey, as trumpets blared, drums were beaten, and the chorus sang. Albert was determined to reach the West Portal without anything going wrong. Finally, and with great relief, the Annexe was reached, and he had a few moments to rest, when he handed off the Orb and Sceptre, and the Crown and Robe were temporarily removed while he made his way to the adjacent restroom to, finally, relieve himself and take a much-needed drink of water. Then the Crown and Robe were replaced and, with Orb and Sceptre back in hand, King Albert exited the Annexe to receive the acclaim of his people, with Paul just behind him.

CHAPTER 64

When Albert appeared before his people, the bells of the Abbey began ringing and wouldn't stop ringing for another three hours, the most demanding moment of the eight bell ringers' careers. That was the signal for bells throughout the city to ring, and not just in Anglican churches, but it seemed every available bell, whether in church, school, or government building, was being rung.

Albert and Paul were soon joined on the steps of the Abbey by Princess Elizabeth and her family, by Connie and her family, by Pauline, Sir Humphrey, the Lord Great Chamberlain, the Lord High Chancellor, the Archbishop, the Dean, the extended Royal Family and, finally, by as many people as could possibly press onto the space while maintaining an open area of respect around the King.

Because the event was being streamed live across the country and the world, the ringing of the Abbey's bells was the signal for bell ringers, prepared in advance for this moment, to ring bells across the kingdom, from the smallest rural church to every cathedral. That was also the cue for bells in the remaining British possessions around the world, and in every Commonwealth country, to begin ringing as well until, in a remarkable sense, the planet was ringing and ringed with the sound of bells – from deeply pitched, massive bells, to hand held school bells – in Africa, Asia, North America, the Caribbean, and remote islands in the Pacific, the Atlantic, and the Indian oceans. Bells rang in jungles, deserts, Antarctic outposts, crowded cities, remote sheep ranches, rural villages. It was a true media event, but it was the bells of the Abbey and London that the King and his family heard. It was a celebratory sound that those who were present remembered for many years, but then something else happened as well, something completely unexpected and unplanned. A single voice across the street started to sing "God Save the King". Not a professionally trained voice, but a passionate and fervent voice:

> "God save our gracious King,
> Long live our noble King,
> God save the King!"

Other voices quickly picked up the melody and that solitary voice was joined by dozens, then hundreds, then thousands of people, at first just in the immediate area, but as people all along the processional route heard the anthem, they joined in as well, and music and words spread person to person as though blown by a brisk wind, block to block, from Westminster to Piccadilly, Oxford Street and Hyde Park, all the way back to the palace itself to be picked up by spectators, guards, mounted horse troops, even the household staff itself awaiting the return of the King. Millions were singing:

> "Send him victorious,
> Happy and glorious,
> Long to reign over us
> God save the King!"

When those inside the Abbey heard the singing, they picked it up as well. The organist quickly found the key, as did the silver trumpets, the orchestra, and the massed choirs, and the tympani joined them. And, again, as the event was being live-streamed, then anyone anywhere on the planet who knew the words could join in or at least could sing the famous old tune.

And so those watching in every pub raised a pint as the anthem continued, joined by those gathered at every Government House to honor the occasion, every capitol, every church, to those on street corners, to those in apartment buildings, senior care facilities, military bases, naval ships and submarines, to those on lonely scientific expeditions; Mounties sang it, students sang it, the world was encircled by perhaps a billion voices all singing the same anthem at the same time, on the daylight side of the planet, on the dark side of the planet, on airplanes in flight, anyplace anyone had access to a telly or a mobile or the internet. The anthem continued through its verses:

"May he defend our laws,
And ever give us cause,
To sing with heart and voice,
God save the King."

An aging naval veteran of the Falkland Islands War, who lived blocks away from the waterfront in Plymouth, back where the rents were lower, stood unsteadily at attention and raised a hand in salute, his fingers gnarled and knobby with painful arthritis:

"Oh Lord our God arise,
Scatter his enemies,
And make them fall."

In another town, in government housing, lived an elderly woman whose son was killed in Iraq. On the table in front of her was a commemorative mug kept treasured in her family for a hundred years since the Coronation of Edward the Seventh, with his picture and that of Queen Alexandra:

"From shore to shore,
Lord, make the nations see
That men should brothers be."

On remote Pitcairn Island, descendants of the H.M.S. Bounty mutineers stood outdoors under a loudspeaker:

"May just and righteous laws
Uphold the public cause."

While in America, the granddaughter of a British woman who married a visiting G.I. not because he repeatedly said he loved her, but simply to get away from the hopelessness of Liverpool [Though she later regretted leaving before the Beatles started up as it turned out the family of John Lennon lived around the corner on Gambier Terrace.] sang the anthem she hadn't thought of for years:

"May peace her power extend,
Foe be transformed to friend."

The young man from Cameroon, a graduate of Cambridge, now teaching Greek at an exclusive college prep school in Connecticut:

"His heart inspire and move
With wisdom from above."

Members of the extended Patel family, preparing to open their first store-front pizza parlor in Leeds:

"Not in this land alone,

But be God's mercies known."

Expats from the Case del Sol to Sri Lanka:

"And Britain's rights depend
On war no more."

The Hong Kong youths singing as a protest against oppression, just before they were brutally arrested and imprisoned:

"Confound their politics,
Frustrate their knavish tricks."

The carillon player at the Scottish Episcopalian Church in Edinburgh, who only had time to play four verses before an angry mob gathered outside and threatened to vandalize the church if it wasn't stopped, which it was:

"May he sedition hush,
And like a torrent rush,
Rebellious Scots to crush,
God Save the King."

One who refused to sing was the new Bishop of Durban, who preferred to occupy himself with reviewing the proposed budget for the coming year. Still, many of his parishioners did sing:

"Thy choicest gifts in store,
On him be pleased to pour."

The young players at a cricket match in Mumbai kept playing as they knew there was a Coronation in far-away England but didn't care. Their parents and grandparents who did watch the ceremony remained ambivalent about their country's colonial past. On the plus side was the legacy of a common language, the rule of law, and the railways and telegraph lines that bound the massive sub-continent together; unfortunately counter-balanced by the British view of India as, primarily, a source of raw materials and, later, after the raw materials such as cotton were processed back in England, then as a market to buy the finished goods. Gandhi proved perceptive in his understanding of how to break the supply chain and make the fragile house fall apart:

"God bless our native land!
May Heav'n's protecting hand
Still guard our shore."

The young transgendered woman lying in the hospital after she was brutally attacked by a gang after school and beaten unconscious. With three broken ribs where she was kicked, a bruised face and fractured jaw, she nonetheless insisted on at least humming along, despite the pain, as she watched the telly in her room:

"Home of the brave and free,
Thou land of liberty."

Meanwhile, in a pub in Llanfynydd, Wales:

"Oh Lord, our monarch bless
With strength and righteousness."

"No bloody monarch of mine," thought a rebellious Welshman as he brooded over his pint, studiously avoiding the telly and refusing to sing with the others. Indeed, he sang a protest song to himself, in Welsh, eagerly awaiting the day when, finally, Wales would be freed from its English oppressor which had the temerity to take his country and give it as a plaything to someone absurdly called "The Prince of Wales." Indeed!

The revised Order of Druids gathered at Stonehenge, wearing their white robes and carrying oak branches, referred to their own gods while singing:

"Thy choicest gifts in store,
On him be pleased to pour."

Not content to stay inside the International Space Station to see the world through a small port hole, the lone Brit astronaut made a spacewalk so she could look down upon the entire planet shimmering beneath her, half in darkness, half in light. The anthem's stanzas came through her helmet speaker, and it seemed as though the entire planet was singing:

"And form one family
The wide world o'er.
Happy and glorious,
Long to reign over us.
God save the King!"

And in the time-honored tradition of saving the best for last, the Abbey's organist had the moment for which she'd been waiting so she could use, for the first time, the new thirty-two foot pipe, called Falstaff for its massive size, as in another time-honored tradition, she literally pulled out all the stops, with the help of an assistant, to create a massive wall of sound she wanted to be heard all the way to Chelsea.

The triumphant anthem finally ended, and Albert stood looking like the very incarnation of the divine spirit that now inhabited him, wearing the Imperial Crown, the Royal Robe of State, and holding the Orb and Sceptre. Photographs of that moment did not do justice to the reality of what those present saw, and what Paul understood completely: he was the consort of a god and felt lifted in the claws of an eagle.

CHAPTER 65

Albert stood there in the bright sunlight for a very long moment, as his people, many thousands of them in the immediate area, cheered him and shouted, "Long live the King!" This was the moment of greatest satisfaction, the culmination of his life, and he knew this moment would never come again and, frankly, he didn't want it to end.

But it did, and the procession for the return to the palace had reformed, with the Royal Horse Guard leading the way. The State Coach pulled up in front of the Abbey; both doors were held open as the King, precariously balancing the Imperial Crown on his head while holding Orb and Sceptre, which he momentarily handed to the Lord Great Chamberlain until he entered the coach and sat upon the brown leather seat as another chamberlain gathered and arranged the royal robe around him. Then he received the Orb and Sceptre, as Paul entered through the other door and sat beside him. The doors were closed, then the return journey began, six miles of it, to enable as many to see their sovereign as possible.

Particularly meaningful to Paul and Albert were the thousands of school children from across the country who, standing and shouting gleefully, were in special bleachers along the Embankment, including a contingent from Durham. Unfortunately, Albert could do little more than smile, encased as he was in the accoutrements of the day. He could turn towards the shouting and cheering multitudes, but even the briefest of nods placed the Crown in jeopardy and he certainly did not want it to fall off as the ancient coach jolted and jostled along London streets.

Realizing Albert's predicament, Paul joked, "If it falls off, can I put it on?"

But he quickly realized the comment was out of place as Albert growled, "You do, and it's your head."

And Paul wasn't sure Albert was joking, so he returned, chastened, to waving and smiling.

It took two hours to return, but while it seemed every muscle in his body was aching, Albert still did not want the procession to end. He had never seen such a multitude of diverse people in one place before and knew he never would again. And all of them, from all over the country and the world, were there to see him, and he would not disappoint them. His job now was to be seen as the rightful heir to the throne. This was his moment of legitimacy, and it was one he only wanted to share with Paul, and while he was facing away from Paul to see his people, Albert was aware of his presence, of his being there, and that was what he needed, and all he needed, to sustain him.

The procession itself was more than a mile in length and took an hour to pass any particular spot. It was a spectacle rarely matched in the country's history, rooted in the people's outpouring of love, respect, and admiration for their sovereign. Finally, the procession passed the Queen Victoria Memorial and headed for the palace gates. The crowds, who had seen Albert leave six hours earlier, saw him return in splendor. Both men were relieved to return. Home at last.

Once inside the enclosure, the mounted troops peeled off to one side while the State Coach proceeded to the portico and finally stopped so the doors could be opened. Albert was glad to hand off the Orb and Sceptre to the Lord Great Chamberlain, who always seemed to be present when needed. Now the solemnity of the morning was gone as Albert walked into the vast entrance hall where, once again, the staff had gathered to welcome the King home and everyone was smiling and most were shouting, "Long live the King!" while the loud acclaim of the crowds beyond the fence was clearly heard as the rest of the procession continued to enter through the gates.

There was one last formality to conclude this part of the day's events, and that was the entrance onto the balcony for one last view of the monarch as, freed from holding the Orb and Sceptre, Albert could finally wave to his people.

But first, he had to mount the long staircase to the grand reception room for a half hour to recover from the stress of the day. The Lord Great Chamberlain assisted by removing Crown and Robe, so he could use the adjacent restroom to again relieve himself. Though trained in how to hold himself, Albert, nonetheless, had a weak bladder that had to be emptied more often than he would have liked, and such breaks were included in the planning for his official duties. When he returned, naturally he was thirsty, and he and Paul sat at a table where, on this pleasingly warm London day, they were served from a pitcher of iced tea, a taste for which he had acquired from an American actor he'd known years before. He took a sip and smiled.

"The English don't know how to make iced tea," he explained. "To most it's simply a cold version of hot tea that needs milk and sugar. Fortunately, we have an assistant chef on staff who trained under a famous American cook in Charleston, and I think it's the best thing she does."

Gradually the other members of the family came into the room as their carriages arrived, and the last of the procession moved away from the front gates so people could gather for one last view of the Royal Family and their monarch.

Finally, when everyone was present, the Lord Great Chamberlain said, "We're ready, Your Majesty," and Albert stood as the Royal Robe was put on him, and the Crown, then the doors were opened, and Albert led the way onto the balcony, followed by Paul, Pauline, Princess Elizabeth and her family, and Connie and her family. They moved forward to the acclaim of the thousands gathered beyond the fence, with their shouts of "Long live the King!", while thousands of hand-held Union Jacks were waved in the air, along with thousands of mobiles raised to record the event. A squadron of R.A.F. fighter planes trailing long spumes of red, blue, and white vapor trails flew overhead. Paul looked up at them with the delight of a child.

The Royal Family stood on the balcony for a long time, smiling and waving, but then it was time to go back inside for formal photographs, not only of the immediate family but also for the vastly extended family who, in one form or other, represented nearly every remaining royal house in Europe. It was this encompassing group, nearly a hundred people of all ages, including the Jamaican contingent, who sat for the royal photographer.

Finally, the Lord Great Chancellor recovered the Imperial Crown and the Royal Robe, not to be worn again until the next Opening Day of Parliament.

Albert was quickly helped to change into a suit so he could make his first broadcast address to the nation. He, naturally, looked slightly tired, but the strength of his voice carried the conviction with which he spoke:

"My dear people, I came to you solemnly and humbly, as your crowned Sovereign, after a ceremony attended by thousands, with millions lining the streets of the procession, and perhaps a billion more watching the event streamed across the planet, and even into space. Today I took my oath to serve you faithfully; to defend our nation and its heritage; and to lead it fearlessly into the future. All this I will do to the best of my ability. As my father before me, and my grandmother, my great-grandmother, and back down a long line of monarchs, I, too, value the Crown as a symbol of our unity beyond political division. I see it as a rallying point as we forge a better future for us all, leaving no one behind; a future of equal opportunity for all; of a truly United Kingdom where, regardless of one's position at birth, we as a people can still, through education, diligence, and hard work, achieve our greatest potential and, most importantly, by working together, by a mutual commitment to make a nurturing, benevolent Britain, we can become more than any of us can achieve on our own.

"To that end, I pledge my life. I begin that long journey not alone, but with the care and support of my dear consort, Paul McGregor, the Duke of Durham. Together, we dedicate ourselves to you, to help create a land of justice, compassion, and growth for all.

"On a personal note, the Duke and I have been touched by the remarkable outpouring of support from so many of you, both in person today and through countless notes and emails received from every part of the Kingdom, and from around the world. Paul and I cherish your kindness, and it will help guide us in the work that lies ahead, and for that we thank you. As we make our way around the country soon, we look forward to seeing as many of you as possible, both old friends and new ones we have yet to meet. Now, good night to you all, and may we join around the bonfires that will light the country from every direction.

"I remain your humble servant, Albert George Alfred Edward."

A family dinner came later, following a suitable period to rest and prepare, in the large banquet room which would be the scene the following night for a much larger formal banquet that Albert and Paul were hosting for world leaders who had come for the Coronation.

It was this first dinner that Albert and Paul most enjoyed. It was a time for Albert to see some relatives not seen in years and for Paul to meet for the first time. Albert insisted the numerous children eat with the adults. He knew this would be a moment they would cherish. The meal was boisterous and loud.

As Albert looked around the long table, he particularly noted the Tsarina, who had requested a private audience, during which she explained that the Tsar did not privately believe the public statements given in his name as to why he was not attending the Coronation. She explained he was forced to make a statement condemning homosexuality at the demand of the Patriarch of the Russian Orthodox Church, a man powerful enough that, behind the scenes, he could influence dynastic change in favor of the Tsar's more conservative and traditional younger brother if her husband moved too far and too fast with his agenda of liberalizing the country.

The Tsarina assured Albert that her husband was eternally grateful to the House of Britain for saving his family during the Revolution and, in better times, would have come personally. As it was, he'd asked her to carry that personal message so there would be no misunderstanding.

Albert, who had been dismayed by the Tsar's refusal to attend the Coronation, was mollified by the Tsarina's explanation, and admitted that, even in his country, politics was often a balancing act, as would be shown in his first address to the Opening of Parliament and prepared by the government, in which he would be required to state some positions and objectives in which he did not personally believe.

Both Albert and the Tsarina were relieved at their rapprochement. She then explained she planned on staying several weeks at Michael's country estate with her sister and expressed the hope that Albert and Paul would visit them there.

"Nothing would please us more," said Albert as he kissed her hand, though he disliked the idea of seeing Michael informally.

At the end of dinner, Albert tapped his water glass with a knife and, when the room was silent, asked loudly, "Did everyone have a good time today?"

"Yea!" cried the children almost in unison, and one energetically added, "Let's do it again!"

And the children repeated the phrase like a chant: "Let's do it again! Let's do it again!"

Albert smiled wearily before explaining that one Coronation is all a sovereign gets, to the children's vocal dissatisfaction, but he hurriedly added that the events of the next two days would keep them more than busy, which was received with cheering.

He looked at Paul, who smiled at him and winked. And then, perhaps for the first time in his life, Albert realized that in this room he was home, and that all those gathered here were his family. Despite the aching exhaustion from the day, Albert felt renewed by an unexpected satisfaction and peace. He stood to make a toast.

"On a personal level, this has been a momentous day. But I am so glad you are here to share it with me. My dear sister [And here he looked at Lizzie with remarkable tenderness] and I, especially after Mummy's death, were raised in isolation as our father was not a social person. We knew there was family out there, beyond the walls, but we rarely had a chance to see you. Your presence here, and your choice to share this moment with us, makes us so very happy, and I believe I can speak for Paul as well."

"You usually do!" interjected Paul from the other end of

the table, as the company laughed and Albert replied, wryly, "Cheers!" before continuing.

"But what I'm trying to say is that each of you is family, and I'm coming to realize that family, no matter what size it is, makes life a shared adventure, and I look forward to sharing it with you."

Then he raised his glass.

"To family!"

And all those present raised their glasses and said, "To family!"

"I also want to recognize my husband and consort, my dearest Paul, who came into my life at a time when I wondered if I would ever know the meaning of love, if there could possibly be anyone to love me and whom I could love in return, and the answer was yes. So, here's to Paul; may we live forever!"

Albert raised his glass again.

"To Paul!"

And, again, the company raised their glasses.

"To Paul!" they said in unison.

"Here, here!"

And the loving glance between the two men told those at the table all they needed to know about the commitment the men shared.

Then a butler entered from a side door and, catching Albert's eye, nodded once, then left.

Then Albert lowered his glass to the table and said heartily, "And now I believe there is a bonfire to attend!"

The children yelled, "Yea!" and then eagerly waited for Albert and Paul to lead the way to the Great Lawn behind the palace where a massive pyre of wood was erected.

In an ancient custom dating back more than a thousand years, the tradition of lighting bonfires across the country to announce the crowning of a new monarch went back to the time of signal fires as a method of communication. Now its purpose was to signal unity as the entire country, from Cornwall to Hadrian's Wall, and from Wales to East Anglia, was to be covered by a web of light where each hilltop fire would be seen by another in a continuous chain. The colleges and universities vied for the largest bonfires, and, in some cases, the piles of wood were fifty to sixty feet high, with the stated goal of being visible from space.

To forestall environmental criticism, fruitless, as it turned out, the palace issued a statement asking that no live trees be used in the bonfires, stressing that only dead trees should be cut, and suggesting this was a prime opportunity for good forest management. The use of scrap or surplus wood from construction sites was also recommended.

Regarding the unavoidable carbon emissions, Albert decided to offset the pollution by planting an entire forest in Northumberland, which some viewed as the King trying to buy his way out of a compromising situation, but then it was the Coronation, and most people understood they would likely never see another. Still, many fires were accompanied by protesters. Albert understood there was no justification for the event aside from tradition, but this was one tradition he wanted to maintain. He pointed out that many bonfires were also set for religious reasons at the solstices and equinoxes as an inheritance that reached back deeply into Britain's past. Besides, fire had always entranced him.

Staff members were standing around the large wooden pyre with unlit torches. Albert took one, as did Paul, and the older children. The torches were lit and set to the shavings that encircled the structure, and which quickly caught on fire, then the torches were tossed on as well. That was the signal, sent through a special mobile app, for all the bonfires to be lit at once across the country, and many were lit around the world as well. Soon, the night sky was ablaze as firebrands rose into the air and the structure turned into a blazing inferno of heat and light. In addition to family members, many of the staff were also present, as well as off-duty soldiers who had been in the procession earlier in the day. Soon, the country was crisscrossed with streams of light like ropes of gleaming pearls, which the Brit astronaut overhead in the International Space Station assured the country could be clearly seen, while an onboard camera streamed images to the planet below.

Everyone present on the Great Lawn, from children to adults, was impressed amid exclamations of oohs and aahs, and the children ran around screaming in delight. One little girl timidly approached Albert and took his hand. Albert was surprised to feel a tiny hand in his and looked down at the child and asked if she would like a better view. She nodded yes, so he picked her up and set her on his shoulders while holding onto her hands. The other children, seeing this, ran to him and yelled, "Now me! Me too!" and Albert ended up lifting every child onto his shoulders, then looked over at Paul and said, "You could help, you know!" So then the children rushed to Paul, and he held them up as well. As the great pile blazed away, King and Duke repeatedly lifted the children until the men were exhausted. Finally, the various parents found their children and said it was time to leave to assorted groans and "Not yet! Not yet!"

By now the fire was beginning to die down, and after the children left with their parents, staff members brought out blankets so those remaining could lay on the grass and watch the structure slowly collapse upon itself, with sparks flowing up into the night sky.

Eventually, Albert and Paul found themselves left alone and side by side on a blanket.

"So," asked Albert, "how was your day?"

"Busy," replied Paul with a smile. "And yours?"

"Mine, too. What did you like most?"

"I loved the State Coach," said Paul.

"It's wonderful, isn't it? Like riding in a golden Baroque wedding cake. We have George III to thank for that. You know, the Americans, understandably, look askance at him, but he was actually a remarkable King, by far the best of the German Georges. Of course, by insisting the Empire stay together he ended up losing America; he lacked the vision of hindsight. My father took the name George to specifically rehabilitate George III, who had an inquisitive mind, who sent explorers around the world, who had a scientific interest in the natural world, who loved farming – while my father probably didn't know one end of a hog from the other [He smiled wryly at this] – and who appreciated both art and craft, as shown by his commissioning of the coach. So, what else did you like today?"

"I loved the fly-over. I thought it was just so cool."

"It was great, wasn't it? I've always liked them myself. And I'll keep that in mind for future events, not that I can have them here every day of course."

"Not even for me?" Paul asked in a coy voice.

"There are limits to my power," said Albert with a laugh.

But then Paul turned serious.

"I was surprised at how you turned on me in the coach for what was just a joke about the Crown."

Albert deeply regretted that moment.

"I don't know what to say. All I could think about was not having the Crown fall off, and I couldn't see that you were joking. It just wasn't a time for me to kid around."

"Well, if you ever do want to have my head chopped off, just please give the executioner a bonus so he'll sharpen the blade for a clean chop."

Appalled, Albert asked, "Where did you hear that?"

"On a BBC costume drama, of course."

"Well, you were watching the wrong show."

And then Albert turned solemn.

"If you wanted to learn how power and rulers really work, you should have watched 'I, Claudius'. That show taught me that the Jews and Christians have it wrong: the greatest sin is betrayal."

And he spoke with such grim determination that Paul started shaking. To change the mood, he smiled, "Next you'll be telling me the Tower is not just a museum."

And Albert, startled by his own admission, went along with the joke.

"That's for the tourists. But there are still cells down below the river level that are terribly damp and cold and that's where Papa kept his older brother."

"But your father didn't have an older brother."

"See how effective it was? In that instance he wasn't mad; just inconvenient." Albert was smiling, and Paul knew it was a joke, but this was a side of Albert he'd never seen, and it frightened him.

Aware of how the moment had turned unexpectedly dark and foreboding, Albert shook his head as though coming awake and sat up.

"I'm knackered. The day has worn me out. Pay no attention to me as I'm just rambling incoherently. Could you take me to bed?"

And he held out his hand. Paul stood, took Albert by the hand, and led him back inside.

Meanwhile, the staff, who had stayed back at a respectable distance and out of earshot, came forward. Some folded up the blankets and took them back inside, while others, with the help of the palace fire brigade, started dowsing the remnants of the bonfire. Then, finally, their day was done as well.

Paul and Albert lay in bed, naked and side by side. But Albert was unable to rest or sleep.

"Paul, sort me out."

So he did.

CHAPTER 66

To make up for the Coronation taking place on the Abbey side of the river, Albert and Paul toured the other side several days later, including public housing, orphanages, a children's hospital, work centers, schools, a mosque, a synagogue, a Hindu temple and a Buddhist shrine, and they were pleased to note that, in general, they were met with cheering and adoring crowds.

The day immediately after the Coronation was reserved for the Nation's Parade and the Parade of Nations. Planning was intensive and took months to organize, with the primary work falling to Albert and Paul's foundation, but it also required input from the palace, Whitehall, a variety of security departments, and a myriad of agencies both within the country and without, as the day's events and participants encompassed the remaining Possessions as well as Commonwealth countries.

Paul quickly felt out of his element and was criticized, as Pauline was as the foundation's CEO, for having had no experience with such a massive project unique in the country's history. Still, Pauline's motto for this and similar situations was, "If you don't know what you're doing, hire someone who does," so they hired the best events organizers in the nation to provide a framework for the parade and for the Nation's Party to be held the following day.

The themes for both events were the same: to celebrate diversity and inclusion. The parameters of exactly what that meant were formulated initially by an executive committee formed of Paul, Pauline, an official from the Prime Minister's office, another from the Lord Chancellor's office, plus one from the Arts Council. Their mandate was not to choose the participants but to organize a selection committee to make those choices. They picked a team representing education and trade unions, the arts, manufacturing and tech organizations, craft and arts groups, and a cross-section of the country's ethnic and religious groups. It was large, diverse, and potentially unwieldy. But its members shared a common goal with no private agendas and set up a website to accept applications from potential parade participants from within the country for the first part of the parade, and from the overseas Possessions and Commonwealth countries for the second part.

It was agreed that the parade would be on both sides of the river and could stretch for six miles, with half for the national section and half for the international participants. At Albert's request, there was to be no formal military presence within the parade, as their day was the Coronation. However, military personnel were encouraged to attend the event as off-duty viewers with friends and family. There was a strong police presence, both uniformed and non-uniformed, and the steel crowd barricades were kept up from the previous day.

The six-mile length was then divided into sections, with space allotted to marching bands, floats, and other motorized entries such as flat-bed trailers and open-air buses to transport participants unable to walk the route due to age or other conditions. There was also space allotted to walking units, so the resulting layout of the parade provided a blueprint for how many different groups could be accommodated. It was basically a question of filling in the blanks on what was actually a very long strip of paper that went around the four walls of the main planning room.

The main categories for groups were chosen to ensure diversity and a representative cross-section from within the country and outside, followed by an open call for participants issued through the media. Quite soon there were far more applications than spaces available. Each applicant organization was vetted by security first for legitimacy, and no terrorist groups or groups advocating the violent overthrow of the country were permitted. After that, slots were filled by lottery, with the idea that walking or motorized groups would be separated by musical organizations such as marching bands. The order of groups was also decided by lottery, with each group requested to have an identifying banner at the front.

Another large banner was to be held at the beginning of the parade announcing the Nation's Parade, with another in the middle announcing the Parade of Nations, with a ten-minute gap between them, primarily so those in the Royal Grandstand could have their own break. Albert insisted on being present for the entire event, understanding it was his coronation that was the causal factor for subsequent events, and that people wanted to see their King, not an empty chair.

Realizing it would be a very long day, Albert woke early and had a, unusual for him, hearty breakfast with the extended Royal Family. Their grandstand had appeared overnight in front of the palace, though it had been built off-site, dismantled, and then taken to the location and reassembled by a small army of workers.

The lottery to determine participants and their location within the parade provided a distinctive amount of equal opportunity without favoritism and, as Paul said, was a remarkable British example of what could be described as an almost Buddhist-like indeterminism in action, though he was careful not to say so in public as there was already enough commentary regarding his spirituality.

There was also the matter of logistics, getting the national participants to London was not a problem, but it was for those flying in or crossing the Channel. Albert and Paul were insistent that no group was to be prevented from coming for lack of funds, so organizations within Britain were encouraged to help subsidize like-minded if financially strapped groups from abroad with airfare. The large number of international L.G.B.T.Q. organizations was a perfect example, as gay groups from around the country raised money to fund the attendance of their international counterparts. Indeed, Albert had ruffled more than a few foreign feathers by insisting that each Commonwealth country and Possession was required to send an L.G.B.T.Q. contingent if they were going to participate. This made it difficult for those countries where homosexuality was still illegal. A few decided to change their laws, but a few decided not to attend.

"No loss," was Albert's only remark. He was already frustrated at the list of countries the government expected him to invite to the formal banquet of world leaders he was hosting the night of the parade. Several of their leaders he privately called "thugs and bullies," though he was careful not to say so in public. Still, the Prime Minister insisted even thugs and bullies had their role in different areas of foreign policy, and so they were to be invited whether Albert wanted them or not.

"Fine," he reluctantly agreed, while stipulating they were to be seated far away from him. He understood that he would have to deal with the fallout from that decision at the next Commonwealth Heads of Government Meeting.

"I'll wear my most effusive smile," he snapped.

Once the parade participants arrived [And getting travel documents for them all was another issue], there was the matter of getting them from their respective airports to their lodgings, and then to the staging areas.

Lodging was a problem, as well as feeding the many thousands of participants. As it was between terms, schools and universities opened their dormitories, gymnasiums, and field houses; and large, indoor athletic and convention facilities were also used. Cots were at a premium. Space was also sought in private homes and apartments throughout the city and beyond, many of which were already booked by Coronation visitors.

The planning for all this was massive, and Paul was frequently overwhelmed even with the assistance of a large staff and would often seek Albert to complain about how badly things were going and how it was going to be a massive failure, and he was to blame.

Inevitably, Albert would laughingly reassure Paul that everything would be fine.

"But how do you know?" Paul would demand in exasperation.

"Because I'm King and I don't put incompetent people in charge of things. Besides, London is my Camelot, where everything works out for the best."

And then he'd always break out into song:

"The snow may never slush upon the hillside.
By nine p. m. the moonlight must appear.
In short, there's simply not [And by now Paul invariably
        joined him]
A more congenial spot
For happ'ly-ever-aftering than here
In Cam-el-ot!"

Sometimes Paul even made up an issue just to hear Albert sing.

Finally, things were ready. All the slots had long been filled in on the parade chart that went around the planning room. All the groups had arrived, except the group from Pitcairn's Island which was running late due to flight delays but did have the

Possession's sole transgendered person to fill the King's request for diversity.

The staging areas were filling up. All along the route, the hydration stations, the food stands, medics and first aid stations, rest areas, portable toilets, everything needed to sustain a small army of participants as well as viewers on what turned out to be a hot, sunny summer's day. Albert had already vanquished Paul's concern about inclement weather by, again, singing about London's Camelot as the place where:

"The rain may never fall till after sundown.
By eight, the morning fog must disappear."

Paul was not always convinced, but he did wonder about Albert's connection with the weather gods when the day dawned into one of the most beautiful in recent memory.

At 11 a. m., with the family assembled in the Royal Grandstand, Albert, followed by Paul, entered and stayed standing at their chairs while the lead band, with players specially chosen from the country's music schools, played "God Save the King" directly across from the grandstand, while the thousands nearby joined in. At the end, after the lengthy cheering finally died down, Albert approached the microphone in front of him and simply said, "Let the parade begin!"

For three hours the component parts of the Nation's Parade passed by, beginning with the banner held by selected participants. Following them was a vast assemblage that included street dancers, Morris dancers, bagpipes, school groups from across the country, trade unions, craft groups, miners, representatives from municipalities from isolated Cornish villages to the City of London, ethnic groups, religious groups . . . Albert had insisted anyone watching the parade on their telly, from anywhere in the nation or Commonwealth or Possession, must be able to see someone like themselves in the parade, and never had so much diversity been seen at one time or place in the country's history.

Albert loved every minute, especially whenever an L.G.B.T.Q. contingent passed; then he'd always proudly stand, smiling broadly, and hold out both hands to greet the participants.

There were countless marching bands, but also Welsh choruses, inner city rap groups accompanied by street dancers, endless groups of school students of all ages, several groups of motorized wheel chairs [With charged batteries ready if needed at the halfway point], plus a variety of floats promoting everything from saving fish, birds, and other wildlife, to housing councils, advocates for clean energy, and more special interest groups than Albert knew existed. He smiled and waved at everyone.

Paul had been concerned about simply attending and watching the parade, thinking he should be in the command center overseeing things.

"No," insisted Albert. "Your place is beside me. You've done your job; now let your people do theirs."

Pauline looked distinguished and radiant. She, too, had been worried, but now it was happening, and she could not have been prouder of her staff in pulling the day off.

At the halfway point, Albert quickly left the stand for the adjacent comfort station and to grab a quick snack and drink before returning for the second half. He was especially pleased at how excited the kids of what was now his Jamaican family were; cheering and applauding as various groups passed. It was a day for kids, he thought, as it was a day for the future.

He was even more amazed during the second part at the

amazing variety of peoples and causes and groups assembled from around the world. He was especially pleased that bringing all of these people together was having a synergistic effect, that it wasn't just a one-off event, because the foundation was making this into a time of networking and sharing, of not just meeting one another but of finding mutual interests and concerns that came from planned workshops as well as chance meetings where mutual interests could develop into shared strategies and plans. Indeed, the foundation planned on having conferences and similar events like the Parade and the Nation's Party every four years, with an emphasis on mutual cooperation and planning around the themes of equity, equality, opportunity, self-help, and care for the planet. There would be regular meetings every other year around the world, and national meetings annually. Albert wanted something lasting to come out of his Coronation, and not just a celebration of the monarchy and its traditions; he wanted the emphasis on unity to provide a better future as well.

As the parade finally ended, with a band of musicians picked from around the world, instead of just going back inside the palace, Albert stayed to meet the volunteers and staff members in the immediate area who helped make the day possible. He asked their names and thanked them for their service. Finally, he and Paul went back into the palace to change.

He had worn a formal morning suit for the parade and changed into formal evening wear for the banquet of four hundred, rather tightly packed together at long tables in the State Dining Room, which was the first time it had been used since his father's death. He knew he was there to be seen and greeted, even by those foreign dignitaries he didn't want to meet, but he graciously had a smile and warm greetings for everyone, regardless of his private assessments.

The menu was varied, with many individual choices

available, which, considering the amount of food to be prepared, led the head chef to contract kitchens across the city to help. The trick was keeping the hot foods hot, and the cold foods cold, until being served. As with the parade itself, the banquet was, frankly, a logistical nightmare. But she and her team pulled it off, including Albert's insistence that, if salmon was to be offered, that it be commercially caught and not served poached, which she knew at least kept it moist without drying out. But she had her secrets and used every one of them.

Finally came the toasts. Albert rose as those present stood with him. During the toast, he paused ever so often so those depending on translations could stay with him.

"I greet you, distinguished dignitaries from around the world, and I appreciate your being here tonight. A Coronation is a time to celebrate not just a tradition brought from the past, but to look forward to the future as well. And that has been the joy, for me personally, of the parade today, and of the Nation's Party tomorrow, which I hope each of you can attend. It's going to be fabulous!

"My father would have welcomed you to a unified Britain; unfortunately, since the Scottish secession, I cannot do the same."

"Live with it!" said an unexpectedly boisterous Scottish prime minister with his Highland burr.

"Actually, I'm glad you brought that up," replied Albert with a smile, "because I think now is the time to mention something we have been discussing for some time. The United Kingdom will return the Balmoral estate to Scotland as soon as the treaty is completed, with two conditions: [Albert ignored the shocked look on Lizzie's face] that the land be used as a national park for all Scottish citizens; and that hunting and fishing are prohibited. Also, that poached salmon is never served there."

"That would be the deal breaker!" interjected the Scottish

P.M., to the amusement of the room, to which Albert only smiled before turning serious again as he looked at those present.

"Some of you have known me all my life, while others I am meeting for the first time. In any case, I hope and trust that we can work together to ensure a fair and equitable world for all our peoples, so they can be safe, healthy, fed, housed, and educated to lead lives of remarkable accomplishment."

Then he raised his glass.

"To the future!"

"To the future!" replied the room in agreement.

"Finally," continued Albert, "I must thank the many thousands of people it took to make this day a success: paid staff, volunteers, the coordination of many government agencies, and non-government organizations too numerous to mention. Indeed, it has taken world-wide planning to pull today off, and tomorrow's events as well. But I want to thank the head of the organizing committee for these two days, Dr. Pauline McGregor, for the remarkable energy and consummate patience she has shown since the project was first conceived."

Albert then turned to Pauline and applauded her, as did the entire room. She acknowledged the applause and then turned back to Albert.

"And finally," said Albert, "I must give credit to my dear husband and consort, Paul McGregor, for his ceaseless work on this project for so many months."

Paul had been seated elsewhere in the room and Albert wasn't sure exactly where he was.

"Paul? I think you're somewhere in this room."

"Over here!" said Paul from his table.

"Whew!" replied Albert with mock relief. "For a second I thought you'd gone out for pizza!" which brought general laughter as so many present were familiar with the King's earlier escapades.

"Not at all," said Paul, "I'm enjoying my salmon," which made Albert grin broadly.

Then, smiling, Albert raised his glass again.

"To Paul. My everything. To the Duke!"

And the room responded, "To the Duke!"

Much later that night, after a long, exhausting day, Albert and Paul lay side by side in bed, naked, but Paul was still not ready to sleep.

"Albert," he said softly. "Sort me out."

So he did.

CHAPTER 67

The next morning, the day of the Nation's Party, Albert and Paul had a hearty breakfast as they knew, once again, that it would be many hours before their next meal.

The plan was that Albert would be primarily consigned inside the Royal Enclosure at the back of the palace that opened onto the Great Lawn. Here, anyone with an admission ticket to the Party could meet him on a first-come basis. It was the closest thing to a royal levee that he would ever have. And while what he most wanted to do was to walk around the grounds and see all the people, all the exhibits and demonstrations, all the performances, and to try all the food – in so far as he was able – he knew his duty lay instead in greeting his people because, despite the day being a showcase for the country's diversity and that of the Commonwealth, still none of this would have happened except for his Coronation. So he was resigned to standing beside Paul in a greeting line for the six hours of the party, meeting people, saying, "Hello. So good of you to come," and shaking hands, then on to the next one, and the next one, and the . . . Yes. It was going to be a long day, indeed.

The grounds for the event covered not only the Great Lawn behind the palace, but the adjacent Green Park and St. James' Park which, for the day, had been transformed into a continuous space by closing the roads that otherwise separated them, and encircling the entire event with fencing. The tall metal fencing that already enclosed the palace grounds was removed in places so people could freely cross to the other sites as well.

The organizers determined that 100,000 people could

comfortably and safely attend the event without inordinate crowding. However, when the website was open for applications, four million, from all over the world, applied. Again, a lottery system was used to determine who got tickets, with a limit of four per application. The winners had to provide a photo I.D., and they were the only ones who could use their ticket, in an effort to prevent scalping the free tickets. Attendees were vetted by security before receiving tickets. Photo I.D.'s and tickets were checked at each entrance, and metal detectors were also used. There were other security measures which were not made public, but which included a facial recognition system. Security was tight, but not always apparent. Still, despite 100,000 attendees, and thousands more staffing the event, the site was considered probably the safest place to be in the country that day.

The same method used to determine the participants in the previous day's parade was also used to determine the performers, exhibits, concerts, and other events for the party. The United Kingdom had its own exhibit, as did the Commonwealth countries and Possessions. There were booths for NGOs of all kinds, with many related to education, health, and environmental issues; there were also cultural and ethnic displays and performances, a huge variety of entertainers, both at various stages as well as strolling performers, including magicians, jugglers, sword swallowers, fire eaters, and Punch and Judy shows. There were many food booths featuring both regional and ethnic cuisines. Since those coming from overseas could not bring food to prepare, they were invited to coordinate with similar ethnic restaurants within the country already serving food from their homelands to provide food prepared by, or at least overseen by, overseas chefs, so the recipes would be as authentic as possible.

While admission was free, food was sold, primarily as a

fund raiser for the sponsoring groups. But to make sure everyone could afford to try a wide range of food that day, those attending who were also receiving some form of national assistance obtained special, one-day government-issued debit cards to allow for a wide range of sampling.

The day began with a truly ecumenical service that included brief prayers or meditative thoughts provided by a cross-section of religions and spiritualities, as well as philosophies that included humanist, existentialist, and atheist groups. The Archbishop of Canterbury later told Albert that it was the most remarkable, as well as the most inclusive, such event in which he had ever participated.

The service was held at a temporary stage to one side of the Great Lawn that also provided a stage for large-scale performances throughout the rest of the day, such as the City of Birmingham Orchestra and the Royal Ballet, as well as many performances of world music.

Albert and Paul attended the service, then went to the Royal Enclosure for their meet-and-greet.

The number of exhibits and performances was truly staggering. It was as if the world itself, at least the one-third of it connected in some way to the United Kingdom, was on display. Many attendees later described it as a veritable kaleidoscope of sounds, smells, and colors, including an amazing variety of ethnic and regional clothing, as well as, since it was a party, costumes of every description, from historically based dresses to outer space and fantasy wear. A few nudists tried to bare all but were quickly wrapped up and asked to leave. Otherwise, there were surprisingly few security issues as people were on their best behavior, just pleased to attend and simply wanted to enjoy the day.

What was later remembered by many was the sheer

delight of often vastly different people sharing themselves freely and openly. There was so much to see and to do and to eat that no one could pretend to have taken it all in, not even with the quickest

sampling tours. The sheer variety of performances, exhibits, demonstrations, and food stands was overwhelming. On various stages one could encounter a Charles Dickens impersonator reading his works; while, needless to say, several theatrical troupes and companies gave both traditional and non-traditional performances of Shakespeare; one queer company acted out creative and erotically-charged interpretations of the Bard's sonnets; while acting companies from Manchester, Leeds, and Liverpool centered on pressing social issues in their areas; and there was space set aside where protesters could explain their positions for or against issues of the day, such as why they were against the monarchy itself, or the European Union, or drilling for oil in the North Sea, or why Wales deserved its freedom.

Strolling performers wandered through the crowds doing magic tricks that enthralled the youngsters, even to age-old tricks like disappearing coins and finding the hidden card.

Musicians performed Purcell and ska; there were West End theatres providing scenes from modern classics and Restoration comedies. One stage alternated Gilbert and Sullivan with Noël Coward songs, which Albert sorely wanted to attend. There was chamber music, rock music, house music, jazz, Jamaican steel bands, sitar music, drumming from Africa, didgeridoos from Australia; available performances seemed endless and the cacophony from so much happening at once was not disconcerting but, on a basic level, remarkably stimulating. It was later recalled as one of the country's great days.

Meanwhile, Albert and Paul continued standing and meeting people who, themselves, stood in line for hours for the opportunity to meet the monarch and his husband. There was the basic etiquette of a bow or a curtsy, then waiting for the King to speak first and for him to extend his hand before taking it. But basically, it was quite informal as Albert and Paul put people at ease, knowing how stressful it could be for most people to meet their monarch for probably the only time in their lives.

No break was planned for the entire six hours as Albert wanted to meet as many as he could. However, at one point midway through the afternoon, he and Paul were surprised to hear children shouting, "Uncle Albert! Uncle Paul!" and they came rushing forward, grabbing Albert and Paul by the hands and then pulling them out of line, even pushing from behind.

"You must see the Jamaican exhibit. Come on!"

Fortunately, those waiting at the front of the long queue to see the King were quite understanding and smiled as Albert apologized and said, "My people are calling!" as he and Paul were taken away. But he took time to stop and explain to the next people in line to "Please stay as I will return shortly. That's not a royal command," he said lightly, "but a royal request."

Those in line were so excited at this unexpected interaction with the King that they willingly waited as Albert calmly looked over at Graham and simply said, "Follow us."

But Graham had already considered this possibility and had many plain-clothes staff on duty. He simply spoke into his head piece and said, "Top dog is on the move," for the team to be alerted, then followed Albert and Paul as they made their way through the crowds which parted before them as they were practically being dragged to the Jamaican exhibit by the family children.

Once there, they sampled the food, which both agreed was fabulous, listened to the musicians and watched the dancing, all while being pointed out as people said, "The King! The King and the Duke!"

While Paul was surrounded by an admiring group as a kind of native son by people who wanted his autograph, Albert briefly looked at the exhibits that celebrated Jamaican life while calling attention to British use of slave labor and the often-fraught relationship between colony and ruling country. At Pauline's urging, and with the Prime Minister's approval, he had already set up a commission to study the issues of reparations and an official apology. Albert also recognized the island would soon be completely independent, and he would be its head of state only for a short time to come. Still, that was a transition he supported.

By now, he'd already been gone for half an hour and, while he would have preferred to spend the rest of the afternoon exploring the grounds with their myriad of exhibits, food, and performances, Albert realized he had to return to the enclosure and to those patiently awaiting his return, so he turned to Graham and said, "Take us back" to the dismay of the children: "Stay with us, Uncle Albert!" But he assured them that he would see all of them later.

"Yea!" they cried in a jagged chorus. Soon Albert and Paul were back in the enclosure to greet the next people in line who had, indeed, waited patiently to meet their King.

And so, it went for the rest of the afternoon, right through to closing. People only reluctantly left, and exhibitors and performers were already starting to close when Albert and Paul finally greeted the last people in line. They were exhausted, but it was also the only time when they could finally wander the grounds and meet the people who had made the day work, like the senior volunteer who had driven from her farm in the Fens to help. They also met the archaeologist from Bristol who was packing up his artifacts and who turned out to be a new member of the revamped Time Team 2.0 series that Albert and Paul often watched on the telly. They also spoke with crew members as they took apart stages and took down the climate-controlled tents where art works had been exhibited, both treasures from the country's past, like Van Dyke's life-sized portrait of Charles the First, through recently made art by school students from throughout the country and Commonwealth. They talked with performance artists taking off their makeup, and with members of the security teams about how the day had gone.

In apparently no time at all, Albert and Paul had spent another two hours on site. Albert later recalled that time as among the best of the entire Coronation Week. In fact, they had very little time to prepare for that evening's event, a concert at London Stadium, a kind of giant variety show, of the best young performers, as well as many who were legendary. Albert and Paul had dressed informally for the day but now changed into full formal evening attire. The event was originally scheduled for Albert's namesake hall but was quickly changed for the larger venue so more could attend, and all tickets, again picked through a lottery, were free.

The show was broadcast around the world and scheduled to last three hours; it lasted four hours. It had a bewildering variety of acts, including a comedian described as the new Benny Hill ["Not bloody likely!" said the King privately]; as well as dramatic readings, songs, dances, sketches; the list went on and on while Albert, by now completely exhausted, nonetheless managed to laugh where appropriate, while always smiling and applauding enthusiastically.

After the grand finale, and the singing of "God Save the King," there was the meeting of the performers backstage who were lined up and waiting to be greeted by Albert and Paul. It was said that Albert looked, understandably, tired and wan. It was with a feeling of relief that the two finally headed back to the palace and soon they were, once again, side by side, naked, and they just fell asleep.

There were other Coronation-related events, but none were as stressful or eventful as these three summer days. Now Albert could look into the mirror, bleary eyed, and realize that, at long last, he was, legitimately, King of England and Wales.

PART III

CHAPTER 68

"I still don't understand why Albert is coming here and why by himself?" asks a perplexed Larry.

"I don't know," replies an equally perplexed Lizzie, "but I don't like it. It reminds me too much of the old, scheming Albert, while I've grown so used to, and am so much enjoying, the new Albert – the caring, affectionate Albert – the brother I always wanted."

They are seated in the rear drawing room. It is a mild day; the wall of glass doors is open to the terrace. The children are gone with Grant, their tutor, on a field trip so the house is quiet.

"Do you think it has anything to do with Toria?" asks Larry.

Lizzie scoffs.

"Of course not. The succession is set; he's said so many times in public."

"But not during Coronation Week," he reminds her, "which would have been a proper time."

"He was a trifle busy then, you must admit," explains Lizzie patiently. "Besides, she was prominently seated at the Coronation, so the connection was clear to everyone. Besides, there's no one else."

"I suppose you're right," he agrees. "Besides, maybe Albert's coming for something good. Maybe he wants to help some way."

Larry was ever the optimist.

"Oh, I like that!" agrees Lizzie, who wants to feel good

about the visit.

"Like what?" she asks.

"Well," and he pauses to consider the options. "Like maybe he wants us to go on a tour of the Commonwealth for him. You'd think that would be a natural step for him after the Coronation, but I haven't heard anything about it, just this upcoming tour of the country that he and Paul are taking."

"Oh, that would be wonderful!" exclaimed Lizzie enthusiastically. "I haven't seen most of those countries since our world tour after Mummy's death. That would be a perfect way to show Toria off: for her to see and to be seen. It would also be a great educational opportunity for the others as well. Yes, I'd like that very much indeed. Of course, knowing Albert, he probably wants us to go to those bleak South Atlantic Island possessions, or those even bleaker South Pacific possessions."

"Well, we'll know soon. As they say, from his mouth to our ears."

Lizzie smiles.

"Is that one of your American expressions?"

"Perhaps," he admits. "I really can't remember."

And, soon enough, they hear the distant, low growl of Albert's helicopter as it approaches and then, much louder, as it lands beyond the gardens on the lawn. Soon he is seated in an armchair before them.

After the pleasantries are over, the three of them sit looking at each other, smiling, with Lizzie and Larry expectant, while Albert is visibly nervous. It is obvious he has something to say, but equally obvious that he is reluctant to speak. This is when Lizzie's doubts about his visit return.

Unable to look at them, Albert turns to stare at the paintings on the nearest wall. And so, it is finally here; the moment he's been avoiding for months. And it wasn't just because he was afraid of Lizzie's reaction. He was, and is, because he knows she is capable of almost anything. But it's more because he hasn't wanted to lose the closeness, he and his sister have reached these past few months, when he's finally had the caring, friendly, affectionate sister he's always wanted, a true pal he could just call up and talk with. He's never had that before, and he knows that what he is about to say, the words he'd rehearsed all the way over and, indeed, has rehearsed for weeks, will destroy their tenuous truce forever as she will be devastated and their close relationship will end. He is about to destroy his sister's plan that if she can't or won't be queen, then at least her daughter will. He knows she will blame him and never forgive him. He is going to destroy her dream so he and Paul can have theirs. It isn't right; he knows that; but he is prepared to do it anyway. The moment is here and now. The door of life's possibilities opens, and he walks through it.

By now the smiles on Larry's and Lizzie's faces have become quite strained, and Lizzie knows she must break the tension before she runs screaming from the room, so she asks if he would like some tea.

"What?" Albert asks, almost absentmindedly as his gaze turns back to her. "Oh, no, thank you. I can't stay long as I must return to London."

Now Lizzie is prepared for something awful to happen, but she has no idea what it could be.

Albert steels himself, and then calmly looks at each of them. The fatal moment is now.

"An announcement will be made shortly," he says, "but I want you to hear it first from me before you hear it from the media."

Now Lizzie and Larry know they will not be touring the Commonwealth.

"Paul and I are having a child."

Larry hears Albert clearly but is so shocked and stunned that he needs time to formulate a reply.

"What?" he simply asks.

So Albert repeats what he's just said.

"Paul and I are . . . "

"Yes, yes, yes," interrupts Larry hastily. "We heard that. But how?"

"Modern Brit technology from Oxford," says Albert, relieved at the opportunity to explain something rather than just confess.

"Our chromosomes have been combined and then injected into an empty egg, which was then implanted into a host mother."

And now, for Lizzie, everything becomes shockingly clear.

"Connie," she says softly. "So that's why she's been in London."

"Yes," replies Albert equally softly.

"That bitch!" screams Lizzie venomously.

"Now Lizzie," replies Larry in his conciliatory tone, but Lizzie ignores him.

"All these times I've seen her, and she's said nothing! All of you have said nothing!" exclaims Lizzie, as the full weight of betrayal oppresses her.

"You, Paul, and . . . "

Lizzie cannot bear to say the name of her greatest betrayer, her closest and, frankly, the only true friend she's ever had, and who never said a word.

"Bastards! All of you are bastards!"

"Lizzie," says Larry in a hopeless attempt to contain his wife's anger.

"That's all right," says Albert placatingly. "I understand how she feels."

She immediately turns on Albert.

"So, you know how I feel? You destroy me, and then sympathize with me? How male can you get?"

"Lizzie," replies Albert in a soothing tone of voice. "This has nothing to do with you and Toria."

"Oh, it doesn't?" she replies scathingly. "How can it not?"

"Because Toria simply moves to Number Two."

But Lizzie sees through that ruse.

"Until you have another child, then another and another, and soon she'll never be Queen!"

"Lizzie!" shouts Albert in his authoritative tone. "It's not always about you!"

And Lizzie is silenced by the force of his voice, which he quickly changes as he keeps trying to placate her.

"I was relieved when you and Larry had Toria. I can't tell you how much pressure there was on me, even as a gay man, to get married simply to continue the line, but then Toria came along and that pressure was gone because she would be monarch. And you know that's what I wanted."

"So what happened to change your mind?" asks Lizzie.

"Paul happened," he replies. "I never expected to fall in love. I was resigned to being a hermit king who lived solely for his people. But Paul thawed my heart and gave it back to me. Yet we live in dangerous times. You can't imagine the number of death threats against us every week. And no matter how good Graham and the security team are, there's always the chance that either of us will be killed, and the survivor will be left with nothing. It would be different if we had forty or fifty years together, and we may, but who knows for sure? If he were to die next week, what would I have?"

"The foundation. Memories. Pictures," replies Lizzie defensively.

"Would those be enough for you if Larry were to die?" asks Albert softly. And Lizzie looks away because now she sees this is an argument she will lose.

"You and Larry have five children!"

And Lizzie realizes this is not the time to tell him about Number Six on the way.

"Why can't Paul and I have just one? If I were straight and married a woman we would have children, and neither you nor Toria would ever be Queen. Why can't we have a living creature we have jointly created, so that, if I'm gone, Paul can still see something of me, and, if he's gone, I can see something of him? It's the continuity we want. Isn't that why you and Larry have children? Not for the succession alone, but to continue some part of each other?"

Yes, Lizzie has lost the argument, because that is precisely why she and Larry have had children. But she can't allow herself to give in, too much is at stake; too much she has fought for, for so long. So, she looks at her brother, who basically has been pleading, even begging, for her understanding.

"I do understand what you're saying, Albert, but the price is too high. Why can't you and Paul have a child yet keep the succession the way it is?"

Albert smiles wanly.

"Because the country would never let me do that. Once I have a child, the question is taken away from me and whatever power I might have in that regard is also taken from me."

Lizzie didn't quite follow his point, so he explained.

"The child of a monarch basically becomes a ward of the state because the succession is too important to be left even to royal parents. In a monarchy, the succession is everything, and the government will ensure the succession is protected. You and I were raised that way ourselves, only we weren't aware of it. But now I see it clearly. I cannot keep my own child from the line of succession. You'll see it after the announcement. The people were fine with Toria as queen as long as they thought there was no other choice but to watch the country's reaction to the news. The people want the monarch to have a monarch. They want a direct line on the family tree, not some side branch through a sibling. Mark my words, Lizzie, the child will be greeted with joy.

"But" Albert continues, "and you may find this hard to believe right now, I love Toria [Lizzie gives Albert a look of disgust, which he ignores and continues], and I don't want to hurt her as I know she will be, since she has her heart set on being Queen. I understand that. [Lizzie looks at him with daggers, which he also ignores] but I have something special to offer."

"A consolation prize?" interjects Lizzie with dripping scorn.

"Actually, no, because nothing can truly replace being Queen, but Toria is smart; she has common sense; and she is compassionate. She truly wants to help people. And what I'm learning is that as monarch I have remarkably little opportunity to directly help my people, which is my driving passion."

"Oh, really?" asks a skeptical Lizzie. "You've hidden it well enough."

Which Albert also ignores, gaining Larry's admiration for Albert's refusal to be taunted by his sister. Larry realizes the once impulsive lad was now growing into a remarkably restrained and self-controlled adult.

"It turns out that being King comes with its own set of restrictions. My days are so filled with things that I am expected to do – by the office, by the government – that I have very little time for what I want to do. I meet foreign dignitaries, tour auto plants and housing projects, wade through the red boxes, so that at the end of the day I look at Paul and asked just what I've done all day that was truly constructive. And there are no good answers. But there is so much that can be done, especially with the Commonwealth countries and our remaining overseas possessions, which mainly seem to be small islands scattered across large oceans. I really have very little idea what is happening overseas aside from politics and skirmishes. I don't know what the needs of their people are; or how we can form alliances to improve their lives, or how we can work together for our mutual benefit. Yes, I do know their rulers, their presidents, but, again, not their people. And, yes, we have an admirable foreign service, but its mission changes based on which political party is in power, and usually our politics are governed by expediency and how useful these countries can be to us. But I want something more. I need someone to be my eyes and ears overseas. And, yes, I know Toria is only eleven, but it's not too early to start preparing her to become my overseas representative. That's what I want her to be."

Lizzie and Larry look at each other, perplexed by Albert's suggestion, yet enticed by its vision as well.

"Now," Albert continues, "She may not even be interested in this, and it's completely up to her, of course, but I hope you'll present it to her as an option to consider when she finally comes out of her disappointment and, yes, her anger towards me. ["And how about my anger towards you?" asks Lizzie to herself] But at some point she will be ready to ask herself what she now wants to do with her life, and as my overseas representative she will find a challenging life, a life that demands all of her creativity and intelligence and tactfulness, all of her ability to make connections and linkages on a global scale. I think it would be fabulous; it's tailor-made just for her. So, would you please, when the time is right, have her consider this? Because it's never too soon to start. She will need language training, world history, diplomacy, and the sooner she starts, the more capable she will be when she finishes university to start her new position."

Albert finally stops, breathless from the excitement of explaining his plan.

Lizzie is conflicted. She can tell that Larry is already taken in by Albert's plan for their daughter's life. But Albert had already had one plan for her – that she would be Queen – and now he already has another plan. Who was to say that in another eleven or so years, when she finishes university, that Albert wouldn't change his mind again? Lizzie doesn't trust him anymore. She also despises him, a rather superficial word for something much darker and more ominous.

Having been unable to look at him as he spoke, she now turns to face him and says simply, "I hate you," without shouting but with forceful intention. "I hate you for coming here and destroying our lives and thinking that some mid-level diplomatic position can buy us off. Well, it isn't going to work!"

By now she is shouting, and her voice pounds off the walls.

"Do you hear me? I hate you!"

"Lizzie," pleads Albert who, despairing at what he has created, looks at Larry for help.

Once again, as often happened when the three of them were together, though almost never since Paul joined the family, Larry realizes he is the adult in the room and knows a diversion is required to keep the two siblings apart.

"So, you say an announcement is going to be made?" he asks brightly.

Thankful for Larry's tactic, Albert says in a relieved tone of voice, "Yes."

"When?" And Albert looks at his watch. "Right about

480

now."

That morning, the palace press office released a brief statement that, at 11 a. m. , an announcement of national importance would be made from the Proclamation Balcony of Friary Court at St. James Palace.

Coming so soon after the Coronation, the announcement caught royal watchers by surprise because they assumed the King would simply be getting on with his duties. So, speculation was immediately rampant, both on broadcast media as well as online platforms like Twitter and Facebook, and the forums dedicated to all things royal. The strange thing was that there was nothing to base speculation on, not a hint of what the announcement might be about. Of course, that never stops speculation, but reporters contacting their palace insiders about what to expect were surprised to learn that either they didn't know or weren't saying, either on or off the record. It was a confounding, nearly unprecedented situation to have absolutely no idea what to expect, and an unnerving one for broadcasters to simply admit they didn't know what was going to be announced, which doesn't make for interesting news.

So, satellite news vans and reporters were quickly dispatched to the palace where they found the street was already cordoned off in expectation of their arrival and vans were quickly parked to begin the setting-up process. Journalists who entered Friary Court found themselves in a news pen, with the rest of the rather small courtyard set aside for the general public, who also started coming in to await the proclamation. They noted large screen monitors set up outside the courtyard along the street to convey the event to those who could not get in. The crowd included royal watchers who kept track of the goings and comings of the Royal Family, as well as the simply curious, and to passing tourists. All of them took the time, while waiting, to speculate on what they were about to hear. And of those professional journalists and the general public, only one person out of all of them got the answer right and he happened to be an American tourist, whose deep and obvious drawl pinpointed him as being from the grand state of Texas. His home was also indicated by his prominent cowboy hat, his fringed shirt with snaps, his hand-tooled leather belt with the motto on the back that said, "Remember the Alamo," and a huge bronze belt buckle of the Lone Star State. Naturally, he also wore Levi jeans and had alligator-skin boots.

And in a loud voice that reverberated off the stone and brick walls of Friary Court, the Texan proclaimed, "I bet that fag King and his niggra boyfriend are going to have themselves a Mandingo baby!"

In an instant, the crowd turned on the man and bloodshed was only averted by plainclothes security guards who surrounded the man to protect him from the enraged crowd and hustled him out to the street and into a security van that took him to a nearby side street in the City where it stopped and waited until the announcement was over. Then the man was released with an admonition that respecting his host country would be greatly appreciated, especially if he ever wanted to return.

He reluctantly agreed, saying the whole thing was un-American, which was merely stating the obvious, and was released. He spent the rest of the day going from pub to pub, telling all within hearing that he was the only man in the country who got it right.

And that day stayed with the man for the rest of his life, long after he returned to Texas. Particularly on the Fourth of July, and only needing a couple of beers, he related yet again to his long-suffering family and neighbors how it took only "one good ole boy from Am'rilla" to get the best of all those hoity-toity, funny talking, faggy Brits.

When the bells of Big Ben tolled the hour, an ornately uniformed Royal Herald entered the Proclamation Balcony, preceded by an equally ornately uniformed quartet of Royal Trumpeters, who approached the parapet, brought their silver mouthpieces to their lips, and blew a majestic fanfare. Then they stepped back as the Herald stepped forward and, in the florid language of his profession, read the Proclamation, which said that King Albert and his consort, the Duke of Durham, were expecting a child to be born in October. The child would be theirs equally and would be the new successor. At the King's request, the gender of the child would be announced at the time of birth. The host mother, Constance Ann Mary Elizabeth, the Duchess of Essex, was doing well. The technology for the procedure was developed by and carried out at Oxford. The christening would take place at the Chapel of St. James, with the Archbishop of Canterbury presiding. After the Herald concluded his remarks, he stepped back and the Royal Trumpeters came forward to play a recessional, then they left.

Unbeknownst to those in Friary Court, the proceedings were observed by Paul, Pauline, and Connie. They stood back from a window in a palace room overlooking the courtyard. Albert and Lizzie had played in that very room as children.

There was a moment of silence, then the courtyard erupted into cheering; everyone cheered – the general public, the media, the security guards, the police – and the cheering was quickly picked up by those outside as well. In fact, wherever people were watching the announcement there was cheering – whether in pubs, cafes, banks, government offices, shops, housing projects, estates, factories – it seemed anywhere there were Brits, there was cheering.

Once again, Albert had correctly understood his people:

they wanted him to have a child, and the cheering was a direct repudiation of the young Princess Victoria. She simply wasn't wanted now that there was a choice, and that was what Lizzie found so hard to bear as she watched the event replayed throughout the afternoon, like someone fascinated by a train wreck.

Every time she heard the cheering again, another nail was pressed into the flesh of her palm just so she could feel the pain. How could she have been so wrong as to think that she, and her child, were wanted? And she hated the fact that, once again, Albert was right. Well, obviously he understood his people while she didn't understand them at all. In fact, she didn't even like them. She hated being touched; she hated shaking hands; she hated small talk from people she would never see again. She did it because she was expected to, but she didn't like any of it, and now she hated all those who repudiated her and her daughter with their inane cheering. But she also had other things to think about.

Albert was still walking across the lawn back to his helicopter when she and Larry called in their press officer to come up with a release when the media would call asking for a comment. They knew it had to be positive and supportive; there could be nothing of envy or anger. The family had to be close ranked and welcoming of the new successor, though admitting it was galling to Lizzie. The release was short and simple, to the effect that Her Royal Highness, Princess Elizabeth, and her husband, the Duke of Sussex, were pleased at the announcement of a child to her brother, King Albert, and to his husband and consort, the Duke of Durham. Having five children of their own [she still didn't think it was the right time to mention Number Six], they understood the joys of parenting. They also wished their cousin, Constance, well on her pregnancy and looked forward to standing together as family on the day of the child's christening. The statement concluded by saying interviews would not be granted nor would submitted questions be accepted.

Next, Lizzie and Larry had to consider how to tell their children, especially Toria, when they came home from their field trip. They agreed to be very positive because they knew that how they responded would be picked up by Toria and form the basis of her own reaction, perhaps coloring it for years. Lizzie understood she was not the person to do this, as she didn't trust herself not to somehow taint even positive words with the wrong inflection, or a grimace, or a sideways glance, that Toria would notice. She was bright and astute after all.

So, it had to be Larry, and both knew he was up to the task as he had a special rapport with his eldest child. Lizzie, then, would deal with the rest of the children, and she already knew how they would react, with utter joy at the idea of a new cousin to play with. Yes, she had the easier task.

But Larry and Lizzie's well-thought-out strategy had no chance of implementation as events were moving beyond their control. They stood waiting on the front steps when the car returned and stopped. A door was flung open and Toria, sobbing, ran past them screaming, "I hate you! I hate you all!" And Lizzie and Larry listened in shock as their angry child ran screaming across the marble floor of the entrance hall, then up the marble steps of the staircase, and then gradually receding down the long hallway to the far end and they heard a door slam shut. They looked at each other and just shook their heads as the other children came bursting out of the car laughing and yelling, "We're going to have a cousin! Uncle Albert and Uncle Paul are having a baby!" and they also ran into the house. Lizzie at least had called that one correctly. Finally, Grant came up, apologetically; "Your Highness," he said, and bowed, then continued.

"They wanted to hear the radio on the way back and it was on every station . . . "

His voice trailed off, but Lizzie smiled gently for he was obviously distraught, and said, surprisingly lightly, "It's all right. They would have found out one way or another. Now see if the kitchen staff can give them some refreshments and then get them out onto the terrace. I'll be there shortly."

Relieved, he said, "Very good, Ma'am", and then went into the house.

Lizzie and Larry looked at each other.

"I'll go upstairs," he said, and she nodded.

He paused at the closed door. He heard Toria sobbing inside, and what he took to be the muffled sound of small fists pounding a pillow. The children's bedrooms had no locks, but Larry and Lizzie had made it clear they would never enter their children's rooms without their expressed verbal permission. So, he quietly knocked.

"Toria," he said softly.

"Go away!" she shouted through her tears. "I hate you all!"

Larry knew that while Toria seemed mature for her age, she was still an eleven-year-old, with all the conflicting passions that implied, so he also knew to tread carefully, and with respect. He waited while she continued to cry, then said, "Toria, we need to talk. Please let me in."

"You lied to me!" she shouted. "You said I would be Queen!"

Then she continued crying.

"I'm going to wait right here until you want to let me in," said Larry softly.

"I never want to see you again!" she shouted, at which Larry smiled to himself, remembering how quickly his own emotions had flared up at her age.

"I'll be right here," he said to the closed door. This time she ignored him, while still pounding her pillow; the muffled sound came faintly through the door.

And so, he waited. Five minutes. Ten minutes. And she was still crying.

Fifteen minutes. Still crying.

But then she stopped. And at eighteen minutes she opened the door, and he entered, leaving the door open. The room was dark. She'd pulled the heavy curtains together, but there was just enough light for him to see her now seated on the edge of the bed, so he crossed the room and stood before her.

"May I sit down?" he asked.

She said nothing but patted the bed cover beside her with her left hand, so he sat and they were side by side. Neither spoke, then she collapsed onto his shoulder, bawling, still a child, and he put his right arm around her shoulders and his left arm across her front and gently pulled her to his chest and held her close. She leaned against him and cried, then said through her tears, "They took my crown, Papa; they took my crown!"

"I know, sweetheart," he said. "Albert came this morning and explained it to us."

"But why?" she asked. "I don't understand," with near panic in her voice.

"Toria, look at me," he said. And she leaned back to see him.

"This may be the hardest day of your life. You left this morning thinking you would be queen. We told you that all your life, and you came back and you're not going to be queen, ever."

She looked at him, teary-eyed, so he pulled out a

handkerchief and gave it to her.

"Here," he said, "Wipe your eyes."

She hesitated, so he added, "Don't worry. It's clean."

And, despite the emotions raging inside her, she smiled, and, at that moment, Larry realized she was going to heal, eventually. She was resilient, like most children her age, so he continued.

"You need to know that no one lied to you. All of us thought you would be queen. Albert made it clear. He was relieved that you would be queen when he thought he was going to be alone his entire life. But he found Paul, and they fell in love, just like your mother and I did, and now, just like us, they want to have a child; they want to create something between them, just as we created you and your siblings. You wouldn't begrudge them having a child of their own, would you?"

And despite her still-flowing tears, Toria shook her head. Relieved, Larry continued.

"But Albert regrets how this has changed the succession since it moves you to Number Two, and he also admits there will be other children to come, so the fact is that you will never be Queen."

And here Toria began to tremble again, and her eyes swelled up with yet more tears, so he quickly continued.

"But he loves you so much, and admires you for your intelligence, your common sense, your creativity, that he is creating a new position just for you."

She picked up on that and looked at him curiously, despite her anger and even grief.

"Albert said his job as King actually keeps him quite confined, with demands on his time that he never expected; he's kept so busy doing things – meeting foreign dignitaries and the like – that he actually has little time to do what he really wants to do, which is to serve his people and make his country the best it can be. And I know you feel that same calling to serve, don't you?"

Toria just nodded.

"So in one sense," Larry continued, "I'm glad this happened because I actually think Albert has saved you from a life of a kind of drudgery that most people would revolt against; I know I would because it keeps you trapped doing things that, frankly, I know you really do not want to do because they keep you from doing what you really want to do, which is to serve. Do you follow me?"

Toria, no longer crying, nodded yes.

"Albert is creating a job just for you."

"Just for me?" she asked, in her child's voice.

"Just for you," he replied. "Your Uncle Albert realizes he cannot get around the Commonwealth countries and the Possessions nearly as much as he would like, and he knows there is much work that could be done in which these lands can work together for their mutual benefit, so he wants you to be that person. He wants you, someone he can trust, to be his personal representative to travel the world – meeting people, working with them – seeing how to make a better world for all of us to live in. Toria," he said nearly breathlessly, "It's visionary. And I agree with him that you are perfect for the job."

"I am, aren't I," she said as a statement, not a question, as she correctly assessed her abilities.

"Yes, my princess, you are. And he will wait until you are ready for the job. You're already going to boarding school this fall. So, if you want this job, and it's not a royal command that you must accept – Albert realizes you must want it yourself – then it's the perfect time to start preparing with the classes you need so that by the time you finish university, you'll be ready. So, will you at least think about it? I know you're still hurting by what's happened but promise me that you will consider it.

He eyed her quizzically, and she responded with the smile he liked so much to see.

"I will think about it," she agreed. Then he brought her close and kissed her on the forehead.

"That's my girl," he said approvingly, then added, "You'll always be my Queen."

They looked at each other with great tenderness.

"I love you, Pappa," Toria said.

"And I love you, princess. Now, you've had a long and stressful day. Try and take a nap, then come down to tea when you're ready."

"All right, Pappa."

He stood up, went to the doorway, and turned back to see that she had already laid her head on the pillow she'd been pounding so vigorously. He smiled and gently closed the door.

Lizzie was greatly relieved that she'd chosen the easier job to do, as her other children were, indeed, ecstatic at the prospect of the first cousin on her immediate side of the family. Unlike Larry, she didn't have to sell them on anything. They simply wanted to know exactly how Uncle Albert and Uncle Paul were going to have a child between them, then they just said they'd ask Aunt Pauline all about it the next time they saw her.

Lizzie agreed, for their sake, that that was the right thing to do, but the very mention of Pauline's name submerged her again in a kind of grieving anger, and a deep sense of betrayal and loss she'd felt since Albert's announcement.

Later that evening, as she and Larry sat outside on the terrace and the children were asleep, the deepening twilight enveloped them. The entire day had been spent in words, first with Albert, then dealing with the children. Now, it was time for her, and it was indeed all over except for the screaming, and she knew she was ready for a good one. She owed it to herself; she'd been good all day. She'd held herself in respectful reserve – for the most part – even as her world collapsed. She needed time alone – just for herself – and she looked at Larry, who understood and simply nodded; not giving permission, but in agreement. And, at that moment, Lizzie realized just how much she loved Larry, and how lucky she was to have met him. For it was he alone, from all the vast number of suitors who sought her hand in marriage – being the most eligible young woman in the kingdom – it was he alone who didn't care that she was the most eligible princess in the world. In the eyes of all the others, she knew they only looked at her and saw a crown; whereas he looked at her and saw the one woman he desired more than anyone else. Indeed, as far as he was concerned, her lineage was mere baggage. He hated the role of being the husband to the spare. He hated the, to him, artificial formality and annoying duties. He'd been an extremely successful businessman who now ran an extremely successful foundation and that's all he wanted to do, besides marrying her and having children. So, yes, Lizzie appreciated him, his thoughtfulness, his care, and she never took him for granted. To her, Larry was a daily gift.

But now she was called for a moment she'd waited all day to experience, so she got up, crossed the terrace, walked down the steps and across the vast gardens, to the much vaster Great Lawn. She passed the indentations in the grass where Albert's helicopter had landed just hours before, when he'd changed her life forever. And she finally came to the lake, with the hill on the far side whose reverberating feature gave the name of Echo to both. Here, she was far enough away from the house that the surrounding forest would muffle her screams as she didn't want to frighten her children, and she didn't want to appear any more unstable to her staff than they probably already considered her.

She paused at the shoreline and thought about the day. The problem was that she knew Albert was right in everything he had said, and, despite herself, she did appreciate the care and concern – the love – he'd shown for Toria with the offer to work with him to make the world a better place. She knew this appealed to her idealistic daughter, as she saw when Toria eventually came down for tea, and realized from her unexpected acceptance and contentment that Larry had indeed been the one to deal with her.

Lizzie felt a bit envious at the close attachment between father and daughter, one she could never enter. And she also felt a tad angry that Toria could so quickly accept a position as roving representative for the crown, instead of the crown itself. Still, Toria had her father's streak of practicality. On some level she would have preferred Toria to still be bawling instead of just giving in. But Lizzie knew she herself would never give in. She would never surrender her daughter's right to the throne no matter how many bones she was tossed. It galled her that a child coming basically out of nowhere could so quickly erase so many plans and so much hope. It just wasn't right. Why did this child even have to exist? And then, with blinding insight, Lizzie knew she had the answer: the child didn't have to exist. If the child was in the way, then get rid of the child. The quickness of the decision belied its complexity because Lizzie abhorred violence, though aware of her own propensity towards verbal brutality. It was her father who taught her that the use of force and violence to resolve conflicts, whether domestic or foreign, was always a sign of weakness and failure, of failing to see a more appropriate and less destructive option.

Here, however, there was no option. Her daughter's life was at stake, her rightful destiny, and Lizzie, having finally unleashed the protective she-bear inside herself, would use fang and claw to protect Toria's future as Queen. Lizzie was a throwback to a much earlier time, like her brother, when so many unthinkable solutions in these modern times now became thinkable.

Of course she couldn't just outright murder the child. Albert, again, was right. Once the child was born, it would be protected by the state as its most valuable asset. Besides, there was no way she could murder the child without being implicated, which would taint her daughter's right to the throne. No one would accept her then. So, it had to be done before the child was born. It had to be murdered in the womb. Well, that could be easy; miscarriages happen all the time. She'd nearly had one herself. But it wouldn't be as easy as simply pushing Connie down the stairs. No, Connie would have to throw herself down the stairs, but with what motivation? Of course! thought Lizzie: with money. It was so simple. Connie was undoubtedly getting paid to have the child. She and her husband always needed money. So how much would it cost for her to throw herself down the stairs? A million pounds? Five million? Ten or twenty? It didn't make any difference. Larry was loaded, and while he would never countenance this kind of plot, Lizzie had access to her own money from him, lots of it, in on-shore and off-shore accounts, much of it just across the Irish Sea.

But what if Connie was still too moral to do that? Lizzie could see that flaw in her. Then only one thing was left: to make Albert himself pay. Yes, that was it. If need be, she would make him regret the day they were born. Vengeance would be hers, one way or another, through the child, or through the parent.

And now, she was ready for her scream. She didn't want a scream of failure and defeat. She wanted a scream of triumph. She planted her feet firmly on the shoreline. Her hands were at her sides, palms turned out to the hill across the water, and then it began. First, a low growl, deep in her chest, like a mother bear defending her cubs. Then it rose, tone by tone. "Ah!" Then she stopped. Then "Ah!" again, still not loudly. She didn't want to wear out her voice too soon, and she still couldn't hear her echo yet. She started a series of fast, short breaths as though she were hyperventilating, with glottal stops. Breathe. "Ah!" Wait. Breathe. "Ahh!" Wait. And each time the sound of her voice rose in pitch and volume until preparation was over and she was finally ready for the big one. She took a deep breath and screamed in a loud, full voice: "Ahhhhh!" And the sound went across the water, slammed against the hillside, and was returned to her. She was surrounded by her voice. She screamed again and again and she was engulfed in a chorus of herself, a cry of vengeance and triumph. She was drowning in the sound of her voice, and she knew that it was good.

CHAPTER 69

Shortly after the announcement, the palace press office released additional information about the procedure, mentioning that, at the King's request, both his personal physician, Sir Sullivan, and his mother-in-law, the renowned microbiologist Dr. Pauline McGregor, had observed the process, while adding that neither would be available for interviews. However, the head of the Oxford team was, and in her very first one, she mentioned that while the technology was developed at Oxford, the principles involved came from work done at the Pasteur Institute in Paris. Reporters following that up found, unsurprisingly, that the French had a different take on the story. A spokesperson for the Institute bluntly stated that both the underlying principles as well as the splicing and implantation technology were both developed at Pasteur, and that Oxford had merely appropriated them without attribution or compensation.

The resulting media brouhaha threatened to become Alfred's first scandal as King, until an anonymous donation was quickly made to the Institute sufficiently large enough for the creation of the Albert Center for Reproductive Research, a stipulation of which was that the English name was to be retained even within France.

When news of that was leaked, the French press had a second scandal with both Le Figaro and Le Monde calling it another example of British colonialism towards its neighbor south of The Sleeve, while, in turn, commentators north of the Channel described it as a tempest in a champagne flute and another example of frogs being frogs. The later phrase was widely derided in public as an example of cultural insensitivity, while the private assessment of much of the country was that it was spot on. The Pasteur Institute quietly accepted the money and the conditions.

This time, unlike their engagement, Albert and Paul decided not to give any interviews as they didn't want to deal with the issue of which father the child would more closely resemble, which they realized was, at the very least, the question of the child's skin color. The other question they wanted to avoid was the succession, and the replacement of Princess Victoria with their own child.

However, it turned out that who the country wanted to hear from most was Connie who, up to this moment, had lived her life almost completely outside the public eye. But no longer: Who was she? Why did she accept the job of host mother? People wanted to know, and Albert and Paul realized it was time for Connie to be unleashed. So they met with her and Marlowe Leigh-Stoke, the long-time head of the palace press office, to discuss the options.

"Connie," said Albert with a Cheshire Cat grin, "the people want to know who you are. Are you ready to tell them?"

Also grinning, Connie said, "Yes, sir, I believe I am."

"Excellent," replied Albert, who turned to Mr. Leigh-Stoke. "So, what do you suggest?"

With the unctuous manner of a high-level appointee gained from working for three monarchs, Mr. Leigh-Stoke said, "Sir, with all due respect to Duchess Constance's enthusiasm, she nonetheless remains an amateur in dealing with the press, so I suggest we begin slowly, with one interview from a small, provincial newspaper, just to get her accustomed to the questions she'll be asked, and to gain familiarity with responding, then we can approach a larger regional newspaper, perhaps the Liverpool Echo, and then, with increasing confidence and success, we can finally approach the large London dailies and the networks."

This idea met with complete silence, as it was most definitely not what the other three wanted.

"But there is so much interest and demand for Connie now that I fear we'll lose the momentum," replied Albert. "I'm thinking of a general news conference here at the palace," and Paul and Connie nodded agreement.

"Oh, most definitely not, Your Highness. These things take time. Gain experience first and then, in a few months – "

"Months?" interrupted Albert. "Months?" he said again, with even more frustration. "The child will be born by then. No, that won't do at all."

He turned towards Connie.

"What do you want to do? Do you feel ready to meet the media?"

Connie knew she was in a delicate position as she didn't want to offend Mr. Leigh-Stoke but, as she was ready to start posting on Twitter, Instagram, and Facebook, she, too, felt the urgency of the moment.

"I can see the logic of Mr. Leigh-Stoke's point."

He looked both relieved and satisfied.

"However, I really think I could be good at this type of thing, and I agree that the time is now."

Mr. Leigh-Stoke was visibly offended and looked daggers at Connie, which she avoided by turning towards the King and Paul, who had decided to let Albert do the talking for them both.

"I would like to see a press conference," he said.

"But, Your Highness," protested Mr. Leigh-Stoke ineffectually, as the King pointedly ignored him.

"Excellent," replied Albert satisfied. "So that's that."

He turned back to the fulminating Mr. Leigh-Stoke and said, "You will set up a press conference and Connie will do it back on the lawn, so arrange for a tent, a stage, chairs for the media, whatever needs to be done. Contact the BBC as we'll need a moderator and we want this broadcast live."

"Live?" protested Mr. Leigh-Stoke. "But what if she says something . . . " And his voice trailed off as the three just looked at him. And, in the ensuing silence, Albert said softly, "Something you'll have to walk back later on?"

Trapped like a frightened deer, Mr. Leigh-Stoke merely nodded assent.

"Then we'll just have to hope that doesn't happen. Oh, I also want your department to tape this as well for the Royal Archives. Is that possible?"

It really wasn't a question. Mr. Leigh-Stoke nodded assent again.

"Good," replied Albert, satisfied. "Then we're done."

Finally, Mr. Leigh-Stoke could not take another affront to his professionalism, so he spoke up.

"Sir, I must protest – "

"No," replied Albert curtly, "There is a short list of people who can disagree with me, and you're not on it. The only thing you must do is get this organized. Now I can count on you, can't I, Mr. Leigh-Stoke?"

Faced with the inevitable, Mr. Leigh-Stoke accepted his defeat, though obviously displeased with it. He stood, bowed abruptly, then left. Then Paul spoke for the first time.

"Albert, you were a little hard on him."

"I know, but I'm coming to realize he's too out-of-touch with modern culture to continue as head of the press office. He seems to have been left behind by changing times. Well, he started in the press office under my grandmother, and that was decades ago, and for my father he was fine. Both Pappa and Mr. Leigh-Stoke were stolid men of tradition, with a fondness for tweed. I'll have to give this some thought."

Paul and Connie looked at each other apprehensively.

Noticing their concern and not wanting to make an issue now of the situation, Albert covered himself: "But I know he can at least do this."

Then he looked at Connie and gave her a big smile.

"Connie, you're on. I hope you're ready for your closeup."

She smiled back.

"Indeed, I am!"

The press conference was set up just as Albert wanted, out back on the lawn, under a large tent, with chairs in the middle for the press corps and media, and space along the sides for cameras.

The event would be broadcast live through the BBC and other platforms, which also supplied its most recognized interviewer, N'gamo Forrester, known as the British Oprah. She and Connie met several times beforehand, both at the palace and at Broadcast House, where N'gamo and her staff gave Connie basic lessons in dealing with the media, as well as with microphones and cameras; the upshot of which was to ignore them and concentrate on the people asking questions. The two of them hit it off, and N'gamo realized the press conference would be immensely popular and a boost to her already stellar career. It was clear the show would be the most popular media event since the Coronation. Indeed, that morning The Sun ran a closeup with the headline, "Connie Speaks!"

Connie arrived early at the trailer set aside for her next to the tent. She took issue with what the makeup person, a nice young man with the single name of Bright, wanted to do for her. He tried several different looks, all of which she rejected, and then got her own makeup from her bag and started applying it herself. She wanted to look as she always did, and especially not with a face that hid more than it enhanced. But Bright quickly got the idea and even made some touch-ups that Connie admitted were improvements. There came the ten-minute call. Bright was leaving just as N'gamo knocked and entered.

"You're going to do fine, girl," said N'gamo. "Just be yourself. That's what people will like about you."

"As though I could be any other way," laughed Connie.

There was another knock at the door. It was Leigh-Stoke, who asked if he could speak with her privately. Connie looked at N'gamo, who nodded, winked, and left. Mr. Leigh-Stoke was obviously not happy.

"It's still not too late to cancel," he said worriedly. "Just claim morning sickness or something."

By now, Connie was no longer offended by him and decided to treat him as an officious uncle.

"I really think it's a little late for that," she said gently.

"I thought you'd say that" he replied rather waspishly, "so I prepared this for you."

He pulled a paper from his notebook and handed it to her. She glanced at it but was confused by what she saw. There was another knock on the door.

"Five minutes!" said a member of the crew.

"I'll be right out!" replied Connie loudly, then turned back to Mr. Leigh-Stoke for an explanation.

"The left column is a list of reporters I've contacted who will ask you the questions in the middle column, with your responses on the right. It's too late to remember these, but you can just read them out."

Connie looked closely at the paper and read several of the questions aloud.

"What was my childhood like?"

"How did I meet my husband?"

She looked at him in amazement and asked her own

question.

"Are you serious?"

"You are an amateur with no experience in these matters. The King was raised dealing with the press. He knows what he's doing."

"And I don't, obviously," replied Connie, having lost all respect for him. Then she stood up, looking down at the rather short man who cowered from her in fear, which she instantly regretted, so she stepped back, held up the paper, and said, calmly, "I know you just want me to do well and not embarrass the Royal Family, and I promise not to make a fool of myself."

Relieved, Mr. Leigh-Stoke bowed slightly and left. Connie threw the paper in the waste can and then there was another knock on the door.

"Time."

She opened the door, stepped down to the ground, and walked a few feet to the edge of the tent, which was completely packed with media types, with an overflow spilling beyond.

Ms. Forrester was already seated on one of two chairs on the stage, which was raised above ground level. A small table between the two chairs had a vase of flowers, a pitcher of water and two glasses, already filled. A staff member attached a microphone to Connie's dress, and a sound check was quickly done as she waited. Connie stood just inside the tent, surprisingly calm, and looked at all the people looking at her, with cameras and microphones pointing at her. She saw Mr. Leigh-Stoke holding up his own copy of the questions and waving it towards her. She merely smiled and nodded, which did not relieve him. She turned back towards the stage. Forrester nodded towards her, the signal to go up the few steps to the stage proper. The lights were bright. There was an air of nervous anticipation. Connie took a deep breath and said to herself, "It's showtime, folks." She climbed the steps, crossed to Forrester, who was now standing and applauding her, then everyone started applauding her. This was the moment for which Connie had prepared. It was why she wore a tight-fitting dress. She stopped at the center of the stage, turned towards the crowd, and held out her hands as though to say, "Here I am, people, all of me." She was a large woman. Then she turned to the side to show her profile, and the pregnant bulge of her abdomen. The room went wild.

Finally, the applause died down, and the two women took their seats. In genuine admiration, Forrester said, "Duchess Constance, I've never seen the media give a round of applause like that for anyone."

"I guess they like my dress," replied Connie with a smile and, from that moment, she had them.

"Before we open things up for general questions," said Forrester, "Let's start with one of my own. Why are you even here today?"

Connie didn't immediately reply but first looked out not just at those in the tent, but she looked at the BBC camera with the red light on and looked at all those watching whether at home, at work, on the telly, laptops, or mobile. She paused as though waiting for the attention of the nation to center on her, then she turned back to answer Forrester's question.

"I'm here today to tell the country why I'm carrying the future monarch. I did it because I was asked by the King and the Duke, and I deem it a great honor. It's true that in one sense the child isn't mine because it carries none of my genetic code, but, in a very real sense, it is my child because it is growing within me, and I take that responsibility seriously. Finally, I want to stop calling this child an "it." The King and the Duke have both made it clear they do not want to know the child's gender until the moment of birth, nor do they want the gender to be revealed before then. However, because of ultra-sound scans, I do know the child's gender. But, in accordance with their wishes, I may refer to the child sometimes as 'he', and other times as 'she'. Of course, if the child is transgendered, then all bets are off, and s(he) will choose their own pronouns."

Gasps were heard from the audience and then titters.

"Oh, great," said Paul, who was watching the press conference on the telly in the palace next door with Albert. "A transgendered monarch. That's just what the country wants to hear about!"

"I think it's fabulous," replied Albert with a satisfied grin. "Now there's something else for them to talk about in the pubs."

"And with that," continued Connie, looking at Forrester, "I guess we can open up to questions."

The moderator just smiled and agreed. Hands were raised. Connie searched for Mr. Leigh-Stoke in the crowd and saw him frantically waving his copy of the question-and-answer sheet. Knowing the problems she would face with him later, she glanced beyond him and picked out a waving hand at random.

The reporter stood, identified himself, and asked Connie the question she'd been waiting for.

"Do you think the child will look like the King or the Duke?"

And Connie answered without hesitation.

"With the child's genetic code being split between them, I assume she will blend features of both. I know that when the King looks at the child, he hopes to see part of Paul in her; and I know that Paul wants to see part of the King in her as well. So, we'll just have to wait and see what pops out of the oven."

There was a scattering of laughter as the media found themselves enjoying Connie and her irreverent take on things, but not all of them. One woman angrily stood up and said pointedly: "But what if the child is too dark-skinned for the country to accept as monarch?"

Forrester interrupted to say, "You don't have to answer that."

"But I want to," said a self-assured Connie, looking at the moderator, "because I know there are people concerned about this."

Then she turned towards the audience.

"And to them I can only say, keep in mind how the monarch is chosen because color plays no role. It's purely genetics. The first-born child of the monarch becomes the monarch and that's all there is to it. It's that direct line going back over a thousand years that's important, and nothing else. And yes, that line is modified by whom the monarch chooses for a consort. Perhaps, in older times when monarchs married into the royal line of other European countries it didn't change all that much. But that tradition stopped in the last century, and now monarchs marry whom they please, and for love, as the rest of us should. It's true that King Albert has married a person of color. Well, good for him, I say, because, for the first time, the country's next monarch will look like many of his people already look. Wherever you go, in any city or town and now even in most villages, you see an amazing blend of colors, and it's refreshing because – I don't know about you – but personally I get so tired of just vanilla. This child – boy, girl, whatever – will look like Britain. This child will be Britain. Next question."

And upstairs in the palace, Albert and Paul looked at each other and smiled. They'd picked the right person for the job.

"But aren't you getting paid for this? And, if so, what does that make you?" asked a man sneeringly.

Refusing to be baited, Connie replied, "It makes me a professional. You get paid for what you do, and I am no different.

It's true that the King offered to pay me for services rendered, and I accepted. It's no secret that my husband and I are always strapped for cash trying to keep our place going, just as many Brits are. It's just that our place is somewhat bigger than most. And I do make a living as a book designer, which I love doing. And it's also true that I would have done this for free; just don't tell him! But, as I said, I consider myself a professional host mother. I've had two healthy children of my own, and I'm far enough away from the direct royal line that I don't receive a government stipend. So, yes, I am getting paid [And here she looked directly at the camera]. King Albert, I know you're watching this, so thank you."

And, indeed watching, Albert replied, "Connie, you are most welcome."

Then Connie took another question.

"What about Princess Victoria. How does she fit into this?"

Connie paused and then answered.

"I know the King was looking forward to having Princess Victoria as his successor, as he has said many times. But something happened – Paul McGregor happened – and both men realized that now they wanted a child between them to carry on the line; they wanted to create a human being who will pass through time and carry parts of themselves into the future. It does change the succession."

"You can bet it does," fumed an infuriated Lizzie as she also watched the press conference.

"But I also know," continued Connie, "that the King admires Princess Victoria immensely, and hopes that, as she grows older, she will become a trusted advisor, especially on foreign affairs."

"But never Queen," said an embittered Lizzie.

"I also know that the King and the Duke regret the impact

of this change on their beloved niece and will do everything in their power to smooth the transition. In fact, they hope that Princess Victoria and her siblings will become fast chums with their new cousin."

"Oh, how bloody thoughtful of them both!" shouted Lizzie at the telly.

To lighten the tone, Connie abruptly changed focus.

"Isn't anyone going to ask me about Manchester?"

Picking up the thread, someone yelled from the back: "What do you think about Manchester's chances?"

"Well, if you must ask, then you don't know me very well. And second, of course they're going to bloody well win!"

And the room started cheering over Manchester's upcoming game in the World Cup finals.

Now Connie was making the transition from being a mother pregnant with the country's future monarch to become both a topical pundit and a new media star, and the mood of the press conference changed accordingly.

"What do you think of the P.M.?" called out someone.

"A woman with a nearly impossible job. Trust me, making babies is easier!"

"America?"

"I wish we still had it. I'd love to take my children to Disneyworld without troubling with passports."

"Your favorite meal?"

"The next one!"

By now the press conference had changed to nearly a friendly, pub-like atmosphere. Connie held the stage for the rest of the hour, answering questions with quips about a vast range of topics. Apparently, she had a ready retort and opinion on most topics, though she clearly stayed away from religion and politics. She knew the room, for the most part, with her.

Finally, N'gamo Forrester – who had done almost no moderation, realizing people were there to see Connie – interrupted to say there was time for one last question.

Connie decided to finally use one of Mr. Leigh-Stoke's plants in the audience, so at least she could later say she had gone along with him to some degree, but it turned out not to be a question she expected.

The reporter held his mobile in the air and said, "There are comments online that you are a vulgar, common, fat woman making a mockery of the Royal Family."

Forrester immediately came to Connie's defense.

"You don't have to answer that," she said again, to provide Connie with cover, but she didn't need it.

"It is true that I am pleasingly plump," Connie explained. "I've always been that way, even as a baby, and I never grew out of it like many do. And I had many issues with body image as I grew up, especially at puberty and after. Kids can be so spiteful and mean spirited. I really wasn't prepared for the comments I got about my figure, so I did all the things that many girls in my position do: diets, purges, overeating, bulimia, cutting."

And at that she held up both forearms. The scars would not be seen at a distance, but she knew the cameras would clearly pick   them   out.

"I nearly died. My parents were so worried they took me to a therapist who saved my life, who helped me to look at myself in the mirror not as a grotesque monster, but simply as a healthy if not hefty young woman. And, gradually, I came to accept my image in the mirror as being who I really am and no longer thinking I should be like one of those impossibly thin models on magazine covers who, back in the 1960s and 1970s, were apparently all named Twiggy. But I had a different path to follow. And it's not like I'm out of shape. I exercise and work out all the time, though lightly now that I'm pregnant. Yet many still call me fat, but that's on them and not on me.

"And, yes, I guess I do fit the stereotype of a woman who is large, loud-mouthed, vulgar and, what else did you say? Common? Yes, I am all of those. And it must be amazingly improbable to some that I'm a member of the Royal Family, but I am, and don't you forget it!" she admonished with a shake of a forefinger.

The tent erupted into cheers and applause. Even N'gamo Forrester stood and applauded. Mr. Leigh-Stoke realized he needed smelling salts while, upstairs at the palace, Albert turned with a satisfied grin to Paul and said, "A star is born."

Connie finally made it back to her trailer. She sat at her dressing table, looked at herself in the mirror, and said quietly, "Girl, you were good."

There was a knock on the door.

"It's me," she heard, "N'gamo."

"Come in."

Forrester quickly entered and shut the door.

"It's a mob scene out there!"

Then they looked at each other, smiled, and hugged.

It was the reward Connie needed. Finally, they pulled apart and N'gamo looked at her with admiration.

"Connie, you were fabulous; just don't take my job!"

"You'll get no competition from me," said Connie. "Doing a press conference is one thing, but for you it's day after day, and the quality is always there. I don't know how you do it. I would wear out in a week."

"Well," explained N'gamo, "We are both professionals, each in our own way. But I know you're going to be busy yourself now as I think everyone will want an interview. I can see the headline now: 'Connie Rules!'"

"I just hope Albert's not too jealous!"

On the contrary, he was ecstatic, as he made clear when she had changed into something far more comfortable, removed her make-up (after taking a selfie because she did like the look that Bright developed) and finally returned to the acclaim of King and Duke. However, Mr. Leigh-Stoke was also there and he was not at all happy. Albert knew he would have to deal with that but, first, he just wanted to be happy for Connie.

"A triumph, Connie, a complete triumph!" exclaimed Albert joyfully. Smiling broadly, she took a deep bow of appreciation.

Paul added, "Connie, you were just fabulous."

And she bowed to him.

"It was like seeing Benny Hill reborn!"

"From you, sir, that is high praise indeed."

Mr. Leigh-Stoke stood to one side, unsmiling and obviously very concerned.

"And you, Mr. Leigh-Stoke? Your opinion?" asked Albert.

Angry at being put on the spot with his obviously contrary opinion, Mr. Leigh-Stoke hesitated.

"You're on that list now," said Albert gently. "Don't be worried."

Mr. Leigh-Stoke still hesitated, but his need to speak overcame his hesitancy.

"I fear my opinion differs, Your Highness."

"Well?" asked the King.

"Sir, Duchess Constance made a mockery of the monarchy!"

The three others tried hard not to snicker as they jointly thought, "A mockery of the monarchy? A mockery of the monarchy?" It sounded like a Gilbert and Sullivan patter song or even a Benny Hill sketch. Still, their faces did not belie what, inwardly, they saw as a very humorous situation.

"Continue," was all the King said.

"With all due respect, Duchess, if you had only taken my professional advice, this never would have happened."

"You mean her amazingly popular success?" asked Albert.

"I mean her debasement of the Royal Family!" retorted Leigh-Stoke. "The way she turned it into a joke the entire country is laughing at."

"I see," replied Albert. "Well, there is obviously a lot to deal with, so perhaps we should continue this tomorrow. Connie, as for you, keep doing what you're doing and do more of it. I think you're perfect. I do like Mr. Leigh-Stoke's suggestion to do interviews with papers and media outlets across the country; do as many as you feel you can handle." [And here Mr. Leigh-Stoke had to stifle his desire to interrupt and explain that it was not at all what he'd said, or at least not what he'd meant to say. By now he was quite confused.]

Albert blithely continued speaking to Connie: "You did an excellent job of explaining the situation and I want everyone to know who you are as the mother of the future monarch. Will you do that for me?"

Newly blushing at Albert's praise, Connie bowed slightly.

"Of course, Your Highness."

Then she turned to Mr. Leigh-Stoke and said, in an attempt to heal the rift between them: "It is my duty to serve the Crown in any way I can, and please understand that I would never make fun of it, just myself, big cow that I am!"

Appreciating her kindness, Mr. Leigh-Stoke smiled slightly and bowed as Connie left the room with her parting words, "I am rather tired."

Mr. Leigh-Stoke also prepared to leave, thinking the meeting was over, but it wasn't.

"I'd like you to stay," Albert told him.

"Of course, sir," Mr. Leigh-Stoke replied, rather puzzled.

"What is your concern about the press conference?" asked Albert. "I thought Connie proved herself to be tremendously effective, and she was remarkably popular."

"That is the point, Your Highness," replied Mr. Leigh-Stoke rather testily. "The monarchy is not a popularity contest."

"But that's precisely what it is," interrupted Albert. "British monarchs haven't ruled by force for many centuries. Indeed, our power, since the Magna Carta, has always come from the people. If the people are against us, the monarchy falls, and my vaunted thousand-year inheritance becomes worthless. Without the people's support I am nothing. I might as well be selling fish and chips. The country is changing, Mr. Leigh-Stoke. My own marriage attests to that, as will our child. And technology is changing the country as well."

He turned towards Paul.

"What's Connie's appeal rating just since the press conference?"

Paul checked his mobile.

"Eighty-five percent."

Albert looked triumphantly at Mr. Leigh-Stoke.

"That's twenty percent higher than my own."

Then, turning back to Paul, he asked, "And what about Connie's new Twitter and Instagram accounts?"

Paul checked again.

"Just within the past hour, her accounts have received 100,000 hits."

"And how many hits did the palace website receive yesterday?"

Paul checked again.

"Nine hundred and eighty-seven."

Albert turned back to Mr. Leigh-Stoke.

"I believe the palace website is under your office."

"Yes, sir," confirmed Mr. Leigh-Stoke, not knowing where this was going. "I have a young person on my team who takes care of it for me."

"Mr. Leigh-Stoke," asked Albert, "how many years have you been in the press office?"

"I've had the privilege of working here for thirty-five years, Your Highness, my entire professional life, and I've had the privilege of serving three monarchs, beginning with your grandmother."

Albert chose his next words carefully.

"Then I suggest, Mr. Leigh-Stoke, that it might be time to consider other plans."

Truly confused, Mr. Leigh-Stoke replied, "I don't follow you, sir."

Brusquely, Albert made his point quite clear.

"I want someone else."

Appalled at this unexpected development, Mr. Leigh-Stoke asked,   perturbed.

"Are you firing me, Your Highness?"

Then, to explain himself, Albert continued, "No, Mr. Leigh-Stoke, I am not firing you. I want you to retire. I am neither my grandmother nor my father. I want someone new at your position, younger, with fresh ideas, who understands modern media."

Mr. Leigh-Stoke protested.

"But I do understand – "

But Albert abruptly interrupted.

"No, sir, you do not, or you would understand the significance of Connie's triumph today. Sir, you do not," he repeated, "And it's clear that you are no longer the right person for the job."

Mr. Leigh-Stoke was stunned but recovered his professional demeanor.

"I've always served at the pleasure of the Crown, Your Highness. I apologize for obviously failing to meet your expectations. I shall certainly resign as soon as I return to my office."

"Not resign!" insisted Albert. "You are retiring, at full pension, all benefits, and with a hefty bonus."

Trying to keep some sense of dignity, the defeated man said, "My prerogative is to pick my successor and provide the necessary training."

"Not this time," replied Albert. "For now, your deputy will run the operation until a successor can be chosen from a nation-wide job search."

Now Mr. Leigh-Stoke felt completely blind-sided and realized this was not a spur-of-the-moment decision but one that, unbeknownst to him, the King had obviously considered for some time. So, with a look of resignation and defeat, he merely said, "Very well, Your Highness." He seemed about to faint.

Concerned, Albert pointed to a nearby chair: "Paul, please." And Paul quickly moved the chair behind Mr. Leigh-Stoke who sat heavily upon it. He took out a handkerchief to daub his face. Paul and Albert looked at each other. This was Albert's first time changing his father's staff, and he knew beforehand that it would not be easy.

"Would you like something to drink?" asked the King.

Looking down before him, Mr. Leigh-Stoke shook his head no, then he raised up to stare directly at Albert, smiling ruefully and said, "I came here with nothing, and from nothing. You may have heard of my father, Sir, Alexander Leigh-Stoke."

Albert thought for a moment, then the pieces fit together.

"One of the most famous lawsuits in English jurisprudence, and surely one of the longest. Over a century, wasn't it?"

"One hundred and ten years, Your Majesty," said Mr. Leigh-Stoke. "It was begun by my great-great grandfather over the perceived impugning of the family name by a bitter family enemy who sought to besmirch our integrity. Suit followed countersuit, and it was passed from generation to generation and, naturally, only the lawyers really won. Basically, my father simply outlived our opponents. They died with no one left to appeal, so my father finally achieved the end he'd fought for his entire adult life. The family's honor was upheld. He won, but legal fees took all the family fortune and estates, so it was a Pyrrhic victory. Last to go was our beloved Cresswell Hall. Were you ever there, Your Highness?"

"No, never," replied Albert.

"One of the most beautiful Georgian mansions in the country. Not large, but perfect, like living inside a diamond. I was raised there and even as a child I realized how fortunate I was to be surrounded by a world of exquisite beauty. But it, too, was sold. Our family had no place to go. Finally, we were offered a small cottage on a neighboring estate. My parents were supposed to work there, but what did my father know about work? He just sat in the garden all day, oblivious and lost. It was my mother who worked as a washer woman for the family that sheltered us, perhaps as a kind of revenge for some unspoken slight. I really don't know. But her lovely, white hands, like living pearls, were turned red, rough, and swollen by lye soap and scalding water, but she never complained. Yet I saw her cry late at night, when she thought I was asleep, and I promised myself I would get them out of there."

Mr. Leigh-Stoke smiled wanly.

"It was very Dickensian. My father was left with his title, his honor, and enough friends to get me into university, and to secure an entry-level position in the press office. Through diligence and application, I rose through the ranks to become chief. And it has been the great joy of my life to serve three monarchs, including yourself, Sir. I see now that, in the words of some American films, this is no longer a place for old men, even though I'm only sixty-three. Still, you need people you trust and who can meet your expectations for a younger, more forward-looking staff. I guess I am rather too traditional for this role anymore. Besides, my wife and I have an enduring interest in Celtic history and archaeology, and there are many, many sites we can explore, and this is the right time to do that. So, Your Highness," And with this, Mr. Leigh-Stoke slowly got to his feet and said with great dignity, "I want to thank you for the opportunity to begin the next phase of my life."

He bowed and prepared to leave when Albert said, "Mr. Leigh-Stoke, you have served the Crown well."

And he held out his hand, which surprised Mr. Leigh-Stoke, but who gratefully took it. "

"Thank you, Your Highness."

Then he bowed, turned, and left the room, shutting the door behind him.

After a moment, Paul said, "That was hard."

"Very hard," admitted Albert.

Paul looked at him sympathetically.

"Shall I stay?"

"No, my dear, I want to be alone," said Albert imitating Greta Garbo's voice. So Paul came over and gently kissed Albert first on the lips and then reached up and kissed his forehead as well, holding his lips to Albert's warm skin as though with lips alone he could relieve Albert's obvious pain, but even his lips couldn't relieve all of it, so he, too, left the room and left Albert to himself.

Albert turned and sat at his desk, then looked to the left where he saw his favorite portrait of his father, only recently hung, replacing George III.

He liked this portrait of his father because it was not the usual stiff, formal portrait, but it showed his father turned in his chair, as though the artist was sitting to the side and had just called to him. The artist captured his father's look of expectation, as though eagerly anticipating the unknown, a moment of remarkable innocence that he carefully concealed in public with a stolid, usually unsmiling, dignified demeanor that he felt appropriate for a King. But Albert preferred the other side; the one he generally only showed his family.

"Papa, you said there would be days like this, days when the weight of responsibility bore down heavily. You said the times of joy were always obvious – the glory, the trappings – but they were always offset by those times when you had to do your duty, even when it hurt. Well, this hurts, Papa, and I'm finally starting to know what you meant. I changed a person's life today, as I did with Lizzie even though, as with her, it had to be done. There was no way around it. But it wasn't easy. Such decisions are always hard, aren't they, and they should always hurt . . . . Oh, how I miss you."

And Albert stayed there, communing with his father's spirit, yet another example of how he really wasn't an atheist at all. Finally, he knew what to do, and he pressed the intercom button on his desk for Clive Daniels, his private secretary.

"Mr. Daniels?"

"Yes, Your Majesty?"

"Are you familiar with Cresswell Hall?"

"The one from the lawsuit? One of the most beautiful

Georgian houses in the country?"

Which reminded Albert that the line of Hanover Georges at least had taste.

"Yes," replied Albert, "That's the one."

"I believe it was the family estate of Mr. Leigh-Stoke, who just left your office."

"Yes, that's right. Have someone approach the owners with an offer to buy. Offer 150 percent of the appraised value."

"Very good, sir."

"If that doesn't work, tell them the King wants it for a royal estate."

"Very good, Your Majesty."

"And if that doesn't work, offer the money and a comparable property, but make it clear the property will be sold."

"Yes, sir."

"And when that is done, have a lease prepared for Mr. Leigh-Stoke and his descendants, for 100 years at a quid a year, terms renewable. Is that clear?"

"Of course, Your Majesty."

"And let me know when everything is ready."

"Of course, sir."

And with that, Albert finally realized just how bloody tired he was. He looked at his father's portrait, then noticed the very comfortable looking sofa beneath it. It was just long enough for him to rest his head on a pillow at one end, with his feet on the armrest at the other end. He quickly fell asleep, under his father's expectant gaze.

CHAPTER 70

"I am going to kill that mutant devil spawn!"

Princess Elizabeth is speaking via phone with Michael Romanov.

"Now, my dear, how you go on," he replies without sympathy.

"I mean it, Michael. The child is dead."

"And how do you propose to do that?"

"Connie always needs money. She's being paid by Albert to have the child. I'll simply pay her a lot more to destroy it."

"And what if she's gotten attached to it? And I don't mean just physically attached, of course. What if she loves it and wants to have it? What if she tells Albert, for example."

"Then I am doomed," replies Lizzie simply. "I'll probably be the next person exiled to Saint Helena. A wretched little rock by the way. I was there when I was eleven and hated it even then. Or he might put me in one of those dark, dank cells at the very bottom of the Tower, basically a stone coffin."

"Well, I'll come visit you," reassures Michael, taking none of this seriously.

"Don't bother," explains Lizzie, taking all of this seriously. "Within two days I'll have gone insane anyway. It runs in our family, our darkest secret, you know."

"Insanity?" asks a startled Michael.

"More like mental instability; we're unbalanced, Albert and me. He just hides it better than I do. I believe it's from our mother, a sweet but fragile soul with loonies in the closets of her family tree. Evidently Papa's love overrode practical considerations such as what if we all turned crazy."

"But you hide it so well," exclaims Michael sarcastically.

"We have tried," replies Lizzie, oblivious to sarcasm. "What would the people say? Besides, crazy royals are not unknown in history."

"Tell me about it," says Michael ruefully. "But back to Connie, what if your grand scheme fails to achieve its goal?"

"Then I make him pay. But I swear that Toria will assume the throne. It's her birthright and her dream."

"Actually, my dear, I think it's more your dream than hers."

"She's just eleven. Her dreams are my dreams."

"Is that the secret of your parenting? Living vicariously through your children?"

"Only in her case," snaps Lizzie angrily.

"But I get the idea that she's actually looking forward to her new position that Albert is creating for her as his personal representative to the world, or whatever it is."

"A second-rate consolation prize for second place? No, I don't think so. Besides, she wants what I tell her she'll want."

"More loving parenting, I see. Now, what I don't understand is what happens even if you are successful. Let's say there is a miscarriage. Don't you think Albert and Paul will keep trying? You can't kill them all."

"What a reputation that would give me, to be found over Connie's slashed body, a bloody knife in my hand with a dead fetus on the floor in a pool of blood."

"That's so manky and positively reeks of 'I, Claudius'. What a BBC mini-series that would make, not that you could reap the benefits, of course."

"You can't criticize me, considering the family you come from."

"Poison is more my family's style – we must have a Borgia

line somewhere – and it has been made into a mini-series, not that I gained anything from it. No, you're more like a female Richard III, killing those boy princes in the Tower."

"That was never proven."

"But it's a great story."

"And one that ended with the downfall of both Richard and his family. But I can't think of anything beyond that child in Connie keeping Toria from the throne. It consumes me. So I'll take care of this first and everything else as it comes."

"Now, having told me your secret plan, are you prepared to pay me, so I'll keep quiet?"

"Michael, you're my best male friend," says a ruffled Lizzie.

"Ducky, I'm your only male friend," explains Michael curtly, and needlessly.

"Actually, you're about my only friend, period, now that I'm not speaking with Pauline after she saw me how many times and never said a word about the child."

"My dear, it's her grandchild and it was a secret. She knew that telling you would destroy this beautiful sister relationship you two have."

"I understand her silence," says Lizzie ruefully. "I just can't forgive it."

Still thinking about money because, like Connie, he always needs it, Michael ponders, "I bet Albert would pay well for this information."

"Don't you dare!" shouts Lizzie, then she pauses. "Would ten thousand pounds help?"

"Make it fifteen and my lips are sealed," replies Michael joyfully.

"Very well, then, I'll send you a check for services rendered or, rather, for services not rendered. I can't believe I have to pay off my best friend."

"Frankly, my dear, I wouldn't have any friends if I didn't buy them."

"Such a sad comment on our times," replies Lizzie.

"Indeed," agrees Michael. "But wait," and he pauses to think. "If I keep quiet about a murder – "

"Miscarriage," insists Lizzie.

"Miscarriage," agrees Michael, "that I know will take place, doesn't that make me an accomplice? I could end up in my own deep, damp cell next to yours."

"Then let's hope I succeed, and no one is ever the wiser."

"If I see headlines saying, 'Royal heir accidentally killed in staircase tragedy,' then I'll know you've succeeded."

"And if you hear I've been sent to Helena, you'll know I'll have failed. And if I disappear completely, just visit the Tower and listen for the faint screams of a mad woman coming up from the lower depths."

"I can hardly wait. Pins and needles, my dear, pins and needles. Ta ta" he says in a sing-song voice.

"Ta ta," she replies.

CHAPTER 71

Paul and Albert were working at their desks; Paul was reading his mail while Albert reviewed a document. Seeing the return address on one envelope, Paul smiled bemusedly, opened it, pulled out the letter, quickly read it, then turned with a bigger smile towards Albert.

"Do you remember Dylan Jones of – "

And Albert immediately joined in as they mutually finished the sentence: "Llanfynydd, Wales!" They laughed, recalling Mr. Jones' phone call, which they took during their first radio talk show that now seemed centuries ago.

"Of course I do," chortled Albert. "How is our Welshman doing?"

"He wants to know when we're coming to visit his town."

Albert was puzzled.

"That's been settled for weeks. I just reviewed the final security details with Graham, and the agenda with Sir Humphrey. We'll take the helicopter and land at the elementary school playground, where we'll be met by the mayor and her husband, Mr. Jones and his wife, and assorted other dignitaries. Then we'll proceed in a motorcade of antique vehicles to the town hall. My, how Papa would have loved being in that procession."

Albert interrupted his Welsh itinerary to remember his father's passion for old cars.

"He loved watching his mechanics work on fabulous Jaguars and Bentleys so he could drive them when we were at Balmoral and Sandringham. He had garages full of them."

Albert glowed at the image of his father at the wheel of one of his antique Rolls-Royces, then picked up the thread of the itinerary.

"Next, we'll be introduced from a balcony at the hall before having lunch, then we'll return to the school for a town meeting to discuss economic conditions and opportunities. And that will conclude our royal visit to Llanfynydd. We'll get back into the helicopter and return here. But all of that must be well known."

"Perhaps," suggested Paul, "he just wants to hear it from you to make sure it's going to happen."

"Then I'll allay his concerns right now. I'll write him myself!"

Albert opened the top right-hand drawer of his desk and pulled out a sheet of palace stationary, with a florid heading at the top and the royal coat-of-arms in colour on both sides.

He got his favorite gold pen, thought for a moment, and then began writing and speaking as he wrote.

"My dear Mr. Jones; How nice to hear from you again. The Duke and I are looking forward to meeting you and your wife in person, and in seeing your town, which I have heard is the most beautiful in Wales."

Albert glanced at Paul to explain that "Every town in Wales is the most beautiful."

Then he continued writing.

"All arrangements are made, and we have indeed saved the best for last on our upcoming royal tour. We especially look forward to discussing with you and your neighbors how well-paying jobs can help keep young people in your area, so they don't need to move to Cardiff or, heaven forbid, here to London. The Duke and I feel strongly about keeping rural Wales economically thriving for future generations. So, we will shortly be with you. Tan gyfarfyddwn ni eto."

Albert looked at Paul.

"That's Welsh," he said gleefully.

"I know it's Welsh," replied a slightly peeved Paul. "But what does it mean and how am I supposed to spell it?"

"Learn Welsh and figure it out yourself," said Albert archly.

Paul reacted by sticking out his tongue. Albert just laughed, then relented and spelled it, though without a translation.

"Now for the pièce de résistance."

He looked at Paul triumphantly.

"That's French."

Paul stuck out his tongue again. Albert then paused to consider how to sign the letter.

"You know that American traitor John Hancock, as he prepared to sign that treasonous declaration, was quoted as saying something like he would write his signature large enough so my near-sighted great, great, great – "

Then Albert paused again, this time to consider just how far back George III was on his family tree but got confused and blithely ignored the issue with a wave of his hand.

"Whatever, so he could read it without his spectacles. So, I'm going to write my signature large enough so a nearsighted Welshman – "

"But how do you know he's nearsighted?" interrupted Paul.

"All Welshmen are nearsighted," replied Albert blithely. "It's common knowledge."

He considered how to place his signature on the blank lower half of the page, then wrote a large, entwined A. R., complete with circular flourishes beneath. He looked at it. It met his expectations, then held it up for Paul, who smiled and said, "I can read it from here."

"Very good," said the satisfied Albert as he pushed the intercom button for his private secretary.

"Yes, Your Majesty?" asked Mr. Daniels through the speaker.

"Here, please, Mr. Daniels."

"Yes, sir."

Clive Daniels entered, bowed, and approached the desk. Albert held up the letter and explained, "This letter goes to this return address," and he motioned for Paul to hand Mr. Jones' letter and envelope to Mr. Bennett, who took them, looked at the address, and smiled knowingly.

"Very good, sir."

"Find an official envelope large enough so the letter does not have to be folded. I want people in Llanfynydd to be impressed at Mr. Jones' connections. Make sure the envelope not only has the palace address on it, but a picture of the palace in colour. If we don't have one, make it so."

Mr. Daniels, long familiar with the King's Star Trek references, smiled tactfully and said, "I'm sure we can find something, Your Majesty."

"Thank you, Mr. Daniels."

The secretary smiled again, bowed, and left, just as an obviously panic-stricken Connie rushed in, breathless and distraught. Paul and Albert immediately stood up and were instantly worried.

"Connie," said Albert. "Whatever is the matter? Is it the baby? Paul, a chair."

Paul was already bringing a chair forward for Connie, who sat down on it heavily, panting and unable to catch her breath.

Paul said, "Breathe deeply, Connie. Take your time."

"Paul, some water," directed Albert. Paul filled a glass from a silver pitcher on a nearby table and gave it to Connie who gratefully drank it all, then held out the glass to be refilled. Finally, her breathing became less labored, and the deep breaths helped relax her.

Albert knelt before Connie and took her hands in his.

"Now, Connie, is it the baby?"

Connie looked at him tearfully.

"No," she said, then changed her mind. "Yes," then changed her mind again. "No." But realizing she was only confusing the men, she shook her head several times quickly and said, "It's not the baby, but it's about the baby."

"Whatever do you mean?" asked a perplexed Albert. Then Connie pulled her hands away from Albert's, retrieved a handkerchief from a dress pocket to wipe her face, and now, more composed, said, "You're not going to like this."

"I don't like it already, Connie," explained Albert. "Tell us what's happened."

"It's Lizzie."

Instantly alert and tense, Albert asked with a near growl, "What about Lizzie?"

"I've just met her." Then Connie stopped.

"And?" encouraged Paul.

Then Connie realized she had to tell everything, so her words poured out in a jumble as she looked from Albert to Paul and then back to Albert.

"She offered me 10 million pounds to fall down the stairs and have a miscarriage."

Stunned and doubting what he'd heard, Paul asked, "She what?"

But Albert knew what he'd heard and instantly understood the implications. "That bitch! I will destroy her!"

"Albert!" shouted Paul. "Stop it!"

Albert, stunned both by Connie's revelation and Paul's

command, stood up, walked to his desk and pounded it with his fist.

"I will destroy her!" he shouted again.

Paul, taking command of the situation, came and stood before him.

"No. You will not!" Now Paul was shouting. "You do anything to harm Lizzie, and I will leave you!"

"You'll do what?" shouted Albert angrily. "You can't leave me!" he thundered.

"Albert!" shouted Paul again, then lowered his voice, but said emphatically and distinctly, with each word clearly separated: "You - don't - own - me."

Then he continued, "As the song says, I'm not just one of your pretty toys."

Albert turned ashen, and said softly, "Paul, my beloved consort. You don't understand. It is not I who owns you, but you who owns me."

Paul looked at him quizzically, while Connie wished she were someplace far away from this unexpectedly intimate moment, and looked everywhere around the room except at them.

"Paul," explained Albert. "You are my rock. My stability. If you leave me, I am lost. I wouldn't die from grief. Monarchs don't die so much as fade into insignificance. But if you aren't by my side, I will never be the monarch I could become. I need you, my love. I need you so badly it hurts. And that's from another song."

He smiled wanly.

Paul smiled back.

"That's the most beautiful thing you've ever said to me, except 'I do'."

Albert held Paul's head in his hands, moved forward and gently kissed him on the lips. Now Connie wished she were someplace else and felt an unwanted intruder at such intimacy. But both Paul and Albert realized there was a very important unresolved issue.

"Albert," said Paul softly. "Lizzie is ill. She needs help. Punishment is not the answer. Obviously, the stress of her disappointment has unhinged her. After all, where could she possibly get ten million pounds?"

"From Larry, of course," replied Albert, "but I know he has nothing to do with this or else he would have told me."

He turned to Connie.

"What do you suggest?"

"Let's talk to Larry and see what he says. He knows her better than anyone."

Aware that Albert was about to contradict her, she added, "Larry is also more objective. You and Lizzie are too much alike. You set each other off. Larry is the one with perspective."

"Very well," agreed Albert, who pressed the intercom button again, this time for his appointments secretary.

"Yes, Your Highness?" asked Mr. Bennett immediately.

"I want you to locate the Duke of Sussex. Call his office in the City and see if he's there. If so, I want him here, now. If he isn't there, find out where he is – anywhere on the planet – and get him here today. Is that clear?"

"Of course, sir."

Shortly, Larry was seated with the three, and after Connie told him about Lizzie's proposal, he kept saying, over and over, while looking at the floor, "My poor Lizzie. My poor, sweet Lizzie."

Finally, he looked up.

"I didn't know she was under such stress. I thought she'd finally accepted the situation. Just last night she was discussing with Toria what classes to take for the fall to start training for her new role. I had no idea she was in this much pain."

He looked back at the floor and said, quietly, "Albert, let me handle this."

"Of course," replied Albert, "because I don't want to. But Larry, understand that this must stop. And, whatever you do, I don't want to see her again until after the birth. If she tries anything like this again – "

"Albert," warned Paul. Albert looked at him angrily for a moment, then calmed down and turned to Larry.

"Just make sure she gets better."

Relieved at the reprieve, and grateful to Paul, Larry said he would, then stood up, bowed, and left.

As he was being driven back to Kensington Palace, where the family was then staying, Larry made a phone call he didn't want to make. When he arrived at the family apartment in the palace, the children were surprised to see him home so early and ran to greet him.

"Papa! Let's go play!"

He knelt to hug and kiss each child and assured them that he would shortly be with them, but first he had to speak privately with their mother. After they'd left, he gave to an apprehensive Lizzie a fierce look that combined anger, disappointment, and pity, which was when Lizzie realized her plan had failed and Connie had talked.

"So, you know everything," she said despairingly.

"Everything," replied Larry, "except why."

"Because I can't bear to let my daughter down. She was to be Queen, not some kind of globe-trotting diplomat."

"She will never be Queen," erupted Larry tensely. "You know that and it's your job to help her make a creative life for herself, not to kill the heir to the throne. Lizzie!" he cried out in despair, "how could you?"

"Because Albert takes everything from me, and the only thing I can do now is hurt him."

Which was when Larry realized what he'd actually known for years but had never wanted to admit, that by marrying the woman he had, he had also joined a family whose twisted dynamics were destroying that very woman. He had tried to build a safe world around her, but the walls kept getting breached, from inside and out.

"So what happens now?" asked a defeated Lizzie.

"You're stressed and fatigued. You need a rest."

"No!" shrieked a terrified Lizzie. "Not that place again! I can't do it anymore! They treat me like I'm some sort of mental defective."

Larry held her tightly.

"Dr. Greene can help you and you'll come back better."

Resigned, Lizzie asked in a flat monotone, "For how long this time?"

"Until the child is born, at Albert's request."

"Albert! Albert! Albert! Will I never be done with him? Will he rule my life forever?"

The unspoken reply, of course, was "Yes".

Now, completely broken, she said, "I'll go pack."

"Just one bag."

"I know the routine," she replied.

That night Albert and Paul were finally in bed, with Albert's head on Paul's chest. Then he sat up and looked at Paul.

"I meant it when I said I can't live without you."

"I know, sweetheart, I know."

"But what if something happens to you? How can I continue?"

"You'll continue because you must, for your people."

Then Albert collapsed, crying, onto Paul's chest. Paul

stroked his head with one hand and placed his other arm across Albert's body.

"There, there, my beloved. I want to tell you something."

Albert continued crying softly.

"If anything happens to me, it really doesn't make any difference."

Albert pushed away so he could look directly at Paul.

"What do you mean?" he asked, perplexed.

"Because I will be with you forever," replied Paul, "at least part of me. And, somehow, I will find a way to let you know. And I'm not talking about faith or belief, because I know those mean nothing to you. I'm talking about a signal, something you will actually experience."

"Like what?" asked a confused Albert.

"I don't know. I'm not there yet," replied Paul with a gentle smile. "But once I am there, I will find a way to connect so you will genuinely know that I will never leave you. It will be like a message from beyond."

"A rattling table, perhaps, at a séance?" asked a now-smiling Albert.

"Perhaps," replied Paul, " but whatever it is, cherish that moment because it will mean that I am with you."

"You promise?" asked a still-skeptical Albert.

"I promise," said Paul with a smile. "Now, come here, my King, and try to rest."

He pulled a still-reluctant Albert down onto his chest and held him close.

Sometime later, when it was still dark, Albert awoke to find he had moved away from Paul and now was halfway off the bed, with a hand and a leg on the floor. Now he was angry, with an anger he realized he'd been denying all day.

"That bitch!" he thought to himself. "That cunt! So, she

wants to murder my son [Because Albert had decided to learn the child's gender without Paul's knowledge] and put her daughter on the throne? She's always envied me! Well, Lizzie, my dear sweet sister, I can't make you suffer now. But if there ever comes a day when Paul can't find out about it, I will make you pay in a drawn-out, terrifying, and agonizing way. You'll wish you'd never been born, because I will become the god of vengeance!"

And with that, Albert pulled himself back onto the bed, and realized he was finally ready for a deep, deep sleep.

CHAPTER 72

The royal tour was a smashing success. Nothing like it had been seen since the glory days of Elizabeth I. Albert and Paul spent nearly three months crisscrossing the country – all the major cities, most of the towns, and many villages were included, spending one or two days in each. And it was more than a meet-and-greet as the men wanted to encounter not just prominent movers and shakers, but people from all walks of life, from a variety of social and economic classes, as well as representatives of various organizations working to improve the lives of the people, in the social services, education, employment, and economic development.

Wherever Albert and Paul went, they were loudly proclaimed by clamorous and admiring crowds. Albert quickly recognized that when he and Paul split up to cover simultaneous events, Paul's crowds were invariably larger and more raucous than his own. It was obvious that Paul had attained a kind of superstar status, but Albert wasn't jealous. He knew that many who had formerly looked at the Royal Family as a bunch of privileged white people now could see one of their own sharing that privilege.

But finally, the tour came to an end. After Cardiff, there was only the town of Llanfynydd, the prettiest of all the pretty towns and villages in Wales. As Albert had explained in his letter to Mr. Dylan Jones, the royal helicopter landed as scheduled at the school yard, to be met by a small welcoming committee of the mayor and her husband, himself a council member, Mr. and Mrs. Jones, and the students, teachers, and support staff of the school, who formed a greeting line that ended at the small motorcade of antique cars that would take Albert and Paul the short distance into town where the King would address a much larger group.

After exiting the helicopter, the King approached the welcoming committee and easily identified Mr. Jones and his wife and approached them first. The man awkwardly bowed, and his wife curtsied. Albert held out his hand and shook that of Mr. Jones.

"My dear Mr. Jones, so we meet at last. I do feel as though we are already old friends."

"Yes, Your Majesty," was all the happy fellow could say. Then the King turned towards Mrs. Jones, who looked as though she'd been gob smacked. "And this must be your charming wife."

Mrs. Jones curtsied again, nearly fell over, and her husband had to rather awkwardly help her to stand. Speaking to no one in particular, Albert said, "We do have that effect on people."

Then he turned to the mayor, resplendent in her official chain and robe of office, which she hadn't worn since last being sworn in.

"Madam Mayor," the King said grandly, "I request admission to your beautiful town."

"As Prince of Wales it's practically yours anyway," said the mayor with a smile, "but yes, you are most welcome here."

The King nodded to her husband as well, then turned to Paul at his side.

"And this," he said needlessly, "is my husband, Paul McGregor, the Duke of Durham."

The group bowed and curtsied to Paul, who still felt uncomfortable at such moments. Albert could tell that he was blushing, which he found delightfully endearing.

The King and Duke proceeded down the receiving line of the school's students, a small group even though it was also a regional school for students from the surrounding countryside. The small number of students made Albert keenly aware of just how few young people still lived in such rural areas to raise families.

The students, in their uniforms, and the boys primly bowed and the girls primly curtsied, and Albert and Paul took time to shake the hand of every student and to greet each one. The girls especially blushed and giggled in front of Paul, and a couple of the boys as well. He also had an effect on people. Finally, they reached the end of the receiving line as Albert gave an admiring glance at the 1921 Rolls-Royce waiting for them, with the owner, a member of the local gentry, proudly standing beside it, with the bonnet raised to show the sparkling clean twelve-cylinder engine. Though not particularly interested in antique cars himself, Albert did admire the powerful engine, as the owner gently closed the bonnet and held the rear door open. Albert paused to investigate the immaculate driver's compartment and told the proud owner that not even his father had that particular model, which pleased the owner no end.

As Albert entered the passenger compartment, he admired the English oak paneling, the English cowhide leather upholstery, and the blue-dyed English wool carpeting. He and Paul settled into the back, while the mayor and her husband took the next car, and Mr. and Mrs. Jones took the third. The students and faculty were to walk a short distance into the center of town. The motorcade drove a few blocks to the town hall. A barricade kept a driving lane open, lined with police from several local municipalities, and, on the other side, there was a large crowd both of residents and people from across the region. The town was small, basically located entirely along the main road, with detached homes on the outskirts, then two- and three-story buildings in the town proper, with shops on the ground floors and apartments above. The windows were filled with cheering people, many waving Welsh flags. Graham had decided that security could be light and discrete. The town band was playing a Welsh march as the motorcade stopped in front of the town hall.

Albert's door was opened, and he and Paul got out to even greater cheers and applause. They climbed a few steps to a wide, broad space where they turned to greet the crowd as the mayor, her husband, and Mr. and Mrs. Jones came up beside them. Albert took Paul's hand and raised it high. The cheers grew even louder, then they turned to follow the mayor inside, passing police at the front doors, and into the entrance hall. Albert and Paul followed the mayor up the broad, open staircase and into the council chamber on the first floor, where the other members of the council were waiting to be introduced. The long council table had refreshments at one end. Double doors opened onto a balcony at the front of the building overlooking the street, where Albert would address the crowd. The band was still playing in the street.

When asked by the mayor if he and the Duke would like tea or something else to drink before proceeding with the schedule, they looked at each other and the King replied that he didn't want the crowd to wait any longer and they could have something later.

Albert and Paul stepped out onto a large balcony, with a high stone balustrade. Paul noticed that Graham was positioned to the right in a corner of the balcony, with his back to the wall and speaking into his headset while checking out the buildings up and down the road. Graham nodded at Paul and smiled reassuringly as this was the last stop of a very long and tiring tour. They were almost home.

Paul and Albert approached the balustrade and looked down at the assembled people. Once again, Albert took Paul's hand and held it up. Paul was on Albert's right side, with Graham somewhat behind them and at the far end of the balcony. To Albert's left, though not in a straight line, as some were closer to the balustrade than the others, were the mayor, her husband, and Mr. and Mrs. Jones, while the other council members came up behind them. The mayor raised her hand, and the crowd quickly grew silent. She nodded down to the band, which started the Welsh national anthem, which the crowd started singing, with many, like the King, in Welsh, with others in English. Paul, not knowing the words, simply stood respectfully. At the conclusion, the crowd cheered again, then the King pressed against the balustrade and the crowd grew silent again, expectantly. Then Albert said, with a booming voice amplified by the microphone in front of him, how glad he was to be back in Wales.

"Rwy'n hapus i ddychwelyd i'm mamwlad."

The crowd broke into cheering again as Albert turned to Paul and winked. The Welsh was expected.

"The Duke and I are here at the specific invitation of Mr. Jones, whom I am proud to call my friend. I daresay he is one of Llanfynydd's finest ambassadors."

The crowd laughed. Albert was enjoying himself. The affair was quite low-key as, at Albert's request, there was no media presence. He wanted the visit to be a kind of family gathering. He had agreed to the mayor's suggestion to allow a reporter and photographer from the local weekly newspaper to cover the event as, even with a small staff, it was still one of the area's leading employers and the King was glad to acknowledge its role in the local economy, though most of its business came from small commercial job printing such as specialty advertising.

Albert continued, "Today, I understand there is to be a town meeting back at the school, so we'll have time to discuss issues that concern us all, like how to provide good paying jobs so your young people do not have to move to Cardiff or, heaven forbid, London!"

Albert never minded repeating a good line.

The crowd laughed, and then the shooting began far down the street. At first, people didn't know what was happening, and in those first moments of confusion and hesitation, Paul heard the words he'd been trained to follow: "Paul! Down!" shouted Graham. Paul knew what to do. He'd known the moment might come when he was to fall to the ground but, for some reason, this time he didn't do what was expected. Perhaps it was something in Graham's tone, or maybe some nearly instinctive reaction, but instead of collapsing to the floor, Paul turned to his right and looked at Graham, who stood, grim and determined, with both hands on his handgun which was pointed up the street in the direction of the shooting. But, as Paul stared, Graham started to turn, and the direction of the barrel came back to the balcony towards Paul, who watched in shock as the barrel moved, as though in slow motion. And Paul knew he was dead. But the barrel moved past him, and Paul realized that Graham was going to kill Albert, who was turning away from the street towards Paul to figure out what was happening.

"No!" Paul screamed and leaped in front of Albert to protect him just as Graham repeatedly pulled the trigger and his bullets struck Paul's chest in a tight circle that killed him instantly. The bullets exited through Paul's back and ricocheted off the stone balustrade; one struck the mayor's husband in the side of the head and killed him; while another grazed the arm of Mrs. Jones, who screamed.

The force of the impact pushed Paul back into Albert, who involuntarily grabbed Paul and held him against his chest. But the weight was so great that Albert collapsed to the floor, still holding Paul, whose legs and feet were to one side, while Albert had one arm under Paul's back and the other across Paul's chest, while Paul's head fell back, opening his mouth, now filled with bloody foam, while his sightless eyes were open.

The firing continued up the street as security team members and police raced towards that end of town. The crowd was screaming in panic and fleeing. The band members dropped their instruments and fled. The 1921 Rolls was commandeered by security and driven around the block to the rear entrance of the town hall.

By now, other security members had rushed onto the balcony and wrestled a yielding Graham to the floor and handcuffed him. His second-in-command was now in charge, and she rushed to the King, still on the floor, still holding the dead Paul in his arms, a pieta of tragedy, and said in a surprisingly calm voice, "Your Majesty, we have to go."

All Albert knew was that Paul was dead.

"I won't leave him!"

There were security guards on either side of him who looked at her for direction. She motioned for others to come forward and take Paul inside.

"No!" shouted Albert.

"Your Majesty," she repeated calmly. "Look at me."

He did.

"We will take him with us, but we must get you to safety."

In shock, he nodded yes and loosened his arms so Paul could be taken inside where the refreshments in their silver containers were shoved to the floor so Paul's still-bleeding body could be placed on the table. Other security team members were on the balcony tending to the dead and wounded.

The King was picked up by one person on either side of him and brusquely brought into the chamber and past Paul's body towards the door that led to the stairs.

"Not without Paul!" shouted the King again, and once again the new head of security nodded agreement, so Paul's body was lifted, leaving a pool of blood on the English oak table and a trail of blood across the English oak flooring as the King, with Paul's body following behind, was taken down the stairs and out the back entrance to the waiting Rolls.

The street in front was now deserted of townsfolk while security and police went door to door inspecting every building; band instruments were on the pavement where they'd been hastily dropped. Up on the balcony, the mayor was screaming at her dead husband while Mr. Jones stood helplessly by his wife as her wounded arm was wrapped until medics could arrive. The shriek of an ambulance was heard in the distance, getting louder as it approached. There was no more shooting.

Behind the town hall, the passenger door of the Rolls was hurriedly opened and a security member got in first and pulled Paul's body onto the blue wool carpeting. The King was then pulled inside and pressed down onto the floor beside Paul, so he wasn't exposed. The car was then driven quickly away. Albert found himself pressed tightly against Paul's body, whose eyes were still open; his mouth still open and filled with bloody foam. Later, the car's owner would find it impossible to remove Paul's blood stains from the carpeting and had it replaced. He kept the stained carpeting in case it was required for some investigation. It never was, so he ended up burning it, and covered the car with a tarp and stored it in an old sheep stable on his estate. After that, he never looked at it nor drove it again.

During the drive back to the school yard and the waiting helicopter, all Albert could do was stare at the shattering reality of death as he was jostled against Paul's gradually cooling body. The sight haunted him the rest of his life.

At the helicopter, Albert was taken inside.

"The bench!" he commanded. "Put him beside me on the bench"

As Albert's seat belt was fastened, Paul's body was laid out beside him and strapped down, with Paul's head on his lap. Albert tenderly looked down at that beautiful, unmarked face, streaked with blood and foam, and finally, gently, closed Paul's unseeing eyes. Then he leaned over and kissed him on the forehead, and then on the lips, as the helicopter lifted off.

The concern was not knowing the full extent of the assassination attempt and not knowing if the conspirators had considered that they might not successfully kill the King in the town but had also prepared to shoot down the helicopter in flight. Still, there was no time for "what ifs" as the pilot went just above tree level and sped towards the southeast and London. Soon, it was surrounded by a protective cocoon of airships. Albert, regal even in mourning, refused to be seen crying. After the two kisses, he remained impassive for the entire journey home. He knew his countenance affected those around him; his grief would come later and in private.

Meanwhile, the lone photographer had sent out his pictures to the world, and the lone reporter had the biggest scoop of her career with the story of the attempted assassination of the King, and the deaths that accompanied it, in what was undoubtedly the prettiest town in Wales.

CHAPTER 73

After returning to the palace, Albert had Paul's body brought up to their rooms and placed on the bed. The staff was in shock, and stood about singly or in small groups, in the forecourt, the entrance hall, and along the great corridor. They looked furtively at the King as he passed, unheeding as they bowed.

Sir Humphrey was waiting apprehensively at the entrance to the royal apartment and noted with relief the care and concern towards the King of the person who was now effectively Albert's new head of security. She was careful with him; attentive to his needs; protective almost as a she-wolf to an injured cub. She had already been on the King's personal security team for some time and she – almost instinctively – knew how remarkably fragile he was now, even if he didn't show it. Still, Sir Humphrey realized the King was safe with her, which freed him for all the other pressing demands the events of the day were forcing upon him. For one, he'd just come from an unsettling meeting with the Prime Minister.

"He must make a public statement!" she demanded. "As soon as possible! People must see that he is all right."

"He is all right," assured Sir Humphrey.

"But how do you know?" she demanded. "You haven't seen him. You're going on reports just as I am, just as we all are. The longer this goes on without his being seen, and without telling the country personally that he is fit for office, the more intolerable and untenable the situation becomes. You cannot imagine the extent of the rumors already spreading on the internet: he's mortally wounded; he's in a coma; he's dead. No, Sir Humphrey, the country must have certainty. The stability of the government, and the financial markets, must be assured. His Majesty must be made available!"

"The King is in mourning!" shouted Sir Humphrey so unexpectedly that both he and the P.M. were surprised.

"I apologize for my outburst," he said, immediately chastened, "but this is the most trying time I have experienced in all my years of service to the Crown."

She waved aside his apology as accepted so he would continue. Sir Humphrey took his handkerchief from his vest pocket to daub his sweating forehead. Predicting events soon to come, Sir Humphrey continued in a protective and calmer voice.

"The King will be in mourning for an unspecified length of time. This cannot be rushed."

"He has twenty-four hours!" shouted the P.M., who didn't mind shouting when she felt it appropriate. Then, calmer herself:

"I understand mourning. And I grieve for the King's loss. I thought the Duke was a fine young man and, in my weekly audiences, I saw they worked well together. His death is a loss not just for the monarchy but for the country as a whole. And the way he sacrificed himself for the King is admirable, or else we would be dealing with a completely different set of issues. So, I'll give the King twenty-four hours to grieve. Have the palace keep issuing bland yet supportive updates, emphasizing that at the end of that period the King will make a public statement – "

"But we can't be sure," interrupted Sir Humphrey.

"Twenty-four hours, Sir Humphrey."

"Or what?" he asked, perplexed.

"Frankly," she replied from her own perplexity, "I don't know, because the country has never been here before, at least not for many centuries. This is unexplored country; but I know indecision cannot continue."

He understood precisely what the P.M. was saying and,

considering the current unsettled state of things, he could see her point.

"The King will do his duty," he replied sternly.

"I know he will," said the P.M. grimly.

Sir Humphrey merely nodded, then left.

And so here he was, watching the distraught Albert go into his bedchamber with the body of Paul taken in on a stretcher, then the door was shut as the security head personally stood in front of it. And that was it for now, as staff members looked bewildered at each other and wondered what could possibly happen next.

That was not Sir Humphrey's problem as he had much to do. He had flown back to the palace from Cardiff, because the last stop in Llanfynydd was more personal than public. He was relieved not to have been caught up in the assassination attempt itself, certainly not for his personal safety, but because he could now be more objective about what needed to be done.

First there was the issue of Graham, who currently was in Cardiff Prison awaiting the outcome of the preliminary investigation. It now seemed there was only one other conspirator, who had drawn fire by shooting from the upper end of town, and then killing himself as his position was quickly surrounded. He had no identification, not even a mobile was found on the body, but he wouldn't remain anonymous for long. Graham was refusing to talk, but Sir Humphrey hoped that he could eventually speak with Graham personally as he found his behavior so completely out of character. This was a man he had valued and admired daily for his devotion to the monarchy. So, what happened? It was as though the Graham he knew had been substituted by someone else, a changeling. Graham's decision to kill the one man he would willingly die to protect was inexplicable.

Sir Humphrey assumed the assassination attempt was limited to the King, but he definitely did not want Connie to miscarry from the shock. Still, he knew she was strong and would hold up even under this distressing news.

Lizzie had been allowed to return home early from her hospitalization because she had recovered so well and so quickly, a decision out of Albert's hands. Now she was with her children in the garden when apparently her entire security team came quickly out of the house, guns out, and surrounded them. The children thought it was some kind of game, but Lizzie, from a lifetime of experience, knew otherwise, then her own chief of security leaned over and whispered in her ear. Her first reaction was shock, but she knew her children were closely watching her, so she smiled instead.

"Bobkins, let's go into the house to play; quickly now, but no running."

Her children eagerly looked forward to whatever fun was in store for them and proceeded back inside the house surrounded by the security guards who kept looking at the surrounding countryside as though expecting an imminent attack. Lizzie led them into the house's interior and the windowless safe room, which usually functioned as a kind of entertainment and playroom. The children looked expectantly at her except for Toria, who was aware and concerned.

"Now bobkins," said Lizzie gaily, "Find something to occupy yourselves while I step outside for a moment."

A security guard stayed with them and others protected the front and back entrances to the house, while still more searched the grounds of the vast estate.

There was actually very little known at that time, but Lizzie was assured that her brother was safe while the Duke was dead.

"Oh, my poor Albert," she thought, recognizing the fearful possibility that always haunted the Royal Family had nearly come true. Then, still to herself: "Paul. My dearest Paul. My sweet, sweet Paul," because she knew how much Paul meant to her brother, but he had come to mean a lot to her as well. And what about Pauline? How could she possibly handle this? Lizzie's ambivalence towards her one-time dearest friend was now gone, and all she wanted to do was get to London, where Larry was, and to be with Albert and Pauline.

"We're going to London, now," she told her security chief.

"I'm sorry, Your Royal Highness, but that is impossible. Until we know the full extent of the plot, my orders are to keep you here."

"But my husband – "

"Is safe at Kensington, Ma'am."

Recognizing that in matters of security she could do nothing but accept the situation, Lizzie resignedly returned to the safe room to tell her children what had happened. However, they already knew from checking their mobiles. As she entered, they ran to her, screaming and clutching her.

"Mummy! Uncle Paul is dead! He saved Uncle Albert's life!"

"Yes, bobkins; it's a terrible, terrible thing."

She held her children close to console them, then caught herself staring at Toria and, really, for the first time, understood how this could easily have been her own daughter, and then she realized that Albert's plans had kept her and her daughter alive. She also realized that if Graham had been successful, then her life and Toria's would now be quite different. And she thought about Graham. Like Albert, she had known him for most of her life. How could he even consider such a monstrous deed? Such utter betrayal? She felt herself trembling and so clutched her children even closer. What she had wanted for her daughter had, inadvertently, nearly come true. Now, in the face of death, she wasn't sure she wanted it at all. And how, she wondered, could Pauline even live after this?

Pauline was in Durham where she still maintained her old home, for now, and was listening to the radio when the music was interrupted for a special news alert. She was standing when she heard it, put both hands to her mouth, and shouted, "My baby! My beautiful baby!" She nearly collapsed but sat down in a nearby chair as members of her security team rushed in, having just heard the news themselves. They rushed her to the army base outside Durham where she was put onto an army helicopter for the flight to London.

Usually, she enjoyed watching the passing scenery from the North to the Midlands. Now, staring out the window gave her privacy, though she knew the others in the compartment were studiously avoiding looking at her. In her mind's eye, her son was still alive. She had planned on returning anyway tomorrow to learn about the last leg of the tour. She had purposely avoided participating, though both Paul and Albert had asked her to accompany them at least to selected stops. But she realized people wanted to see the dashing royal couple and not an older generation.

This was the moment she had dreaded, the moment she'd feared would come, ever since her son fell in love with the Prince. She was aware of the hatred against Paul on the internet; the vows to destroy him because of his sexuality, his race, his "upstartness", his, well, everything, because everything about him seemed to offend some people who said they wouldn't stop trying to get him until he was dead. And now he was. She was not at all surprised that Paul had sacrificed himself to save his beloved husband. She knew how totally he had surrendered himself to Albert; she knew he must have considered his life was a small price to save Albert's. Sacrifice was in his nature; that, and the idea of duty to a cause. In Paul's case, Albert was both duty and cause.

But Graham? She couldn't understand that. Though she really hadn't known him for long, she knew his dedication to Albert was complete. In fact, she knew Graham would readily give his own life to save Albert, and Paul as well. So, none of this made sense. What had happened to take him so far from the man she knew? A man she now doubted she had ever known.

What she did know was that she was not alone. She thought of Connie and the child of Albert and Paul growing inside her. Such continuity was vital to Pauline, and now it was the one thing she had to sustain her in the grief of her loss.

When the helicopter landed at the palace, she was immediately taken upstairs. She saw the staff looking at her, with care, concern, and bewilderment on their faces. She'd been informed that Albert was inside his chambers with Paul's body and refused to let anyone enter. She also realized that she was the only person he might be willing to see.

She saw Sir Humphrey standing outside the bed chamber. He stared at her and simply shook his head. He didn't know what to do; he hoped that she did.

She looked at the new security chief at the doors. So much had changed so quickly. The chief looked straight ahead, but Pauline felt her concern as well, and knew that something, almost anything really, had to be done to move beyond this paralysis. She paused only for a moment, then knocked.

Instantly Albert shouted from inside: "No! No one knocks! No one enters!"

Undaunted, Pauline said to the man beyond the closed doors, "It's me. Let me come in."

Then Albert shouted from the pain of unexpected bereavement, "My baby is gone!"

Calmly, Pauline replied, "He's my baby, too, Your Highness. He grew inside me. I gave him birth. Now, I will stay here, outside your chamber, until you are ready to see me."

She motioned for a chair to be brought for her.

"However long it takes – an hour, a day, a week – I will stay here, and no one will enter until you open the doors."

Then she sat down on the chair and waited. She waited all night and until early the next morning when Albert was finally ready to share his grief. During those hours, the King was heard shouting and stomping the floor, repeatedly. Those outside looked at each other apprehensively when it started, and then in amazement at how long it continued. Only Pauline remained impassive.

Finally, at dawn, the doors were unlocked, slowly opened; and a specter appeared. Everyone there, even Pauline, gasped. The King was dressed only in his long-tailed white shirt, with a large circle of Paul's blood in the center, now dried to an iron-oxide tint. But it was his overall appearance that both shocked and caused consternation, for he had taken handfuls of white ashes from the fireplace and poured them over his head. They coated his face like a mask. It was completely white except for his eyes, which were terrifying in their blank intensity, as though he didn't know who he was, or where. The pale ashes on his face were streaked from crying, which was understandable. Harder to comprehend were the rivulets of red blood across his face and down his shirt; then it became clear that he had torn clumps of his hair out by the roots, with bits of skin and hair on his shoulders. The King, it appeared, had shattered from recent events. At this sight, both horrific and terrifying, hope for the King's recovery vanished; and even Pauline doubted her ability to help this lost soul.

But he wasn't completely gone. He recognized her and said, "You. You alone." And then to the guard, "No one else enters."

"Yes, Your Majesty," she replied, her duty keeping her composure intact.

Albert turned and went back into the room; Pauline followed and closed the doors behind her.

Softly, Sir Humphrey quoted one of his favorite passages from one of his favorite books: "Taken with both hands the fire-blackened ashes, he poured them down upon his head and defiled his handsome face, and he lay outstretched in the dust, a great man in his greatness, and with his own hands he defiled his hair, tearing at it."

"What's that, Sir Humphrey?" asked his assistant.

"From The Iliad, you dunce," said Sir Humphrey with surprising vehemence to the young man beside him, hired for his computer and networking skills and not for his knowledge of classical literature.

"Where the hero Achilles mourns the death in battle of his beloved Patroclus."

Then he finally turned to look at his assistant and instant-ly regretted his words, said in stress and shock, for the young man was obviously hurt and humiliated.

"My dear Mr. Overstreet, I do apologize."

But the young man brushed off the apology by vehemently saying, "He is my King, too!"

And then Sir Humphrey realized he'd taken his fatigue, stress, and worry out on this young man who obviously loved the King as much as he did. That was when Sir Humphrey finally allowed himself to feel the full depth of the emotion he'd hidden so well, so he thought, until this moment; indeed, he was nearly overwhelmed by what he recognized was nearly complete despair. That was when he also realized – and not for the first time – that perhaps he'd been at this long enough, and perhaps too long. It was a kind of final acknowledgment that it was time to leave this work for a younger generation with more stamina than he was evidently capable of anymore.

After the doors were shut behind Pauline, Sir Sullivan came forward to enter, but the security chief moved to block his way.

"No one enters," she said, repeating the King's command.

"But I'm his personal physician. I must see him!" he insisted. "I have a right to see him."

The security chief merely crossed her arms and stood tall, a silent sentinel before doors she was guarding with her life.

Sir Sullivan was taken aback; he was not used to having his orders rejected. Sputtering and not knowing what to do, he looked pleadingly at Sir Humphrey for assistance, but Sir Humphrey merely shook his head, which was when Sir Sullivan reached the place that some doctors admit only with reluctance, that his salves and lotions, pills and liquids, were only of use to heal the body, not the soul. Stepping back, Sir Sullivan realized, however reluctantly, that Dr. McGregor, whom he now admired after having worked so closely with her during preparations for the royal conception, was indeed the only person who could put the shards of the King's psyche back together.

The room was dark. Albert had closed the heavy curtains and the lights were out. Still, as Pauline's eyes adjusted to the gloom, she saw Albert standing at the bed, waiting for her to join him. Of course, the bed was the one spot on the entire planet where she did not want to be and, looking back in later years, she realized this was the most difficult moment of her life, when she had to force herself to look at the dead body of her child.

She reluctantly stood beside Albert. Paul's body was naked and, except for the concentric pattern of bullet holes in his chest, looked as though he was merely sleeping. His arms were at his sides, his head on a pillow. All it took were the right words of a mother: "Awaken, my son. Come back from your sleep and join us."

But she realized he would never awaken again.

"Look what they've done to my baby!" cried Albert. "Look what they've done!"

And he turned to her and hid his face on her shoulder and cried openly, nearly defiantly. And she put her arms around the broken man and held him close to her, and then she realized it was finally time for her to mourn as well. So, they shared their mutual grief.

Finally, Albert turned again to look at Paul.

"How can I live without him? He was my everything. We were going to have a lifetime together; and now cut off like part of my body. Pauline, I can't do it. I can't live without him. I can't function without him."

"Albert," said Pauline gently, "Paul sacrificed himself precisely so you could continue, so you could live and be the King, he knew you are. If you fall apart, if you forsake your duty, then you destroy the trust my son had in you, and his sacrifice would be meaningless. Is that what you want?"

"But I can't do it by myself. Not yet. It's too soon."

Refusing to let him drown in grief, she walked to the windows and pulled back the heavy curtains; early morning sunlight flooded the room, and Albert groaned as it struck him as though physically hit.

"No! No! No!" he bellowed in a surprisingly theatrical voice. "Not yet!"

Pauline turned back to see Albert had covered his eyes

with his hands. Calmly yet forcibly, she said, "Your duty requires it. Your people require it. And I require it."

He ignored her. Not knowing how to get him just to move, she looked out beyond the windows for a clue, and then the road to Albert's recovery was clear.

"But Albert, my dearest Albert, you don't have to do it by yourself," she said gently. "And you and I can't do it by ourselves either."

He looked at her questioningly.

"Come, my King," she said confidently. "This is something you must see."

And slowly, reluctantly, Albert approached the tall windows and looked down across the courtyard to the street beyond the gates. It was filled with people, hundreds, possibly thousands of people, all just standing there and looking up at the palace. Even at this distance, he could see the worry and consternation on their faces; and he knew they were worried and concerned about him.

"Albert," said Pauline with authority. He looked at her with the questioning innocence of a child. "Those are your people. They're concerned for you. They mourn your loss with you. And we are going down there to be with them."

"No," he resisted. "Not like this. I'm the King. My people cannot see me like this."

"Then let's clean you up and make you presentable."

She took him by the hand, and he followed her like a child into the adjacent bathroom, where she unbuttoned his blood, hair, and ash-covered shirt and carefully pulled it off. Then she sat him on a chair by the white marble basin and filled a pitcher with water. She looked down at his scalp and saw the holes still oozing blood. She gently leaned his head over the basin.

"This will sting," she said as she poured the water over his head. But he didn't cry or even moan. He just sat there as she poured pitcher after pitcher of water over him, and they both watched as the blood, hair, and ashes mingled in the white basin and then flowed down the drain.

"Away," she thought to herself. "Go away; go down to the Thames and out to sea so I can cleanse and redeem this man."

She took a cloth and gently wiped his head first, then his torso. Then she gave him the towel so he could finish drying himself off as she searched through his wardrobe for something appropriate to wear. No, not formal mourning attire; that would come later. She quickly found what she was looking for, his now-famous, blue-striped Oxford shirts. She took one off its hanger, then opened a drawer and pulled out a pair of tan slacks. Brown loafers only, as socks were too much trouble right now.

But how to cover his head? No hat, but something else. She pulled open another drawer and there, beside the black armbands left over from his father's funeral, she saw a black silk scarf. Just the thing, she thought. She folded it diagonally to make a large triangle, then, after Albert had put on the shirt and slacks, Pauline placed the long, flat side against Albert's forehead and tied the ends together in back and over the lower end point of the triangle, just as she'd recently seen a biker wearing in Durham. Well, if it's good enough for Durham bikers, then it's enough for their King, she thought, inadvertently starting a new trend for the fashionably aware.

Finally, Albert was ready, but he paused before the full-length mirror to look at himself. He was slouched over and despondent but, as Pauline watched, he raised himself up. He regained his dignity, like an actor standing in the wings prepares to make an entrance in character. He became a King again. He looked at her and nodded. He was ready. So, they walked to the doors but, just as they reached them, she felt him hesitate as doubt returned. This was the moment she knew when he could either confidently face his people, or hide from them in terror.

"Remember Paul," was all she said, and it was enough. He pulled himself up again and nodded to her. It was time. She opened the doors and waited as he made his entrance.

Those waiting outside were afraid, yet expectant. And their hearts lifted at the miracle of seeing their King return. And then Pauline stepped forward, and just as their relief at seeing the King was palpable, so was their collective gratitude to her: "You brought him back."

Pauline looked over at Sir Humphrey, who simply mouthed the words, "Thank you." And she just nodded before turning to the security chief to say, "We're going outside."

The security chief instantly understood and motioned to one of her staff to take her place at the bedchamber door so she could follow the King and Pauline, and then to two other team members to join her. She also spoke softly into her headset to prepare those waiting below.

Albert held himself erect, but was quite weakened by stress and exhaustion, so he paused and said, "Would you take my arm, Dr. McGregor?"

"With pleasure, sir," replied Pauline as she slipped her arm through his. They slowly made their way along the great corridor. The staff, relieved at the King's return, bowed gratefully as he passed, leaning on Pauline. Albert didn't notice them as he concentrated on walking carefully, marking his steps. He hesitated only at the top of the stairs. So many were watching he could not afford to stumble now. Then he realized this was simply another entrance, so he walked down that long flight of stone steps he'd known all his life and reached the entrance hall. The Household Guards stood at attention as he and Pauline crossed the courtyard and approached the gates, where Albert finally looked up and saw the multitude beyond. There was no traffic on the roadway, only a vast crowd of people hoping to see him, needing to see him. The gates were opened. He paused again but only for a moment.

"My people are here to see me," he explained to Pauline, as she continued supporting him lightly, still not feeling steady enough to walk unassisted. As they passed through the gates, Albert realized that the entire nation was before him: all ages, genders, races, blends of races, sexualities, social classes, economic classes, the wealthy, the poor, all were there because they were concerned for him. Then he stopped because he wasn't sure what to do next, but Pauline knew: she led him to the left, in front of the tall, cast-iron fencing, to a huge mound of floral bouquets, and people kept adding more flowers even as he approached.

Pauline bent over and picked up a bouquet, read the card, smiled, and handed it to Albert.

"Paul, we love you," was all it said.

Then Albert picked up a bouquet himself and read its card.

"I'm a queer, transgendered, multi-racial techie from Devonshire and you give me strength."

And then he read another: "I am a 62-year-old white heterosexual veteran from Cornwall who has fought in three conflicts and one war, but I've never been more proud of being an Englishman than I am today. Your ultimate sacrifice will never be forgotten."

And then, another: "I feel as though you are the grandson I always wanted."

And another: "I am a Jamaican man old enough to be your father, but we Jamaican boys must stick together."

And Albert and Pauline stood there for a long time, reading the tributes and cards, pausing to smell the bouquets, amazed at their bright colors that gradually brightened their spirits, but finally Pauline said, "Your Majesty, over here."

And they walked further along to what seemed to him to be a large pile of stuffed animals, and most of them seemed to be one style that Albert couldn't immediately identify so he reached over and picked one up. It was small and fit easily into his palm. Pauline leaned over and said, "It's Rainbow Unicorn, and obviously it's now his emblem."

There were hundreds and hundreds of them, thousands it appeared. And as Albert stood there looking at them all, he felt a tug at his shirt and looked down to see a small girl who had stepped forward from her parents and held out her own Rainbow Unicorn.

"Please, Your Majesty," she said in a child's sing-song voice. "Take mine."

And he put down the one he was holding and knelt beside the girl, with her parents looking proudly on. He noticed hers was attached to a lanyard, which she wanted to put around his neck, so he bent his head over and she placed it over his head. It lay against his chest at approximately the same spot where bullets had ripped through his beloved, and his eyes filled with tears as he put his arms around the child and held her close. That was the first iconic photo of the day.

Then Albert stood up with the child still in his arms, and saw the sea of faces looking at him hopefully, expectantly, then he carefully passed the child to her father so he could hold out his hands to those nearest to him, not to shake hands, but to grasp hands, to feel the warmth of human contact, to feel his people's strength come into him. And they were respectful. They bowed or curtsied as he approached but maintained a distance until he took their hands and, as the Americans say, he worked the crowd. And Pauline joined him. They spent two hours holding the hands of strangers who were no longer strangers. And in all that time, not a single word was spoken. There was complete silence. No one had ever experienced anything like it. But finally, Pauline looked over at Albert and realized just how exhausted he was, though he would not admit it.

Then she looked over at the security chief, who had remained cautiously nearby with other members of her team and members of the Household Guards, and signaled that it was time to go. The security chief spoke into her headset, and a path was cleared back to the entrance gates.

"Would you mind taking me back to the palace, Your Highness?" asked Pauline as she held out her arm to the King.

"Of course, Dr. McGregor," he said gallantly as, once again, he took her arm, and they walked slowly back to the entrance gates. But he stopped before going inside and turned around as Pauline slipped her arm from his and stepped back so the King stood alone, yet not alone at all. Then he bowed his head towards the mass of people before him, and remained bowed for a long time, and that was the second iconic picture of the day.

Albert finally raised his head, and Pauline returned to take his arm, and they made their way back inside, up the stairs and down the corridor to the King's apartment. Despite his near complete exhaustion, Albert now did recognize those around him and nodded towards each one, a nod of gratitude and thanks, while they, in turn, were grateful for his return. Finally, they stood at the doors opened to the bedchamber, and neither knew what to expect, or what they would find. The security guard bowed his head as the King entered with Pauline and closed the door behind them.

The lights were on. Paul's body was gone. The bed was freshly made with linen sheets and a folded blanket at the bottom. Albert, aching with exhaustion, took off his clothes and simply let them fall to the floor. Pauline just smiled, "Well, he is the King," she thought to herself.

She pulled back the sheet and covered Albert up as he got into bed. She walked to the doors but, before leaving, looked back. Albert had moved to the upper end and wrapped his arms around a pillow. Now he would be sleeping alone. She left the doors open as she walked away, knowing they would be gently closed behind her.

CHAPTER 74

Two days after Paul's death, the King met with Sir Humphrey, the Archbishop, and Pauline to discuss the funeral arrangements. The King insisted on a state funeral in the Abbey; the others were opposed. He pounded his desk with his fist and shouted, "But he is the Royal Consort!"

Then he paused, and said in a much lower and meeker tone, "He was the Royal Consort."

There was a long pause.

"I want to do this for him," he said almost pleadingly.

"If I may speak, Your Majesty?" said Sir Humphrey.

Albert nodded, almost begrudgingly.

"There are issues of logistics and economics coming so soon after your father's funeral and the coronation" explained Sir Humphrey, in what he hoped was a soothing tone. "This morning the P.M. – "

"Damn the P.M.!" shouted Albert abruptly. "How she hounds me!"

And the three realized that he was still quite fragile.

"The Government," continued Sir Humphrey in a placating voice, "will pay for a formal thirty-six-hour lying-in-state in Westminster Hall, on a scale similar to that of your father."

Which mollified Albert somewhat.

"The funeral procession will follow [He purposefully omitted the destination], led by the Northumberland Regional Pipers, followed by a battalion of the mounted Royal Guard. The Duke's casket will follow on a caisson, with you, the Duchess, and Princess Elizabeth and her family."

"Princess Elizabeth will still be in treatment then," explained Albert pointedly, "so it will just be the Duke of Sussex and the children."

"Her absence will be questioned," said Sir Humphrey.

"I have it on good authority that she will not be ready for prime time, as the Americans say. Just explain that an on-going medical condition prevents her attendance."

The Archbishop was the only one unaware of the new tension between the siblings. He looked questioningly at Sir Humphrey, who merely shook his head to avoid the situation.

"Very well, sir" said Sir Humphrey resignedly, preferring to leave the Archbishop puzzled for now, then he continued.

"The Lady Constance, due to her pregnancy, and her family will be in a landau. Various governmental and national figures will follow, including the P.M., then Commonwealth representatives including a large Jamaican contingent [Which made Pauline smile in anticipation] and, finally international dignitaries. Then another mounted battalion will follow, and, finally, the Eighth Regimental Band. Between the lying-in-state and the procession, it's possible that more than a million people will attend."

That also mollified Albert.

"And the destination?" he asked quietly.

Sir Humphrey hesitated only slightly.

"The Chapel Royal at St. James, Your Majesty."

And there it was, clearly laid out. The three waited apprehensively. Albert looked grim.

"If I may, Your Majesty?" asked the Archbishop.

"Of course," replied Albert coldly.

"If the funeral is held at the Abbey, I would be bound to give a complete and traditional Anglican service and, frankly, I don't think that would do justice to the full range of the Duke's spirituality, about which he and I had several lengthy discussions. But if the service were to be held at the Chapel Royal, then I have the freedom to recognize the breadth of his vision."

He paused for the King's consideration.

"Pauline?" asked Albert, looking at her.

She didn't hesitate.

"I agree with the Archbishop. Paul felt pomp and ritual belonged to you and certainly not to him. I like the idea of the Chapel Royal."

The three looked at each other apprehensively. The King looked down at his desk while considering the implications before speaking.

"So, you are agreed?"

"Yes, sir," the three concurred.

And he looked at them: "Then make it so."

They bowed, and the Archbishop and Pauline were already through the door when Albert spoke up, "Sir Humphrey, a word."

Sir Humphrey turned to stand before the King's desk. Albert spoke just one word: "Graham?"

"Still at Cardiff, Your Majesty. Still refusing to speak. Still refuses a lawyer. However, the investigation, while still ongoing, is leaning towards two counts of murder, as well as attempted murder and high treason."

Albert looked away and sighed. He was still using the black silk scarf to cover his head, which made him look disconcertingly like a pirate, or a biker. Then he looked back at Sir Humphrey.

"And Mrs. Jones?"

"Doing well, sir, and out of hospital."

"Anything the family needs – "

"Of course, Your Majesty."

And the funeral for the mayor's husband?"

"In two days, sir."

"I'm going."

"Is that wise, sir? Maybe it's too soon . . . " And his voice faded away, but Albert quickly replied.

"Two are dead because of me, and one is wounded. I must be there."

"Very well, Your Majesty," acquiesced Sir Humphrey, who then waited to see if there was anything else, as the King appeared lost in thought.

"Is there something more, sir?" he asked gently.

Albert came back from wherever he had been.

"No, Sir Humphrey, that will be all."

Sir Humphrey bowed and turned to go, but before he reached the door, Albert said, "Sir Humphrey?"

The old man turned back towards his sovereign.

"Yes, Your Majesty?"

Albert smiled a genuine smile and said, "Thank you."

Sir Humphrey bowed again, then left. As the door closed behind him, Sir Humphrey felt better than he had in days, and decided it was probably too soon to think about retirement.

CHAPTER 75

He wasn't scared when he entered the helicopter, or when it lifted off, or as it flew across the country. The fear only came as it flew over the Welsh hills, and Albert noticed his clammy hands, his sweating, and his rapid heartbeat. Though he'd never been in battle, Albert knew he was experiencing a kind of P.T.S.D. as he neared the place where his life changed forever. He knew people in the cabin were, at least surreptitiously, glancing at him as Pauline sat beside him in the black dress and formal coat from his father's funeral. It was she who had encouraged him to come today. Everyone else, including Sir Humphrey, thought it too soon. So, he didn't want to justify their concerns. He knew what people were already saying about him, calling him the Mad King. He really should have removed that portrait of George III sooner, as though somehow it had infected him. So, no, he could not show his fears to those looking for symptoms. Fortunately, Pauline put her hand over his and said gently, "Albert, you'll do fine."

And that was all it took for him to relax, but he didn't look out the window again.

The helicopter landed once more in the Llanfynydd school grounds, only this time the welcoming committee was just the deputy mayor. School was still dismissed following the shooting, and the students were expected to attend the funeral with their parents.

Albert heard the town band rehearsing somewhere in the building as he approached with Pauline and Sir Humphrey. This time it was not the joyful Welsh marches of just a few days earlier, but the dirges they would play at the head of the procession from the school to the church graveyard, picking up residents as it went to the church at the other end of the street. But, first, he would meet privately with the mayor, and Pauline with Mr. and Mrs. Jones, then they would switch.

The deputy mayor greeted the King and Pauline with a bow, then led them into the school. He stood outside a classroom door, knocked and, without waiting for a response, opened it and said, "Mr. and Mrs. Jones."

Pauline's look at Albert acknowledged this was going to be difficult, then she entered, and the door was shut. Next, the deputy mayor took the King to the next classroom, knocked at the door, opened it, and said, "The King."

Albert entered, wearing the formal morning coat of his father's funeral, except now he was hatless. The mayor was seated, wearing black, with a veil pulled back over her hat. She rose only with difficulty and, as she attempted to curtsy, she started to collapse. Albert rushed forward to hold her with both hands, so she didn't fall to the floor. She was so embarrassed at causing such a breach of protocol that she kept saying, "No, Your Majesty. Please, no," as Albert helped her sit again in her chair. Then he pulled up a nearby chair for himself and sat down across from her and took both her hands in his. He looked directly at her, as she broke down and started crying, still embarrassed. She looked down to hide what was so obvious.

Albert, gently holding her hands, let her cry so they could share the mutual loss of their husbands, then he said, softly, "I am so sorry, Madam Mayor."

Questioningly, she looked up into his face as he continued, "I am so sorry to bring such tragedy to your beloved town with these unspeakable deaths. When Mr. Jones called us on the radio talk show and invited us here, we were both excited at the opportunity to do something positive, to help, and so we'd looked forward to the trip for the longest time. To have it end so shockingly and with such finality . . . ."

And the King stopped talking, momentarily overwhelmed with his own grief before continuing, "but I swear to you, Madam Mayor, that whilst my beloved Paul is no longer with us, nonetheless I will continue our mutual goal to do whatever we can to make Llanfynydd and this region a place where its young people can stay and thrive."

The mayor looked at him gratefully, then looked away again. There was another period of silence, then Albert said softly, "Tell me about him."

And then the mayor sat up and pulled away her hands as she told about childhood sweethearts, raised only houses apart, who fell in love and went to university with the idea of going to London for their careers, then deciding instead to return to their rural town to help as they could, with her husband a teacher and she a politician. Then, when he retired, to join her on the town council. And that's where the story ended because it brought her up to the moment of his recent death.

Then Albert took her hands again and, looking directly at her, said, "You and I can make the changes you and your husband wanted to see. It's true that people often overestimate the power I have, but I promise that if I have specific ideas to benefit this area, then I'll present them to the foundation to see what can be done."

The mayor looked at him gratefully and nodded just as there was a knock at the door.

"Come," said Albert, and Sir Humphrey entered to say, "It's time, Your Majesty."

Albert nodded, released the mayor's hands and stood up. She also stood, gracefully and unassisted this time to curtsy with dignity as he left. As he passed Pauline in the hallway, they looked at each other to silently acknowledge that while this was indeed difficult, it was also why they were here.

As Albert approached the next classroom, the deputy major opened the door and said, again, "The King."

Albert went inside where Mr. and Mrs. Jones attempted, awkwardly, to rise from their chairs, designed for the smaller bodies of young students. Mr. Jones was wearing perhaps his one good suit, from the other day, though now with a black armband on it. Albert took both his hands in his and held them tightly; neither man spoke, though it seemed to Albert that Mr. Jones was concerned about something. Then he let go of Mr. Jones and turned to his wife, with her arm in a sling, to ask, "And how are you doing, my dear lady?"

Mrs. Jones held out her good hand to grasp Albert's outstretched hand and told him, as though continuing an ongoing conversation, "I told them I didn't want to be admitted, Your Majesty. I told them to just patch me up and send me home, but they didn't listen, and they kept me overnight with my dear husband asleep in a chair beside the bed and that's not good for his back."

Albert smiled.

"Well, I'm sure they just wanted to be careful," he explained.

"I have no doubt about that, Your Majesty, but it was a hardship none the less."

Albert smiled and held out his hand to the school chairs behind them and it was only with difficulty that they sat down again, sinking heavily onto the low wooden seats. Then Mr. Jones buried his face in his hands and started crying.

"It's my fault, Your Majesty, all my fault. If I hadn't made that bloody phone call and invited you and your lad to come here, none of this would have happened. So, it's all my fault, you see?"

And he looked at Albert with such anguish that Albert quickly took the man's hands in his own and said, "Now I won't have any of that, Mr. Jones. As I just told the mayor, you invited us here to help, and I will see that it's done just as the Duke, and I intended. This tragedy was unforeseen, especially from a man I trusted implicitly, and we will not let his madness stop that admirable goal. But, again, as I told the mayor, I cannot do it alone, and I need your help [and here he looked directly at the two tear-stained faces before him], and that of your neighbors to come together and develop practical solutions for a better future. This shared horror will not stop us. Mr. Jones, I understand you served in the military, so this is a new way to serve your country. Will you help me?"

And Mr. Jones looked proudly into Albert's face and said, "That I will, Your Majesty, that I will."

Then Albert firmly pressed the man's hands between his own and said, "Good for you!"

Then he turned to Mrs. Jones and asked, "And will you keep him on task to make sure he does that for me?"

And she smiled and nodded just as there was another knock on the door.

"Come," said Albert again, as Sir Humphrey entered, bowed, and said, "It's time, Your Majesty."

All three struggled to get up, helping each other to rise from their chairs, as Sir Humphrey stifled his natural tendency to assist the King, realizing it was Albert who wanted to help the aging couple.

Outside the school, the band was assembled on the main street, then Albert, Pauline, and the others were shown to their positions directly behind them by the deputy mayor, with Sir Humphrey joining them. Security was discrete, forming a perimeter outside the town to keep the curious away so the residents were free to participate in the day's events, and without media, except for, again, the local reporter and photographer.

Looking at the buildings along the street, Albert noticed black bunting had replaced the red, blue, and white of the previous visit. The residents, either wearing black or with black armbands, waited on the pavement in front of their houses for the procession to reach them. The band started its first hymn, and the procession began. Albert held out his arms to Pauline on one side and the mayor on the other, and they linked their arms through his, with Mr. and Mrs. Jones on either side of them. As the procession moved forward, the villagers fell in behind and linked their arms together as well. It reminded Albert of pictures he'd seen of marches in the American South when protesters formed an interlinked mass of people with a common goal that these Welsh people shared today: "Violence will not win because we are better than that."

Albert only faltered as the procession approached the town hall with its balcony where his life forever changed. He knew those with him who had also shared the balcony that day were faltering as well. Then Pauline said loudly, "Remember our loved ones." And Paul appeared to Albert not as a dead body with sightless eyes and a shattered chest, but alive and laughing again, just as the mayor's husband appeared to her. Albert and the mayor recovered their strength and pride and walked with heads raised as they passed the building and they refused to let its tragedy overwhelm them. They simply looked beyond it and, as they did so, the town hall disappeared from sight and thought.

The procession continued adding people as they stepped off the pavement to join the constantly enlarging group as it reached the end of town to pass the building where Graham's accomplice had fired the diversionary shots that gave him the few moments he needed to assassinate the King. Albert knew it from pictures he'd been shown, and its brick facade was pockmarked with bullet holes, and all the windows were shattered. But he made it disappear as well by looking ahead so it simply vanished.

The procession by now had reached the graveyard with its low stone wall. Albert looked over the wall and saw a mound of earth beside an open grave. The mayor saw it as well and faltered. Albert leaned over and simply said, "Courage." Then she picked up the pace.

By now the band had reached the front of the church where the vicar waited beside the open double doors. Those in the procession gathered around as the last dirge stopped and the band, joined by the organist from inside the church, joined in to play the old Welsh lullaby, "Suo Gân," which the people started singing both in Welsh and English. Albert sang it in Welsh.

> Ni chaiff dim amharu'th gyntun,
> Ni wna undyn â thi gam.

> Nothing shall disturb your slumber,
> Nobody will do you harm.

When it was over, the vicar went to the King, bowed, and said, "We are honored to have Your Majesty join us today."

Albert replied that he was honored to be there and, with his love of old architecture, added that he wanted to return in different circumstances so he could study the church more closely. It dated to the twelfth century and a time when the local population was much larger than now, so there was plenty of room for everyone. The double doors, of heavy oak planks, were held together with hand-forged iron nails with studded heads, while massive and florid strap hinges attached the doors to massive pintles set into carved stone casings on either side.

The vicar explained that an alderman would show the King and his party to the front row. Albert nodded, entered the stone church, and noticed the coffin at the far end. But he also recognized that the mayor did not hesitate as she walked beside him to the front of the sanctuary to take their places, remaining standing at the wooden chancel rail as the organist and the band continued to play and the church gradually filled with parishioners. Finally, the vicar stepped up before the altar and turned to face the congregation.

The service began with a hymn. Albert looked behind him and noticed everyone else had or were sharing hymnals, and he asked loudly, "Don't I get a hymnal as well? I do read music, you know."

The mayor smiled, reached down and pulled a hymnal from a wooden holder and turned it to the right page, as others in the group got their own hymnals. She held it out to the King, and they shared it together. Placated, he leaned over and said softly, "I'm told I've a pleasant light baritone voice." She smiled and the two found the correct place and started to sing.

The service continued, and then came the sermon, in which the vicar spoke of the need to maintain unwavering faith in the face of incomprehensible tragedy, with the consolation of knowing that loved ones would meet again in the hereafter. Albert was not consoled. Later, at the graveside ritual, the coffin was lowered into the ground and the undertaker handed out flowers to drop onto the coffin, which was then gradually covered with shovels full of dirt. The mayor, whose black veil now covered her face, put a hand to her mouth and merely shook her head as she bid farewell to her husband. Albert took her other hand and held it, and then the funeral was over. The plan called for a return procession to the school where a wake would be held in the cafeteria.

Albert had been looking forward to this as he had never attended a wake and wanted to be part of the communal commemoration. The mayor excused herself and went over to say something to the deputy mayor and the vicar, and Albert saw them turning towards him, as though waiting for something to happen. Then he realized that many of the villagers were looking at him questioningly, as though there were some kind of issue, when he realized he was the issue. Albert knew he was welcome to attend, but he also knew his presence as King would hinder the event and make it something formal and more inhibited than the townsfolk would want. He knew they wanted a traditional wake with its boisterous singing and drinking and sharing of stories. So he leaned over to Pauline, standing beside him, and said quietly, "We should leave."

Understanding his concern, she agreed. Albert looked over at Sir Humphrey and gave him the signal they used at events, the signal that says, basically, come here. So Sir Humphrey approached the King, who said quietly, "Come closer and say something in my ear so it appears that you have a message for me. We need to leave and I need an excuse."

Sir Humphrey leaned over and said, "Good idea, Your Highness."

Albert nodded as though acknowledging Sir Humphrey's message, then approached the mayor.

"I am so sorry, Madam Mayor, but I've been informed that something has come up, and I am needed back in London. Please make my apologies to the others, and we'll keep in touch."

The mayor, relieved, curtsied gracefully and this time without hesitation. Healing had begun.

"Of course, Your Majesty. We are grateful you could be here."

He nodded to her, and soon the helicopter lifted off and headed towards London. Albert looked out the window at the Welsh hills passing below. He turned to Pauline and said, "I was afraid on the way over, but now I'm not. I don't know why."

She merely smiled and placed her hand over his. She was pleased this day had gone well because, after all, there was one more funeral to attend.

CHAPTER 76

It was after 3 a. m. the morning of the funeral when the last of the mourners paying their respects to the Duke finally passed on either side of Paul's catafalque in Westminster Hall. For three days they had solemnly passed by, waiting for hours in a queue that at one point crossed Lambeth Bridge and even wrapped around St. Thomas's Hospital. Now, the doors of St. Stephen's Entrance were finally closed and, at last, the great hall was silent and the four officers of the Brigade of Guards continued to stand in attendance at each corner of the bier, with the plumes of their shining metal helmets falling down around their faces as they bowed their heads in honor of the deceased, white gloved hands on the hilts of their swords, with the points on the floor. The polished leather of their thigh-high black boots gleamed in the soft light from the chandeliers high overhead, and the even softer light from the four tall beeswax candles on their floor stands, one at each corner of the catafalque.

It was reminiscent of the late King's lying-in-wait, with four Yeomen from the Tower standing off the risers in their striking, Tudor-era uniforms of gold and red, with their oddly flattened and heavily-fulled black wool hats, and their pikes held upside down with tips on the flagstone floor.

There were also two members of His Majesty's Bodyguard of the Honorable Corps of Gentleman-at-Arms, of which Sir Humphrey was a member, and he had already held watch here.

Three days earlier, before the waiting queue was admitted, there was a private viewing for the Royal Family. Albert was at the center, with Pauline on one side, and a very pregnant Connie on the other, with her family, and Larry and his children beyond

Pauline; Princess Elizabeth was still in treatment.

Albert stood before the catafalque, with a wreath of white flowers – roses and lilies – to each side. Albert finally accepted that the Royal Standard would not be permitted to cover the oak coffin as Paul was not of royal blood, so the standard of the House of Britain was used instead, with its red lion on a gold field, which Albert knew was a particular favorite of Paul's.

For his father's funeral, there had been the Crown, the Orb, and the Sceptre on top of the Royal Standard. It took some time before Albert decided what he wanted placed on Paul's coffin. He contacted the Master of the King's Music and requested a hand-illuminated vellum copy of "I sat down under his shadow" to be framed and laid on top of the standard. After the procession to the Chapel Royal and the funeral itself, the vellum copy would be removed from its frame and placed inside Paul's coffin for the cremation, an act which Albert and Pauline had both agreed was most appropriate as neither wanted to think of that beautiful body corrupted by decay and time.

Paul was the first member of the Royal Family to be cremated. Albert and Pauline planned, at some point, to take his ashes back to Durham and release them from the footbridge below the cathedral into the River Wear, perhaps part of him would even reach the North Sea, returning to the ever-creating spirit that was part of his animistic belief.

Albert stood with his hands crossed in front, but then he fell to his knees, a motion so quick and unexpected that, initially, there was general concern that he was collapsing. However, it was quickly recognized that he was in a position like that of prayer and, indeed, as Albert had worshiped Paul in life, so he worshiped him in death. Not knowing what else to do, the rest of the family started to kneel as well though Pauline, recognizing the difficulty of Connie's kneeling at her late state of pregnancy, motioned for a chair to be brought for her and, somehow, within that vast and empty space, a chair was found and brought to her, and she gratefully sat heavily upon it.

As Pauline knelt beside Albert, she heard him say softly to himself, "What hope for us remains now he is gone?" It was a quote she couldn't place, but it was a line that, somehow, came to Albert from across the years as he had last read it more than a decade earlier in a book of Elizabethan dramas.

And, indeed, it was all Albert could think about while kneeling before the coffin containing the shattered body of his slain beloved. Albert was alive but would remain alone, his widowhood happening so quickly and unexpectedly. He realized as he knelt that these were among the last times he would have Paul near him, yet so still, so cold.

Kneeling itself became an act of resistance in which, even though Albert was alive and Paul was dead, they were nonetheless together in a timeless moment that kept the outer world at bay, and where he wanted to remain forever with his beloved and never have to leave him or share him.

Over and over, Albert said to himself, "Not yet. Not yet. I cannot leave you just yet."

He refused to let the world move on, as though he could stop the sun itself. And yet Albert knew time was passing, that the world was waiting for him so it could move on, but still he thought, "No! Not yet! Too soon! Too soon!"

He knew that after rising to his feet and leaving the hall, the doors would open to the waiting queue beyond, and that Paul would become theirs, and the world's, and part of history as well, as he already was, of course, and without Albert's permission.

Finally Albert realized that continued resistance was futile because even monarchs are subject to fate, which seemed to be pounding on the doors, and so, in one of the hardest moments of his life, he abruptly stood up, bowed his head one last time towards the bier, then turned and walked across the stone floor and up the stone staircase. But he stopped at the landing, paused, then turned back to see that magnificent room as though for the last time.

Westminster Hall was one of Albert's favorite spaces, with its amazingly engineered hammer beam ceiling, with its carved heads at the ends of the horizontal chestnut beams, and the rafters disappearing upwards into the darkness above. He looked down at the catafalque with its honor guards standing in attendance and suddenly realized there was yet another way he could honor his dead.

He urged his valet: "Perfect. It must be perfect."

His valet understood the King's manic states.

"Yes, Your Majesty," as he prepared the King's dress uniform. Fortunately he'd had time to make sure that everything was, indeed, perfect, including the proper and exact placement of the various ribbons, medals, and commendations, as well as the polished black belt, the polished sword in its polished scabbard, the polished shoes, and everything, cape included, immaculately cleaned and pressed so that the creases themselves stood out like sculpture.

And so it was that, shortly after 3 a. m. on the morning of Paul's funeral, the King unexpectedly appeared in full dress uniform at the top of the stairs that descend to the flagstone floor of Westminster Hall. The officer on duty gazed, startled, at the unexpected sight and immediately worried that she must have done something terribly wrong to warrant a royal visit.

For his part, Albert was relieved to note it was the same commanding officer who had been on duty when he visited with the family three days earlier. Seeing her flustered, Albert rapidly approached. She came to attention, saluted, and he saluted back, an act he had fortunately practiced over the past three days so he wouldn't appear an amateur. It was amazing what one could learn on YouTube. Then he leaned close to her and said, "A word, Captain, if I may?"

"Of course, Your Majesty."

Then he explained why he was there and the favor he had to ask of her. He understood that a request from him was usually taken as a command, but he really meant it when he said he did not want to somehow be out-of-place with his request, and that he would abide by her decision if she found it too irregular.

"Not at all, Your Majesty," she replied graciously to his relief. She walked over to one of the Brigade of Guards and quietly spoke to him. He looked over at the King, then nodded and, sword in hand, walked to the nearby wall, where he resumed his position. The duty officer motioned for the King to come over and take his place where the officer had stood.

"How long is the watch?" asked Albert.

"Four hours, and it just changed, so most of it is ahead," she explained, then added hesitantly, "The guards have practice doing this because it's not easy."

Rather than taking offense at the tactful implication that he might not be up to the task, Albert merely smiled, "I've been practicing, too."

The captain smiled in turn, then Albert added, "If, by chance, I do not meet your expectations, I trust you will charge me with the appropriate demerits."

Then he paused to consider what he'd said.

"Maybe that's Scouting and not the military?"

"Yes, Your Majesty," she agreed.

"Then put me in the brig, if necessary. The Tower isn't far away."

The captain continued smiling.

"I don't think that will be an issue, sir."

She returned to her post as Albert removed his sword from its scabbard and placed its gleaming point on the floor; put his white gloved hand on the hilt, then bowed his head.

He wanted to pass the coming hours without thinking, because to think meant thinking of sorrow and loss and tragedy. He decided to meditate as Paul was teaching him; then he caught his mistake – still so frequent in these early days of widowhood – that Paul had been teaching him, before . . . before the world changed. His mantra was simple: "Paul." He loved the very sound of it, with its hard opening consonant, the lingering, soft closing consonant, and the vowels in the middle like a bridge from one end of time to the other.

By saying the word slowly, by drawing it out, he joined with his beloved, so he closed his eyes to shut out the world and said to himself, "Paul," while breathing in, then "Paul" while letting go; the breathing in; the letting go; the breathing in, the letting go, in constant repetition, "Paul – Paul – Paul." Over and over and . . . .

Then Albert became aware of the captain talking to him, as from a distant place, so he opened his eyes.

"Did I fall asleep?" he asked, greatly concerned.

"Not at all, Your Majesty," she said gently. "Your shift is over."

Surprised, Albert looked up and saw the vast hall filled with soft morning light, then looked back at her.

"Was I all right?" he asked, fearful of failing.

"You did well, Your Majesty. The Duke would have been pleased."

And those were the kindest words he heard all week. She saluted him, and he returned the salute. He placed his sword in its scabbard and proceeded towards the stone staircase, not at all surprised to see Sir Humphrey waiting for him up on the landing and smiling gently. Albert passed the Guard whose position he had taken as the man returned to the catafalque. Albert gasped as the man looked like Paul and was nearly as beautiful. Though it was against protocol, the man briefly looked directly at Albert and gave just the briefest hint of a smile before passing on. For some reason, Albert found his breathing labored and it was only with great difficulty that he made it to the top of the stairs, as he heard Sir Humphrey say softly, "A most appropriate tribute, Your Highness."

His valet was waiting when Albert returned.

"How did it go, Your Majesty?"

"Everything was perfect," replied Albert, which was all he needed to say.

Soon he was in bed, alone, but there was only time for a brief nap before he had to get up again to dress for breakfast with the family before the day's events began. He was relieved at not being able to deeply sleep, because the last thing he wanted to dream about was either the dead Paul, or the living Guard.

CHAPTER 77

In future years, Albert could not recall the day of Paul's funeral in strict chronological order, but as a series of images and sounds, more impressionistic than detailed. There was the morning breakfast, with an unexpected question from one of Larry's children.

"When is Mummy coming home? Papa says you're making her stay away. Why are you doing that?"

Caught unaware, but instantly angry, Albert gave Larry a "if looks could kill" stare, and the assault made Larry look down at his plate. Then Albert instantly regretted such aggression on this particular day and covered it with what he hoped would be perceived as a benevolent smile.

"I think what your father meant to say is that I am greatly concerned for my dear sister's recovery, and I want her to get all the help she needs for as long as necessary so that when she does return, she will be so much better."

Then he turned towards Larry and said, with exaggerated politeness, "That's what you meant to say, isn't it, Larry?"

Then Larry stared at Albert with a look combining relief, embarrassed chastisement, and barely submerged resentment.

"Yes, of course, Albert. That's precisely what I meant to say."

Satisfied, Albert returned to his food, though he had no appetite, and neither did the other adults at the table – Connie and her husband, Pauline – all of whom were silent and even shocked at the whipping scene they'd just experienced. The meal progressed in silence until another of Larry's children asked, "Is Uncle Paul really dead?"

To which Toria, with the certainty of the young, replied, not waiting for Albert to speak, "Of course he is. That's why we're going to his funeral."

Albert agreed.

"Toria is right, Sarah. Uncle Paul is dead."

Persistently, the child next asked, "And his body was in that coffin with the guards around it?"

Perhaps surprisingly, Albert was not angered or upset by this question either, as it gave him a chance to truly accept the finality of the situation, and he glanced sadly at Pauline before turning back to the child.

"Yes, Sarah, his body was in the coffin, and today we will follow the coffin from Westminster Hall to the Chapel Royal for the actual funeral service, then his body will be cremated, and Aunt Pauline and I will take his ashes back to Durham where we'll put them into the river."

As he said this, he looked again at Pauline, who had the merest hint of a resigned smile.

Young Sarah persisted in her questions.

"So, you'll never see him again?"

Albert replied with a fleeting smile of his own, "No, Sarah, I'll never see him again."

Then Henry, another of Larry's children, spoke up, "But our minister says that when you go to Heaven, we meet our loved ones again. Aren't you and Paul going to Heaven?"

In the face of such childlike curiosity, Albert remained an unexpected font of patience as the other adults wondered how he would reply.

"Not everyone believes that" he said kindly yet firmly. "I believe that death is final and that Paul and I will never see each other again."

"Albert," interrupted Larry. "The children respect you as a

role model. Please don't undermine their faith, especially on this day, as I'm trying to get them through a situation that's difficult for children to understand."

Refusing to be angry, Albert carefully explained to his brother-in-law, "Henry asked me a question, and I simply answered it. I'm not going to deny my beliefs, or lack thereof, to reinforce your own."

Grimly, Larry nodded. Albert had already turned back to the children.

"Surely you understand that there are many different kinds of beliefs, and that we don't all believe the same things?"

The children all nodded with agreement.

Then Albert expansively added, "While it is true that, as King, I am the head of the Church of England, the fact remains that, privately, I differ from the doctrine of your Anglican minister, just as your Uncle Paul did. Surely, we can all agree to differ and to respect our differences, can't we Larry?"

And, refusing to be pulled into a confrontation with Albert on today of all days, Larry said resignedly, "Of course, Albert. Lizzie and I have raised the children to be independent thinkers.

To which Albert replied with a broad smile, "So, there we are, children."

Then little Sarah had another question.

"Will Mummy come back to live with us again?"

A dark cloud temporarily crossed Albert's face, quickly replaced with a benevolent smile.

"That's the plan," he said magnanimously to reassure the group, while thinking to himself, "For now."

A short time later, Albert and the rest of the family waited outside Westminster Hall as Welsh Guards, arms interlocked across shoulders to more steadily distribute the weight of the coffin, carefully brought it out front to the waiting gun carriage, pulled by a team of matched horses. The procession began with a company of bagpipers, followed by a long line of the King's Troop Royal Horse Artillery, resplendent in their uniforms and helmets. Then came the gun carriage, with the coffin still overlaid with the banner of the House of Britain, a wreath of white lilies, and the framed illumination. Albert and Pauline followed the carriage on foot, with Sir Humphrey and the Prime Minister behind them. Despite Connie's insistence that she could walk the two miles back to St. James, Sir Sullivan insisted she ride, so she and her family were in a horse-drawn open landau, while Larry and his children followed in another, so the youngest ones wouldn't have to walk either.

Albert later remembered the solemn crowds, the tearful faces, the streetlamp posts draped in black, and with many buildings also draped in black. Certain areas along the way were reserved for the media and Albert was aware that he, dressed in formal mourning attire, was being watched around the world. Flowers were tossed towards the gun carriage, as well as Rainbow Unicorns. Evidently all of Europe was sold out and special flights to England were arranged from factories in India as they worked around the clock to meet the demand.

Albert knew the world wanted to see how he would handle the death of his beloved, and he handled it well, with gravity, dignity, and even a kind of pride. Pauline looked resplendent, with her face fully veiled, unlike the Prime Minister who only wore a hat. The day was sunless, though at least without the rain which had been forecast.

A drum brigade preceded the cortege, with its steady repetition of sixty-five beats to the minute. Black cloth encircled the bass drums to muffle their sounds, accompanied by snare drums and a single bell from the Abbey, rung every minute.

Those attending the funeral had long had their seats when

the procession arrived shortly before 11 a. m. and more Welsh Guards interlaced their arms to carry Paul's coffin to the chancel of the Chapel Royal. There were no trumpets this time, but organ and choir formed of cathedral singers from throughout the kingdom. As the coffin was carefully laid on the bier, it was precisely 11 a. m. and Albert entered as everyone stood and sang, accompanied by organ and choir, "God Save the King."

Albert remembered little of the service, though he appreciated the care the Archbishop took during the homily to include significant references to Paul's animism and, naturally, the Archbishop included traditional Anglican references to the persistence of the soul. Albert sat unmoved as the Archbishop also explained what he had discussed with Pauline, of how her son returned to the divine creating spirit to be reborn among the living. The Archbishop had carefully crafted his message to be one of consolation to the bereaved, but Albert remained untouched.

The rest of the day eventually went completely out of focus, and Albert later had no idea what happened. What he did recall, with painful clarity, was being alone that night in bed, realizing he had a lifetime of loneliness ahead of him, and he wondered if he would forever mourn Paul, as the first Victoria forever mourned her own Albert, and who even hoped, by stopping time and keeping everything the same, that somehow he might eventually return. Albert was not so optimistic. He finally fell into a deep, deep sleep, and dreamed vividly of the dead Paul, and the live Guard.

CHAPTER 78

Shortly after Lizzie was finally released, she was informed that Albert wanted to see her. Despite her trepidation, she also saw this as a way to make amends for what she would always refer to as "her spell". The doctors said she was recovered, and she felt ready to regain her place and duties as a working member of the Royal Family. She was eager to prove that what had happened was simply a momentary lapse that now was behind her. This meeting was her first opportunity to show that her rehabilitation was successful.

Still, she paused at the entrance to Albert's office, an understandable moment of hesitation and doubt before entering what she could only think of as the lion's lair. Yes, she was afraid, but, nonetheless, she bravely entered, smiling, and was relieved when Albert looked up from his desk where he was working to return her smile. Yes, she was greatly relieved as Albert rose, came around the desk, and held out his arms to hold her close to him. Yes, she thought, she was forgiven; that was all she needed to know.

"My dear Lizzie," said Albert as he kissed her on the cheek, before holding her out at arms' length, "Let me see you."

And giddy with delight at this unexpectedly warm greeting, she turned around and then curtsied like a girl.

"You're looking fine," said Albert appreciatively. "How do you feel?"

"Like I've been reborn," she admitted.

"Excellent," replied Albert, "because I've got a job for you."

As this was the first time Lizzie had seen her brother since

Paul's death and the attempted assassination, she knew she had to say something.

"I'm so sorry about Paul's death, and to think that he would die saving you from Graham."

Albert's face instantly darkened, and Lizzie realized, too late, that, inadvertently, she'd already made her first mistake.

"It's hard, unbearably hard, without him," admitted Albert. "Now I know how Victoria felt at Albert's death. I fear I may not recover."

"But Albert," Lizzie started to say, when Albert interrupted her.

"It's how you would feel if you suddenly lost Larry and the children."

Which was when Lizzie felt horror creeping towards her like a black panther on a dark night.

"Why, Albert," she said surprised and shocked, "how dreadful. Why would you say such a thing?"

"Oh," he replied, instantly apologetic, "It's just an analogy, a point of reference. Nothing more."

Determined to move on, Lizzie said she understood that it had to be a terrible shock.

"Yes, it has been," admitted an apparently contrite Albert, "but he wanted me to continue in case anything happened to him. We just didn't think it would happen so soon," he added with a slight, mournful smile, but he quickly moved on, as though to cover a momentary weakness. "That's why I want to see you."

Lizzie was relieved to see Albert looking ahead instead of looking back which, as she well knew, could become a bottomless pit from which he might never return.

"So, you have work for me? The doctors said returning to my duties is beneficial."

"Of course," said a now ebullient Albert, "and I've got just the ticket. Let's sit down and discuss it."

"Of course, Albert," replied Lizzie, as they sat beside each other on the sofa beneath their father's life-sized portrait. She looked at Albert expectantly, as he continued.

"As you know, for some time I've wanted to expand the powers of the monarchy that have been chipped away for centuries until we are little more than figureheads of state."

Puzzled at where this could be going, Lizzie just continued looking at him as he continued.

"Part of that, as you know, is my plan to have Toria eventually become my personal representative to the Commonwealth and possessions."

Lizzie winced slightly as she was reminded of what could have been, and what should have been, but her curiosity and desire to please made her eager for him to continue. And so he did.

"But that will take many years as she grows into the position, and I want someone now to represent the Royal Family and what better person than you, my very own sister?"

He stopped triumphantly. She was taken aback at what he was offering her as a chance for them to work together, and the chance for her to regain her place as an integral part of the family.

"Why, Albert, I'm touched that you would consider me."

"You're perfect for the job!" he added brightly.

"And, of course, I accept," she replied. "I just hope it can be done close to home as I've only just returned and would like to spend time with Larry and the children."

He just looked at her, and she realized there was more to this than he'd said so far.

"It's not in Wales, is it?" she asked jokingly, then realized that was her second mistake, so she quickly continued.

"Unless it's that town where – "

And then she paused, not knowing where to go now, except just to continue and make it as positive as possible.

"Of course, that would be a great opportunity. I'm sure I could do a great deal of good there . . . ."

And then she paused again as Albert still said nothing, but then he did.

"Actually, it's a bit farther away than Wales."

Now perplexed, and with growing anxiety, she asked with trepidation, "Then where is it?"

And she never forgot his look of complete triumph when he replied, "The Falkland Islands!"

She exploded, "The Falklands!", but then everything became clear, this whole charade.

"You still blame me, don't you? You haven't forgiven me. This is your revenge."

Now Albert's face darkened again.

"You wanted to kill our child and, perhaps with a different host mother, you would have succeeded. I will never forgive you."

Now Lizzie knew the danger she was in, and that there was no escape. She was trapped.

"But Albert," she said pleadingly, "I was ill. I didn't know what I was doing."

With a sneer, Albert replied, "Is that what you told the doctors? Or is that what they told you to say, hoping I would just let it go? That's what Paul told me to do; just let it go. And I told him I would, but Paul's dead, so I'm no longer bound by that commitment, and now I'm going to make you pay because you knew what you were doing. You took a calculated risk, but you failed, and now you're mine!"

Lizzie knew she was lost, so she tried to negotiate.

"But the Falklands are no place for my children!"

"No," agreed Albert, "which is why they are staying here."

And now Lizzie was aware of the full depth into which she was descending.

"You're taking my children!?" she screamed.

"They're the succession, as you keep pointing out. For their own security, they are staying here in Britain, where they will be well taken care of. You can take the one you are carrying, of course."

"How do you know about that?" asked a mystified Lizzie.

"My dear sister," replied a triumphant Albert, "I know everything about you. Now, Larry can go with you or stay here, as he pleases. He can run the foundation just as well down there as he can here. I'm pretty sure there's internet access. And as your children come of age, they can decide whether to join you or not, if they still remember you," he added viciously.

Then she turned on him.

"Albert, you're a monster."

Unfazed by her accusation, Albert merely corrected her.

"I am not a monster, my dear sister; I have become Death, the destroyer of worlds."

And he said this with a malicious intensity she had never seen in him before, and she knew her life was over.

"Of course," he added, "You may not like the Falklands, and I can understand that, so there are options. For example, if you like the South Pacific, there is Pitcairn Island, but, if you prefer the Atlantic, then I can suggest St. Helena. Every year on the anniversary of Napoleon's death you can wear a copy of his hat and put your hand in your waist coat like this – "

And he slid his hand inside his shirt to imitate paintings of the emperor.

"But this is a real job, Lizzie. I do need you. You've proven, both with your family and your foundation, that you have organizational skills useful to me. You will be my representative, and you can make of the job what you will."

"What if I refuse?" asked Lizzie with a smoldering intensity.

"That is an option I would not recommend," replied Albert airily. "In that case, there is another hospital waiting for you, a long-term facility much farther away than your last placement, which I understand has effective drug therapy for your condition. Very long term. In fact, I daresay you will never leave."

All hope was gone. Albert continued.

"You will be accompanied to your apartment at Kensington, where you will say farewell to your children. Try not to turn them against me too much. Tomorrow, you will be accompanied to the Falklands on a military flight. Your new life awaits. I hope you enjoy it. We shall not see each other again."

With that, Albert stood, went to his desk and pressed a buzzer. On the intercom, his new security chief asked, "Yes, Your Majesty?"

To which Albert replied, "Princess Elizabeth is ready to leave."

"Yes, sir."

The woman recently promoted to replace Graham entered and stood before Lizzie, who made no move to stand, so the junior guard stepped forward to get her up when Lizzie abruptly stood.

"I can walk by myself!" she said imperiously. She gave Albert a look of hateful intensity, but he had already returned to his desk and his work. She took a long look at the room which, in a better world, would have been hers, then her shoulders slumped, her head bent over, and she more shuffled than walked from the room.

Albert really wasn't looking at the papers before him. He was haunted by how the meeting had gone. It had gone as planned, but his complete revenge was not as satisfying as he'd hoped. Lizzie was still his twin and would remain bound to him until death. He realized he would never be freed from her. They were inextricably part of each other, and he found that difficult to bear.

He pushed the buzzer for his secretary.

"Yes, Your Majesty?"

"Admit Michael Romanov as soon as he arrives. I expect he will be late as usual. I think he's been on Majorca."

"So, I understand, sir."

Michael couldn't figure out why Albert wanted to see him, and especially not in his office as though it were an official meeting. The two had never been more than distant cousins, except when Michael supplied his coach house as a trysting site, and look how that ended. Well, he would know soon enough.

Albert did not rise when Michael entered; in fact, he didn't recognize him at all. He continued working at his desk while Michael stood before him. It almost seemed like a game of one-upmanship that irritated Michael until Albert suddenly slammed his fist on the desk and shouted, "How could you be so stupid?"

Caught off guard, Michael stood there speechless, with no idea what was happening. He just looked at Albert questioningly, so Albert explained.

"Did you think we would not find out about your money laundering? About your dummy corporations set up around the world whose one purpose was to siphon funds out of England to avoid paying taxes. I had no idea your holdings were so extensive, or that you were so devious in hiding them."

Michael was unapologetic and replied starchily.

"And why, may I ask, is the King at all concerned with my

business dealings? Have you nothing better to do?"

"I'm involved because of this," replied Albert as he opened a file on his desk and turned it so Michael could see it, yet who, frankly, couldn't care less what it was. He sniffed, without even looking at it.

"And what's that to me?" he asked imperiously.

Albert pointed to it.

"That, dear cousin, is the agreement between your great-great-grandfather Nicholas, and my great-great-grandfather Edward, specifying the conditions of asylum which your family agreed to when my family saved your royal arses from the revolutionaries."

Now taken aback, Michael said quietly, "I didn't realize there was an agreement."

"No, obviously you didn't because you have blatantly violated it with your criminal activities. The agreement states the Romanov family in exile will faithfully uphold British law and, if found guilty of violating those laws, can be returned to Russia."

"And your point?" asked Michael, still unsure as to where this was going.

"Well, you violated and so you are being returned."

"To Russia?" asked a disbelieving Michael. "You're joking!"

"Not at all," replied Albert calmly, in full control of the situation. "It's perfectly justified for someone guilty of being an accessory to the attempted murder of a royal heir."

Michael finally understood, and he started to worry.

"What do you mean?" he asked quietly, hoping to postpone what he knew was coming.

Albert pushed a button on his console, and the voices of Michael and Lizzie filled the room.

"I am going to kill that mutant devil spawn!"

"Now, my dear, how you go on."

"I mean it, Michael. The child is dead."

Then Albert released the button and looked at Michael triumphantly. Michael was shocked.

"You bugged my phone? How dare you!"

To which Albert angrily replied, "How dare you learn of a plot to kill my child and not tell me!"

"It was not my affair!" shouted Michael defensively. "Besides, she was just ranting. She wouldn't follow through on it."

Now Albert shouted at him, "She offered Connie ten million pounds to have a miscarriage, and you knew about it. Do you want to hear more of the recordings?"

Michael just shook his head, defeated.

"So, what happens now?" he asked in a flat tone.

"You will be returned to Russia and never set foot in England again."

"What about Mother?"

"We know she was not involved, so she can stay here."

"It will take time for me to convert my holdings into cash."

"Well, that's just it," explained Albert. "It turns out that what you owe Inland Revenue in unpaid taxes equals the value of your assets. Everything has been seized. You have nothing."

Michael looked at him furiously.

"You're a monster!"

Calmly, Albert replied, "So I've been told."

Then he continued, "Since the government doesn't want your estate but what it's worth, I was able to buy it all – land, buildings, contents – at their fair market value. I especially like the Fabergé eggs. You can see that a lot has happened during your trip to Majorca. I assume you found some hot young men to occupy your time and bed."

Michael said nothing, still stunned at what was playing itself out.

In a more expansive mood, Albert leaned back in his chair and explained, "Paul always liked your estate, and I'd hoped somehow to buy it for him once he became Duke for his country seat. Now that he's gone, his mother will live there, while I'm keeping the coach house, for old times' sake. I do appreciate your letting us use it."

Michael bowed quickly and stiffly, without grace.

"Now," continued Albert, "I've spoken to your uncle about all of this, and he is not pleased to have you return. Despite the Tsarina's protestations that he is not homophobic, it seems he is. I think all that Russian Orthodoxy really has affected his mind. Anyway, he doesn't want you in either St. Petersburg or Moscow, and he also has no interest in supporting, as he called it, your decadent Western lifestyle."

"So, what am I supposed to do? How am I to live?", demanded Michael sharply.

"He's found a job for you."

"A what?" shouted Michael.

"A job," replied Albert, now thoroughly enjoying himself. "Many people have them. You're going to be managing a government import-export office in Vladivostok."

"Where?" shouted a disbelieving Michael.

"I hear it's beautiful in summer, all two weeks of it," said a smiling Albert. He pushed another buzzer on his desk and this time two security guards entered, each carrying a suitcase.

"Now," explained Albert, "These men will accompany you to the airport. Your remaining possessions are in those two suitcases. We don't want to pay extra for additional baggage. There, they will hand you off to Russian security who will accompany you for the long, long flight to Vladivostok. Goodbye,

Michael; we shall not see each other again."

He returned to the work in front of him. Michael gave him a look of intense hatred, then turned to leave with one security guard ahead of him, and one behind.

Albert continued to work, a satisfied smile on his face, until Sir Humphrey was admitted, who came forward, bowed, and quietly asked, "Was any of that really necessary?"

Instantly furious, Albert hit the desk with a fist and shouted, "How dare you question me!"

Then he paused at the shocked look on Sir Humphrey's face and smiled ruefully.

"If you didn't like what I just did, you're going to hate what's coming next."

Sir Humphrey hesitated – as on the brink of his own deep chasm – before asking what it was.

"I want to see Graham."

The old man felt like he'd been gob smacked, a coarse, common phrase he'd never used before, but one that, in this case, seemed totally apt. Then he shouted, also out of character for him.

"Completely out of the question, sir!"

Albert looked at him determinedly, yet Sir Humphrey was equally determined and raged on: "It goes against established protocol. It's completely outside constitutional boundaries. The Prime Minister will never approve it. It will cause a political crisis. It goes against centuries of legal precedent which you clearly understand."

Albert continued to look at him impassively.

"I want to see Graham," he repeated.

"And why do you want to see the man who ultimately betrayed you? Who killed your husband, and who tried to kill you?"

"Because" Albert said calmly, "he is the man who ultimately betrayed me, who killed my husband, and who tried to kill me."

Sir Humphrey paused, then said softly, "It's impossible, Your Majesty."

"Damn you!" thundered Albert as he struck the desk with his fist in a, by now, well-known act of frustrated anger. "I'm the King! Nothing for me is impossible!"

As though explaining the facts of life to an unbelieving child, Sir Humphrey said calmly, "No one is above the constitution, sir, not even you; an historical fact of which you are well aware."

He stared piercingly at Albert, who turned away and looked at his father's portrait. Then he turned back and said, from a depth of despair, "I know, Sir Humphrey, but I also must know why he tried to kill me. How could he, of all people, turn on me like that? How could he, of all people, kill Paul?"

And, to his credit, Sir Humphrey did not turn away from that despair.

"So far, he hasn't said a word. But he will."

"But don't you understand?" said Albert in both plea and protest, "He won't talk to anyone but me. You know that. And I can never rest until I know the reason why, not if I live another fifty years."

Now Sir Humphrey did turn away to avoid Albert's begging look, as Albert continued.

"You know there can't be a trial. This is not some common and sordid murder case . . . Well," he paused, then admitted, "It is sordid, but the monarchy cannot be dragged through the publicity because the monarchy will not stand. The people will be so revolted at what they hear, at revelation upon revelation, of betrayal upon betrayal, at the highest levels of the Royal Family that is supposed to be a positive role model, not this shameful farce. All support for the Crown will drain away. That cannot be allowed to happen."

"I am well aware of that," said Sir Humphrey resignedly. "And so is the P. M. We've already discussed this."

"I had thought of a pardon – "

Then Sir Humphrey quickly interrupted: "But pardons are for after a conviction, not before it."

"Hear me out," explained Albert. "If I pardoned Graham and he were released, how long do you think he would last out there before he was murdered? Death in that sense is justice that cannot be obtained through our current judicial system."

"But – " interrupted Sir Humphrey again, who was just as quickly interrupted, again, by Albert.

"Yes, yes, I know, the people would never understand his release after such a heinous act. Also, and I know this is a point you would stress, he could just as easily become a poster child and possibly even a leader for all the anti-royal feeling in the kingdom. So, I'm stumped. What do you suggest?"

Albert looked pleadingly at Sir Humphrey, who was surprised that Albert hadn't seen the only solution himself, especially after all the times he'd joked about putting people in the Tower.

"It is true, Your Majesty, that we don't live in Henry's time, so beheading and the Tower are out. Yet there is a modern equivalent," and he paused. Albert looked at him questioningly.

"One of which your sister is well aware," continued Sir Humphrey, leading Albert to the point where he began to understand.

"A psychiatric hospital?"

"An ultra-secure, ultra-secret military psychiatric hospital, Your Majesty."

Albert never doubted Sir Humphrey, but he was surprised to learn such a facility existed.

"We have one of those?"

If Sir Humphrey were French, he would have said, "Naturellement." Since he was British, and of a certain class and education, he said, "Naturellement."

"But wouldn't that require a hearing?"

"Yes, but in this case, it will be a private hearing before the Star Chamber."

"The Star Chamber?" burst out Albert, nearly laughing. "There hasn't been a Star Chamber in hundreds of years!"

"Ah, but there can be. Completely secret; composed of select members of the Privy Council and military judges at the highest level. It will be completely legal, completely out of the public eye, and he will never leave," and here Sir Humphrey paused to dramatically emphasize his final word: "Never."

"Oh, I like that," said Albert smiling. "And the Prime Minister approves?"

"Actually, sir, it was her idea."

"Better yet. And the public is told . . . ?"

"The truth, of course, that your would-be assassin and the murderer of the Duke is undergoing a psychiatric examination at a restricted military facility, which will take an undetermined length of time, and then, at some future date, the government will release a statement to the effect that Graham has been deemed mentally incompetent to stand trial and needs long-term psychiatric care. No visitors. No interviews. Ever."

"I like that very much indeed," said Albert, finally satisfied. "Make it so."

"Yes, sir," said Sir Humphrey, relieved at the outcome, but just momentarily. He didn't even have time to turn around before

Albert added.

"And I will see Graham."

Sir Humphrey sighed because he knew there was no way around this issue, yet with a private Star Chamber hearing to resolve Graham's fate, at least now it was possible.

"At the military prison," continued Albert, "I will see Graham in a windowless room, by myself, just the two of us, with no one-way glass, no cameras, and no microphones. Do you understand?"

"Of course, sir," replied Sir Humphrey graciously.

"Do you understand?" repeated Albert, more insistently.

It was only then that Sir Humphrey bristled, and Albert realized he'd pushed too hard. Albert then just nodded as Sir Humphrey bowed once more and left.

A military guard stood at attention outside the metal door. Sir Humphrey waited beside him as Albert approached. The guard saluted, then stepped aside. Albert looked at Sir Humphrey quizzically, who nodded once.

Albert stood in front of the door, knowing Graham was on the other side. Albert stared at the door, and Sir Humphrey saw a wave of such flushed hatred and anger on the King's face that it scarcely appeared human, but then it passed. Albert's normal skin color returned as the emotion drained away, replaced with such glacial passivity that Sir Humphrey seemed to be staring at a wall of ice. Then Albert opened the door, and saw Graham seated at a table, handcuffed to a metal ring attached to the table so he could not lunge at Albert and attack him yet again. The two men stared at each other for the first time since the balcony. Both were expressionless. Then Albert entered the room and shut the door behind him.

The guard returned to his position in front of the door, while Sir Humphrey sat down on a nearby chair to wait. He waited less than ten minutes, then the door opened, Albert came out, impassively, with no recognition of Sir Humphrey, and walked down the corridor towards his waiting helicopter, never to see Graham again.

Sir Humphrey motioned to two other military guards who entered the room, released Graham from the steel ring while keeping him handcuffed, then led him to the door where Sir Humphrey stared at Graham and Graham glared back, impassive, calm, unfathomable, then he was led away. Sir Humphrey continued staring at Graham until he and his guards reached the end of the corridor and turned a corner, then he was gone. Sir Humphrey would see him once more, at the meeting of the Star Chamber, then Graham would be lost to history, with not even a public notice of his death, decades later, after which he would be buried on the hospital grounds in an unmarked grave in a plain wooden coffin to become worm food.

For now, Sir Humphrey turned back to the guard.

"Wait out here," he said, then he entered the room and closed the door. He crossed quickly to the table, reached underneath, and removed a small tape recorder, put it in a coat pocket, then left to join Albert for the return trip to London.

Sir Humphrey sat in the garden of his London home. He knew better than to listen to the recording in his Whitehall office, which, at his request, was under constant surveillance. Here, however, he was truly alone, so he put the recorder, an old-fashioned one with a micro-cassette tape, not a digital model, on the table beside a manual typewriter. He turned on the recorder and listened to Albert's entire conversation with Graham, then he transcribed the conversation onto typing paper to make a single copy. He didn't want to use his computer because even if he deleted the file after printing it, he knew it could still be retrieved, and this was for no one's eyes but his own.

Then he removed the batteries from the recorder and removed the mini-cassette tape. He discarded the batteries so they could not leak through the years and destroy the machine. He placed the tape, the recorder, and the single transcript into a large manila envelope labeled, "Top Secret – Not to be opened for fifty years after the death of King Albert." He later gave the envelope to the Royal Archivist who placed it into a box also labeled "Top Secret" and with the same instructions, which was placed on the top shelf of a remote section of the Archives, its contents known only to the King and, unbeknownst to him, to Sir Humphrey as well, both of whom were long dead by the time the contents eventually came to light, and the motive for the King's attempted assassination on a Welsh balcony was finally opened. Albert's and Paul's son was King by then and ordered the faded transcript to be brought to him.

"My poor, poor fathers," was all he was heard to say.

Then he, against his better judgment, decided to show the transcript to his younger sister, Princess Pauline Elizabeth Victoria Mary. And, unbeknownst to him, or to anyone, it was the princess – who preferred her second name and was called Lizzie within the family – who had, somehow, inherited the family's darker, unstable side. It was this Princess Elizabeth who then, late one night, entered her brother's bedroom and lay beside the still unmarried, sleeping King. It was she who pulled out the knife hidden in the folds of her white night gown, and it was she who repeatedly stabbed her brother while hissing softly in his ear, "Devil spawn! Devil spawn!" until his heart was shredded and he was dead. It was she, covered in her brother's still-warm blood, who then ran down the long, long corridor shouting victoriously, "Vengeance! Vengeance!" and it was she who was shot numerous times as she lunged, knife in hand, to attack the first person she approached.

A surreptitiously taken photograph of the crumpled, dead body as it lay on the red carpet, inlaid with its gold monogrammed and entwined letters of "P R," was broadcast to a horrified nation as it awoke to the morning news. Parliament hotly and angrily debated for days whether the monarchy, despite its tradition and thousand-year-bloodline, had finally outlived its usefulness. It was perhaps the most momentous issue in Parliament's long history. When the question was finally moved, the deciding vote to retain the monarchy was, ironically, cast by the grandson of Solomon Pembroke, now himself the King's Champion, and who had loyally and faithfully served his rural constituency for decades.

The choice of a new monarch was as obvious to the country as it was satisfying to the elderly Princess Victoria, who had diligently served two monarchs before her.

"This is for you, dearest Mummy," she thought, as St. Edward's Crown was carefully placed upon her head at the Coronation. Lizzie had died decades before on St. Helena, with her devoted Larry beside her.

One of her first acts as Queen was to pardon the late Michael Romanov, whose adopted son still lived in Vladivostok and who gratefully accepted Queen Victoria's offer to return. While his father's former estate remained the seat of the McGregor family – Pauline having remarried, with a new line of descendants by the time of her death – Toria had known for some time that Albert had retained part of the Balmoral estate in his own name, which she gladly deeded to Michael Romanov's son. She also returned the Fabergé eggs, which meant far more to him than they ever had to her.

And so, the kingdom (no longer a United Kingdom as Wales had finally voted for independence) entered a new age of prosperity. The dark side of the Royal Family would remain submerged for some decades to come, like a great whale gliding silently underwater, before it would breach the surface again.

CHAPTER 79

Albert and Pauline stood beside each other on the footbridge over Durham's River Wear, with the nearby cathedral looming high on its promontory. Both banks were lined with hundreds, possibly thousands, of people, as well as the media. Albert knew this had to be a public event, to help the nation heal, but, as far as he and Pauline were concerned, they were the only people there.

Albert held the marble urn as Pauline opened the lid and pulled out a clear plastic bag holding Paul's ashes. They looked at each other, hesitating, wanting to delay what must be done, then Pauline opened the bag, held it beyond the railing, and emptied half of its whitish contents into the air. The heavier bits of bone sank quickly to lay on the silt below. The lighter ash seemingly floated in the mild breeze, tumbling in the air, glittering at times like the dust of diamonds as it gradually fell gently onto the surface of the water on its sluggish way to the North Sea.

Then Albert handed the urn to Pauline and took the plastic bag, held it out over the water, and dropped the rest of its contents into the air as, again, the heavier bits of bone dropped sharply into the water, while the lighter ash was borne away on the wind.

The crowd was completely silent as the people watched but said nothing. Only Albert and Pauline spoke.

"Goodbye, Paul," said Albert softly.

"Farewell, my beloved son," said Pauline, as they watched the last of the ashes gently lay on the river for their journey to the sea.

"Ashes to ashes; dust to dust," said Albert, mainly to

himself, then thought grimly, "At least Christianity got that part right."

For a moment they stood side by side, thinking of transformation and loss, and how quickly and unexpectedly things can change. Then Albert placed the empty bag back into the urn, replaced the lid, and took it from Pauline as they walked up the hill to the cathedral, where they were met at a side door by the Lord Bishop, who bowed first and then took the urn from Albert and gave it to an assistant.

"A lamentable day, Your Majesty," said the Lord Bishop.

"Indeed," agreed Albert.

"Would you like to see the mock-up for the proposed memorial plaque?"

Albert looked at Pauline, who shook her head "No," saying she'd already seen it. She was spending more time in the area now at her new estate.

"I would like that," said Albert, as Pauline continued: "What I don't understand was why Michael Romanov had to leave the country so quickly. It's like he just walked away."

"Well," said Albert, without a hint of a smile, "these things happen."

Which was when Pauline realized this particular thing didn't happen by chance, but she never inquired further.

The relatively new Lord Bishop then said, "This way, Your Majesty."

Albert looked again at Pauline who, hearing the choristers rehearsing, said she'd prefer to go inside and listen. The cathedral and grounds, at Albert's request, were closed to the public for this occasion.

Albert nodded, then motioned for the Lord Bishop to lead on. Inside, they went down a broad stone staircase to a lower level, then followed a corridor to the spot where the mock-up was attached to a wall.

"It will take some time for the actual bronze plaque to be made, but we wanted to put this up so people can at least see it, as there is a great deal of interest."

The men stood before the carved wooden replica of the plaque, and Albert read the inscription: "Paul McGregor, Duke of Durham." Then there were the years of his birth and death. "Outstanding chorister. Durham native. Benefactor. Beloved husband and consort of King Albert. A blazing meteor taken from us far too soon."

The words affected Albert more than he'd expected. He closed his eyes as a wave of pain and loss swept over him. The Lord Bishop tactfully stared at the plaque until Albert opened his eyes again. Then the Lord Bishop gently asked, "Maybe Your Maj-esty would be interested in seeing the shrine of St. Cuthbert? It's just down the corridor."

"Of course," replied Albert, wearily and without enthusiasm which the Lord Bishop noted. bThe men continued standing before the plaque as the L ord Bishop explained,b "It b was long after the saint's death when he appeared to your ancestor, King Alfred, after the Vikings had invaded the Kingdom of Wessex and forced him to flee with his remaining supporters into a distant marsh land where they found refuge on an island and things looked very bleak in-deed. In a vision, Cuthbert encouraged Alfred to continue the struggle and not lose hope or faith in his eventual success. And, in-deed, Alfred and his army left their watery shelter, overthrew the invaders, and Alfred's progeny eventually created a unified En-gland."

"I do know the story," said a miffed and quite sensitive Albert. Unperturbed, the Lord Bishop continued, "When the coffin was opened, much later, it was found that the saint's body remained immaculate and uncorrupted, just as when he died. A true miracle. And even today, it is said the saint gives succor to those in need of consolation."

Then Albert's anger flared.

"Am I in need of consolation?" he growled belligerently.

Refusing to be baited, and with consummate tact, the Lord Bishop looked directly at Albert and said, softly and calmly, "I think you are wounded, sir, and have suffered a grievous loss from which you will not soon or easily recover."

Caught unexpectedly by the Lord Bishop's sympathetic understanding, Albert was mollified by such perceptiveness and merely nodded agreement.

"Now, Your Majesty, I shall leave you for a few minutes. The shrine is further down this corridor."

He bowed and left Albert alone. Albert heard him going back up the stairs. He looked again at the proposed memorial and was quickly lost in the reality of his pain when he heard several youths loudly coming down the stone steps. Obviously, choir practice was over. He didn't want to be seen and recognized, so he looked around and saw a dimly lit passageway in the opposite wall and quickly entered it, moving back into the darkness. The choristers approached, evidently on their way out of the building, but they stopped first, and one read aloud the inscription on the mock-up. Several tittered and laughed at the phrase, "beloved husband."

"Bloody poof!" said one older lad.

"And our bloody queer King as well," agreed another.

"I think it's sweet," said one younger boy.

"That's because you're a bloody poof yourself!" shouted the older lad, who roughly shoved the younger boy, and then he and the others laughed and ran off.

Albert watched from the darkness of the hallway as the boy straightened himself up, looked at the inscription again, and then said aloud, "I still think it's sweet," then rushed off to join the others.

Albert stood in the darkness, then realized he was in the same darkened passageway where he'd first kissed Paul so many centuries ago, or was it just yesterday? He put both hands against the damp, cold stone wall and, leaning forward, pressed his lips gently to the unyielding stone, not at all like the soft warmth of Paul's lips; no, not at all.

He pulled away, feeling only loss, and entered the lighted corridor. He wasn't ready to go back upstairs, so he turned towards the direction of the saint's shrine, if only from historical curiosity.

He reached it quickly, a chamber set against the cathedral's outer wall. Beyond a low railing, the saint's tomb was set into the floor, covered by a single, large, flat stone carved with the saint's name. Albert stood outside the railing, looking at the stone in the floor, when an unexpected anger overwhelmed him and he easily stepped over the railing, stood at the stone, and then spat upon it. A large glob of spit flew through the air and smacked onto the floor.

"You vile creature!" exclaimed Albert with loathing and fury. "You with your immaculate body while the charred remains of my beloved float to the sea. How dare you!" he shouted. "If you are truly capable of miracles, you would gather his ashes and bone and restore them into that beautiful body I cannot live without. Do that for me, and I'll proclaim you a saint indeed. But you can't, can you? Because you're just a pile of dust and bone yourself, no matter what the good Lord Bishop believes. But you and I know otherwise, don't we? Still, if you're nothing, then I am nothing, too. How can I go on without him? How can I help my people without him?"

Then an immense fatigue overwhelmed Albert and, unable

to continue standing, he sank to his knees on the stone floor.

The cathedral was completely silent except for a single chorister still practicing upstairs. Albert closed his eyes, still kneeling, then realized he knew that lad's voice. And, somehow, it became louder and louder, as though coming nearer and nearer. Then, with a gasp, he realized it was unmistakably Paul's distinctive voice and no one else's. It was Paul's voice coming closer, getting louder, and then Albert realized, with another gasp, that Paul was singing the very song he'd sung for Albert the first day they met. He was singing "I sat down under his shadow." And now his voice was so loud that Albert knew Paul was in the room with him, then Paul was joined by other voices to harmonize the melody, only they weren't other voices, they were all Paul's voice; he was all the voices singing together, and the voices were all around Albert, and then the voices were inside him. Paul was inside him, then Albert heard the flapping of wings from far above, then talons firmly yet gently grasped his body, holding him tightly, then Albert gasped as he was lifted high into the air, up through the cathedral. Above him, a great eagle was lifting him towards the sky. Albert looked down, totally without fear, to see the cathedral below. The eagle lifted him higher, and Durham was below; then the massive wings continued flapping as eagle and Albert rose even higher, until the countryside lay below them as a vast panorama, then Albert heard Paul say, "Entre, ici, ami de mon coeur."

Paul paused, then added, "That's French."

"I know that's French!" replied an exasperated, yet also exhilarated, Albert. And they continued to soar aloft, and he wanted the soaring to never end.

A hand tentatively touched his shoulder.

"Your Majesty?"

It was the concerned voice of the Lord Bishop.

"Are you all right?"

Slowly, reluctantly, Albert opened his eyes. The Lord Bishop was kneeling beside him, with Pauline standing nearby, equally concerned. Albert was laying on the stone lid of the saint's tomb. Evidently, he had slumped over.

Albert considered the question before replying.

"Yes," he concluded, "I am."

He tried to get up but was too unsteady to stand on his own.

"Help me," he said, and with the Lord Bishop and Pauline on either side to assist him, he slowly got to his feet. He took a few tentative steps with their help, then raised his hands to indicate he would continue alone. He stepped over the railing and into the corridor, then headed towards the stone steps. He felt trapped inside that vast building and needed the freedom of open air.

Future historians of Albert's reign recognized something significant happened to him during that visit to Durham Cathedral, but he never spoke of or referred to it, and so whatever happened there remains a mystery to this day. However, it's clear that the Albert who emerged from the building was not the Albert who entered it, and that he underwent some kind of transformation, as though emerging from a chrysalis. Before that experience, the question was frequently raised as to whether Albert would ever be able to master the passions that so often overwhelmed him. Could he gain the self-control and discipline necessary to dedicate his life to the role fate had destined for him, and so become the monarch to his people that he was capable of being? After Durham, that question was never asked again.

CHAPTER 80

Connie later said that Paul Junior was the easiest birth she ever had.

"He just slipped right out!"

Then came the photo op as the Royal Family left St. Mary's Hospital to a cheering crowd of hundreds, indeed, thousands of people, plus a huge media contingent, all eagerly awaiting the first public viewing of the future monarch.

First, Albert, Connie with Paul Junior, and Pauline greeted and thanked the waiting hospital staff – doctors, nurses, orderlies, and others – who helped with the delivery, then they faced the cheering multitudes. Albert carefully took Baby Paul from Connie and proudly held him up to proclaim, "He looks just like his father!" No explanation was necessary as to which father that was and, as a result, many bets were lost, and many bets were won, on that distinction.

Thus began Paul Junior's introduction as the most eagerly awaited baby of his generation, for whom interest was not just national, but worldwide as well. Indeed, during the coming weeks and months, an entire cottage industry grew up to provide a seemingly endless variety of baby-related souvenirs and memorabilia that put his likeness on everything from silver spoons and teething toys to old-fashioned scrapbooks, in which could be mounted the apparently endless release of weekly photographs from the palace which became available as prints and downloads and followed Baby Paul through his subsequent developmental stages of crawling, standing, and then his first word, which sounded suspiciously like "Ma-Ma."

Those following Paul Junior's gradual development could

also insert the weekly numbers into their scrapbook as he constantly increased in length and weight. Then there were the pictures of son with dutifully caring father, a role Albert quickly assumed, with Paul Junior and Albert playfully together on the carpet of the royal heir's playroom; Albert looking lovingly at his son as he slept in the suitably ornate bassinet installed in Albert's office as he insisted on spending at least two hours a day with his child. There were even pictures of Albert changing diapers at the changing station also installed in his office. He made sure those photographs were not too revealing.

While Connie primarily breastfed Paul Junior, she also pumped milk for storage so that Albert could warm it and bottle feed his child when needed, though Connie remained a continual presence. It had been decided that she would stay with Paul Junior until weaning, when she would finally return to her own family, with Pauline to care for the child after that. There were far fewer pictures of her with her grandson, at her request, because, unlike Albert, Pauline never felt comfortable with what she considered media intrusion into her private family life, though she was fully aware that there were few aspects of Paul Junior's life that would ever be truly private.

Later would come pictures of Baby Paul in the palace gardens with his father; Baby Paul's first helicopter ride; and Baby Paul at Windsor and Sandringham.

Albert was determined that Paul Junior would grow up in the family business and be familiar with its demands and routines from an early age, so he held P. J. on his lap while working at his desk and even read dispatches to him from the red boxes, knowing full well that the infant had absolutely no idea what was being said. Still, it was important for Albert to instill in his son what it meant to be King, as his father had done for him.

By both nature and nurture, and with a great deal of help

from science, P. J. was called into being by fate, destined for a unique role as though summoned by all the men and women who preceded him.

Yet Albert knew his son had a choice. Being monarch was a voluntary duty. Once assumed, it was assumed for life, but there was a choice, despite the expectations placed on a royal heir. There could be nothing worse for the country or the monarchy than an embittered and resentful King who did not want to be King. That would destroy the monarchy itself, and Albert was determined that would not happen on his watch, or on that of his successor either.

Paul Junior had to want to rule for the system to work. Albert recognized the possibility that his son might want to do something else, and he was actually good with that, which was why another child was necessary, a girl this time, by choice, as he and Paul had already discussed, something to be arranged during the combining of genes and not, this time, left to chance. And Connie had already agreed to be a host mother, one more time.

Still, the thought that P. J. might want to be a doctor or a musician or a craftsman was unsettling to Albert because there were already so many of them whereas a monarch, by definition, was unique, and Albert wanted his son to be fully aware of the special challenges and rewards of being King. There was, literally, no other job like it, at least in his kingdom. It demanded one's full attention and capabilities. There were many jobs in which one could serve, but none in which one could serve so many, or to do so much good for an entire country. Albert did not understand how anyone could possibly walk away from such an amazing and challenging calling. Indeed, he could not recall a voluntary abdication in the history of the monarchy; involuntary removals and revolts, yes, but the role of monarch was one that, for a thousand years, had willingly, even forcefully, assumed, though with widely varying degrees of success.

So Albert didn't worry that his son might refuse the job or fail to do his duty, but he did worry, daily, about whether his son would respect him, which Albert wanted more than anything else. He had respected his father and grandmother for being who and what they were. And he wanted to make sure that P. J. would know about his namesake so he would respect the father he never knew. That would be easy considering the kind of man Paul had been. But what terrified Albert, when he admitted it, was the possibility that, at some point, P. J. would look at him with disgust and say, "My father Paul sacrificed himself for you?" That, Albert knew, on a gut level, would be unbearable and would tear him apart. Albert was fiercely determined that he would never hear those words, so he carefully decided how he needed to act, as both father and King, to hear the other words he needed his son to say: "Now I understand."

That was what so often haunted Albert as he looked at himself in the mirror each morning: "Can I measure up? And how can I bear it if I don't?"

CHAPTER 81

Sir Humphrey arrived early for his appointment with the King and found the Archbishop already waiting in the antechamber to the King's office. Neither was surprised, and they greeted each other with the wry, knowing smiles that come with long acquaintance.

As Sir Humphrey sat down, not as easy as it once was, he turned to his old friend and said, simply, "You, too?"

The Archbishop nodded and continued to smile.

"It's time, don't you think?"

Sir Humphrey agreed.

"I always wanted to leave at the right time, but now I worry I may have waited too long. You and I have served three monarchs in various capacities, but this third one has nearly done me in."

"Indeed," was the Archbishop's laconic reply, then he asked, "What are your plans?"

Then Sir Humphrey looked truly happy.

"I've always wanted to travel. Of course, I've seen many countries through the years, but now I want to visit places without wondering how we can use them to further our own purposes, without wondering how they can be shaped and molded to fit into our foreign policy, economic development, or defense plans. I want to simply enjoy an exotic locale on its own terms and simply for itself."

"And where, precisely, do you want to go?"

And Sir Humphrey, nodding towards the King's office, said, "Any place where his picture isn't on the currency."

The Archbishop chuckled sympathetically.

"And what about you?" asked Sir Humphrey.

"My wife and I own a small lock tender's cottage in the Cotswolds, across a canal from a five-hundred-year-old grist mill. Our place is archetypal: half-timbered, thatched roof, flowers in window pots, lace curtains, and no phone. I'm even getting rid of my mobile."

"Good for you," exclaimed Sir Humphrey.

Just then Gerald, the King's appointment secretary, approached them.

"The King will see you now, Sir Humphrey."

Sir Humphrey rose slowly and with obvious difficulty, then turned to the Archbishop.

"Wish me luck."

"I do indeed," replied the Archbishop. "At least he can't cut off our heads."

"With this King, I'm never sure," said Sir Humphrey, only half-jokingly, and the Archbishop merely nodded as he watched Sir Humphrey enter the King's office and heard Albert exclaim, "Sir Humphrey, since when do you need an appointment to see me?"

Then the door closed.

The Archbishop looked at the framed photographs of King and heir on the table beside him.

"At least he's a loving father," thought the Archbishop, as the shouting started. The King was clearly heard through the heavy wooden doors.

"You're leaving me? How dare you! Out! Out!!"

Then a pale, perspiring Sir Humphrey came back into the antechamber, looking both dazed and shocked, as the Archbishop, concerned, asked, "Are you alright?"

Sir Humphrey wiped his forehead with a handkerchief and merely said, "It went as expected. I just thought of Morocco!"

Despite his own consternation, the Archbishop smiled and stood to take leave of his old friend. They looked at each other, then the Archbishop held out a hand, which Sir Humphrey warmly grasped.

"Until we meet again," he said.

"Indeed," replied the Archbishop, "Hopefully in better circumstances."

Sir Humphrey merely nodded and then turned to go.

"And so ends a lifetime of service," thought the Archbishop as he watched his friend leave. Both men had finally reached the point already recognized by Mr. Leigh-Stoke, that this palace was no place for old men.

"The King will see you now."

The Archbishop hadn't noticed Gerald's approach.

"Is my head safe?" asked the Archbishop jokingly, then instantly realized the man had no sense of humor, at least in this situation. Chastened, the Archbishop rose and followed him into the King's office. Albert was standing behind his desk, looking out a window, when he turned to the Archbishop, who bowed, as Albert said, "Et tu?"

The Archbishop simply stared at him as Albert sat at his desk.

"So, I'm to be left alone, am I, without my two most trusted friends and advisors? Don't worry," he assured the Archbishop with a slight smile, "I'm done shouting."

Relieved, the Archbishop explained it was time for the King to have his own handpicked people from his own generation, not apparently out-of-touch elders inherited from his father. Albert understood but still didn't like it.

"What am I to do without you both?"

"You'll carry on, as you are meant to do."

Albert looked rueful.

"I do regret shouting at Sir Humphrey."

"Then perhaps you should let him know that" suggested the Archbishop gently and tactfully.

"I'll think about it," was Albert's reply, not exactly curt, but not encouraging either.

Then silence enveloped the room as each considered a future without the other. The Archbishop finally spoke.

"I could give you a list of possible replacement candidates, but I think you've already made your choice."

Albert said nothing, so the Archbishop continued, "He's a good man, and it's time for Durham to sit at Canterbury again."

Then there was more silence as neither wanted the meeting to end, and neither really knew how to end it. Finally, the Archbishop said, "It's been an honour and a privilege to serve you, Your Majesty."

Albert looked at him questioningly.

"You'll still do the christening?"

"Of course, Sir. Dr. McGregor would never forgive me if I didn't."

"Damn Dr. McGregor. I wouldn't forgive you!" replied Albert with a smile.

Against his better judgment, because he feared triggering Albert's wrath at a moment when they were close, the Archbishop still took the risk.

"Never turn her against you, Your Majesty."

His concern was justified, because Albert turned furiously upon him.

"And why would I even consider doing that?"

Undaunted, the Archbishop placidly explained, "She is your lodestar now that the Duke is gone."

He was relieved to see Albert agree, as his anger fled as easily as it had come.

"I understand," he said quietly.

Then the Archbishop took another risk when he added, "The Duke will always be with you."

Albert turned to avoid the Archbishop's stare, and the older man realized the King was looking far away, as though reliving a perilous trip to a distant land from which he'd miraculously and surprisingly returned, then he faced the Archbishop again.

"I understand that, as well, Your Grace," Albert said quietly.

"Then I look forward to the christening, Your Majesty," said the Archbishop to close the meeting. Realizing their time was over, Albert rose and came from behind the desk to stand in front of a man he'd known all his life. They looked at each other, then the Archbishop held out his arms and Albert came forward and the Archbishop held him close. It was not a time for tears as the men found themselves in a different place than tears; a time not of holding on, but of letting go. Yet they held each other one last time, a farewell to so much between them – funerals, marriage, the coronation, with the christening still to come – as grief and celebration mingled in memory, then they pulled apart.

The Archbishop bowed and, in return, Albert bowed to him, a gesture which the Archbishop cherished for the rest of his life which would not be much longer.

Soon Albert was alone, truly alone, and he realized this was his moment, with his own people around him, people he would choose and not merely inherit. It was still early in his reign, and he wondered if his name would be applied to an entire age, like Elizabeth or Victoria, or would history judge him harshly as one of the bad monarchs, another George IV, heaven forbid? Or would he simply be yet another mediocre monarch, too numerous to mention?

History's assessment of him was one of the few things he could not control. He did want his son to be a better monarch than he could ever be a major reason Paul Junior's second name was Arthur. But there was so much Albert wanted to achieve and had planned to achieve with Paul. But now Albert knew he was alone and would stay alone. On some level he knew his reign would be long, and he had many more years to live. Years, hopefully, of great accomplishment as he served his people to the best of his ability. He wanted to leave his country better than he found it, and he had found it in good condition, but there was nothing that could not be improved. Things were a long way from perfection, and there would still be plenty left to do for his son and for those who would come after.

And what about the monarchy itself? How long would it remain relevant? What if his people decided, even during his lifetime, to do away with the institution? Was there a place where has-been royals went to die? Hopefully not to France, or to America either for that matter. Yet the monarchy, in its thousand-year history, had survived so much. The important thing was not to get in the way, but simply to be there, the continuity of a line that also evolved. That was the neat trick he had to balance, as did all good monarchs.

As to his place in history, and its judgment, its assessment of how much he had achieved or how badly he had failed, that was simply part of a future that he would never know, the unanswerable question mark of his life. What he did know was that he was King; that his son would soon be christened; and that tonight he would sleep in an empty bed.

CHAPTER 82

It was the day before the christening, and Pauline went to see Albert. As the doors to his office were open, she walked in unannounced, Gerald merely nodded his head as she passed, and then she stopped abruptly, shocked by what she saw. Albert was seated at his desk and, leaning over him, in a most intimate manner as she had seen Paul do numerous times, was a young man unknown to her. They were studying a document, and Albert looked up as she entered and smiled brightly at her.

"Pauline, come in! I want you to meet my new adjutant, Capt. Macaulay. I met him at Paul's lying-in-state where he was on duty."

Then the young man looked up at her, and she caught her breath as he could have been Paul's brother. He stood up, smiled as well, and came around the desk towards her, bowed, and said, "Dr. McGregor, Duchess, it is a real pleasure to meet you. I admired your son so much."

To herself, Pauline thought, "I guess you still do, even to taking his husband."

Yet always gracious, she simply said, "Thank you, Captain" with a smile less than full; and shook the outstretched hand. Realizing he'd somehow failed Pauline's initial assessment, the captain turned to Albert and said, "I'll work on these figures and get back to you, Your Majesty."

"Of course," said Albert, himself quite aware of , and surprised by, Pauline's reaction.

Capt. Macaulay bowed to the King and to Pauline, then left the room, tactfully closing the doors. Pauline turned to Albert and said, with icy disgust, "You couldn't even wait a year?"

Albert replied calmly, "Pauline, he fills my bed, not my heart."

Then, wanting to explain more informally, Albert went to the sofa, sat down, and motioned for her to sit beside him. Reluctantly, she did, but when he reached for her hand, she kept it firmly in her lap and stared straight ahead, avoiding him.

"Pauline," said Albert softly, "I live in a big, empty house, with a big, empty bed, and I don't like being alone. You know Paul was the only man I ever loved, and he's the only man I will ever love."

Yes, she knew that.

"And you know that he is always within me and will be with me until I die."

She knew that, as well.

Albert continued: "What Capt. Macaulay doesn't know is that he is merely temporary, maybe a year at the most. Then I'll replace him with another young man, and another, for as long as I want. There will be a long line of them, but there will never be another Paul as he owns, and fills, my heart completely."

She knew that, too. Pauline finally turned and looked at him   tenderly.

"And I want you to know, Albert, that part of my resentment is simply jealousy, because I, too, have a big, empty house, with a big, empty bed, and there are many times when I want someone beside me as well."

"Then make it so," said Albert gently.

That was what she needed to hear.

CHAPTER 83

Albert asked to see the Archbishop before the christening.

"Yes, Your Majesty?" he asked.

"Thank you for taking time to see me," said Albert. "I hope I'm not interrupting your preparations."

"Actually," replied the Archbishop, "A christening is one of the simpler rituals. I'll merely dip a hand in holy water, touch it to your son's head, say a blessing, and then my wife and I are on our way to Dorset."

"Which is why I want to speak to you," explained Albert, which made the Archbishop nervous as he hoped the King would not press him to stay on.

"I wonder," continued Albert, "if sometime my family and I – Pauline, Paul Junior, and I – could visit you and your wife in retirement? Your house on the canal sounds lovely and, frankly," he continued ruefully, "I don't have many friends, and with Paul gone, there are times when I miss just being social."

Surprised at this unexpected confession, the Archbishop said tenderly, "I speak for my wife when I say we would be most honoured to have you visit, and it would be a pleasure as well."

Albert smiled gratefully as the Archbishop continued, "I must tell you, however, Sir, that my wife, whilst an excellent cook, doesn't do fancy dishes. We have simple fare."

"Just as long as it's not poached salmon," said Albert smiling.

And, ruefully recalling too many meals of poached salmon with the late King, the Archbishop said, "I assure you there will be no salmon, Your Majesty."

"Then I will be able to thank God for that," said a grinning Albert, before turning serious.

"I saw Sir Humphrey before he left for Morocco."

"So, he told me," replied the Archbishop. "He appreciated your words."

Albert merely nodded.

The christening was a small, intimate family affair held at St. James' Chapel Royal. There was just Connie and her family, Toria, Pauline, Albert, and Paul Junior, wearing the lace christening gown made for the children of the first Victoria. Albert held his son as the Archbishop dipped his hand into the holy font, with its water from the River Jordan, then he gently placed his hand on the child's head and said, while looking at Pauline, "In the name of the creative spirit that animates all life, I christen thee Paul Arthur Albert George."

Then everyone, except the Archbishop who, indeed, left immediately after the ceremony with his wife for Dorset, returned to Buckingham Palace for their presentation on the balcony. While waiting, Connie gently passed Paul Junior to Albert, saying, "This is your moment."

The father nestled his son in the crook of his left arm, leaving his right hand free. Then the doors were opened, and Albert saw the vast, cheering multitude beyond the fence. He strode out onto the balcony, paused, then realized the intensity of the cheering was unsettling his son. Not wanting him to cry, Albert carefully placed his right hand on his child's head, leaned over, and said softly, "My dearest son, this is what we do. All this is for you."

And with his right hand, he motioned in a vast arc from left to right. Then he started the royal wave, but realized this was a learning moment, so he gently took his son's tiny hand in his own, and, together, they waved. It was the perfect photo op.

By now Albert was joined on the balcony by the others, and all began waving to the vast crowd before them. That was when Albert heard the sound for which he'd been waiting, a distant roar but rapidly getting closer. Then he said, as to the air around him, "Paul, this is for you."

And the first fighter planes flew low overhead, in tight formation, with their multi-hued vapor trails. There were lots and lots of planes.

Fini

21 Août 2021

Rough and Ready, Pennsylvania

Selected translations

Many thanks for Fiona Powell of Pennsylvania and Trefor Williams of Wales for the Welsh translations.

"L'oeuvre d'art a besoin de temps et de silence."
"A work of art needs time and silence."
Rainer Maria Rilke

Part I, Chapter 25
Page 111

Rwy'n falch o'ch cyfarfod. Rwy'n blês eich bod wedi galw.

Mae Cymru yn agos im calon.

I am pleased to meet you. I am glad you called.
Wales is close to my heart.

Mae'n ddrwg gen i ichi golli eich mab.

I am sorry for the loss of your son.

Page 112

Mi edrychwn ni ymlaen iddo. Wnawn ni ddim gadael ein cyd Gymry i lawr.

Wnawn ni ddim gadael ein cyd Gymry i lawr.

We look forward to it. We will not let our Welsh people down.
Goodbye for now.

Part III, Chapter 4
Page 414

Tan gyfarfyddwn ni eto.

Until we meet again.

Part III, Chapter 5
Page 425

Rwyf mor falch o gael bod yn ôl yn yr henwlad.

I am so happy to return to my homeland.

Part III, Chapter 12
Page 485

"Entre, ici, ami de mon coeur."
"Enter here, friend of my heart."
Stendhal

Sources

Several works proved invaluable in guiding me through often arcane royal rituals, in particular *The Story of the Coronation – King George VI and Queen Elizabeth – 1937*. Edited by Sir John Hammerton. Printed 1937 in London by The Amalgamated Press, Ltd. An exhaustive resource which I tried not to copy directly to any great extent.

Other resources consulted were:
1. "Goodbye, Diana", People Weekly, September 27, 1997.
2. "Invitation to a Royal Wedding", Kathryn Spink, Colour Library International, 1981.
3. "The Funeral of King George VI", The Sphere, February 23, 1952.
4. "The Coronation of Her Majesty Queen Elizabeth II - Approved Souvenir Programme". Published 1953 by King George's Jubilee Trust.

Acknowledgments

The author is indebted to those who read and commented on sections of the book, including Fiona Siobhán Powell, Trefor Williams, Neil Palmer, and Rituparna Das. They were invaluable in helping me avoid some glaring mistakes.

He is especially indebted to Cindy Inkrote, proof reader and copy editor extraordinaire, whose influence is present on every page.

Dedicated, first, to Austin Knowles, a proud Irishman, and to Ian Palmer, a proud Scotsman, both anti-monarchists to the end. And second, to my parents, Harold C. and Kathryn Kirkpatrick Graves, who never stopped believing in me even when I gave them good reason.

Two selections from Noël Coward's *The Girl Who Came to Supper* by permission of Alan Brodie Representation Ltd.
Acknowledgment is made for using the following material:
"I'm getting married in the morning" from *My Fair Lady*, words by Alan Jay Lerner, with one pronoun change. The Alan Jay Lerner Foundation has been notified of these uses.
"Camelot" from the musical of the same name, words by Alan Jay Lerner. See above.
"Tonight" from *West Side Story*, words by Stephen Sondheim. Universal Music Publishing Group, which holds the license for Sondheim's work, has been notified of this use.

Made in the USA
Columbia, SC
16 April 2026

81764614R00371